Urban intervention,
street art and public space

Editors: Pedro Costa, Paula Guerra and Pedro Soares Neves

Urbancreativity.org

Title:
Urban intervention, street art and public space

Editors:
Pedro Costa
Paula Guerra
Pedro Soares Neves

Graphic Design:
Pedro Soares Neves

©Authors and Editors
February 2017
ISBN: 978-989-97712-6-0

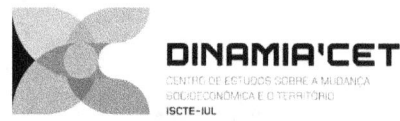

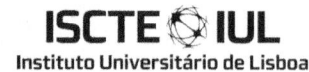

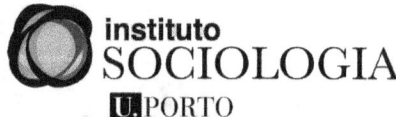

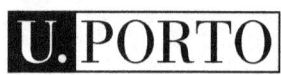

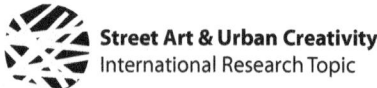

Table of contents

About the Authors

Ágata Dourado Sequeira (PT)

Ágata Dourado Sequeira holds a PhD in Sociology in Instituto Universitário de Lisboa (ISCTE-IUL) / DINAMIA'CET-IUL, Portugal. Has a degree in Sociology and a Master's degree in Sociology of Art and Communication with thesis on the reception of public art. Is currently developoing PhD research on street art and the social construction of public space. Main research interests include public spaces, public art and street art, artistic careers, urban sociology and sociology of art and culture.

Elenise Cristina Pires de Andrade (BR)

Elenise Cristina Pires de Andrade is biologist, with PhD on Education. She works with Edivan Carneiro de Almeida and Milena Santos Rodrigues on the research group "Trace", UEFS, dealing with experimentations on media, education and philosophy. Elenise is professor at Departamento de Educação da Uefs (Feira de Santana, BA).

Edivan Carneiro de Almeida (BR)

Edivan Carneiro de Almeida is a pedagogue. He works with Elenise Cristina Pires de Andrade and Milena Santos Rodrigues on the research group "Trace", UEFS, dealing with experimentations on media, education and philosophy. Edivan is teacher in elementary education II and high school.

Glória Diógenes (BR)

PhD Professor of the Graduate Program in Sociology, of the Department of Social Sciences of the Federal University of Ceará (UFC), Coordinator of the Graduate Program in Sociology of the UFC, Coordinator of the Laboratory of Youth (Lajus) of the UFC and founder member of Luso-Brazilian Network of Researchers in Arts and Urban Interventions.

Leticia González Menéndez (ESP)

Holds a PhD in Art History from the University of Oviedo and a degree in Fine Arts from the University of Salamanca. She was a predoctoral researcher in the Department of Art History and Musicology at the University of Oviedo and has developed her Doctoral Thesis, *Genealogies of creative action in public spaces. New proposals in the Asturian art*, funded by the "Severo Ochoa" program of the Foundation for the Promotion in Asturias of Applied Scientific Research and Technology. He was a member of the research team "The waterfront Gijon. New assets in the public space "(UEFS 2007-61140) from the University of Oviedo and has worked in others as" Art, Globalization and Multiculturalism "(HAR2010-17403) of the University of Barcelona and the Institute of Philosophy at the University Porto within the team, "Philosophy and Public Space" (RG-PHIL-North-Porto-502-1272). Currently, she is part of the Laboratory of experimental electronic Gijon (LEV).

Luisa Tuttolomondo (IT)

Phd student in Territorial Planning and Public Policy at Iuav University of Venice. She graduated in in Cultural Planning at the University of Modena and Reggio Emilia with a thesis on the promotion of social participation among children in the Occupied Palestine Territories. Her main research interests concern the analysis of participative processes involving youngsters and adults, deliberative processes, evaluation of social interventions and local sustainable development. She also collaborates with Next - Nuove Energie x il Territorio of Palermo where she is responsible for ethnographic research, field research, action research, territorial animation and participative events management.

Madalena Corte Real (PT)
Madalena Corte-Real (Cics.Nova) holds a PhD in Urban Studies (doctoral programme from NOVA University of Lisbon and ISCTE – University Institute of Lisbon) and has a background in Sociology. At present, her main areas of interest are urban tourism, inequalities in the urban context, territorial interventions, urban social movements and local governance, as well as cultural production as a key element in the appropriation and transformation of space.

Maria João Monteiro Gomes (PT)
Maria João Monteiro Gomes (Cics.Nova) studied Landscape Architecture (Agronomy Institute of Lisbon- UTL). She holds an MSc in Human Ecology (Évora University) and recently completed her PhD in Urban Studies (doctoral programme from NOVA University of Lisbon and ISCTE – University Institute of Lisbon) investigating the city as a dynamic and continuous social production of space through the experience of walking.

Milena Santos Rodrigues (BR)
Milena Santos Rodrigues is a pedagogue. She works with Edivan Carneiro de Almeida and Elenise Cristina Pires de Andrade on the research group "Trace", UEFS, dealing with experimentations on media, education and philosophy. Milena works with early childhood education.

Paula Guerra (PT)
Sociologist, Ph.D. in Sociology, Professor at the Faculty of Arts and Humanities of the University of Porto, Researcher at the Institute of Sociology (IS-UP), Centre for Territorial Management and Geography Studies (CEGOT) and Griffith Centre for Social and Cultural Research (GCCR). She is the head researcher on the KISMIF project – Keep it Simple, Make it Fast! (PTDC/CS-SOC/118830/2010), which is composed of a multidisciplinary team and has as its central objective the reinterpretation of youth urban cultures in contemporaneity, centred on popular music.

Pedro Costa (PT)
Pedro Costa is an economist with a PhD in Urban and Regional Planning. He is Professor in the Department of Political Economy at Instituto Universitário de Lisboa (ISCTE-IUL) and Director of DINAMIA'CET-IUL, where he coordinates the research line on 'Cities and territories'. He works mainly in the areas of cultural economics, territorial development and planning, focusing most of his recent research on the study of creative dynamics and their relations with territorial development.

Pedro Soares Neves (PT)
1976, Lisbon. Multidisciplinary and post graduate academic training in design and architecture (Barcelona and Rome), and Lisbon Faculty of Fine Arts research Center CIEBA schollar. Specialized in participatory methodologies and informal visual signs in public space (eg, Graffiti and Street Art). PhD student, lecturer and urban designer / consultant at metropolitan and city scale, Winner of the first prize for the "No Rules Great Spot" Oporto. Co creator and professor of "Non commissioned Public Art" workshop and scholar in Science and Technology Management in Faculty of Fine Arts University of Lisbon. Founder of the AP2 (Portugese chapter of IAP2, International Association for Public Participation), APAURB (Portuguese Urban Art association), and of the Lisbon Street Art & Urban Creativity Conference and ongoing associated International Research Topic (urbancreativity.org). Member of the UNESCO Chair in Intangible Heritage and Traditional Know-How: Linking Heritage at the University of Évora.

Ricardo Lopes (PT)

Ricardo Venâncio Lopes (Portugal, 1989) is architect, photographer and researcher. Lopes is currently developing a PhD in Architecture of Contemporary Metropolitan Territories. In the field of architecture, he has been developing projects with different logic's and characteristics in Portugal, Angola, Guinea-Bissau and Brazil. As photographer, Lopes has been travelling around the world, always looking for different "stories" behind the camera lenses. As researcher, he is author of many publications, presentations and artistic interventions in the field of urban studies, architecture and creative culture.

Polona Lupinšek (SL)

Born in Maribor, Slovenia 1989. Bachelor degree in European and Mediterranean Heritage at Faculty of Humanities, University of Primorska (2011). Bachelor thesis entitled Urban Pattern of the Peripheral Squares of Koper. Master degree in Ethnology and Cultural Anthropology at Faculty of Arts, University of Ljubljana (2015). Master thesis entitled Street Art in Indonesia: Messages of the Streets of Jogjakarta. Certification in Batik Textile gained at non-degree study at Indonesian Institute of Arts Yogyakarta (2014).

Rachel Souza (BR)

Rachel Souza is a founding editor of Revista Chão magazine. She holds a Masters Degree in Visual Arts from the Federal Fluminsense Univeristy (UFF) and is currently pursuing a Ph.D. in Sociology at the Rio de Janeiro University Research Institute (Iuperj).

Voica Pușcașiu (RO)

Voica Pușcașiu has a Bachelor's degree in Art History and a Master in Philosophy, Culture, and Communication, both from the History and Philosophy Department of the "Babeș-Bolyai" University in Cluj-Napoca, where she is currently a PhD researcher. Her thesis is concerned with the reception of artworks in public spaces, namely the differences between commissioned and un-commissioned pieces such as Graffiti and Street Art. Her other interests include the social practices through which certain artifacts become icons, exploring the effect the viewer's emotional connection has towards an object's success. Lately she started to explore the field of Digital Humanities and using its specific tools in her research.

Part I. Setting the scene

Chapter 1
Introduction: Urban interventions, street art and public space

Pedro Costa, Paula Guerra e Pedro Soares Neves

The relation between urban interventions, street art and public space have been marked by wide debates and academic discussions in recent years, which have been fueled by diverse moves in several artistic art worlds, including the expansion of site specific artistic interventions, the movements towards community involvement on art production, the increasing visibility of graffiti and street art and the diversification of its practices, or the imbrication between architectural work and artistic intervention on public spaces, amongst many other examples. Specifically, whether they are ephemeral or temporary, or whether they come from within or outside the communities in which they are developed, these interventions in public space have been introducing in recent years a new perspective on what is the city, and the urban life, through creative dynamics that reflect territorially embedded mechanisms, but also particular social and cultural process which need to be better studied. Public space, being a privileged place for interaction and encounter but also for self-expression and symbolic affirmation, is naturally the arena for the development of interesting processes in this field.

Often transformed in an entertainment and consume-based place and understood through the lens of the tourist gaze, and being an expression of the contemporary globalized world, public space can also be seen as the place for the expression of the difference, the transgression and the arena for liminality processes and for the expression of the diversity of identities, as it always have been through history. While the boundaries between time and space, public and private, real and virtual are being blurred by contemporaneity, the importance of the territorially embedded mechanisms that support artistic practice and of the significance territoriality conditions of the social and cultural processes that are beneath them do not cease to increase, and drive us to the need of further inquire on these problematics.

The progressive change in the relation of the artistic practices with territories and, mostly, with urban space, reflects what E. Soja (1989) describes as the "spatial turn" of the arts and sciences in the 1980's, configuring a renewed understanding of the relation between the social and the spatial, which translates in a wide diversity of urban interventions in the public spaces of the cities.

The territoriality of the artistic phenomena, profusely described in the literature which studies the relation between cultural activities and territorial development (cf. e.g, Scott, 2000, 2014; Costa, 2008; Costa and Lopes, 2013), proves that artistic urban intervention has become increasingly linked to local attributes of place, which is assumed with constitutive significance itself, being urban interventions concerned to dialogue with the territories in which they are developed, in order to question, refunction and contest prevailing norms and ideologies, and to create new meanings, experiences, understandings, relationships and situations (Pinder, 2008).

It is important to remember that the territoriality of artistic practices owes much to the work of Howard S. Becker through his pioneer concept of the art world (Becker, 1982; Crane, 1992; Guerra and Costa, 2016). Many of the chapters of this edited book transport us likewise to the concept of scene - one which was developed later, by the end of the XXth century. Through post-subcultural theory, in which the defense of artistic, musical and cultural scenes played a tremendous role, the territory came in as a crucial variable of artistic production) (Bennett and Peterson, 2004; Bennett, 2008). The notion of cultural scene was developed from the concept of art world, such as Howard S. Becker proposed it (see Bennett and Peterson, 2004: 3). According to several authors, this concept can articulate very functionally the dimensions of local and global contemporary dynamics. It is born in the context of the theories called 'post-subcultural studies', to determine several sociocultural activities which are clustered by location (normally a neighborhood, city or urban area) and/or type of cultural production (for instance a style of music) (Bennett, 2004: 223; Straw, 2004: 411). The work of Straw (1991) was seminal in this. He offers a sophisticated analysis of the interaction between music, taste and identity, exploring the idea of translocalism, that is, how clusters of different agents musically and geographically disperse can be involved in collective cultural practices thanks to the ability music has to transcend physical barriers. Since then the concept has been progressively used in the analysis of the production, performance and reception of popular music, taking into account time and space coordinates (see Guerra and Costa, 2016).

Space is truly a critical factor when approaching musical scenes (Guerra, 2013, 2014 and 2015). Its practices and relationships are inscribed in space, and in constant articulation with other social processes. Cultural scenes have a very urban nature (Blum, 2001: 10), but are not circumscribed to cities. Due to new communication technologies and to the mobility of physical supports – such as cassettes, CD's and vinyl – as well as gigs and tours, the limits of each scene have expanded. On the one hand, more people can access, for instance, recorded music. On the other hand, nowadays technology, besides making processes more accessible, warrants a quality similar to the old recording processes. Thus, musicians and bands do not need the support of major labels to get the attention of the public, doing all things needed autonomously, from recording to publicizing their music. The development of the Internet made the communication between bands and fans easier – accelerating the scene dynamism, its beginning and development, up to its disappearance. Scenes can be brought up in urban contexts as well as in rural ones, and in areas of rural-urban contiguity. They can come up in both centers and periphery. Moreover, the bond between scene and fixed physical location has become more tenuous – today a scene can be translocal and even virtual (Bennett and Peterson, 2004; Guerra, 2014 and 2015).

The "urban intervention and street art" "scenes" and "creative milieus" are undoubtedly marked by these processes. On one hand, this importance of space and of territory is clearly marked in the way the attributes of place and its socio-economic and cultural contexts influence the artistic creative practices and the cultural fruition. But on the other hand, the importance of place and of its specificities can be translated in the assumption of an embedness in territorially-based processes which are themselves in the genesis of creative processes (including the characteristics of the local production/consumption systems, their governance mechanisms, and their representations systems), where aspects such as the symbolic attributes of place and its morphologic characteristics are central, and the informality-based processes and liminality mechanisms that specific places can offer can be the difference on unlocking particular gatekeeping processes in the local-global art-worlds of contemporaneity, through the development of creative atmospheres and reputation building processes that anchor local creative milieus in global dynamics (cf. Costa, 2008, 2012; Costa and Lopes, 2013) and that are particularly significant for the development of which A. Scott designates as the cognitive-cultural capitalism (cf. Scott, 2008, 2014).

The origins of this book and all the process that conducted to it reflect this reality. It has its direct origin on an international call for papers, issued by Pedro Costa and Paula Guerra, which aimed to give body to a publication on the thematic of creative milieus and cultural scenes in contemporary urban spaces. The organizers of that publication were surprised by the great quality and interest of the proposals for papers which were presented, even if many of them were not focused specifically and directly on the "creative milieus" and "urban scenes" approach they were looking for. Interestingly, many of the papers raised the issue of the relation between urban interventions (particularly street art approaches) and public space. That was so stimulating that the authors, drawing also upon previous work on that area, decided to give birth to another project, complementary to the edition of the original idea of book, which would be specifically focused on issues of urban interventions, street art and public space. For that, they joined Pedro Soares Neves, which have been working for years in the field of street art and urban interventions, is executive director of Urbancreativity international research topic on Graffiti, Street Art and Urban Creativity, that among other publish the Street Art & Urban Creativity Scientific Journal (Neves, P.S. Ed. 2015, 2016). The diversity of contributions put together in this book acknowledges the variety of debates and perspectives that mark contemporary discussions on the relation between art and public space, with particular reference to the case of graffiti and street art, which attracted most of the contributors that came from various disciplines and backgrounds.

At a time when disciplinary boundaries are progressively blurred and new creative dynamics are emerging with new approaches in public space, we aim naturally to emphasize the importance of these themes in the development of the contemporary city, as well as in the current work of artists, urban planners and cultural mediators. This must acknowledge the increasing diversity of (artistic) urban intervention on public space. On one hand, this diversity is expressed in the variety of artistic expressions that embody these interventions: street art / graffiti, performing arts, visual arts, sculpture, (ephemeral) architecture, festivals, etc. On the other hand, this diversity is expressed on a variety of forms that embody these processes: formal/informal, institutionalized or not, legal or not mainstream/alternative, legitimized or not, etc. We are not interested to enter here in the huge conceptual debates about what are urban interventions and what is street art, or about the different typologies we could define within contemporary artistic urban interventions on public space. For simplification, we assume that we are generally speaking of interventions that have an artistic purpose, that is, that mobilize intentionality on that field, and that are developed on urban territory, specifically in what can be considered the public space.

It is worthwhile to notice that these artistic urban interventions became progressively "central" in contemporary societies and in academic reflection (but also in policy and planning practices), particularly in recent decades, due to a diversity of mechanisms, which include (i) the increasing centrality of public space on daily life practices, through more hedonistic and conviviality oriented lifestyles; (ii) the progresses on art history and artistic schools trajectories, giving space to more open and de-sacralized practices, as well as to more community and site-specific oriented types of artistic work; (iii) the rising awareness by policy makers and public administration of the social, cultural and economic importance of urban intervention movements as well as of their impacts and their usability as tool for development; and (iv) the growing social demand for these practices, linked to the movements towards the de-sacralization of arts, the enhancement of performativity, (self)expression and cultural diversity and the development of civic participation and grassroots community building processes.

Naturally it is not our aim to cover all these debates and discussions in this introduction, but just to set the scene for the discussions that will be made in the following chapters. In order to enable a better framing of those discussions, there are just three main alerts which we would like to highlight prior to entering in those debates.
First, is the notion of the fluidity of the concept of public space, which crosses with the debates on the notions of public space and public sphere. More exactly, we shall be aware of the multiple crossings (public/private; collective/personal) which conduct us from the notion of public space to the one of public sphere. In practice, we have a public sphere which crosses the public/private divide or the collective/personal divide with the several attributes which usually define the public space: (i) its property or management (e.g public space if managed or owned by public institutions); (ii) the way it is appropriated or used (e.g, public space if there is access or conditions of appropriability in it); and (iii) the interested in the name of which it is used (e.g, public space as a public good, or as a common asset, mobilized for public interest).

Assuming this degree of complexity, urban interventions can be seen as developed in a variety of public spaces, with diverse characteristic, which are in practice different components of the public sphere. Besides, the liveliness and multiplicity of uses of public sphere is conditioned and determined by a diversity of factors, such as urban morphology, (sub)cultures, socio-demographic composition, socio-economic conditions, artistic skills and knowledge, conviviality and sociability practices, regulations and norms, etc.

A second alert which we would like to leave here relates to the debates on the relation between urban interventions on public space and territorial valorization. Naturally urban interventions are not neutral and any artistic intervention have impacts in social, economic, cultural or environmental fields, which are diversely felt and perceived by the diverse stakeholders involved in that process, in that territory (the artist, the community, the urban authorities, the cultural institutions, the cultural mediators, their art worlds, etc.). The discussion on this relation between urban intervention and valorization can be seen at two different levels. On one hand, considering the contribution of artistic urban interventions to urban development and the mechanisms of transmission of that (that is, considering the multiple functions of urban intervention at the light of the several dimensions of sustainable development: promotion of economic efficiency, social equity, environmental quality, civic participation, identity expression,…). On the other hand, considering the ways urban intervention lead to the valorization of place, in diverse (material and symbolic) arenas (artistic intervention promotes territorial valorization – or de-valorization – at multiple fields: economic, symbolic, cultural, etc.). The wide debates around the contemporary trends to instrumentalization of arts, or the discussions on the role of artists and creatives as (marginal) gentrifiers of our cities are certainly linked to this umbilical relation between artistic intervention and valorization of place.

Thirdly, we would like to alert to the need to understand and cope with the territoriality of the dynamics associated to urban intervention. Creative dynamics are often embedded in specific territorial realities (e.g cultural quarters, brownfield locations, regenerating areas, etc.) and in specific governance forms (see, e.g. Costa and Lopes, 2013) which are fundamental for the vitality and the sustainability of those territorial systems through time. This implies that there are fragile equilibria which can be compromised by artistic intervention in the public space if these interventions are not solidly grounded on a deep knowledge of that territorial system. The relationships between these urban interventions and the reputation building mechanisms that are generated on those systems; between these urban interventions and the use conflicts that are verified on those systems; and between these urban interventions and the institutionalization process that can occur triggered by those practices; all of them are crucial to the sustainability of those areas as loci of creativity and artistic dynamic. As several studies have shown (e.g. Costa and Lopes, 2106, 2016a), conflict and informality are important drivers for artistic vitality in particular parts of urban space, such as cultural quarters or other, and public sphere plays there an important role in the nurturing of the creative milieu, which need to be constantly managed through the power relations between the agents involved. Besides, these kind of regulatory processes, in their diversity, have naturally also implications, both to the public policies as well to the art worlds themselves, as can be exemplified by the analysis of the case of local policy towards graffiti in Lisbon (Costa and Lopes, 2015; Neves, P.S.,2015).

Having these alerts in mind, several branches of discussion can be identified and can structure the debates which will be held in this book. We draw our attention to four of them:

> a) the way urban interventions confront the concept of public space (or public sphere) and the current challenges to its broadening (e.g, with social media networks,...); public space notion is constantly challenged at several levels: in the social practices as mean of artistic work and self-expression (e.g. new art work platforms), as mediation mechanism (e.g., photo reproduction and documentation of street art), or also as reflexive instrument in the dialogue with the city (e.g, for educational purposes);

> b) the way artistic urban interventions and street art contribute to the production of urban spaces and shape the social practices that occur in them and contribute to the evolution of the collective and individual representations of those places;

> c) the way artistic interventions and art practices transform and symbolically shape urban spaces, that is, the ways they contribute to the resignification of public spaces (and which artistic mechanisms are used to that);

> d) the way they enable reflexive processes and co-creation of knowledge, empowering the communities and promoting development processes (e.g., using urban interventions reflexively for educational purposes, academic and research targets, or urban planning processes).

These four reasoning lines are the backbone for the analysis conducted in this book. Following this introductory chapter, which just sets the broad scene for the discussion that will be held in the next texts, we have four distinct parts in this book, which refer to each of those four thematic branches in the analysis of the relation between artistic urban interventions and public sphere.

First part, entitled "Arts, life and everyday live: broadening the public sphere(s)", deals with the issue of the relation of creative practices with urban public sphere, deepening and deconstructing the notion of public space and the way artistic and daily life creative practices challenge it, through specific territorially embedded mechanisms. Three chapters constitute this first part of the book.

The first of them, entitled "Transfers between the Urban and the Human. Inhabiting the City from the Public Art" (Chapter 2), delivered by Letícia Gonzalez Menéndez, brings us a discussion on artistic practice in public spaces, perpectivating public art practices from an anthropologic point of view, through which the author aims to demonstrate how "creative action" reminds "latent" to the experience of the "common" that the author considers redefines public place as a space for the collective experience, and discusses how this mechanisms can contribute to the livability and the formation of alternative "communities of feeling" in the urban realm and to the production of the practices and the representations of "living in the city".

After this, the chapter delivered by Glória Diogenes (Chapter 3: Youth, Media and Social Networks: contemporary subjectivities) allows us to see this broadening of the relation with the public sphere in practice through a different point of view. Basing on a ethnography of cyberspace research in Orkut social network, the author notices an hybridism between the virtual public space and the city's public space, exploring the practices and representations of organized soccer fan groups in this digital social network, through the analysis of their profiles. Through a survey on these youth profiles, studying a population which lives, in their majority, on the outskirts of Fortaleza, Brazil, the author explores the way the rivalry between soccer teams' fans groups mobilize and represent their feelings in the cyberspace and the way these youth groups represent and produce their public image.

Finally, chapter 4 ("'I come from Porto and bring a Porto in me': essays on a cartography of affections in/of the city"), by Paula Guerra, presents us another way of exploring the boundaries of the public sphere and the impacts artistic practices can have on it. The author describes the result of a project which was developed in 2012 in Sé neighborhood, at Porto, Portugal, which mobilized local inhabitants on a research action process which was based in the development of individual cartographies as a tool for the empowerment of young adults in their local communities. Drawing upon the situationist idea of derive and psycogeogrpahy practices, the youths involved in this project were producing a new relation with their community and their territorial insertion through the recollection of images and the setting up of an exhibition which challenged their perceptions and images about the historical center of the city where they lived and to reconstruct the symbolic and affective landscape of the spaces they were used to know.

The second part of the book ("Urban interventions, representations, and the (re) production of urban space") brings us three approaches to the way artistic practices and urban interventions in the public arena contribute to the production of urban space, and how they shape urban landscape and the social practices that develop in it. Ágata Dourado Sequeira's article (Chapter 5: "Ephemeral Art in Impermanent Spaces: The effects of street art in the social construction of public space") centers in the analysis of street art in the urban context of Lisbon metropolitan area, in Portugal. Through a study which inquires essentially the relation between street art, the image of the city and the spaces in which it is developed, and the role of the actors and institution which shape those practices, the author argues that street art can contribute both (and simultaneously) to the (re)creation of the image(s) of the city and to the promotion of critical discourses on the urban public space and the powers that shape it. It is argued that this is made in a way which is related to the increasing visibility and broader social legitimization of this art world and that is, in parallel, accompanied by a reconfiguration of institutional processes, involving a diversity of actors, from street artist to promoters or public institutions.

Departing from a diverse empirical reality, the city of Palermo, in Italy, Luisa Tuttolomondo, on chapter 6 ("Between formal and informal practices to manage the city: the role of street art in the Old town of Palermo") deals with similar issues. Having in mind the evolution of the Old Town in the center of Palermo, the author emphasizes the complex dynamics of interaction between the more formal and the more informal practices of urban management and of civic participation which took place in this area of the city in recent years. It is particularly studied the discourse around some of the public sphere problems known and identified in this part of the city, considering the practices of the use of its public urban spaces, and the ways actors involved interact in public arena. Acknowledging the diversity of forms that the street art manifestations have assumed in the center of Palermo, the author recognizes the diversity of their impacts on the public space, spanning from the consolidation of pre-existing dynamics (such as the configuration of the place as "underground" or bohemian") to the promotion of change in the use of urban spaces (and its symbolic ..) in other cases.

Finally, on chapter 7, Madalena Corte Real and Maria João Monteiro Gomes drive us through the case of "Camilla Watson photography and its impact in the social production of public space in a neighborhood (Mouraria) in the inner city of Lisbon". The authors aim to investigate how the photographic work of Camila Watson in this changing old neighborhood of central Lisbon has affected the social production of space of this district. Confronting the experiences of the residents and of the visitors of this quarter regarding the project and its results, the authors try to perceive how different constructed realities are molded by this artistic practice and to compare them at the light of the respective contexts. Both narratives are articulated with the continuous and ongoing change process that affects the neighborhood contributing to (re)create images that consolidate and validate the (diverse) social representations of space.

The third part of the book ("Public art and the resignification of public space") deals with the mechanisms through which artistic interventions transform and symbolically shape urban spaces, but now departing more from the "artistic action" perspective, than from the "urban" point of view, and confronting distinct examples and case studies, in very different points of the globe, which bring us the power of artistic practice on urban space through the specific case of street art and graffiti interventions.

Polona Lupinsek's article (Chapter 8: "Untitled"), leads us to Yogyakarta, on Java, Indonesia, to show us how the artistic practices in this field have been shaped by the specific socio-political and cultural context of the country and the local atmosphere of the city itself. The author argues that the artist relation with the community has evolved both in the engagement relation that they build with local population and at the way this is reflected in artistic work they produce. The increasing on the visibility of street art, in very diverse forms, on a society where it was essentially invisible, leads mostly to socio-political benefits (more than artistic or economic, at this phase, the author argues), contributing to the empowerment of the communities involved and the increase of social awareness at different levels.

On Chapter 9 ("Urban Visuality through Stencil"), Rachel Souza, drawing upon a diversity of examples of stencil interventions throughout the world, puts herself in the point of view of investigating the aesthetics and semiotic dynamics of stenciling within the public arena, examining the aesthetic elements that arise from this artistic practice as public space intervention. Urban visuality is used as an entrance point to explore city as "collage" and the artist himself as a "bricoleur" in what refers to stenciling practices. Drawing upon this framework, the author identifies symbolic overloads and the resignification of symbolic aggregations as two sign-line elements of the stencil's insertion in the city.

Finally, on chapter 10 ("The Writing on the Wall: Embraced or Despised"), Voica Puscasiu drives us to the debate on the differences between graffiti and street art, discussing these social constructed concepts and exploring the symbolic differences as well as the social, economic and cultural effects that the diverse perceptions about it bring to the respective communities, and confronting the potential for the "establishment" of these artistic practices in what concerns to the receptivity of art markets and institutions.

To close the digression held on this book, part four ("Research action in practice: urban interventions and knowledge co-creation") brings us two cases which illustrate in practice the ways urban interventions can enable reflexive processes and the co-creation of knowledge with the communities, generating empowerment and enhancing development processes, through the use of image-based instruments.

The first of these examples is brought by Elenise Cristina Pires de Andrade, Edivan Carneiro de Almeida and Milena Santos Rodrigues in Chapter 11 ("Graffiti, street, delirium: arts defiances". The authors, drawing upon a Deleuzian perspective, bring us the questionings that arouse by the confrontations which were enabled by three events held at 2014 in Feira de Santana, BA, Brazil: a graffiti event on a public school wall; an event about street art on a museum; and an academic meeting which provoked the crossovers between different knowledges and expressions, mixing students, teachers and artists and confronting them with the pluralities of the city and its potential for a diversity of encounters. The authors explore the potential of these images and their analysis to defy pre-defined thoughts and to think reflexively about the field of research and university extension programs on education and their relation to the city.

Finally, on chapter 12 ("Beyond the visible on decoding the layers of a cultural quarter: Photo-essay on a reflexive urban intervention") Pedro Costa and Ricardo Lopes take us to the results of one urban intervention they conducted in 2012, assuming a research-action based methodology, at Bairro Alto, the main cultural quarter of Lisbon Portugal. This intervention aimed to explore the reflexivity of this district users' and to promote the discussion on the codification layers of a cultural quarter, as well as on the conflicts that are inherent to them, on the appropriation of public space, both at material and symbolic arenas. In this paper, which is presented in the particular format of a photo essay, the authors bring us a set of images that show us some of the results achieved with artistic this happening, which enabled them to explore the different layers of (in)visibility and liminarity that are present in the informal urban context that usually characterize the creative milieus which develop in cultural neighborhoods.

References:

Adz, K. (2010), Street Knowledge, London: Harper Collins

Arantes, A. (1997), "A guerra dos lugares: fronteiras simbólicas e liminaridade no espaço urbano de São Paulo". In Fortuna, Carlos (org.), Cidade, Cultura e Globalização – Ensaios de Sociologia, Oeiras: Celta, pp. 259-270

Bassani, J. (2003), As linguagens artísticas e a cidade: cultura urbana do século XX. São Paulo: FormArte

Bishop, C. (2012), Artificial Hells: participatory art and politics of spectatorship, London New York: Verso

Becker, H. S. (1982), Art worlds. London: University of California Press.

Bennett, A. (2004), "Consolidating the music scenes perspective", Poetics, 32(3-4), pp. 223-234.

Bennett, A. (2008), "Towards a cultural sociology of popular music", Journal of Sociology, 44(4), pp. 419-432.

Bennett, A. & Peterson, R. A. (eds.) (2004), Music scenes: local, translocal and virtual. Nashville: Vanderbilt University Press.

Blum, A. (2001), "Scenes". Public [online], 22/23, 7-35. Retrieved from http://www.publicjournal.ca/.

Brissac, N. (2002), Arte/cidade: Intervenções urbanas. São Paulo: Senac

Campos, R. ; Brighenti, A. M.; Spinelli, L. (2011), Uma cidade de imagens: Produções e consumos visuais em meios urbanos. Lisboa, Editora Mundos Sociais

Cartiere C., Willis S. (2008), The Practice of Public Art. New York: Routledge

Costa, P. (2008), "Creativity, innovation and territorial agglomeration in cultural activities: the roots of the creative city", in Cooke, P. and L. Lazzeretti (org.), Creative cities, cultural clusters and local development, Cheltenham: Edward Elgar, pp. 183-210

Costa, P. (2012), "Gatekeeping processes, reputation buiding and creative milieus: evidence from case studies in Lisboa, Barcelona and São Paulo", in Lazzeretti, L (Ed.), Creative industries and innovation in Europe: Concepts, measures and comparatives case studies", Routledge, pp. 286-306

Costa, P., Lopes, R. (2013), "Artistic intervention in public sphere, conflict and urban informality: an international comparative approach to informal dynamics in cultural districts", Cidades, Comunidades e Territórios, nº 2, Junho de 2013

Costa, P.; Lopes, R. (2015) "Is street art institutionalizable? Challenges to an alternative urban policy in Lisbon", Métropoles [En ligne], 17 (2015)

Costa, P.; Lopes, R. (2016), "Artistic Urban Interventions, Informality and Public Sphere: Research Insights from Ephemeral Urban Appropriations on a Cultural District", DINAMIA-CET Working Paper nº 2016/

Costa, P.; Lopes, R. (2016a), "Dos dois lados do espelho: diálogos com um bairro cultural através da intervenção urbana", DINAMIA-CET Working Paper nº 2016/

Crane, D. (1992), The production of culture – media and the urban arts. Londres: SAGE.

Flynn, A. (2016), "Subjectivity and Obliteration of Meaning: Contemporary Art, Activism, Social Movement Politics", Cadernos de Arte e Antropologia, Vol. 5, nº1, 2016, pp. 59-77

Guerra, P. (2013), A instável leveza do rock. Porto: Edições Afrontamento.

Guerra, P. (2014), "Punk, expectations, breaches and metamorphoses: Portugal, 1977–2012". Critical Arts, 28(1), pp. 111-122.

Guerra, Paula (2015), "Keep it rocking: the social space of Portuguese alternative rock (1980–2010)". Journal of Sociology, 51(1), pp. 230-276.

Guerra, P. & Costa, P. (2016) (eds.), Redefining art worlds in late modernity, Porto: Universidade do Porto.

Klanten, R. and Hubner, M. (Eds) (2010), Urban interventions: Personal projects in public spaces, Berlin: Gestalten

Lopes, R., (2012), Intervenções artísticas efémeras e apropriação de espaço público em contextos urbanos informais: análise de cinco "bairros criativos": Bairro Alto e Cais do Sodré, Gràcia, Vila Madalena, Brick Lane e Kreuzberg SO36, ISCTE-IUL, Lisboa

Miles, M. (1997), Art, space and the city – Public art and urban futures, London: Routledge

Miles, M. (2012), «Uma cidade póscriativa?», Revista Crítica de Ciências Sociais [Online], 99 | 2012

Neves, P.S., Ed. (2015) Street Art & Urban Creativity Scientific Journal, Vol 1, Lisboa

Neves, P.S, (2015) "Métodos de inventario aplicados al arte urbano de Lisboa" MURAL Street Art Conservation, Nº2, Madrid, 2015, p. 36 – 37

Neves, P.S., Ed. (2016) Street Art & Urban Creativity Scientific Journal, Vol 2, Lisboa

Pinder, D. (2008), "Urban Interventions: Art, Politics and Pedagogy", International Journal of Urban and Regional Research, Vol. 32.3, September 2008

Scott A.J. (2000), The Cultural Economy of Cities. New Delhi, London- Thousand Oaks: Sage

Scott, A. J. (2008), Social Economy of the Metropolis. Cognitive-Cultural Capitalism and the Global Resurgence of Cities, Oxford: Oxford University Press

Scott A.J. (2014) "Beyond the Creative City: Cognitive–Cultural Capitalism and the New Urbanism", Regional Studies, 48:4, 565-578.

Shove, G. (Ed) (2012), Banksy: You Are an Acceptable Level of Threat and if you were not you would know about it, Durham: Carpet Bombing Culture

Shove, G., Potter, P., Jones, S. (2010), Untitled III - This is street art, Durham: Carpet Bombing Culture

Soja, E. (1989), Postmodern geographies: the reassertion of space in critical social theory, London and New York: Verso

Straw, W. (1991), "Systems of articulation, logics of change: communities and scenes in popular music". Cultural Studies [online], pp. 368-388. Retrieved from http://strawresearch.mcgill.ca/straw/systemsofarticulation.pdf.

Straw, W. (2004), "Scenes and Sensibilities". E-Compós [online], 6. Retrieved from http://www.compos.org.br/seer/index.php/e-compos/article/view/83/83.

Traquino, M. (2010), A construção do lugar pela arte contemporânea. Ribeirão, Portugal: Húmus

Part II.
Arts, life and everyday live:
broadening the public
sphere(s)

Chapter 2

Transfers Between The Urban And The Human, Inhabiting The City From The Public Art

Leticia González Menéndez

Abstract

The contemporary city has experienced transformations that have conditioned ways of thinking, perceiving and living public spaces. The urban condition has an essential anthropological component that, in many cases, it is ignored; obviating the substantial transfers between the human and the urban. In this connection, we understand that artistic practice can be an effective catalyst from which we rethink the city through perspectives closer to action and experience. This study puts forward a genealogical coverage throughout the principle operative models of the artistic practice in public spaces and, more specifically, the intention is to deepen in the methodological basis of public art from an anthropological point of view. For that, we defend the necessary reinterpretation of the concept "living" and, in particular, the perspectives relating to the embodied experience in which the body and the affection are particularly important. We will check if such positions from the deconstruction of public art can activate new spatialities maintain latent relationships between participation in creative practice, the redefinition of public spaces and the genesis of other aesthetic policies. Thus, we try to demonstrate how the creative action remains latent the experience of "the common" that redefines public space as a place for the collective experience as well as contributes to the livability an the formation of alternative "communities of feeling" and "living the city".

Keywords: Art, public, inhabit, human, urban, spatiality, city

1. Transferences between subject, art and city

Urban transformations that happened in the last decades have had the development of new production and reproduction models of the city[1] as a fundamental consequence. Nowadays we keep witnessing an enlargement of the human condition that is Fostering other manners of inscription of territories and individuals[2]. From the contemporary art world this changes have been experienced in a relevant way. Creative action is an essential part of mechanisms and devices that move images, subjects, sign or spaces along.

Bearing this in mind, our proposal tries to reflect on different trans-disciplinary connections between the urban and the human from a contemporary art perspective. Specifically, we try to analyse the "public art" category which is understood as a model that links essential elements in the public space production and, what is more important, as a part that melds its symbolic reproduction. For this, we take the concept of "inhabiting" as a catalyst for the transferences between space and subject. We set out a critical point of view about the conceptual settings of "public art" with the aim of exposing how new ways of experimentation can be established from the creative ac-

---

1 The transformations experimented by cities since the decade of the 1960s have moved through such a extreme courses that, according to Soja, "what existed thirty years ago, today is in practice unrecognisable". However, we continue witnessing to a constant evolution that has favoured –thus, provoking interest– other study models for the city that have given way to new analysis models and conceptual settings. This way, "this process of geo-historical development is an integral question an a leitmotif in every study about human condition. What is suggested here is that wherever critical attention is focused, something new about postmodern urbanism is to be learnt". Soja, Edward, 2000, pp. 17-24

2 We take this concept from Bruno Latour. This means that an "inscription" is a basic transformation given when "an entity materialises in a sign, in a archive, in a document, in a piece of paper, in a trace". Latour, Bruno, 2001, pp. 365-366.

tion, not only the building and appearance of the city but the heterogeneity of the urban. We take three action key lines: a) Reconsidering the ways of "conceiving" public space through plastic arts; b) Promoting experience as the axis in the construction of space and the origin of other ways of city "perception"; c) Reflecting on the ability of art as a means of inhabiting the urban that makes new forms of living and social interchange possible.

Summing up, we suggest a critical perspective about the ethical-aesthetic processes that happen in urban spaces and, finally, we question the possibility of inhabiting the city in a creative and different way of understanding public art.

2. The urban space production. Putting space first

Cities represent a specific way of human settlement in which life styles are structured by means of a set of specifically urban production methods (Soja, Edward, *Op. Cit.,* p. 60.). The production of this speciality blends physical constructions and social relationships, thus creating a material and symbolic environment that is essential for life. This way, its social production[3] is given by three levels. Fist, a field that consists of spatial practices –specific forms that are "perceived" and can be mapped and measured–. Secondly, there are conceptualizations that at the same time activate a "conception" of the urban space by symbolic representations. Finally, a third level whose operation is based in the "experience" as it participates in the plurality of human action, configuring a "space entirely lived, a place of experience and structure agencies, individuals and collectives" (Soja, Edward, *Op. Cit,* p. 40.). With all of this, following Henri Lefebvre assumptions (Cfr. Lefebvre,1974), we can realize that urban space –always in a direct relationship with the subject–, is composed by a sign network "whose signifiers are made by special forms and whose meanings are ideology contents" (Castells,1972, p. 155.).

Nevertheless, the transformations that these "three spaces" have experienced –according to Edward Soja, "the modern metropolis transition to the expansive post-metropolis"– suggest two basic problems. On the one hand, space production of the current city has became a "neoliberal expression that understands its development in production, distribution and massive consumption terms" (Naredo, 2000, p. 27). That is, space production is based on the free accumulation and the dispossession[4], being just one more consumer product –a space of control– that uses the instrumentalization of urban space "perception" and "conception". On the other hand, these changes have affected the relationship between space and individual, this is, the "inhabitant" is transformed into an entity without rights on the common spacialities produced and experimented by itself. Consequently, the modes of living, the anthropological dimensions of the urban condition, and in a special way, the "inhabiting" concept, have been devaluated.

To this complex picture we should add the broad problems associated with the technological development which turn the metropolis into a hybrid, volatile and fluid entity (*Cfr.* Castells, 1999). This condition of constant redefinition keeps open the different action critical lines that defend attending the infinite capabilities that can (and must) happen in the urban reality. However, in this way, the urban continues to be an active being that –and this is why it is interesting– can be described as sensitive[5].

In any case, following Robert Frank' ideas, "if the city is the world which the human have created, it is also the world in which is henceforth to live" (PARK,1967, p. 3) and taking into consideration the fact that urban space is always a product of human action, the question is clear: What is the difference between the urban and the city?

---

3 The social space production is given thought the constant interaction between "macro" and "micro" perspectives; an inherent combination among large-scale buildings and other that blends in the common life. Such assumptions, essential in the contemporary cities, cannot be nested and, for this, both perspectives must cohabit without being nested.

4 David Harvey, according Robert Brenner, describes how global capitalism experiments different problems of overproduction. In this regard, Harvey understands that this kind of mechanism is nothing more than the demonstration of a whole series of financial operations that attack "the commons". At the same time this methods threaten the public space dynamics, outperforming and privatising it thought different strategic. HARVEY, David, *The new imperialism*, Oxford, Oxford University Press, 2003. Spanish edition: "El nuevo imperialismo. Acumulación por desposesión", en *El nuevo desafío imperial*, Buenos Aires, Clacso, 2005, pp. 99-129.

5 Martin Heidegger or Gaston Bachelard has used this sensitive condition to understand the space. In both perspectives the concept "inhabiting" is as a catalyst that makes sense, both conceptualizations of space –in the case of essential for the being-in and being-with– as the modes of production space in Heidegger. We cannot forget that " (…) but poetically, man inhabits this earth"

What separates the human and the urban? And more specifically, what is the difference between the production of urbanity and the urbanization?

3. Between the Human and the Urban conditions

Differences between the city and the urban have been defined in a particular way by Henri Lefebvre during the decade the 1960s. We start from a particular basis: While the city is a group of bodies (streets, roads, buildings, etc.), the urban is a "lifestyle" that keeps its autonomy to some extent. "Lo urbano está marcado por la proliferación de urdimbres relacionales descolocadas y la urbanización es el proceso consistente en integrar (planificar) la movilidad espacial de la vida cotidiana"[6]. In any case, the urban is given through energy transferences that behave and are reorganized constantly in spacialities and temporalities.

Nevertheless, the space and the time in the modern city are reproduced through urban space (public space) and its conception and perception are given through the agency of concrete locations and recognition processes. In other words, these procedures are specific to the urbanization. On the other hand, the urban –which always goes beyond temporalities and demarcations–, turns into a social power where practices, experiences, situations or interactions are accumulated in a de-territorialised manner. Urbanization distances itself from urbanity inasmuch as the urban can and must "reconocerse como una labor, un trabajo de lo social sobre sí mismo, como la sociedad urbana haciéndose y deshaciéndose una y otra vez"[7].

Thus, the urban is not only "used" but it must be "inhabited" in all its dimensions. Not in vain, according to Martin Heidegger, the exercise of inhabiting is close to the human construction process but it is always linked to the basic "region" (Heidegger, 1994, pp. 127-134) of the existence. If human beings exist it is because this "region" implies a potential (an uncovering) to generate actions, experiences or sensations. In other words, "inhabiting" is being present, giving space, being affected, touching and being touched by all that surrounds us; it is producing the spatiality (both collective and individual) that the subjects can experience in multiple ways. Therefore, inhabiting is subjetivation, being-in and being-with the world. In this order of things, we cannot afford to ignore that the construction of urbanity is at the same level as the construction of humanity. This gives way to a relevant question: we must rethink urban experiences and understand them as sensitive experiences, beyond their representation, in order to recode them as new models of representation and presentation of the common spaces in the cities. Taking into account that "the spatial practises are the ones which practice and segregate the space and make it social"[8], it is advisable to raise one of the essential foundations in its construction: places. We must be aware that the actual order has used forms of territorialisation and re-territorialisation (other ways of perception and conception) and that places can no longer be inhabited –neither constructed in a Heideggerian sense– for this, critical theory understands that the only available potentiality of the concept is its condition of living and changeable force in which the citizen becomes in a mutable "user". Consequently, is in the power of the urban where "gestures, words, memories, symbols and senses[9]" happen more freely.

> «Todas estas corrientes coincidieron en entender que lo urbano debía ser al tiempo receptáculo y motor de la creatividad humana. La calle pasaba a ser, de su mano, un lugar plástico en el que la paradoja, el sueño, el deseo, el humor, el juego y la poesía se enfrentaban, a través de todo tipo de procesos azarosos y aleatorios, a la burocratización, el utilitarismo y la falsa espectacularización de la ciudad»[10].

6 Delgado, 1999, p. 23. Translation: "The urban is marked by the proliferation of dislocated relational networks, and the urbanization is the process of integrating (and planning) the spatial mobility of everyday life".

7 Delgado, 2000, p. 45. Translation: "recognize itself as a social work back on itself, as the urban society making and unmaking again and again".

8 Delgado, 2013, [en línea] disponible en la *url*: http://www.oasrn.org/pdf_upload/el_espacio_publico.pdf

9 Delgado, Manuel, "El espacio social como patrimonio" en *Arquitectura tradicional y entorno construido*, Manuel Luna y Manuel Lucas (eds.), Roman, Trenti, 2002.

4. The constructions of public spaces and the primacy of representation

The city space production has experienced what is known as a "representation syndrome". That means, "la imagen de la ciudad se ha convertido en una cierta organización del espacio que muestra las condiciones de toda percepción, condiciones estéticas en todos los sentidos del término"[11]; this is, there is a priority of representation over presence (*Cfr.* Trías, 1997) and, for that, a superior understanding of instrumentalization of things perceived and things conceived.

. One of the basic action strategies in the construction of public space is the conceptualization of "urban landscape". To be clear on this, urban landscape is not the city but the image of itself, which is extracted by us, in an individual or collective way (Maderuelo, p. 575). That means, through image-centrism and from what is noteworthy to watch contemplating the re-territorialisation of the spaces (*Ibídem*). In that way, urban landscape is formed by dominant symbolic structures that create an urban code that is stereotypical, apolitical and normalized urban code. The macrophysics of this order reduce the concept "landscape" and transform it into a floating significant that structures the hegemony of the urbanization.

«La calle y la plaza son, en este sentido, objetos de un doble discurso. Uno es resultado de un diseño urbanístico y arquitectónico políticamente determinado, la voluntad del cual es orientar la percepción, ofrecer sentidos prácticos, distribuir valores simbólicos (…) Un segundo discurso es el de la sociedad urbana misma, la de los usuarios –productores– de lo urbano. Son ellos quienes tienen siempre la última palabra acerca de cómo y en qué sentido moverse»[12].

The urban landscape, by setting borders and demarcations, tries to establish a method that allows a correct readability and sufficient "aesthetic spatiality" in the city. Different patterns are pursued in order to get the "peaceful" coexistence among, for example, monumental sculpture and other elements such as architecture, signposts, street furniture, gardens, etc. This encourages a tandem between plastic and urbanism whose clear goal is organizing and creating spaces and searching the aesthetic representation; in the words of Paul Zucker, the pictorial sensation (Zucker, pp., 232-237). However, despite of these experiences looking for a link between the citizen (user and viewer) and the urban experience, the latter is limited to monitoring the edges properly marked for it only. Thus, the urban imaginary and the landscape have become standardized social facts and, in this way, "any place is potentially transformable into public or private space" (Deutsche, 2001, p. 320).

In this context, the artistic practice has gradually been integrated in the urbanization field, keeping the task of developing cognitive maps, in a way that has helped the growth of the informational spatial (and aesthetic) configurations present both in individual and collective city memories. Hence the importance of the art that has participated in a strategy development or in other processes such as wayfinding[13] or gentrification. This approach has encouraged a clear idea: the public space art needs to be part of the landscape environmental cognition of the metropolis through different cognitive and perceptive connotations[14].

---

10 Delgado, Manuel, "En busca del espacio perdido", en Territorios de la infancia: diálogos entre arquitectura y pedagogía", Isabel Cabanellas y Clara Eslava (Coords.), Barcelona, Graó, 2005, p. 14. Translation: "All of these trends agree in understanding that the urban must be receptacle and motor of human creativity in both senses at the same time. The street becomes, in this way, a plastic space where paradox, dreams, desire, humour and poetry face all kinds of random and aleatory processes against bureaucracy, utilitarianism and the false spectacularization of the city".

11 *Ibídem.*, p. 24 -25. Translation: "City image becomes in a certain organization of space that shows the coditions of all the perception processes, aesthetic conditions in all the senses of the term".

12 Delgado, 1999, p. 182. Translation: «Street and square are, in that sense, objects of a double discourse, one is the result of politically determined architectural and urban design, which wants to guide the perception, to offer practical senses, distributing symbolical values (…) A second discourse is related to the urban society itself, the space of the users –producers–, they are those who always have the last word on how and in what direction to move".

14 Understanding as perception the elements that operate directly in relation, dialectal or not, to the subject itself and its cognition (from the environmental point of view) refers to that "not present", the memory or the inserts in that same process.

Consequently, art in public spaces has operated essentially as a framework that establishes a specific relationship with the place, it has organized modes of experience and has a direct influence on their significance. In short, it has been used as a device of social and urban planning that provides a hierarchical aesthetization and processes of control, development planning and cultural policy.

5. The role of art in public spaces. Public Art category

We start from an essential fact: The different technocratic ideas (Marchán Fiz, 1986, p. 279) and the artistic world experiment an approach to the development in the late capitalism model which is parallel to that of the late capitalism. Thus, although in the 1950s it was popular to look for other formal and expressive models of urban artistic creation (Krauss, pp. 30-44) –we must remember the critical importance of Situcionism in Europe– the 50s also proved to be a period of economic expansion that, as we have seen, gradually established the standard uses and forms of public spaces.

In this regard, while contemporary art abandoned galleries and production centres, looking for new signification spaces, a complex procedure began to manage the installation of this art pieces in the city from different points of view. Given the social scale –subsequently economical scale– of these actions, the management of the artistic practices was crucial. The government aim –they continue to be the manager of the "public" specialities– was relocated artistic practice in order to make it more participant of economic structures, embedded in large-scale development, that the great metropolis was experimented[15].

In many cases art has been used, from its monumental conception, to recover what was believed to be a lost identity. An interesting paradox that gives meaning to a patrimonialization that tried to import a new collective cultural heritage steeped in supposedly shared values and whose ultimate goal was to create new models of governance[16]. The strategy was to produce Art and to reproduce new values of the merging macroeconomic order. "Monumentos y ornamentos de los que, hoy, (tampoco) se cuestionan su lugar, su sentido y su función en el conjunto de la ciudad. Y de una ciudad de la que se olvida o ignora que no sólo es representación sino presencia o que no sólo es arquitectura, si no estructura» (LANCEROS, 2000, p. 20). Therefore, a new artistic model, out of private spaces and typical of the new urban spaces, was encoded. "Art" and "Public", two polysemic notions, were linked.

In this way, a new perspective[17] raises "public" as an adjective which should be attached to creative action. Not in vain, one of the most common interpretations refers to, or a concept close to, "contrary to private" artwork, or those works located "outside" the stipulated venues. Given that "the public" is still a floating signifier[18], "the attribute refers to the regulated operation of a control device that is equipped with the monopoly of the legiti-

---

15 We put this consideration and use the notion of "reintegration" consider the fact that certain practices and speeches had managed to distance themselves from their own institutional strategies.

16 Montaner, Josep María, "Traumas urbanos: la pérdida de la memoria", Conferencia pronunciada en *Traumas urbanos. La ciudad y los desastres* desarrollado en el CCCB de Barcelona del 7 al 11 de julio de 2004, [on line], available in *url*: http://www.cccb.org/rcs_gene/memoria_perdida.pdf. Translation: "Monuments and ornaments whose place, meanings and function in the city are not questioned nowadays, forgetting or ignoring the fact that they are part of a city which is not only representation but also presence, not only architecture, but structure"

17 The objectives of conceptual art remained so overshadowed by the lack of theory and art criticism that they did not hesitate to proclaim the end. Thus Benjamin Buchloh himself said that "The triumph of enlightenment of conceptual art, its transformation of audiences and distribution, its abolition of object status and commodity form, at best would only be short-lived and would soon give way to return of the ghost-like re-appropriation of (prematurely?) displaced painterly and sculptural paradigms of the past". Buchloh, Benjamin H.D., "From the Aesthetic of Administration to Institutional Critique", in *Gintz, L´Art conceptuel*, París, Musée d´Art de la Ville de París, 1989.

18 We understand the "floating signifier" as an entity that has different loads of significance in the different contexts in which it appears. At certain times, those meanings can be diluted, transformed or lost. We should clarify that Chantal Mouffe and Ernesto Laclau in *Hegemony and Socialist Strategy* said that these signifiers were linked to attempts to dominate the field of discourse around "nodal points". They are privileged discursive "elements" which partially fix the meaning of the signifying chain, formed inside "an intertextuality that overflows" and whose main characteristic is its ambiguous and polysemic nature. *Cfr.*, Montero, Soledad, "Significant gaps and disputes over the meaning in political discourse: an argumentative approach.", in *Journal Identities,* No. 2, December 2012 and Butler, Judith, Laclau, Ernesto, Zizek, Salvoj, Contingency, hegemony, universality. Left wing contemporary dialogues, Buenos Aires, Fondo de Cultura Económica, 2000.

mate use of spatial violence –and we add, symbolic violence" (Habermas, 1999, p. 56). We must remember that it is no longer possible to accept that such spaces are public, because "they are, like any other social space, restricted and dominated by private economic interests and controlled by the State through urban planning[19].

On the basis of these assumptions, Miwon Kwon made a relevant reflection focusing in the interest that art suddenly raises in the local governments from 1960: «while these shifts represent a greater inclusivity and democratization of art for many artists (…) there is also the danger of a premature and uncritical embrace of "progressive" art as an equivalent of "progressive" politics (…) Why is it now that it has become a favoured model in public arts programming and arts funding)» (Kwon, Miwon, 1997, pp. 95-109).

"Art will become a mechanism of dehumanization and re-significance of the new spaces of the cities, used as a tool to legitimize urban policies in favour of the always acclaimed "recovery" or "appreciation" of the urban landscape and defended as an action in favour of the interest of the citizens. These artworks will receive the generic name of "Public Art"[20].

Despite the impossibility of establishing a chronological axis in the origin of this plastic category, the classic line of argument[21] dates the origin of the concept in 1965, year of the birth of *Art in Public Program,* created by the *National Endowment for the Arts.* The aim of this institution was "to assist communities in their efforts of increasing public awareness of contemporary art" (Fernández Quesada, Blanca, *Op. Cit.,* p. 182.). The creation of the *Art in Public Program* also tried to implement cultural aspects and public artwork[22]. Therefore, it is particularly important to note that the development of these "public" practices was justified, in most cases, because of the social and economic imbalance of the cities[23]. If the art and urbanization discourses continue to use the "public art" concept nowadays, it is precisely because of the emergence of institutions such as the *General Services Administration (Cfr.,* Lovell, 1991, pp. 30-49*)* or the *NEA (Ibídem.)* and, obviously, the economic benefits of these processes of public works.

A comprehensible and strategic classification was founded over the decades, based in three fundamental points[24] of which we will highlight two. An "art in public places", referred to those projects that bring together all kinds of urban sculpture or statuary; that is for «decorate or enriched urban spaces, especially plaza areas fronting federal buildings or corporate office towers» (Kwon, Miwon, *Op. Cit.,* p. 20). On the other hand, an "art as a public space", which keeps a certain interest in the place where the works are located –a good example of this is the proliferation of Site-Specific artworks– whose aim is to «sought greater integration between art, architecture, and landscape» (*Ibídem.*). The main conclusion is that these programs have not questioned the intrinsic relationship between the urban and the human and, more specifically, they have abandoned the necessary anthropological dimensions between art, subject, and city.

After all the debates that have been generated around this issue over decades, a key question remains: "we try to figure out the difference between a work which is "public art" and one that is not, especially if both appear in a (supposedly) public space" (Maderuelo, Javier, *Op. Cit.,* p. 164.). So, following Rosalyn Deutsche, we consider necessary to observe succinctly what is behind of the concept "public" and, especially, to try to understand the potential of certain creative urban practices.

---

19 Deutsche, Rosalynd, "Público", Conferencia en el curso Ideas recibidas. Un vocabulario para la cultura artística contemporánea, en el *Museu d'Art Contemporani* de Barcelona (MACBA), 19 de noviembre de 2007.

20 Other denominations: Street art, art in the city, urban art, context art, site-specific art, public locations, public space design, environmental art, landscape art, contemporary public sculpture, mural art, art: names as they appear ornamental, commemorative art, multimedia art, community art, art therapy, art heritage, political art, public art critic, art public interest or new genre public art. Quesada Fernández, 2005.

21 One that defines the boundaries and borders of an official "public art", standardized and institutional

22 As a state property.

23 The goal is to return to play attention to art in public spaces was again attend trends advocating the creation of places for citizens, they dissolved the previous attacks had grown fierce urbanism.

24 It should be noted that, despite being subjected to further review, this scheme continues to maintain its validity in the analysis and current studies.

With this, in the late 1990s a new creative force appears with a democratic spirit. Its top priority was to recover the "right to the city" and the creative construction of urban spaces. A new dimension of Public Art appears: art with public interest, which Suzanne Lacy called *New Genre of Public art* (Lacy, Suzanne (ed.),1994). This approach goes deeper into the social and anthropological dimensions, referring to the inherent link between artistic practice, space and subject. This holistic understanding moved the classic tendencies (urban statuary) with formal artistic behaviours, and focuses more on processes that improve their modes of action in matters of experience and expertise. In other words, "inhabiting" common spacialities.

6. The strategies of the new public art

In this order of things, the decade of the 1990s started full of critical tendencies whose objective was to redefine the classic conceptualization of classic "public art". There was one other practice that tried to point at the havoc caused by the new aesthetics politics and, at the same time, to highlight its self-sufficient and critical character:

«as a practice within the built environment, public art participates in the production of meanings, uses, and forms for the city. In this capacity, it can help secure consent to redevelopment and to the restructuring that make up the historical form of late capitalist urbanization. But like other institutions…it can also question and resist those operations, revealing the supposed contradictions of the urban process» (Deutsche, 1988, pp. 3-52.).

This kind of reflections questioned that art had the mission of creating new forms of conceiving or perceiving the city. Further than that, the bet was an art with public interest and, obviously, the basic precepts for the creators and collectives were bring back the democratic assumptions to the urban spaces that should be common and public again. The users capacity to construct and inhabiting the city with urbanity (*Ibídem.*, p. 11.) was looked for. In short, «public art should not be restricted to artworks placed in public plazas but should encompass relationships and dialogue» (VV.AA., 1984).

«¿is something common the public art?, ¿in which way public art could represent the audiences, taking into account the audience multiplicity?, ¿is the public art community based the most appropriated for the urban environment than the monumental art?, what the effect could this artworks have over the cultural institutions, over the pubic art, over the contemporary art, over the education?, What could public art contribute to the community?, Could arte strengthen the community and influence the society?» (Jacobs, p. 281).

The new public art strategies tried to recover the art capacities in communicative integration between the user and the urban spaces. It doesn't should be forgotten that "the democracy is understood as a obligation to "practise" the communication in the public arena (take the world and action)" (Wodiczko,1992). The famous "calls to action" of critics and artists as Lacy or Gablik sought to get back the human and ecological of what could already be understood as an ethic-aesthetic turn of the urban artistic practise. The basic objective was bringing back the humanity to the public spaces in a constant privatization through the citizen's participation. That means, this tendencies tried to recode the "inhabiting" the city. The politic component was fundamental and, in much cases, defining. Hal Foster understood, according to Laclau, that the processes as "differential articulations" (Laclau, 1983 and *Cfr.*, Laclau, 2000) as they not only question doubt the image production patrons but also highlight the direct experience. In any case, the artists and collectives in the early 90s tried to recover the diversity, the debate, and the conflict in contrast with concepts such as "urban planning" or "order" according to the classic public art. In such a way that, if we "consider culture as a place of conflict, the strategy to follow is new gramscian resistance or interference –right here and now- broke the hegemonic code of cultural representations and social regimens" (Foster, Hal, 2003) That was the challenged.

The essential idea was inducing public art in the real public sphere; that means, a total "awareness of the structural position of the thought and the material efficacy of its practise inside of the social whole, seeking to produce a concept of politics relevant for the present" (Clark, p. 145). In other words, interweaving the urban and the human condition, considering that the later is close to the aesthetic experience: "(…) the sensibility models, the ways of perception due change and, at the same time, the object with which relates changes as well" (Michaud, 2007, p. 17).

Consequently, this practices tried to highlight a vital impulse that sleeked to transcend the powers over the life, exalting "the power of life as a answer to this powers (...) opening doors to the proliferation of freedom, the production of subjectivity and the invention of new forms of fight. When the capital seizes the whole life, life reveals as a resistance" [25].

7. Redefining the new ways of inhabiting through the public art, conclusions

The operability of the new public art takes shape in front of a multitude (VIRNO, 2003, p. 14.) whose common basis is always a series of "affective realities that reproduce desire and pleasure" (*Cfr.* Negri, 1993.), individual and collective. In short, if public art is articulated through changing orientations, it can be interpreted as impulse modulations but always in a dynamic of associative multi-component relationships. According to Felix Guattari, it is all part of a "subjective emancipation" or "heterogenesys" (Guattari, 1996. p. 47). A metamodel that generates different new ways of self-government[26] as well as helping to escape from certain biopolitical processes.

This way they insisted on the defence and the maintainment of collective enunciations, which came from a "multiplicity" closer to the socius more than the asignifying intensities, *autopoiesis*, a new concept of ethic-aesthetic autonomy "closer to an affection logic" more than to an expression ensemble logic, against a policy of significance. So the works of a new public art should operate as genuine hackers, as existential "ritornello" (Guattari, Félix, *Op. Cit.,* p. 28). One way of understanding the spatiality and the environment from the gesture and the act and its subsequent repetitions which "always come back as another thing." (Deleuze, p. 247.). That is, "the whole range of aesthetic expression matters that trace an area and are developed in territorial motives" (*Ibídem*, p. 328). These complex universes have tried to propose an existential shift in order to promote "a singularity of a semiotic content –in a Dadaist way- to re-organize mutants focus of subjectivity" (Guattari, Félix, *Op. Cit.,* p. 32).

New public art should be a "device for the articulation of a collective enunciation[27]. Thus, the molecular change of sensitivity should organize a new understanding and a new structure of art, going away from the parameters that usually subjected it. It should be understood as an extending aesthetic process that amplifies the scope of the artistic to an extensive "creativity", not serialized or reified from the various devices. This ethical-aesthetic should propose new ways of living, of understanding, of collectivity; that is, it should be participate of the eco-sophical parameters according to Guattari: creative forms of existence whose ultimate goal is the self-enrichment of the subjective relationships with the world. In other terms: new forms of "inhabiting".

Unbridled creativity in the urban must operate, as well as public space, as a strong flow of energy. Its power should reside in reshaping the active participation in the social field, using expressive forms of "living", that should try to encourage those three key points of the Guattari Ecosophy: the subjective, transforming it into multiple subjectivities; the ecological, with new ways of experiencing, rearranging, and understanding both physical and existential territories, as well as social relations.

Taking into account these transformations of the aesthetic condition, the levels of application, performance, and functionality of art vary considerably, generating not only ephemeral and critical practices but also a new emancipated "user" (*Cfr.* Rancière, 2010). In this case, "the aesthetic is the structuring of a specific space, the constituency of a particular area of expertise, posed in the ordinary objects that respond to a common decision of subjects considered capable of designating these objects and arguing about them (*Ibídem.,* p. 14.).

---

25 Negri, Antonio, Interview in FSU-Nouveux Regards, august, 2004. [on line] in *url*: http://colaboratorio1.wordpress.com/2009/11/14/sobre-foucault-toni-Negri-2004/.

26 After noting the growth of emancipatory movements we can say that, two decades after the death of Guattari, society has a fundamental concern for reclaiming subjectivities. Therefore, it becomes necessary to remove the comprehensive visions and mechanisms of subjective emancipation, especially at a time when mechanic reconfigurations are increasingly devastating.

27 Holmes, Brian. "El dispositivo artístico, o la articulación de enunciaciones colectivas", en *Brumaria*, n° 7, [on line]: in *url:* http://www.brumaria.net/textos/Brumaria7/12brianHolmes.htm

Consequently, new public art maintains a latent radicalism of the experience in the urban space, transgressing the traditional discourses (*Ibídem.*, p. 11.) and holding the idea, popularly led by Jacques Rancière, of redistributing the sensible again. Let's not forget something fundamental, "the original field of aesthetics is not art but reality" (Buck-Morss, 2005), so it follows that the aesthetic is always embedded in the public sphere, where the politic field is clearly juxtaposed with the ethical field. Art, therefore, reaches to the specificity of itself and refers to the sensorium[28] (Rancière, Jacques, *Op. Cit.*, p. 20), again and again.

"Art is not the establishment of a common world through the absolute uniqueness of the form but the rearrangement of objects and images that form the already given common world, or the creation of situations aimed at changing our look and our attitudes towards this collective environment. These micro-situations, barely distinguishable from those in ordinary life, presented in a more critical and denunciatory ironic and playful way, tend to create or recreate bonds between individuals, to provoke confrontation and new participation modes" (Ranciére, Jacques, *Op. Cit.*, p. 11).

Therefore, public art should be part of building feeling communities. In any case, the objective of the public art is not to "decorate" public spaces, tackling the most complex objective of critically producing or releasing –in the public space–, in the public domain (BREA, 2004, p. 65). This seems to have an essential mission: to produce "devices capable of critically reorganizing these conditions of registration dissemination and social practice." In short, "we can not define as a public art any behemoth that is installed in an urban environment but only those artistic and cultural practices that have precisely the production of a public domain as a mission"[29].

Even so, a project that involves the fracture of town planning is difficult, but that is the mission of new public art: to try to search for new answers and not redeem itself of the urbanity discourse. So, it transforms into "devices, assemblages, abstract machines, which make the meeting between citizen and public dialogation as common as possible" (*Ibídem*).

---

28 The artwork is defined by its sensorium. Thus, "the property of being considered as art does not refer to a distinction between modes of doing, but a distinction between modes of being. This is what is meant by "aesthetic": the property of being art in the aesthetic regime of art is no longer given by the criteria of technical perfection, but by the assignment to some form of sensible apprehension. The statue is a "free look". In other words, a sensitive heterogeneous form in contrast with ordinary forms of sensory experience. It appears through a specific experience that suspends the ordinary connections not only between appearance and reality, but also between form and matter, activity and passivity, understanding and sensitivity. "

29 BREA, José Luis, "Transformaciones contemporáneas de la imagen-movimiento: *postfotografía, postcinema, postmedia*", en *Revista Acción paralela*, n° 5, 1999, [on line]: in *url*:http://www.accpar.org/numero5/imagen.htm

References

Brea, José Luis, (2004), *El tercer umbral. Estatuto de las prácticas artísticas en la era del capitalismo cultural,* Murcia, CENDEAC.

Buchloh, Benjamin H.D. (1989), "From the Aesthetic of Administration to Institutional Critique", in *Gintz, L´Art conceptuel*, París, Musée d´Art de la Ville de París.

Butler, Judith, Laclau, Ernesto, Zizek, Salvoj, (2000), Contingency, hegemony, universality. Contemporary dialogues on the left, Buenos Aires, Fondo de Cultura Económica.

Castells, Manuel, (1972), *La question urbaine*, Paris, François Maspéro.

Castells, Manuel, (2002), *The Information Age: Economy, Society and Culture. Vol. I: The Rise of the Network Society*, Oxford, Blackwell.

Clark, Thimothy, "Clement Greenberg´s Theory of Art", in Critical Inquiry, vol. 9, n° 1, p. 145.

Deleuze, Gilles y Guattari, Félix, *Mil mesetas,* Valencia, Pre-Textos.

Delgado, Manuel, (1999), *El animal público. Hacia una antropología de los espacios urbanos*, Barcelona, Anagrama.

Delgado, Manuel, (2005), "En busca del espacio perdido", en Territorios de la infancia: diálogos entre arquitectura y pedagogía", Isabel Cabanellas y Clara Eslava (Coords.), Barcelona, Graó.

Delgado, Manuel, (2002), "El espacio social como patrimonio" en *Arquitectura tradicional y entorno construido*, Manuel Luna y Manuel Lucas (eds.), Roman, Trenti.

Delgado, Manuel, (2000) "Etnografía de los espacios urbanos" en *Espacio y territorio: miradas antropológicas*, Danielle Provansal (coord.), Barcelona, Universidad de Barcelona.

Deutsche, Rosalynd, (2001), "Agorafobia", en *Modos de hacer, Arte crítico, esfera pública y acción directa*, Salamanca, Universidad de Salamanca.

Deutsche, Rosalynd, (2007) "Público", Conferencia en el curso Ideas recibidas. Un vocabulario para la cultura artística contemporánea, en el *Museu d'Art Contemporani* de Barcelona (MACBA), 19 de noviembre.

Foster, Hal, (2000), "Recodificaciones: hacia una noción de lo político en el arte contemporáneo", en *Modos de hacer. Arte crítico, esfera publica y acción directa*, Ediciones Universidad de Salamanca.

Guattari, Félix, (1996), *Caosmosis*, Buenos Aires, Manantial.

Harvey, David, (2003) *The new imperialism*, Oxford, Oxford University Press.

Habermas, Jürgen, (1999) *Historia y crítica de la opinión pública*, México, Gustavo Gili.

Heidegger, Martin, (1994), *Construir, habitar, pensar, Conferencias y artículos*, Barcelona, Ediciones del Serbal.

Jacobs Mary Jane, (2000), "Extramuros", in Los manifiestos del arte posmoderno, Anna María Guasch (ed.), Madrid, Akal.

Krauss, Rosalind, (1979) *Sculpture in the Expanded Field*. Rosalind Krauss, October, Vol. 8.

Kwon, Miwon, (1997), For Hamburg: Public Art and Urban Identities" in the exhibition catalogue Public Art is Everywhere, Hamburg, Germany, Kunstverein Hamburg an Kulturbehörde Hamburg.

Latour, Bruno, (1999), *Pandora´s hope. Essays on the Reality of Science*, Cambridge, Massachusetts, Harvard University Press.

Lovell, Vivien, (1991) "Public Art Commissions Agency", en *Les dossiers de L´Art Public,* n° 6, Paris, Art Public Promotion.

Maderuelo Javier, "El paisaje urbano", en *Estudios geográficos*, vol. LXXI, n° 269.

Marchán Fiz, Simón, (1986), *Del arte objetual al arte del concepto,* Madrid, Akal.

Michaud, Yves, (2007) *El arte en estado gaseoso: ensayo sobre el triunfo de la estética*, México, Fondo de Cultura económica.

Montero, Soledad, (2012), "Significant gaps and disputes over the meaning in political discourse: an argumentative approach", in *Journal Identities,* No. 2, December.

Naredo, José Manuel, (2000), "Ciudades y crisis de civilización", en *Documentación social. Revista de estudios Sociales y de sociología Aplicada*, nº 119, abril-junio.

Negri Antonio, (1993), *La anomalía salvaje*, Barcelona, Anthropos.

Laclau, Ernesto, (1983) "Socialism, the People, Democracy: Transforming of Hegemonic Logic", en *Social Text,* nº 7.

Lacy, Suzanne (ed.), (1994), *Mapping the Terrain: New Genre Public Art*, Seattle, Bay Press.

Deutsche, Rosalyn, (1988), "Uneven Development: Public Art in New York City", en *October*, vol. 47, winter.

Lanceros Patxi, (2000), "la estética de la ciudad", en Exit book, nº 7.
Lefebvre, Henri, (1974), *La production de l'espace,* París, Anthropos.

Quesada Fernández, Blanca, (2005), *Nuevos lugares de intención: Intervenciones artísticas como una de las salidas a los circuitos convenciones*. Estados Unidos, 1965-1995, Barcelona, Universidad de Barcelona.

Park, Robert, (1967) *On Social Control and Collective Behaviour*, Chicago, Chicago University Press.

Rancière, Jacques, (2005), *Sobre políticas estéticas*, Barcelona, Museu d'Art Contemporani de Barcelona y Servei de Publicacions de la Universitat Autónoma de Barcelona.

Soja, Edward, (2000), *Postmetropolis: Critical Studies of Cities and Regions*, Oxford, Basil Blackwell.

Trías, Eugenio, (1997), *El artista y la ciudad*, Madrid, Anagrama.

Virno, Paolo, (2003), *la gramática de la multitude,* Madrid, Traficantes de Sueños.

VV.AA. (2004), *Wayfinding Behaviour. Cognitive mapping and other Spatial Processes*, Reginald G. Golledge (ed.), Baltimore, The John's Hopkins University Press.

VV.AA. (1984), *Insights/On Sites: Perspectives on Art in Public Places*, Stacy Paleologos Harris (ed.), Washington D.C., Partners for Livable.

Wodiczko, Krysztof, (1992), "Instrument personal: Democràcia com a espai public", in *Krystazof Wodiczko*, Barcelona, Fundación Tapies.

Zucker, Paul, *Town and Square, from the Agora to the Village Green*, New York, Columbia University Press.

Chapter 3

Youth, Media and Social Networks: contemporary subjectivities

Glória Diógenes

Abstract

A real youngster!!!
Doesn't skip classes, kills the teacher straight away1;
Doesn't eat honey, chews the bee;
Doesn't drink milk, shakes the cow;
Doesn't write, scribbles;
Doesn't kiss, sucks the tongue;
Doesn't hug, grips;
Doesn't laugh, chokes;
Doesn't speak, yells;
Doesn't cry, shouts;
Doesn't love, enjoys;
Doesn't ask, demands;
Doesn't sleep, naps;
Doesn't wear condoms, has it plasticized!
(A 16 year old's Orkut profile – Fortaleza, Brazil)

The present investigation is part of a trajectory I began trailing during my doctorate studies (on youth – gangs, urban groups) and in further research (on organized soccer fan groups and funk parties) carried out with CNPq grant. My objective is to understand the ways in which youth affections are shared on the Web. This paper presents the first steps of a survey on youth profiles in the Orkut social network, with most members living in the outskirts of Fortaleza, Ceará, Brazil. The research aims at identifying connections, representations and expressions of youth cyberspace practices, encouraged by extreme feelings such as love and hate among organized soccer fan groups, supporters of the major teams in the state of Ceará. I intend to broaden a comprehensive research carried out earlier, now shifting its scope to the ethnography of cyberspace. In regard to the organized soccer fan groups, we notice a hybridism between the virtual public space and the city's urban space, condensing proximity and distance. We ask the following questions: having in mind the mobilization of excitement aroused by rivalry between these groups, how are such extreme feelings represented in cyberspace and how are these youths' profiles and public images designed?

Keywords: Photographies, cultures, philosophy of difference

1. Fragments of intense feelings

In the prelude of his *A Lover's Discourse: Fragments* (1981, p. 1), Roland Barthes enounces the reasons for the choices of what he names "dramatic" method – hearing what there is of "unreal", that is, intractable, in the lover's voice. According to the author, *Dis-cursus is*, originally, the action of running here and there, comings and goings, *démarches*, intrigue – *figures*, words that are not to be understood in their rhetoric sense, but rather in their gymnastic or choreographic acceptation, in a much livelier manner – the body's gestures caught in action. As an Internet user, amidst rich research and work experience with youth groups, I was constantly "added" to Orkut user's page by the most diverse people in the universe: students, hip hop activists, taggers, members of organized soccer fan groups, the homeless (yes, they go to *cyber cafés*), music bands and so many others.

In the beginning, out of curiosity, I visited profiles, observed user's names, photos and the descriptions in profile pages. From the start, something caught my attention: when they were young, especially those who identified themselves as 18 and older, in their description of themselves, in their profile page, we could almost always identify the "dramatic" method described by Barthes. The use of superlatives, hyperbole, impact elocutions, radical opinions, as the epigraphy in this paper, express the intensity of the most varied *affection* in the scenario of virtual relationships. According to Ortega (1998, p. 11), the intensity represents "the temperature of the spirit" and sketches another dimension of time to come, simultaneously, event and *devir*. And because they move in time and space, because they do not need the organic body as support for their expression, virtual affection is able to flow faster and without boundaries. "The amorous *dis-cursus* is not dialectical; it turns like a perpetual calendar, an encyclopedia of affective culture" (Barthes, 1981, pp. 4-7).

Thus, we decided to carry out an extensive virtual ethnography aimed at mapping out expressions of intense, passional affection among the youth. In our initial investigation – also considering the themes investigated by students carrying out research at undergraduation, masters and doctorate level – we accessed four scenarios of youth cyber experience: *organized soccer fan groups*, *taggers* and *burners*, and *gothics*. At a very preliminary stage, as our first attempt of analysis, we presented the affection of organized soccer fan groups, their means of subjectification, and what we consider *self-media. And what led us to mapping out affection?*

Feeling implies an evaluation of matter and its resistances, a direction *(sense,* also "meaning") to form and its developments, an economy of force and its displacements, an entire gravity. But the regime of the war machine is on the contrary that *of affects,* which relate only to the moving body in itself, to speeds and compositions of speed among elements. Affect is the active discharge of emotion, the counterattack, whereas feeling is an always displaced, retarded, resisting emotion (Deleuze & Guattari, 1997, p. 79).

Our interest lies in following the flow of emotion that populates and intensifies the use of virtual environment/cyberspace by the youth. Like Lemos (undated), we believe that the rebels of cyber culture find ways of outflowing all their vitality (for better or worse) through the use of microelectronics technologies. It is such affection trails that mobilize our efforts to undertake a virtual ethnography. After all, wouldn't the dimensions of *online and offline* life be just the means of intense experiences/experiment and production of subjectivity?

2. A borderless polyphony: youth movements and subjective modulation

Just like every good researchers', our duty is to follow tracks that have been trailed watching out for shortcuts, curves, winding patterns, and flows that project other routes for observation. A search that becomes even more challenging when it involves visiting the crossroads of research on the youth, their passional affection and the production of contemporary subjectivities in the scenario of virtual relationships. It means assuming that the focus of youth experience no longer lies in delimited spaces, once "nowadays, the youth experience a social condition in which the arrows of linear time cross the spiraled cyclic time" (Pais, 2006, p. 9) – a time that flows in space, arteries of nomad tracks. Such are the lines that compose the enunciation plans in the text that follows.

In 1989, Janice Caiafa published her research on the *punk* movement in town, even before Abramo's (1994) emblematic book about "*punks* and *darks* in the urban show". At that time, Caiafa stresses that in order to carry out her ethnography she had to nomadize with the *punks* "along the alleys in Lapa, on buses in the outskirts of town, on the [train] tracks, across empty lots" (1989, p. 16). Besides the logic of the movement, she gradually noticed that the interviewing process was outdated and grasped a kind of lexicon among *punks* that could only be understood "in conjunction with other movements, including their dance, music, appearance and routine gestures [...]" (1989, p. 17). Their body signs, gestures, and facial expressions compose, in Caiafa's ethnography, what we here denominate *self-media*. [1]

In my doctorate studies on the cartography of gangs, groups and the hip hop movement (Diógenes, 1998) we identified a peculiar logic in the routs trailed by these segments in town. They are bodies in transit that seem to carry the signs of neighborhoods, tribes, likes and preferences, wherever it is possible for them to meet and carry out public representations.

The gangs' territoriality is fluid, changing, crossing the physical-geographic boundaries of periphery neighborhoods. It follows the flow and the lines of flight (Guattari & Rolnik, 1986) of modern metropolis. Gangs' territoriality presumes movement intended to transpose the anonymous condition [...] (Diógenes, 1998, p. 148).

Juvenile bodies used to constitute and constitute still a changing map of the metropolis. The flow transposes the *invisibility* of neighborhoods in the outskirts of the city and creates a changing map of the city, identified and trailed only by those who agree with the logic of the movement. The dynamics of gatherings among gang members is processed through movement/displacement. One may state that despite the youth's use of their body and its practices as billboards of affiliation, of ways of being and thinking, of social networking, many of the studies in this field focus primarily on the observation of delimited contexts of practices.

And what leads us to evoking and highlighting juvenile signs to investigate a field related to subjectivity? Generally speaking, as we introduce subjectivity into the analysis, an effort towards face to face investigation, a research scenario of qualitative nature constituted in the narrative frameworks, is understood. Moreover, as states Pais (2006), before that moment we regard *juvenile cultures in two ways: through socialization or its routine expressions* (performances). Basically, we focus on "routes confined to the characteristics of the very space that determines them" (2006, p. 7). We operate an anthropology that is, in general, constituted via the embedment of time and space, producing subjectivities of clear cultural contexts.

And, when it regards a virtual ethnography of juvenile networks in the Internet, both time and space are transformed into a nonlinear logic, through what Guattari names "machinic processes"[2] (1999, p. 177). In the case of a cyber-anthropology, "synchronicity replaces the unit of place and interconnection, the unit of time" (Lévy, 1996, p. 21). As Negri properly points out, "the human being's work of production of a new subjectivity is integrally consistent in the virtual horizon progressively widened by the new communication technologies." (1993, p. 175).

Virtuality acts as an instance of widened possibilities of the self, of capture and incorporation of symbols *available* for processes of production and publicizing of subjectivities. It is no longer about identifying one-dimensional subjects, catalyzers of identities with body and psychic contours; the challenge lies in recognizing enunciations and media of an "*I*" made possible by the existence of so many other "*I*"s. That is the most recent challenge in juvenile research and in expanding what we call subject and public sphere – as highlights Lévy (1996, p. 15), when assuming the virtual based on its etymological sense, that is, virtual originated from Latin *virtualis*, in turn derived from *virtus*, strength, power to which we would add *of affection*.

---

1 Adriana, A. develops research on cyberpunk movements and their imbrications in contemporary culture; she highlights such culture permeates and is permeated by the technological thinking. Guattari and Deleuze present a "hydraulic model of nomad science and the war machine, on the other hand, consists in being distributed by turbulence across a smooth space, in producing a movement that holds space and simultaneously affects all of its points [...]" (1997, p. 28).

2 Guattari and Deleuze present a "hydraulic model of nomad science and the war machine, on the other hand, consists in being distributed by turbulence across a smooth space, in producing a movement that holds space and simultaneously affects all of its points [...]" (1997, p. 28).

In her latest book on *Digital social networks*, Santaella (2010), in a dialogue with Coldry (2004), highlights that the possibilities for discussing actor-theory network (ANT[3]) and the social media have been little developed. In general, when we speak of the media, the TV has gained primary attention. The Internet as a medium is a scarcely explored field of research. In that sense, the investigation effort interconnecting youth, media and virtuality demands new unfolding of the researcher's view. It means creating a *communicational ethnography* that "experiments an individual's transit, that seeks to represent his compact psychic and logical identity, to a *multividual* capable of developing a multiplicity of selves (*body-selves*) in fluid, plural and multiple perspectives" (Canevacci, 2009, p. 232). And quite on the contrary, here, in this very field of youth investigation, instead of taking symbols whose sole quality would be to represent these subjects, individuals, our task will be to identify the production and making of new agency (Guattari, 1999) of enunciation, of self-multiplicity.

The machines themselves, the computers, "are nothing other than *hyperdeveloped* and *hyperconcentrated forms of certain aspects* of human subjectivity" (Guattari, 1999, p. 177). What kind of subjectivity is constituted within the scope of the individual and collective agency mediated by communication in the Internet? First of all, whatever the domain, as Guattari emphasizes, "technical, biological, semiotic, logical, abstract" (1999, p. 178), they all support protosubjective processes, named modular subjectivity. As we will see next, our interest rests in identifying through the Orkut intense *affection* of members of organized soccer fan groups, modulated by confront and encounters among supporters of a same team and of rival teams.

3. Social networks and organized fan groups

As Souza and Rocha (2010, p. 30) appropriately pointed out, "the Orkut is a fascinating network of invention and display of subjectivities, of diaphanous hybrid-identities". As with the subjectivities, the cities create and multiply symbols of production of the geographic space and of their own actors' routes and spheres of belonging. A hybridism that also merges real and imaginary; actor and space/time. Cities have lines, routes and urban designs that can be continuously retraced and redefined in social networks. Virtual communities – if that is what we are to name them when it regards youth dynamics of Organized Soccer Fan Groups (OSFGs) – expand the space for the social actors' public display and projection of identification signs. In the case of an OSFG, the [weak or strong] bonds between members make it easier to establish and join a community [in the web].

"The Web is especially appropriate for the development of weak and multiple bonds. Weak bonds are useful for providing information and opening up new opportunities [...]" (Castells, 2009, p. 445). Bonds created amongst strangers facilitate the contact between people. A new geography of time and new possibilities of spatial mobility are produced in the Web. "Space shapes time in our society thus inverting a historic trend: fluxes induce atemporal time, places are bound to time" (Castells, 2009, p. 557).

When Internet social networks are concerned, not only the space is another but also the actors constitute themselves under a distinct logic of closeness and association. Recuero (2009, p. 25) explains that "due to the distance between those participating in a social interaction, major characteristic of computer mediated communication, the actors are not immediately discernable. Thus, an actor may be represented by a weblog, a photo log, a twitter or even by an Orkut profile."

Another facet of the public sphere is consolidated in the virtual environment and seems to, at last, fulfill more vigorously the desire for speed and movement particular to the juvenile body. The OSFGs rapidly appropriate themselves of this field of action and territorialize cyberspace. Guimarães Junior (1998) carried out ethnography in "multimedia virtual sociability environments" and, in this mainstay, stressed the challenge faced when developing field research in different communicational structures.

---

3 "According to Latour (2005, p. 129), in ATN "networks don't designate anything outside that would roughly have the shape of dots connected by lines, something similar to the telephone, highway and sewage networks [...]. It qualifies each actor's ability to make the other do the unexpected" (Santaella, 2010, p. 47).

A cyberanthropology can be perceived, in the way it is sketched here, that is eminently supported upon the interpretation of communicative phenomena that appear as given [phenomena] [...] What the field study can actually provide (and, in fact, does) is evidence of the existence of a communicational structure underlying the differences resulting from the specificities of each environment. It is evident that such structures are also influenced by and interact with structures used in the "off-line" life of urban groups, what makes the theme even more complex and, consequently, more fascinating (Guimarães Junior, 1998, p. 20).

The communicational structure to which Guimarães Junior refers enables that each member of the organized fan groups use enunciation signs, *self-media*, which retro feed, modulate and promote subjective agency. These are subjects in their multiple faces and possibilities of existence, subjects who act like places intercrossed with experiences, free from the weight of a given name's restricted *locus*. "The megalopolis creates a compulsive seduction of an anonymous *other* [...] in the interaction of virtual messages that present bodiless alterity, but are overly active as mental stimuli." (Ferrara, 2009, p. 134)

These are not necessarily anonymous subjects, but subjects emptied of the *official name*, personality support, so as to be able to give movement and speed to innumerous stimuli. On the contrary, it means forging new names – as do gang members and street bunches – a bundle of possibilities of self-expression and of sociability couplings.

4. Virtualization of the body and *self-media*

We had to ask for permission, and it must have sounded strange, to join the virtual communities of the organized soccer fan clubs of the major teams in Ceará. Curiously, I was immediately accepted. We followed not just the topics posted by these communities and their discussion forums but also kept a log of innumerous Orkut profiles whose identification included a fan club name, for instance: "marilia 100% cearamor". We visited the first and most numerous three communities of each one of the teams as well as nearly five hundred profiles' IDs that brought the club name.

Unlike many research on social networks, we did not retain our focus on the virtual spaces for supporters' sociability, on the fields of interaction or on the bond between members. Our interests reside in the outflows of affect, subjectivity modulation and enunciations of the self regardless of the dual social relation, of an "I" interacting with an "other" that it may indicate. Though for Recuero (2009, p. 44) the deterritorialization of bonds means the development of new spaces for interaction, we set to sail the open sea, not necessarily attained to points, bands, fields and bond structure.

We regard the fan clubs virtual experiences as rhizomes and map expressions. That means locating the environment of relationships amongst the members in an open space, "connectable in all of its dimensions; it is detachable, reversible, susceptible to constant modification" (Deleuze & Guattari, 1995, p. 32). A space established by lines, without finish lines or limits – just movement. Dornelles (2004), having observed the sociability desired through chats, points out that the individual's experience in cyberspace is as dramatic, emotional and complex as is face to face interaction. By other means, social networks not only possess modulations similar to those of social relations outside the virtual environment but also produce and power emotion *croquis* to be acted out in face-to-face contexts.

In the present research's terrain, our interest lies on perceiving the "entangled bodies" (Serres, 2001), once "nobody can regard change if not associated to mixtures [...] hence the change in titles, in alloys, in fabric and maps, hence the change through drawings and reactions, camlet upon camlet, miscegenation" (2001, p. 23). That is so because virtualization is always associated to reinvention, to multiplication, to vectorization, to a heterogenesis of the human being (Lévy, 1996, p. 33). Thus, the construction of the OSFGs' profiles, the love for the team, the love and the expressions of hate directed to the rival fan groups, are entangled in the live movements that shake and enunciate the actors of social networks. Such movements, exchanges, express only "a visible surface that the ATN can transform in reportable [...] for such it is necessary to go beyond the homogeneous repertoire of the human being on one side, and the mechanisms, on the other, in order to delineate hybrid anthropomorphic, physiomorphic and technomorphic [repertoire] [...]" (Santaella, 2010, p. 48).

They are subjective lines of construction that expand, combine and mix up the body's possibilities; of the technique for making feasible the *formulation* of new existential territories – a body which can pass through the various points of the "organized fan groups in the Orkut" rhizome and reinvent new lines and figurations of the self.

Away from the mechanic logic and invested by the new digital regime, the contemporary bodies present themselves as data processing systems, codes, ciphered profiles, information bundles. So, given to the new beats of techno-science, the human body seems to have lost its classic definition and analogic solidity: inserted in the digital conveyor belt, it becomes permeable, projectable and programmable (Sibilia, 2002, p. 19).

All the feelings in the world seem to fit in that field; in it the over spilling, the excess, the self-complacency, the transmutation of the *solid* codes of sociability are enabled, once it is the body that updates the variation between time and space. The body will perform what Gil (1997) sees as the capacity to function as transduction of signs, as the "support for symbolic exchanges and correspondence among the various codes in the presence [...] the body is the permutator of codes" (1997, p. 23). It is the body that transposes the signs between the various folds of (*online and offline)* experience, it is the one that updates the *profile and*, so, composes and promotes continuous permutation between the inside and the outside and the possibilities of introduction/presentation of the "*I*".

It is important to stress that bodies transcend the wrapping preconized by medicine, the physic materialization of what is established as existence statute. As Lévy points out, "various contemporary scientific schools rediscovered *a* nature in which beings and things are no longer separated by an ontological iron curtain" (1993, p. 138). The bodies of the youth members of the fan clubs skip here and there, incorporate names, colors and images available for operating the most curious merge, in an analogy with Sennett (2001), between flesh and technology.

5. IT IS TUF[4], IT IS CEARAMOR[5]: supporter's subjectivities, fan groups' media

This text will focus on three cases that exemplify the expression of what we call here *intense feelings*: the *Fanautico,* the [useless] supporter expelled [from a community], and profile that sends signals on what it means to be young-supporter. Visiting an Orkut community named "FanauticO+CearamoR", we identified an unusual mixture of feelings of love and hate translated into mediatized signs.

"FanauticO + CearamoR![6] Home > Communities > Others > FanauticO + CearamoR!

Description: **Call the zoo, call the mortuary wagon!** **Tell them Cearamor, it killed the lion!** **Because I know Cearamor doesn't refuse!** **Lion killer and tufgay's ass fucker!** **Tuf is gay, gay, gaaaaay!** **www.torcidacearamor.com.br** **I just can't hide,** **my feelings for you Ará you Ará,** **I can't, I can't, I can't, I can't.**	**All I know is,** **that the young girl trembles,** **[The] hell disobeys,** **Unconsciously we spank,** **Small hands dance and swing,** **When they pass I follow behind** **All I know is...** **Being FANÁUTICO is really cool...** **Êô, Êô..** **I'm FanáuticôÔô,** **I'm FanáuticôÔô."**

---

4 TUF stands for Torcida Uniformizada do Fortaleza, Fortaleza's Supporters in Uniform.

5 Cearamor is Ceará+amor (love), pronounced as one word.

6 We've decided to maintain the original fonts as they appear in the Orkut once we consider such elements to be constituents of the authors' and their communities' language and communication strategies.

Which body does the supporter refer to when he says: "All I know is that the young girl trembles/ [The] hell disobeys/ Unconsciously we spank"? He is probably referring to the team, but with mixed feelings of love and hate. [The] *Fanáutico* is a killer, disobeys hell, sucks his rival's vital energy and reduces him to *tufgay*. Notwithstanding, despite the cruelty he directs his enemy, [the] *Fanáutico* stresses a curious love discourse having the body as support: *small hands dance and swing*.

The place for his outburst is celebrated, letter by letter: "All I know is... Being FANÁUTICO is really cool...". The subject uses the body, creating a pedagogy of gestures of what a fanatic supporter would be like, as a sign transduction (Gil, 1997). Finally, after putting his message through, in a sigh of satisfaction he proclaims THE pleasure of being a *Fanáutico!* That enunciation subject – [the] *Fanáutico* of CEARAMOR – creates stylistic, designs a *modus facendi of the* virtual supporter. Sibilia (2008, p. 295) considers that "everyone and anyone, being conveniently styled as artists of themselves, in order to be able to transform themselves into a character, the greatest paladin possible. Such construction of the supporter's body, of his behavior, needs to be regarded in the social networks, through repetition and suggestions for cries of affirmation, as signs of intensity capable of affecting the body-reader facing the computer screen: "Êô, Êô... I'm FanáuticôÔô, I'm FanáuticôÔô". As states Sibilia (2008), artists of themselves, transformed into characters-icon of what is meant to be aroused in the *other*, of what is meant to be subjectively constructed.

It is also worth calling attention to the rebel tone that gains power in *Fanáutico*'s voice, echoing timelessly, with no interpositions of the *striated space*[7]. The rebel *Fanáutico* expresses himself like a parodox, some err, an inversion of codes: *[The] hell disobeys*. All technologies create new rebels. The English "luddites", who in the beginning of the Industrial Revolution in the 18th century broke machines out of fear of being replaced by them, were the first "techno-rebels". Many things have changed ever since. The cinema gave voice to the "baby-boom" generation's "rebels without a cause". Today, new rebels use the micro-electronic technologies. If the Industrial Revolution witnessed the emergence of the luddites, cyber culture will witness that of cybernetic front: the "cyber-rebels". The most important figures are the "phreakers", the "hackers", the "crackers", the "cypherpunks", the "ravers" and the "zippies". These are the new "cowboys" of the electronic frontier (Lemos, undated).

The new "cowboys" of the electronic frontier express the need to preserve, mainly in forums and topics of TOF[8] communities, the masculine/'macho' *ethos*, as if it was impossible to unify in one single actor the image of supporter dissociated from the heterosexual pattern. That is the reason why a member of the rival fan group is initially *gay*, as affirmation of his fragility, his *lack*. The CEARAMOR supporters' community, named "CEARAMOR the largest in the Northeast" is constituted of 14,279 members and has a moderator whose profile is "Anderson", who is entitled to not only accept or reject new members, but also to assess the posts and select those opinions and attitudes that should or should not remain public. One of the significant topics, regarding to the narrowing of the construction of valid and invalid subjective apparel for the building of the supporter's image can be appreciated in "Anderson"'s reasons for excluding members from the community.

"[Deleted Topics]" *Here are the names of all topics excluded from the community and the reasons for such. Any doubts, talk to moderation.*

Anderson
Topic:
Supporters of ceará are hunks
Reason: Useless topic.
Creator: ' ÑÅÑÐØ"
The next day, ÑÅÑÐØ replies:
"22 may

' ÑÅÑÐØ
Useless my ass...
Don't you think I can find a pussy here?
Once you have your 'woman',
can't I have my 'man'?"2 jun

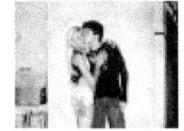

Anderson
yes, ok. But then send a message to the person you want, or chat.

---

7 The "striated space", the metric space, ruled, encoded, institutionalized appears, in Deleuze and Guattari's (1997) concept of nomadism, juxtaposed to the "smooth space" like the [open] sea, whose turbo effect can arise at any point.

8 TOF stands for *Torcida Organizada de Futebol* – Organized Soccer Supporter Groups.

These kinds of things aren't suitable for the community, but I'll do something directed to that specifically." In the dialogue between ' ÑÅÑÐØ and Anderson we can observe the production of a body that suits the image of the fan's warrior *ethos*. In Anderson's profile, a quote of Adolf Hitler signals the perception the mediator possesses of the construction of a moral standard, of a *bio power* (Foucault, 1988) related to the state of being CEARA-MOR: "Make the lie a big one, simplify it, continue stating it and eventually everyone will believe it". The expression of the homosexual desire is "useless" to the construction of the perception of "community feeling" (Castells, 2003) and, fundamentally, to the subjective construction of the supporter's body in and out of the social network. Canevacci (2005, p. 31), investigating the *juvenile mutation of metropolis bodies* signals the irruption of new technologies. Amongst the stud of provocation designed by Canevacci is the idea pertaining to *incorporated technologies:*

The body's natural components – an ambiguous affirmation *per se* once each one of the body's traces as well as itself entirely has always been crossed by powerful symbolic meanings (and that is why one can never mention the biological body alone) – were progressively subtracted from the naturalist dimension of the 19th century to open up and articulate in a myriad of micro-technologies, micro-processors, and chips that can be substituted with temporary prosthesis (2005, p. 31).

Such metamorphoses, mixtures already specified by Santaella (2010), also take advantage of social network tools to signal the body's limits and possibilities. There is an alternative space to be created by Anderson, as written in the reasons for "members' exclusion", which will be destined to ÑÅÑÐØ; in that *community* there can only be one of the mutation plans: the supporter's. That's why it's necessary to state it in the Orkut and highlight identification codes, engage in self-inscriptions. Souza and Rocha report the "confessional tone almost always observed in the writings. In many *Orkut* communities such tone is strongly evoked" (2010, p. 199). Here, in the fan groups space, the confession consists of restating, modulating, repeating the signs of the supporter character, of the public construction of multiple singularities of what that character may and should represent.

The need for the actor of a social network fan group to vociferate, repeat, amplify his visibility (*Fanáutico*) becomes evident, the need to engage in an image prophylaxis (what cleans up or dirties the community), *of the nature and usefulness of the supporter's ethos,* and to make seen and valued the media that characterize, inscribe and inform about the juvenile supporter's 'face' and 'attitudes'. The profile of supporters whose fan group's name is included in the profile name almost always stamps out a long self-report, as the epigraphy that introduces the following text and example:

"luiz 100% **cearamor,** A lot of trouble in this life, Place: Caucaia, Brazil *see whole profile About luiz*

The young don't fight.........................they kick asses	"The sky was clear,
The young don't go to parties...............they go to gigs	The moon kind of golden...
The young don't drink.......................... they lush	There, on the field, me and her,
The young don't fall............................. they pass out	And nothing else could be seen!
The young don't make love.................... they fuck, screw, bang	Her soft skin,
The young don't understand.................... they get it	Her butt exposed,
The young don't smoke.......................... they light up	And I caressing
The young don't eat .... they swallow	Her soft back...
The young don't go in......................... they break in	Not knowing how to begin,
The young don't kill.......................... they destroy	Watched her slim body.
The young don't ask.......................... they demand	Decided to put my hands on it
The young don't engage in conversation.......................... they confab	On her soft breast...
The young don't defecate....................... they shit	I was scared!
The young don't urinate.......................... they piss	My strong heart beating,
The young don't spit......................... they gag	While slowly ,
The young don't pass gas................ they tear ass	Her firm legs opened up...
The young don't leave................. they get outta ...	Victory!
The young don't type......................... they key in	I did it!
The young don't complain..................... they protest	Things then got better...
The young don't curse.......................... they tell you to fuck yourself	At least this time,
	The white liquid spurted!
	Finally it was all over,
	But I almost had to be carried out on a stretcher!
	That was how for the first time...
	I milked a cow!!!
	What did you think it was?"

luiz 100% cearamor enunciates from the beginning: "a lotta trouble[9] in this life". And as there are no half-
-measures for *a rabid fan*, a fanatic fan, he states he is 100% **cearamor**. We can verify his writings of himself
represent a "luiz 100% cearamor" way of being and stating his intense feelings and the codes that represent and
institutionalize the multiple possibilities of being 'the youth'. We can observe that almost everything is trespassed,
not part of the conventional plane, highlights an intensive existence rule. Sibilia considers: "Such fascination brought about by exhibitionism and voyeurism thrives in a society automatized by an individual with narcissist touches,
who needs to see his beautiful image reflected in the other's eyes in order to be" (2008, p. 302).

I ask myself: the invisibility to which they are referred, in daily life, does the youth in the periphery, members of OSFGs (Organized Soccer Fan Groups), find in the Orkut network faster tools for social insertion and self-
-mediatization strategies?

Could we initially consider such a detailed list of self-predicative a kind of narcissistic and pompous billboard? The tone characterizing the profile description slips in a given moment and leads the reader to perceiving the
mess, the ambiguity to which the antagonist perception of the modulation of being young is referred: "*The young
don't curse........................ they tell you to fuck yourself*", linked to a romantic aura:

The moon kind of golden...
There, on the field, me and her,
And nothing else could be seen!

Various parts of luiz 100% cearamor's profile and of the youngster that appears in the beginning of this
paper, highlight the slippery, intense, excessive, and polysemic nature of his introduction of his "*I*" young-sub-
ject: The young don't *skip classes, kill the teacher straight away; The young don't kill .... they destroy.*
The word sets up communication in the Web. It is as if the colossal nature of the words could cross the body
that inhabits the other places of the *emptied* anonymous body. And the maximum of Segundo Canclini is confirmed: "even when seated, the body crosses borders" (2008, p. 44). The cyber culture's body operates an invisible
proximity: Hence, as Rifiotis (2002) suggests, "the field experience in cyberspace becomes ever closer to a co-
-presence situation" (Rifiotis, 2002, p. 10), not forgetting to problematize, naturally, the mediation of communication via computer, the various software and codes that are negotiated, built and shared, being verbal, written, via
body expressions, or others (2008, p. 31).

A co-presence that is made easier by the "alterity emptied of a body" referred to by Ferrara (2009, p. 134) constitutes, via such emptiness, a high speed space for the "transmutation of signs" (Gil, 1997), the production of collective agency and of the supporter's image. Such "mobile geography" certainly demands from the ethnographer
a production of a new body and of a new "design of feelings" (Serres, 2001, p. 47). It makes it necessary that the
virtual anthropologist engage in a continuous exercise of crossing borders – an ethnographer who can move on
maps that are constantly changing across topics, communities, and forums that can be deleted in a second. An
anthropological saga that can visit *affects* inhabiting words, drawings, colors, and an endless number of *tools*, in
the subjective productions of *self-media*.

Keeping in mind that the map does not reproduce an unconscious closed in upon itself; it constructs the unconscious. It Fosters connections between fields, the removal of blockages on bodies without organs, the maximum
opening of bodies without organs onto a plane of consistency. It is itself a part of the rhizome (Deleuze & Guattari,
1995, p. 22).

We have only but trailed some points in the map, in an initial exercise of connection of fields. Hearing the "Fanáutico" cry as if the body acted as a co-presence of the team entering the field. Perceiving that in the locus where
apparently anything can be created, where the *fake* threatens to cover the veils of the truth, even so ÑÅÑÐØ has
his participation excluded and considered "useless". See in luiz 100% cearamor's profile the perception of words
inhabited by shadows:

---

9 Very common slang among the youth in the periphery which means: fight, conflict, mess.

That was how for the first time...
I milked a cow!!!
What did you think it was?"

That may be the greatest challenge regarding acting in cyberspace, the awareness that "it is always by rhizome that desire moves and produces" (Deleuze & Guattari, 1995, p. 23). That imprecise locus of space that leads the anthropologist to formulating time and again the question: *What did you think it was?*

References

Abramo, H. (1994), *Cenas Juvenis: punks e darks no cenário urbano*. São Paulo: Scritta.

Amaral, A. (2008), Subculturas e cibercultura(s): para uma genealogia das identidades de campo. *Revista FAMECOS*, Porto Alegre, n. 37, dez.. Retrieved from: <http://revcom.portcom.intercom.org.br/index.php/famecos/article/view/5553/5037>.

Amaral, A. *Visões perigosas: para uma genealogia do cyberpunk. Os conceitos de cyberpunk e sua dissiminação na comunicação da cibercultura*. Retrieved from: http://www.razonypalabra.org.mx/anteriores/n52/6Amaral.pdf.

Barthes, R. (1981), *Fragmentos de um discurso amoroso*. Rio de Janeiro, F. Alves.

Canevacci, M. (2005), *Culturas extremas: mutações juvenis nos corpos das metrópoles*. Rio de Janeiro: DP&A.

Canevacci, M. (2009) *Comunicação Visual*. São Paulo: Brasiliense.

Caiafa, J. (1989), *Movimento Punk na Cidade: a invasão dos bandos sub*. Rio de janeiro, Jorge Zahar.

Canclini, N. (2008), *Leitores, espectadores e internautas*. São Paulo: Iluminuras.

Castells, M. (2003), *A Galáxia da Internet*. Rio de Janeiro: Zahar.

Castells, M. (2009) *A Sociedade em rede*. São Paulo: Paz e Terra.

Deleuze, G. & Guattari, F. (1995), *Mil Platôs: Capitalismo e Esquizofrenia*, v. 1, Rio de Janeiro: Ed. 34.

Deleuze, G. & Guattari, F. (1997), *Mil Platôs: Capitalismo e Esquizofrenia*, v. 5, Rio de Janeiro: Ed. 34.

Dornelles, J. (2004), Antropologia e internet: quando o "campo" é a cidade e o computador é a "rede". *Horizonte Antropológico*, v. 10, n. 21, pp. 241-271.Retrieved from: <http://www.scielo.br/scielo.php?script=sci_arttext&pid=S0104-71832004000100011&lng=en&nrm=iso>.

Diógenes, G. (1998), *Cartografias da Cultura e da Violência: gangues, galeras e o movimento hip hop*. São Paulo: Annablume.

Diógenes, G. (2003) *Itinerários de Corpos Juvenis: a festa, o jogo e o tatame*. São Paulo: Annablume.

Ferrara. L. D. Cidade: fixos e fluxos. In Trivinho, E (Ed.), *Flagelos e Horizontes do mundo em rede*. Porto Alegre: Sulina, 2009.

Foucault, M. (1988), *História da sexualidade: a vontade de saber*. Rio de Janeiro: Graal.

Guattari, F. (1999), Da produção da subjetividade. In Parente, A (Ed.), *Imagem Máquina*. Rio de Janeiro: Ed. 34.

Gil, J. (1997), *Metamorfoses do corpo*. Lisboa: Relógio D'água.

Guimarães Junior, M. J. L. *Etnografia em ambientes de sociabilidade virtual multimídia*. 1998. Retrieved from: <http://cfh.ufsc.br/~guima/papers/etn_palace.html>.

Lemos, A. *Ciber-rebeldes*. Retrieved from: <http://www.faced.ufba.br/~edc287/topicos%20e%20textos/redes/etica/rebelde.html>.

Lévy, P. **(1993)**, *As tecnologias da inteligência: o futuro do pensamento na era da informática*. Da Costa, C. I (Translator). Rio de Janeiro: Ed. 34.

Lévy, P. (1996), *O que é virtual?* São Paulo: Ed. 34.

Lévy, P. (2003), *Cibercultura*. São Paulo: Ed. 34.

Ortega, F. (1998), *Intensidade: uma história herética da filosofia*. Goiânia: UFG.

Negri, A. (1993), Infinitude da Comunicação/Finitude do Desejo. In Parente, A. (Ed.), *Imagem Máquina*. Rio de Janeiro: Ed. 34.

Pais, M. L. (2006), Buscas de si: expressividades e identidades juvenis. In De Almeida, M. I. & Eugenio, F. (Eds.), *Culturas Jovens*. Rio de Janeiro: Jorge Zahar.

Recuero, R. (2009) *Redes Sociais na internet*. Porto Alegre: Sulina.

Santaella, L. & Lemos, R. (2010), *Redes Sociais Digitais*. São Paulo: Paulus.

Sennett, R. (2001), *Carne e Pedra: o corpo e a cidade na civilização ocidental*. São Paulo: Record.

Serres, M. (2001), *Os cinco sentidos: filosofia dos corpos misturados*. Rio de Janeiro: Bertrand Brasil.

Sibilia, P. (2002), *O homem pós-orgânico: corpo, subjetividade e tecnologias digitais*. Rio de janeiro: Relume Dumará.

Sibilia, P. (2008), *La Intimidad como espectáculo*. Buenos Aires: Fondo de Cultura Económica.

Souza, E. & Rocha, T. (2010), *A vida no Orkut: narrativas e aprendizagens nas redes sociais*. Salvador: EDUFBA.

Chapter 4

"I come from Porto and bring a Porto in me": essays on a cartography of affections in/of the city

Paula Guerra

Abstract

The city has long been used as a framework to understand the profound changes which the urban tissue has continuously suffered. In the late 19th century and throughout the 20th century the core issues concerning social-urban contexts were the binding power of the city, its capacity to bring individuals together, or, symmetrically, the way it broke off community allegiance, the new oppositions between centre and periphery, and the marginalization of sectors of the city. What we experience today is in part the extension of this process: pouring from a set of principles which guide late capitalism, our age has likewise reified certain principles of city life and urban intervention (such as the complex notion of "need") and made them into monolithic interpretations of urban communities. Going in part against this idea, and drawing from the situationist ideas of *psychogeographie/ sociogeographie* and *derive* as well as defending the need to educate individuals to take on their rights to the city, in this work we seek to synthesize an investigation-action project undertaken in 2012 with local inhabitants of the Sé Bairro in Porto (Portugal). With it, we seek to argue that individual cartographies serve as a tool for empowering young residents to take on their communities as part of their lives, expressing a familiar and everyday context through visual and sound symbolism.

Keywords: city planning, territorial stigmatization, *derive*, right to the city, affective cartographies

1. Glorification of the city *dèrive*

> Implicit in the analysis presented here is the contention that the large city is integrated neither by virtue of its citizens' sharing a common "social world" nor by the formal instruments of an anomic "mass society". How, then, is it integrated? To some extent, it is not; that is, value consensus is less likely to exist in larger than in smaller communities. Rather than unanimity, there is "multinimity". (Fischer, 1975, p. 1337)

The project "Sou do Porto e trago um Porto em mim" [*I come from Porto and bring a Porto in me*] (FLUP/ INV3248), integrated into the general framework of "INOV – Urban Polycentrism, dynamics of innovation and knowledge"[1], focused on understanding the various ways in which symbolic and cultural expressions could shape the urban tissue, as well as how creativity could serve as a participatory tool. It was organized in the context of the Open Call "Manobras Porto" [Porto Manoeuvres], which was undertaken by several cultural and scientific agents of the city. (Alvelos, 2013, p. 22).

The project sought to capture certain visions of the city through the privileged lens of the social actors which frequently experience it, simultaneously giving a chance to these individuals to express their own sense of what Porto is or should be. Embedded in this, lies the idea of the situationist *dérive* – the uncertain wandering through the city, through space, through the streets – which makes a path through the city out of interests, desires and fears of the population (cf. Figure 1).This was done in our work in two aspects: through visual recordings using a photovoice approach, and through audio recording, seeking to expose the various soundscapes of the city. In this paper we will be focusing more explicitly in the visual component of the project, giving way to the young residents of the city – perhaps the ones with least political voice, and more socially invisible – to showcase their everyday-lives. The participants were selected intentionally by their location in the Porto historical centre – that is, their living in Sé[2] - their age (16-25 years), as well as their pattern of social-cultural inhabiting of the city (their social-cultural origins, whether or not they are old or new residents, etc). The sample was gathered through cultural and recreational associations, as well as through privileged informants in the streets. This ethnographic incursion sought to give visibility to the perceptions and representations of spaces in a strategy directed towards self-bounded communities and their identity-defining spaces – while simultaneously seeking to promote in the individuals their similarities and their community bonds.

---

1 The project "Sou do Porto e trago um Porto em mim" [I come from Porto and bring a Porto in me] (FLUP/ INV3248), was integrated into the general framework of "INOV – Urban Polycentrism, dynamics of innovation and knowledge" and was organized by the Institute of Sociology – University of Porto (IS-UP), Centre for the Study of Geography and Territorial Planning (CEGOT) and Porto Lazer (CMP) and took place between the 1st of July and 20th of October 2012 under the coordination of Paula Guerra. It was organized in the context of the Open Call "Manobras no Porto" [Porto in Manoeuvres], which was undertaken by several cultural and scientific agents of the city. As stated in their book: "the Manobras no Porto was a vast cycle of ideas, events and expressions that flourished in Porto's Historical Centre throughout 2011 and 2012. The project stemmed from the belief that the inhabitants and visitors to the Historical Centre are themselves social, cultural and creative agents – and that an investigation of them could lead to the discovery and the rooting of new models for living, regenerating and connecting with the City's multiple everyday-lives. In a context where the most diverse studies have pointed out how the creative dimension works as an asset towards urban development, Manobras nonetheless sought to transcend a strictly economical reading of this: development is simultaneously a process woven onto narrative, anthropological, geographical and emotional fields. From within these fields, a proposition of a cultural nature of urban individuals may grow effective roots beyond its immediate resonance in space and time. While it is true that the most varied cultural events have managed to project the cities that host them and therefore generate economic impact, studies on viability have systematically forewarned a weak impact throughout and beyond the length of these events." (Alvelos, 2013, p. 25). We thank in this chapter the participation of the following junior investigators in recollecting photographs and sounds, as well as in assembling the exposition: Daniela Oliveira, Filipa Cavadas, Francisca Mesquita, Frederico Babo, Rita Araújo, Rodrigo Nicolau de Almeida and Tiago Teles Santos.

2 The 'Sé' parish in Porto is so named due to the "Sé" Cathedral near it. Built in the XII century in a romanic style and suffering various changes over time, it is the center of Porto, as the city grew around it over the centuries. As of the Law nº11-A/2013, the Sé parish was integrated in the Union of Parishes of Cedofeita, Santo Ildefonso, Sé, Miragaia, São Nicolau and Vitória. It provides a key insight into the life of the city and its history – due to its association with marginalized activities such as drug trafficking and prostitution from the 80s onwards, it has suffered a progressive degradation and social stigmatization.

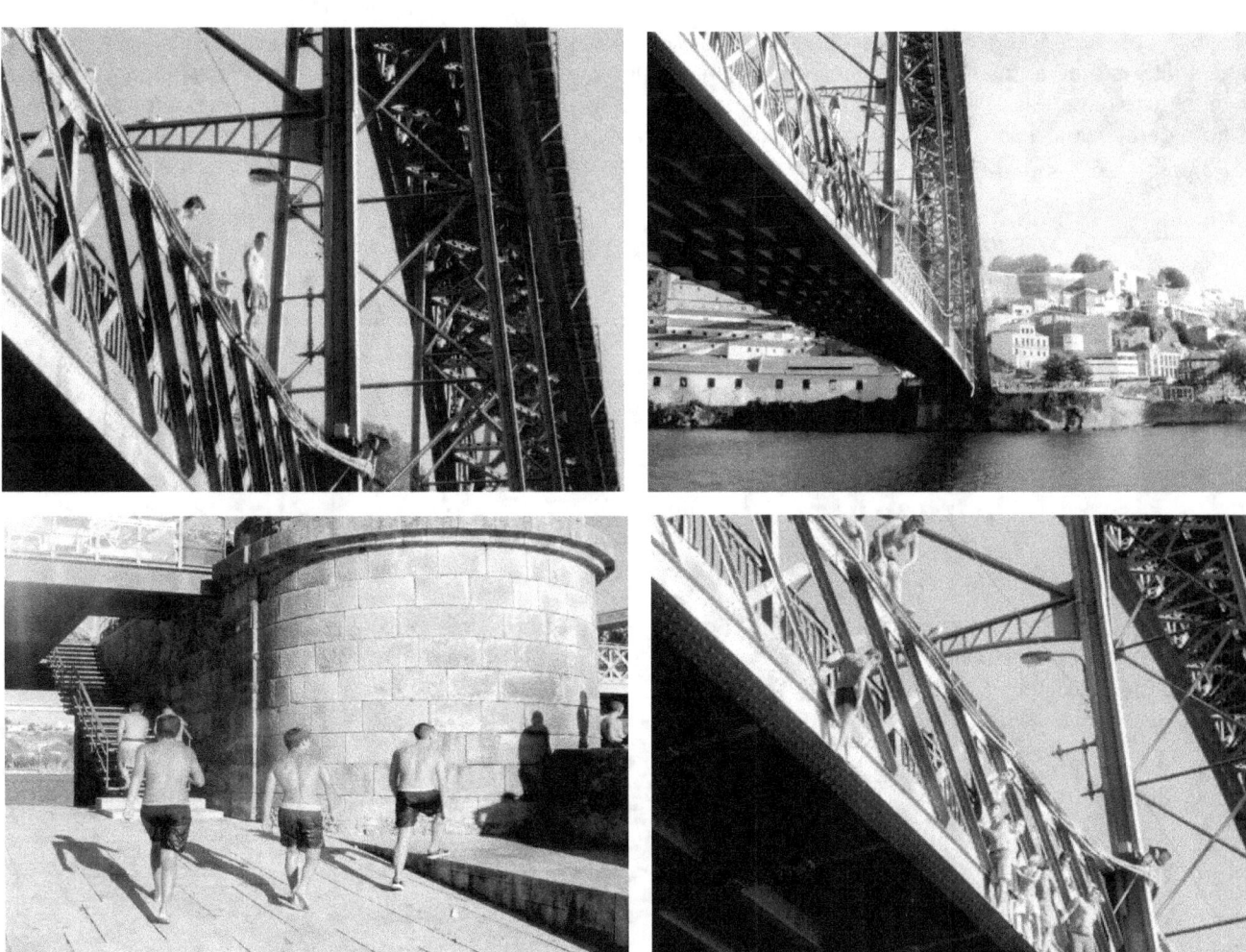

Figures 1 - Images of the social space of young people from Sé through their jumping into the Douro river, Source: Project "Sou do Porto e trago um Porto em mim" [*I come from Porto and bring a Porto in me*] (FLUP/ INV3248) | 2012.

Towards this latter end, we sought to produce a coherent identity to the project, which could be felt as binding, and one which was indicative of the Porto historical centre (Figures 2 and 3). We created a logo which served as an image of affection and belonging, as well as an identity brand which served as unifying mark of the project. The question of street allegiance and neighbourhood – which is vaguely alluded to in the logo – was chosen as motif due to the participants strong bonds to their own location not only on a national, regional and municipal level, but also on a microterritorial level, with the formation of very small "affective communities" (Fortuna, 2012).

Parallel to these processes of internal cohesion, it is of our interest to look at levels of exclusion, namely in their relation to disqualified territories, like the Sé parish. The economic transformations of the late 20th century, in particular, brought with them multiple ways in which the social question was changed – increased precarity, uncertainty, dissemination of poverty, widespread unemployment, among others (Castel, 1995). The impact this had in city life and urban structures, or rather, in the processes of exclusion associated to them, was remarkable. We face urban structures with a certain complexity, polycentric, marked by development and expansion of enterprises with multiples uses – and as the capital tends towards greater accumulation, so the city becomes a progressively more dualistic space in itself (Guerra, 2012). The tendency of these inequalities, in what concerns us, is to create "dead spaces" in the city, that is, spaces which were subjected to profound dynamics of territorial stigmatization (Wacquant, 2002). These tend to crystallize in forms of urban and social segregation of their individuals which are not only habitational, but cultural, and symbolic (Hamnet, 1997) – and yet, these same residents provide in themselves alternative ways to conceptualize their life and their belongings (Guerra, 2002). These processes interest us, in so far as they are strictly related to the myriad of movements which bring people into Sé, and likewise how this tends to lead the residents to have less political voice. In turn these are followed by greater selection-segregation processes, in specific in certain social categories, such as youth, who are at times excluded from school, work, job and the dominant culture (Paugam, 2003). With this in mind, our central theme could not be clearer: to give voice to these individuals.

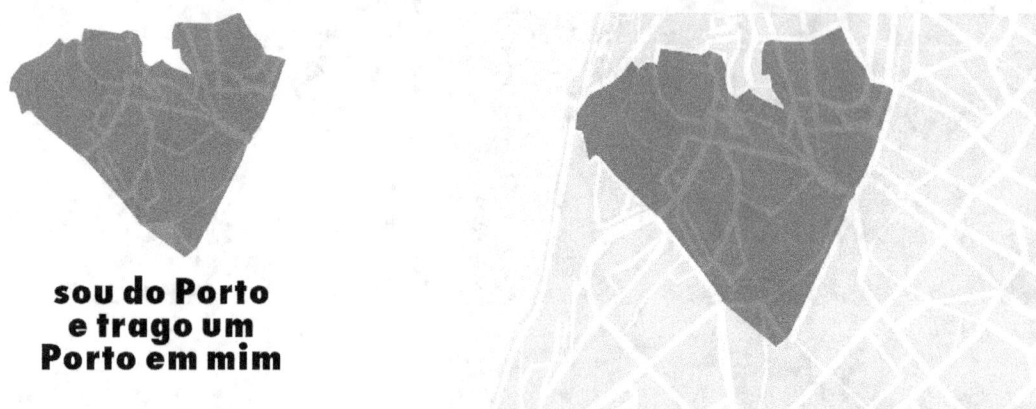

Figures 2 - Logo and branding of the project "Sou do Porto e trago um Porto em mim" [I come from Porto and bring a Porto in me], Source: Project "Sou do Porto e trago um Porto em mim" [I come from Porto and bring a Porto in me] (FLUP/ INV3248) | 2012.

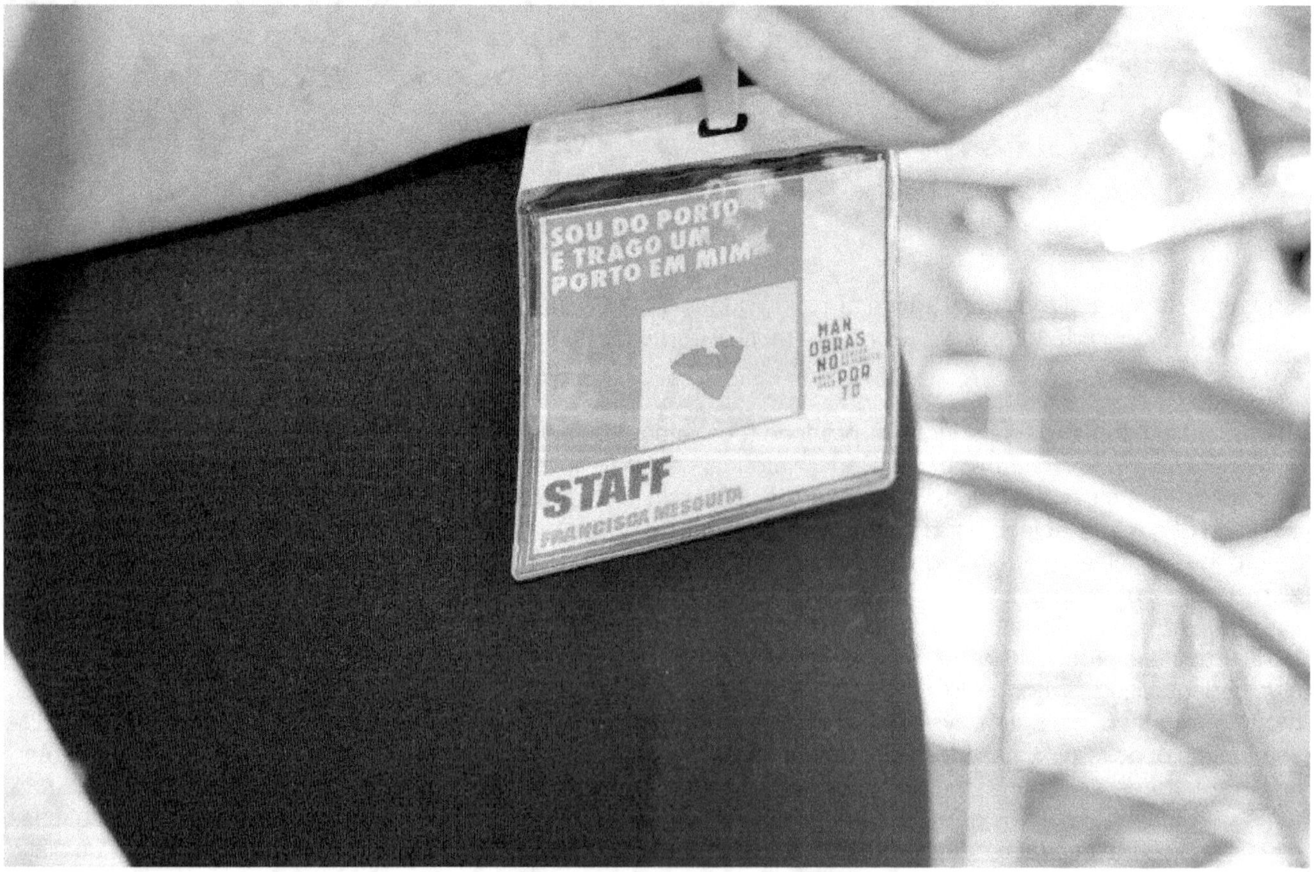

Figure 3 - Badge of the project participants, Source: Project "Sou do Porto e trago um Porto em mim" [I come from Porto and bring a Porto in me] (FLUP/ INV3248) | 2012.

This chapter will be structured as follows: first, we will present a general approach of the core theoretical issue at stake here as well as the context of affective cartographies in the city; second, we will provide the presentation of the methodological framework which guided the project; thirdly, we will have the confrontation with the actual cartographies and the way they were appropriated in public space; and finally, we shall elicit a brief evaluation of this *derive* into the world of the young residents of Sé as a first step towards an effective right to the city. In designing such a *psychogeography* – or rather, a *sociogeography* (Santos, Marques & Guerra, 2014) – we place the living city as the core of the series of dynamics of segregation, polarization, disqualification and exclusion, which are lived in the city of Porto and in general in the contemporary urban tissue.

2. Towards a right to the city

> In periods of social and economic change it is usual for big cities to be put in the position of "accused". (…) this "accusation" [of its integrative power] that is pointed towards them is probably rooted in an old social imaginary, of which Babel is one of the first expressions: Babel is the perfect archetype of the great city that gathers men in an emancipatory project in relation to God and Nature. The building of Babel was possible because men had an absolute means of communication – "the same tongue and the same words" - and a new technology – "the bricks were their stones, the mortar was their cement" (Ascher, 1998, p. 141).

We stand today in a context where urban interventions often stress the need for individuals to feel integrated in the city, for them to have housing, a job, cultural networks, strong ties and to be able to have a sense of alterity. All of these complex dimensions often tend to be conflated into a single and at times reified motto: "Everyone should have a right to the city". This phrase – one of the most well-known slogans of the fight towards an active citizenship in the city in the last 50 years – echoes the idea that all individuals should have space to live in the city, in all its various meanings. It traces its history back to Henri Lefebvre's homonymous "Right to the City" (1968), where it was birthed with a political as well as social agenda, seeking to establish the core identity of the city-dweller, as well as to promote his active engagement with the city (Lefebvre, 1968/1972). However, over the course of these years, the vagueness (or perceived vagueness) of the concept has at times turned it into more of a discursive tool than a conceptual framework towards which one should aspire (Souza, 2010). This brings us to two central questions: first, what are the main characteristics of the city of today? And second, what rights do we entail when we say that individuals should have a "right to the city"?

Far from the industrial revolution, and its debates over the loss of community (Durkheim, 1997; Tonnies, 1957; Wirth, 1938; Simmel, 1987) or the rural-urban distinction (Redfield, 1954; Sorokin, 1969; Weber, 1966), the 20th century evolution of the city led it to become central stages of social and cultural transformation of individuals as well as ideas. The tensions between globalization and local culture are of particular notice when we address the current context of cities such as Porto, with a traditional role as community-building spaces, which has continued into late modernity in ever more complex ways (Guerra, 2012a, 2012b). The pressure exerted over cities (often by the municipal power) to become what Molz called "homogenous heterogeneity" (2011, p. 39) – that is, the tendency for big cities to be 'different' in the same ways, with cultural, religious and social attractions which at times resemble one another - can in part be felt in economic and cultural terms, as housing, local development policies, as well as land price speculation drive complicated motions and movements of population in the heart of the cities (Guerra, 2003). These processes are intricately tied to globalization, and produce specific configurations, in a context where downtown areas turn into contradictory spaces which mix identities and localism with anonymity and disappearance (Guerra, 2003, 2002) and where tourism imparts specific looks and transforms the city in a process of continuous feedback (Urry, 2002).

This process is likewise tied to the appearance of active forces of globalization which have pushed the identity focus of the city into flows. Namely, as Appadurai (2004) notes, ethnoscapes, mediascapes, technoscapes, financescapes and ideoscapes collectively work to produce a social imaginary in which individuals are no longer simply citizens, but belong to wider systems of meaning. As such, both the potential and the risk for communities and individuals in cities is expanded (Appadurai, 1990), and brings new challenges for urban policy and intervention.

We sought to focus on the city as it is appropriated by youth, in their belongings and filiations to the urban tissue, regardless of their status as students or workers. This factor stems from various reasons: the repeated waves of moral panic associated to youth and their (sub)cultures, tribes and groups, in acts of delinquency and vandalism; the fact that one's condition as inhabitant comes more than anything else from the importance of the house to human realization; that housing is in many cases more than just lodgings, implying a certain emotional association and the creation of bonds of security, mystery and pleasure with one's home. All of these make the young a privileged demographic in the city, intensely focused by the social spheres of the city, highly free in their appropriation of the urban space, and at the same time deeply rooted in their homes.

As we have noted, our approach focused on the Sé neighbourhood [Portuguese: *bairro*], at the heart of a city with a long history of social and urban stigmatization. Sé is in practice the "backdoor" of touristic Porto, a place of informal economy, commercial traffic, dealing of narcotics, and (illegal) fluxes of immigrant people. It is a community space strongly marked by a closing and disqualification left by Porto's history.

Insofar as the construction of a self and a personality is related to one's home, this can be seen as a sort of second body (Guerra, 2003). We can at times speak of individuals who are lodged somewhere, but who do not inhabit that place. To inhabit a place is in certain ways to be that place, to allow it to change and be changed by the self, as well as for it to be a location where the social actor exerts power – in short, it means to turn a house into a home. This home can likewise be seen as part of an individual's personal and collective project, taking us back into the contexts and groups of which the individual is a part of. More and more, the home is today a space where people map out the complexity of everyday life, organizing family, kinship and community life, while at the same time it is the place where individuals project their emotions, values, rituals and tastes. In short: the home is the "beating heart" of an individual's experience of the city.

Knowing that the entity which we call "neighbourhood" is not the natural framework in which individuals experience the city, it is nonetheless a crucial matrix to analyse the individual experience of their own homes and of the ties that are formed there. We can think of these as three levels of everyday life: the city, the neighbourhood and the home, complement and complete each other. As such, the crisis of urban life is first and foremost the disaggregation of home and city, where the home becomes more and more a space of fragmentation and precarity. And it is in this context that we should turn to other social realities in an effort to understand, learn and help them in realizing their potential for expression.

Taking from Harvey, the right to the city is "far more than the individual liberty to access urban resources: it is a right to change ourselves by changing the city." (Harvey, 2008, p. 23). In Lefebvre, it arises as a critique of a certain mechanicist view of the city as a space for collective consensus or for conflict, realizing that it is not only in the production systems but also in everyday life that the structures of power are reproduced: in the overarching individualism, in the mystification of objects, in the alienation of work and needs, the individual separates himself from his productive value, but also from his life-space (Lefebvre, 1968/1972). The author emphasized precisely that the city is not reducible to its size, to its population density, or to its urban concentration, nor is it merely a space of cultural or economic expression, but that it is rather a space of human interaction and social-political construction (Lefebvre, 1970). The right to the city is then, in a more specific way, the right not only to space in the city, to economic participation, to cultural expression (though all of these are crucial), but first and foremost the right to have a voice in the city (Lefebvre, 1968/1972). As such, it follows that there is potential for urban life in all individuals, and that the city ought to be collectively constructed.

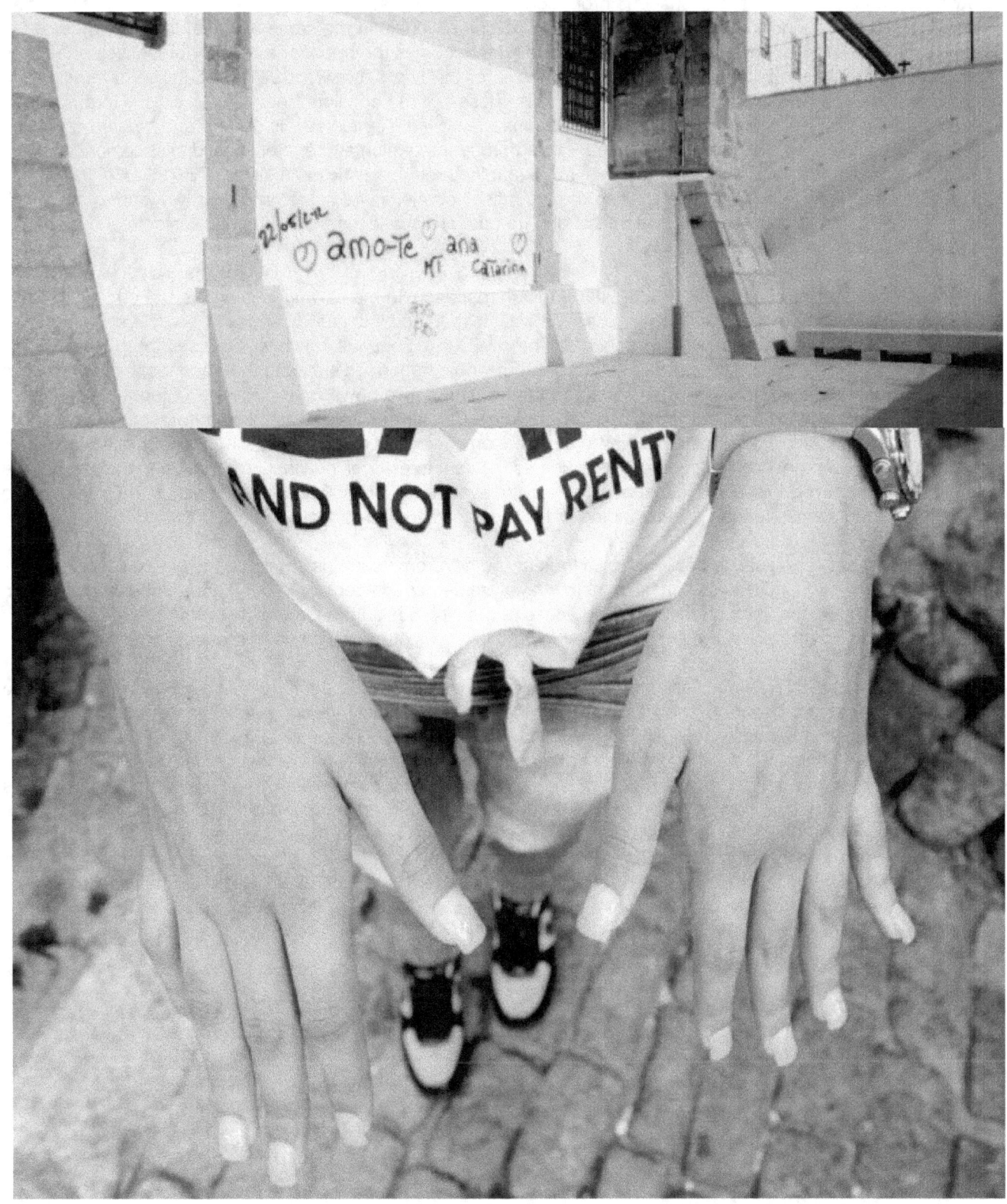

Figures 4 - Marks of belonging and affection, Source: Project "Sou do Porto e trago um Porto em mim"
[I come from Porto and bring a Porto in me] (FLUP/ INV3248) | 2012.

However, the way in which social space is produced is equally of issue here, as it becomes clear that a social-urban intervention cannot peer into the living space of all individuals in the same way (as, for all purposes, the space is not constructed in the same way). The issue here becomes the boundaries of the "objective space", the "subjective space", and what may come as a synthesis of the two (Lefebvre, 1981). In Lefebvre's terminology, in his monumental "The Production of Space" (1981), these are the conflicts between *le perçu* – that is, urban space as it is perceived by individuals in social relations – *le conçu* – space as it is understood by cartographers, geographers and urban planners – and *le vecu* – the "thirdspace" which aggregates individuals memories, ideas, thoughts, symbols and which can be accessed, for example, through artistic expression. This notion of thirdspace proved tremendously influential in conceiving the interstitial locations which are not objectively found but which are "concrete abstractions" – or better yet, through Thomas' pragmatic lens, offer themselves as real due to their effects (Thomas & Thomas, 1928).

Moreover, drawing from Soja (1989, 1996, 2000), this thirdspace – in many ways analogous to Foucault's (1971) concept of *heterotopia*, or "space of otherness" – is what is marked by *spatiality*, and is in a way constructed and reconstructed in accordance to the other spaces of the city. Unlike Foucault, however, Soja sought to conceive the thirdspace as including all otherness and selfness into a single notion. This means that it cannot simply be seen as a mental conception, but rather as a glimpse to the transformative power of the city - by integrating individual expectations, it produces a sort of "imaginary city"). Soja – much like Harvey, Castells and others – also emphasizes the role that ideology and structure play in the creation of city and city-dwellers, noting that today's cities are a product of 20th century politics and ideas as much as they are a result of individual reproduction of everyday life (Soja, 2000). Moreover: to see this thirdspace through the eyes of the individuals who experience the city is also to have a privileged access to their understanding of the world as situated in a given social position.

The distinction between spaces beckons us to look at the city from its intrinsic logic (Löw, 2012), seeking to unravel the way in which individuals conceive the city and create expectations of it, seeing it and hearing it in from their own social position, through their age and sense of identity. Seeking to unravel the many cities inside Porto, we turn towards some of the more radical and controversial views of the city: the International Situationist.

Though problematic in many of its assumptions – as was criticized at some point by their own leader, they tended towards a drunken glorification of obscurity (Debord, 2003) – Situationism emphasized the need to see the city as more than its linear structure, claiming the need to subvert traditional capitalist structuring of the city and exchange it for more fluid urbanist thought – the notion of *unitary urbanism* (Chtcheglov, 1957). The idea of multiple *psychogeograhies*, which obey a certain path taken through the city (a *derive*), seek to give voice to the individuals of a city, through a description of their personal vision and, later, a reconstruction of the city according to these principles (Coverley, 2006). One such way – and the one we chose – is to capture a certain "view" of the city, which likewise follows another radical principle of the situationists: the *dètournement*, that is, the turning of dominant symbolic expressions against the city as a form of protest (Debord & Wolman, 1956). As we shall see, the transformative power of the individual who captures his personal view of the city, is strongly subversive, transforming what it observes into socially situated icons.

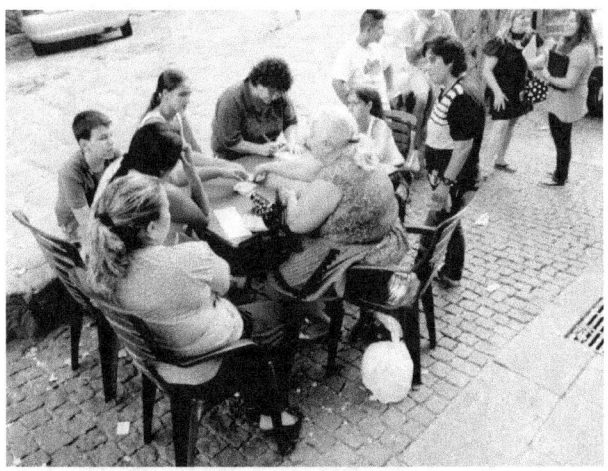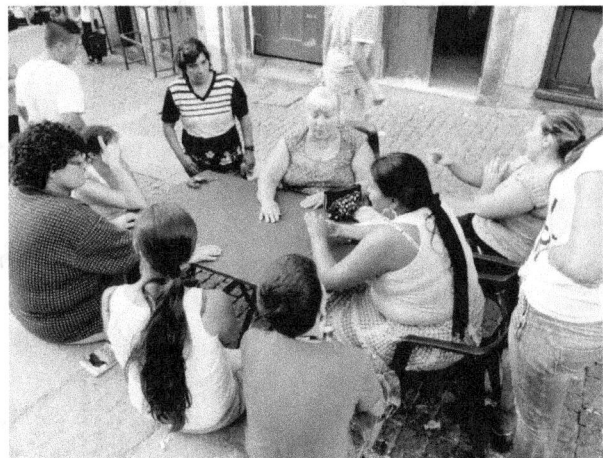

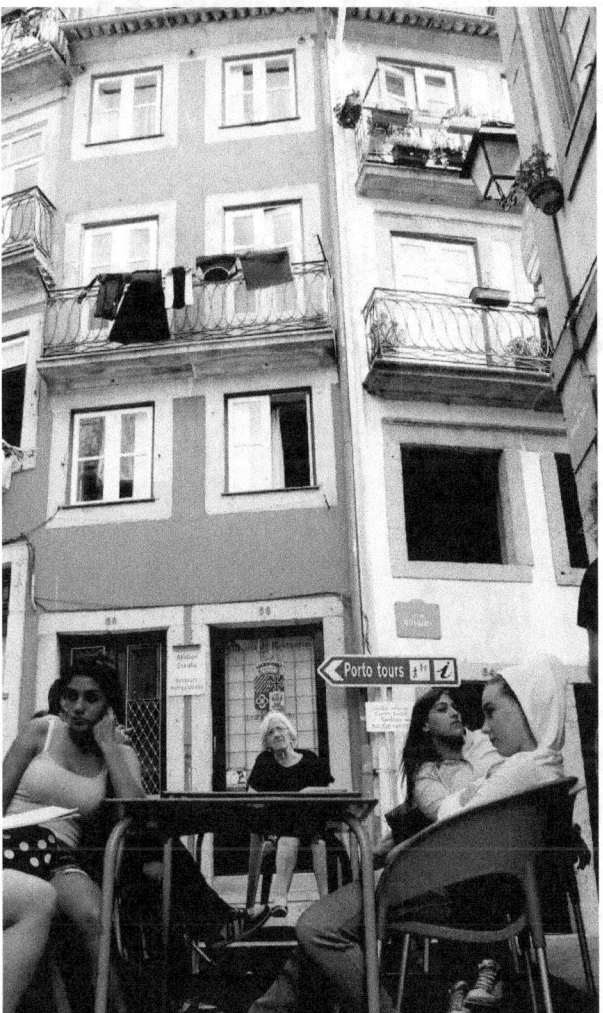

Figures 5 - Sociability and interactions Source: Project "Sou do Porto e trago um Porto em mim" [I come from Porto and bring a Porto in me] (FLUP/ INV3248) | 2012.

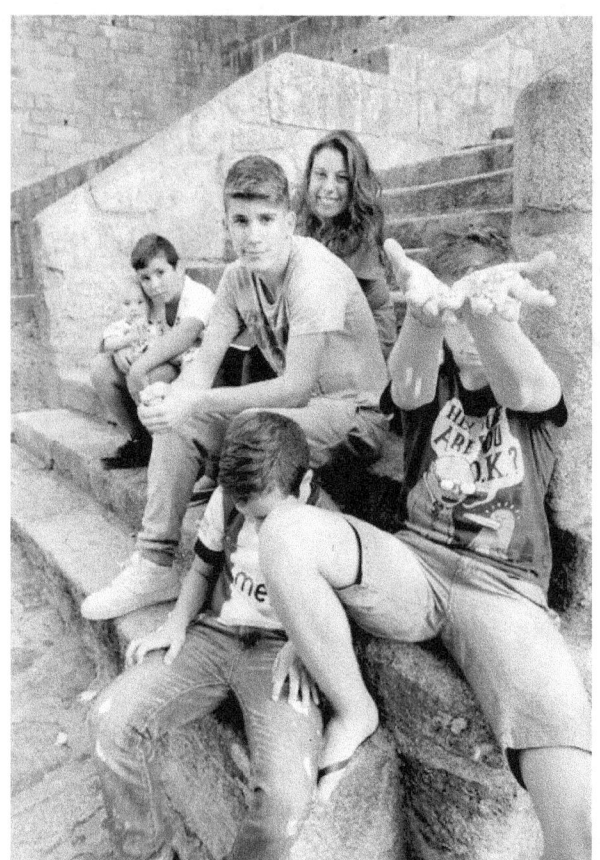
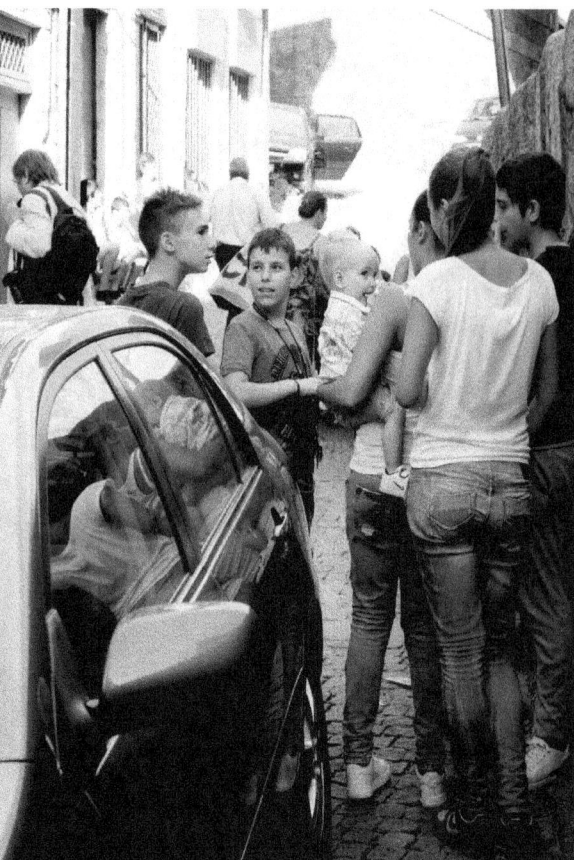
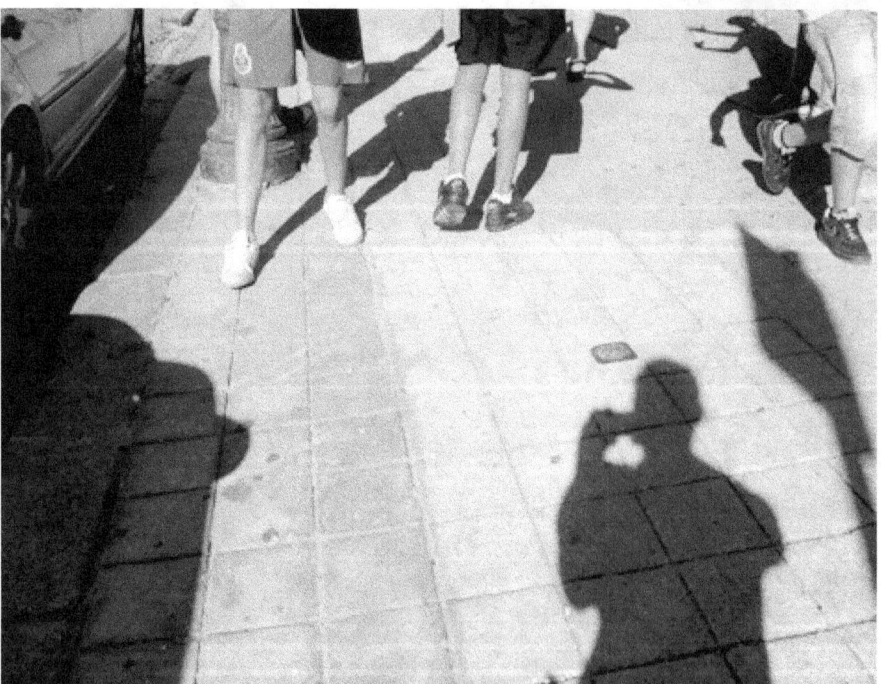

Figures 6 - Positions and demarcations Source: Project "Sou do Porto e trago um Porto em mim" [I come from Porto and bring a Porto in me] (FLUP/ INV3248) | 2012.

In short, we can now answer fully the two questions originally posed. On one side, we have a profoundly trans-formed city, the complexity of which requires us to look at the neighbourhoods and the homes to provide sufficient detail in our analysis; on the other side, the right to the city is first and foremost a right to participate actively in the city, and to transform it whilst being transformed by it. It stems from these two core ideas that in advocating the right to the city in such a context as Sé, we should choose to give voice to the individuals in their relation to their street, their neighbourhood and their homes, seeking to understand their belongings, while at the same time promoting their visions of the city as marked by specificity. The construction of a symbolic lexicon which identifies the imagery and reference values of its inhabitants becomes crucial in this. These semiotic properties are not in any case new, and have been frequently pointed out as something immanent in cities (Ledrut, 1986) and which structure individual lives in a double hermeneutic. This is the same as saying that the meanings which we produce to a city influence the way in which we experience it, while these experiences in turn structure the meaning we make of it. This is, in short, the core issue at the heart of the cartography of affections which we will present here.

3. Processes, captures and interactions

> "In fact, these two cities [that of men and of God] are entangled together in this world, and intermixed until the last judgment effects their separation" (St.Augustine, Civita Dei, 1913: 46)

To fully experience the city, one needs to actively engage in it, which requires a social pattern of reference in terms of rights and duties – a social identity. Erving Goffman distinguishes between two such types: the *virtual* social identity, built through a sum of the information gathered in interaction as to what makes the "self" – physical aspects, reputation, ways of talking, ways of dressing, etc, and *actual* social identity, that is, that which is con-structed by authentic and personal traits of the individual (Goffman, 1982). It is precisely in the interstices – where the social view of the individual does not match his own self-perception with great friction – that stigma comes to exist. Built around the more negative aspects of social identity, these moments of interactional contrast slowly turn themselves into marks of disqualification and exclusion, as well as become associated with stereotypes (Guerra, 2003). Our starting point was the ritual interaction of the streets of Sé, by its residents, where we sought to find an arena of meaning, belonging and affection towards the lived city, as well as place where stigma is resisted and questioned in multiple ways. As our *exergue* seeks to make clear, these processes which elicit are profoundly marked on one side by the profound dualisms which they carry, and on the other, by their inseparability – they are part of the same continuum.

In this respect, we should note the tendency for these young people to engage in various discursive strategies in regards to the streets. Looking at their description of the social spaces of Porto, there is a strong feeling of a need to "defend" the locations, especially noting how some of the "ruas" [streets] in case (for instance, Rua Escura, Rua do Miradouro, Travessa de São Sebastião, Rua da Banharia) belong to a somewhat marginalized area of the downtown centre, and seeing as how certain symbolic associations tend to form in these spaces. In particular, we can find some of the coping strategies proposed by Wacquant (1998, 2002) – from an elaboration of microdif-ferences or lateral denigration ("I wouldn't recommend the location as old people and junkies are always nagging young people", Patrícia[3], 23 years, Rua do Miradouro) a retreat into private or family life ("I like being here as it is where my friends and family are – I don't much care for the rest", Joana, 24 years, Rua da Banharia), to a defence of neighbourhood life ("I like living here because here people are humble, simple and overall nice", Bárbara, 22 years, Rua do Miradouro). Alongside these, we can find numerous mentions to both positive and negative as-pects, whilst one thing does stand out: younger people tend to privilege their individual life, claiming the impor-tance of family, friends and their place of birth as crucial marks, whilst older individuals stress more often the role of the community, the importance of other residents and the social perception of the street. This likewise brings into relevance the fourth line of our analysis: the *self*.

---

3 All names presented here and forthwith are fictitious so as to protect the identity of the social actors.

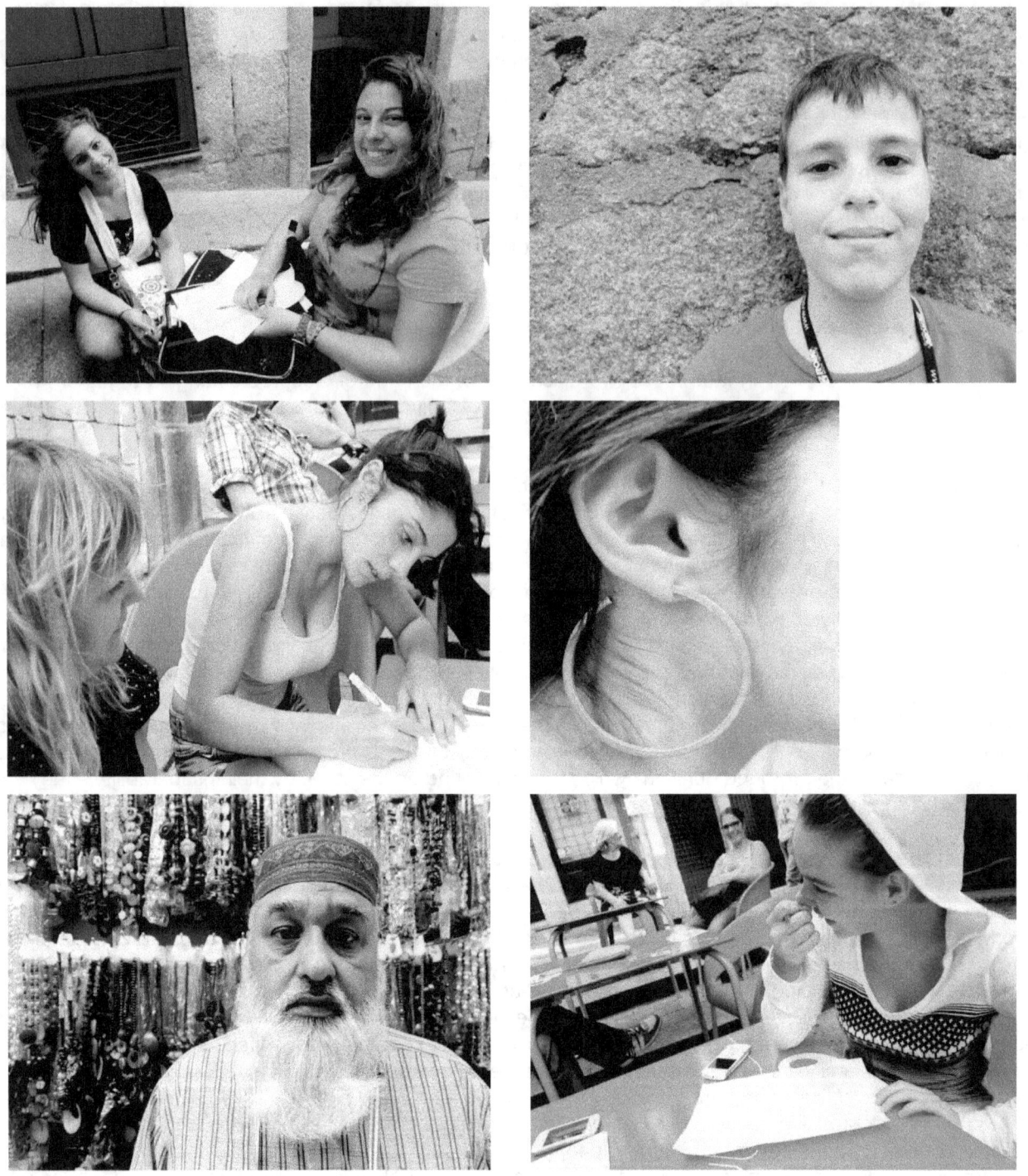

Figures 7 - Information gathering process, Source: Project "Sou do Porto e trago um Porto em mim" [I come from Porto and bring a Porto in me] (FLUP/ INV3248) | 2012.

Our incursion in these territories attempted to be ethnographic. The challenge of this involved a transgression of what is regularly thought as the classical techniques of information gathering and recollection in the social sciences: on one side, it elicited the shunning from attempts to "measure" social reality, while at the same time seeking to capture the "thick description" (to borrow Geertz' term, 2008) of urban reality in the form of signs, discourse and sounds which escape classical social theory (Cohen, 1993). The ethnographic focus drives us to focus on the micro-sociology, on the senses, the plurality, and the difference; in the words of Machado Pais, this path means to "cosy oneself to the warmth of understanding, shunning away from the icy peaks of explanation which, insensitive to the plurality of the lived, raise barriers between phenomena which in all truth bear reciprocal relations." (Pais, 2002, p. 32). In the interstices of everyday-life, the lived, the social, their multiple and invisible *arts de faire* (Certeau, 1980), ethnographic research can in a way activate the senses of the investigator by directly stimulating him in interpreting the people in action, their social networks, their discourses and interactions and their participation in everyday activities of ritual, essays and aesthetic, rather than drawing from secondary sources (Cohen, 1993). Traditionally, for sociologists, ethnography has also meant to participate actively in the everyday lives of analysed groups – though in recent times, it has come to serve as a sort of "umbrella term" that encompasses most qualitative methodologies, such as direct and/or participant observation, but also interviews, life stories, focus groups, videographic and or photographic document analysis – in short, all instruments which analyse the daily body life of the social actors. The arts and music in particular seem to be in perfect syntony with ethnography: "much like music, ethnography is an interpretative practice: it requires participation and improvisation; its presentation invites a multiplicity of meanings as well as self-reflection." (Grazian, 2004, p. 206).

Our ethnographic approach counted with the help of students from the 1st and 2nd cycle of studies of Sociology of the Faculty of Arts and Humanities of the University of Porto[4], which both helped in the ethnography, communicating with the social actors and helping them in having a clearer idea of what was expected of them, as well as in producing reflections on the role of the city as a place of identity in contemporaneity. Their role as mediators allowed a closer connection to the social actors, especially given the proximity in ages in some participants and students. These students were also responsible for the cataloguing of the photos, as well as helping in administering them in their respective social contexts. Social relegation – to which we have already alluded, and which has also been called "territorial stigmatization" – is a mark of such spaces as Sé, which works by an urban concentration of situations which involve disaccredited social groups, excluded from work and the consumption society. The need to look at this situation as a social and global phenomenon – as we have done – should not however forgo a more municipal and regional focus. In fact, looking at the housing policies in Porto, namely those of rehousing, as well as the intervention of public and private organisms with action in this dominion, one can see how practices of socio-spatial segregation work by "jamming" local policy drawn by the population (Bourdieu, 1999). In the case of Porto, as Fonseca Ferreira (1994) notes, the "transplantation" of population from ground level houses to vertical buildings, tearing apart crucial relations such as neighbour ties and replacing them with anonymity, as well as setting them in the periphery of the city, tends to lead to a fast physical and social degradation, the constitution of ghettos, closed enclaves, and "exiled neighbourhoods". These are essentially "holes" in the urban and social fabric: we can see in the media representations that they are often blamed for criminality, drug dealing and urban insecurity. To actively engage in ethnography in these spaces provides not only a relevant challenge to the investigator, but also an epistemological challenge to the notions frequently associated to them (Cohen, 1972).

The visual recollection was done through a photovoice approach, stressing the importance of participatory art in these youth contexts. Social actors were given a photographic camera and told to capture specific everyday moments of their lives which they considered particularly meaningful, which they thought particularly indicative of their way of life or which reminded them of their place of residency in any way – in sum, they were told to capture photos which in some way meant "Porto" for them (Appleyard, 1973). The choice of this sort of method, a modern classic of urban intervention, is aligned with the critique which has often been directed towards the monist statistical and geographic information (population, activities, networks of transportation): that there seems to be a "fear" of cognitive methodologies, perhaps due to a need to establish social life as distinct from individual-psychological experiences of it, but which leads to the neglect of socio-emotional functions, desires and aspirations, as pointed out by Eppler and Burkhard (2004).

---

4 Under the Bologna process, the 1st cycle of studies corresponds generally to a BA, attributing in the case of Sociology 180 ECTS. The 2nd cycle corresponds to an MA, and attributes 120 ECTS.

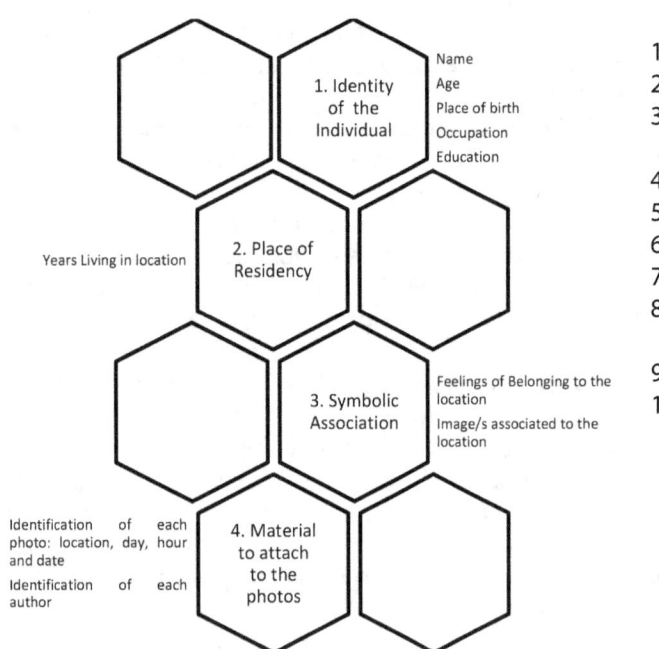

1. Identity of the Individual — Name, Age, Place of birth, Occupation, Education
2. Place of Residency — Years Living in location
3. Symbolic Association — Feelings of Belonging to the location, Image/s associated to the location
4. Material to attach to the photos — Identification of each photo: location, day, hour and date; Identification of each author

1.   Monuments, heritage and toponymy
2.   Music, inscriptions in space, graffiti and tags
3.   Localism and belongings (street, house, door and window house, pets)
4.   Periphery and city relegation
5.   Youth identity marks
6.   Lived-space and economic dynamism
7.   Social space of the street and neighbourhood
8.   Porto, Portugal, football and local, regional and national identities
9.   Multiculturalism and new values
10. Tourism and the discovery of Sé

Figure 8 - Guidelines for incursions of the young residents in the Porto Historical Centre

It is in this context that the more interesting structures arose: in particular, we can find 10 key themes that encompass most photographs, from most frequent to less frequent themes, (to which we will return in the next section): Looking for instance at figure 6 we can see how these themes appear at times in multiple photos: at the same time the groups of young residents form in a peer association which is part of their identity as youths in a dynamic city, they are involved in the neighbourhood life, and at the same time the presence of city landmarks points to the ways in which this heritage is appropriated by them. We can likewise identify that these themes are in tune with our three dimensions of analysis (the city, the neighbourhood and the home), with equal importance to the individual as sources of meaning to their lives.

This matter of affections and belongings of young people, culminated in an intervention in the public space which confronted the "real" space with the individual representation, in an interplay between the real and the represented, placing the image next to the object it represents (for instance, putting the image of the shop front next to the shop front). This moment sought to intervene directly in the city, in a way, drawing each individual's city – in the uses that each people makes of them, at times creating interesting contrasts between multiple individuals. Through this, there was an attempt to transform reality through the creation of "noise", in giving value to something routinely and indifferent, and individuating objects (*the* door becomes *that* door). Concurrently, we edited the soundtracks of the everyday lives in an electronic format (*podcast*) on a website[5]. Through the recollection of nearly 500 photographs and 50 sound blocks, we sought to put the project title and motto in practice: I come from Porto and I bring a Porto in me.

4. The symbols of life
"Life, my dear, is illegible. It appears and disappears as goes. There is no mind that breaks it apart: it comes in the language of nothing, birthed in the body as the day, as if the day and the life of the individual were parallel fabrics." (Tavares, 2011, p. 373).

From what we have said it follows that we see the construction of the social world as inseparable from the representations of the actors who participate in it, and who produce and reproduce incessantly the cultural values of a given time-space setting. Recognizing the bonds between the reflexive structures present in young people and their surroundings, as well as the varying geometries of that relationship, seems like a good starting point to attempt a definition of what can accurately be described as an axiom of micro-sociology. In this section, we will

5 This refers to the website of "Rádio Manobras": http://radiomanobras.pt/

attempt just that: to present the photographs captured by young people in their own personal space, and to produce a thematic approach of the senses, affections and belongings they develop towards it. Reacting against a supposedly homogenous vision of their social world, these young residents present a diversity, a complexity, and at times a resistance against standardization, that produces its own version of normality and is filled with affection and symbolism.

It is likewise important to mention the growing relevance which images have had in the last decades, which stems from a rising number of optical, visual and audiovisual apparatuses which profoundly change the way we think and represent the world (Pais, Carvalho & Gusmão, 2008). While some important fields of investigation such as anthropology, and to a less degree sociology, have taken these resources as bases of investigation, these have for all purposes been considered marginal (Campos, 2011a; Pink, 2006). Effectively, this sort of logocentric[6] approach to writing has only recently started to erode, due to the aforementioned processes (Campos, 2011b).

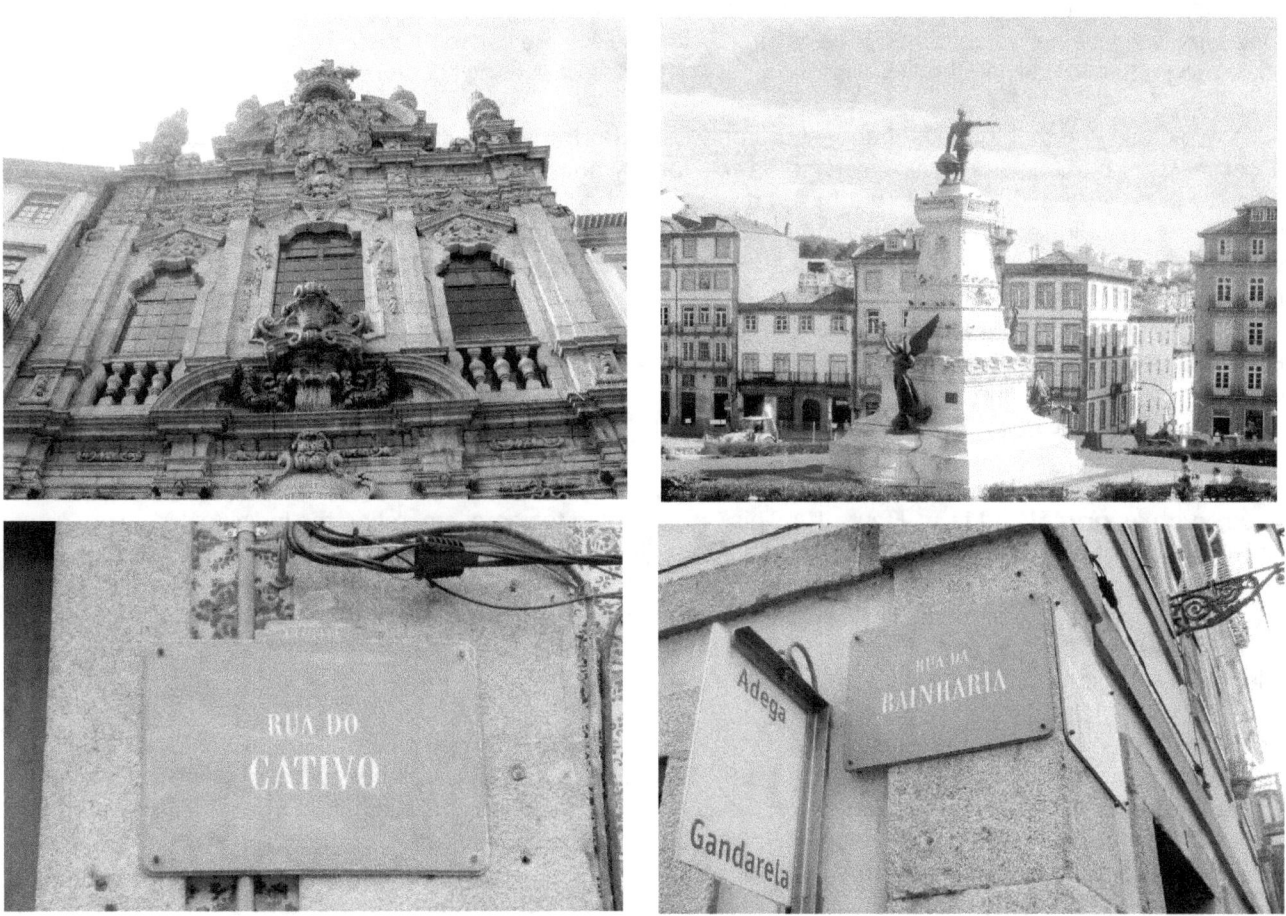

Figures 9 - Monuments, heritage and toponymy, Source: Project "Sou do Porto e trago um Porto em mim"[*I come from Porto and bring a Porto in me*] (FLUP/ INV3248) | 2012.

Images – in the wider sense of the word, encompassing not only the physical or virtual representation, but also what is represented – are in their essence profoundly polysemic, having various semiotic layers. As the line promoted by Barthes (2009) and Eco (1970) emphasizes, visual cues are at the heart of the way in which individuals interpret social life – and likewise, studies such as those done by Hebdige (1979) have emphasized the way in which subcultural life is markedly expressed through vision. For instance, taking the case of punk, the image lay at the heart of the movement, from the way that individual dressed to graphic objects such as fanzines, disc covers

---

6 We take this term to its meaning in the framework of Derrida's analysis, that is, meaning a system which makes itself knowable only through a *logos* – a reified belief which serves as transcendental signified of a given set of assumptions. In Campos (2011b) this role is taken by writing, in opposition to image and sound, in analytical terms.

and demo tapes (Triggs, 2010). These objects, generally produced through a DIY *ethos*, sought at the same time to defy the dominant semiotic discourse, and to produce its own alternatives. This eventually led to it being "swallowed" by the cultural industries, with a certain "domestication" of its visual and audiovisual aesthetics (Guerra & Quintela, 2014). These processes are not innocent: they are the result of our living in what has been called an ocularcentric society (Jenks, 1995) and they accurately demonstrate the relevance taken by images. This is on its essence the transition to a new "visual culture" which stems from the expansion of technology and visual languages, taking a specific role as a "primordial form of intercultural contact" (Campos, 2011a, p. 37).

Images are in a way also a profoundly contextual feature. They exist to an individual only in certain moments, and in certain ways. Drawing from Schütz (1996) understanding, the image exists in a given *lebenswelt* (life-world) and is always the intention of an individual (that is, there must always be an individual to capture the image; otherwise, though the object may stay, there is no image of it). Far from a principle of causality, and taking the *verstehen* approach, as well as a semiotic framework – to interpret ourselves the sense of social reality - we took to analysing 500 photographs, identifying the key themes in the life-worlds of our social actors.

In this, we could see that the most frequent theme was (1) **heritage, monuments and toponymy** (Figure 9). The Sé cathedral is particularly relevant, serving as the toponymous identification of the neighbourhood, and as a source of pride for the individuals. That this sort of object should be the most frequently depicted by the youths we contacted should tell us something of the importance that such landmarks have for individuals in general, and perhaps for inhabitants of relegated areas in specific. The heritage is crucial in terms of how the young residents of Sé position themselves: their relation to the city through a central landmark connects them not only to the "mainstream city", but also to the individuals which inhabit it. At the same time, this concern with heritage also has deep roots in a transitional understanding of the city: how monuments are a legacy from the past which ought to be preserved for future generations. This is crucial in working against the social relegation to which the neighbourhood is subjected – in short, the Sé works as a sort of bridge to a socially inclusive city.

The second most important theme in terms of photographic presence was (2) **music and the inscriptions in space, such as graffiti and tags** (Figure 10). This fact, directed towards integrating the individual in an imaginary community (Appadurai, 1990) is hardly surprising: the role that youth cultures have come to assume as axes of structuring the social life of individuals in the city grants them a transversal nature (Guerra, 2010), as common factors beyond the structure of the neighbourhood. As we can see in Figure 4, the individuals identify these marks with the city, select them as part of their everyday-life, and integrate them as theirs as much as they do their street, their house or their room.

At the same time, in a tangent, a different theme tackles the issue of the self: **(3) localism and belongings** (Figure 11), in what is more personal and unique (their objects, their doors, their pets, their room). If youth cultures serve as measures of unity, these come as marks of specificity, individualism and distinction (Pais, 2003). They are, in short, something which marks the personality of the individual. This dualism – youth culture and individual – are two ends of the same process of constructing the self: on one side, that which binds youth together (and in a way sets them apart from the rest of society), and on the other that which makes them individuals.

Fourthly, **we can see (4) the image of the periphery and of social relegation** (Figure 12), of the abandonment of spaces and buildings which are left behind. These images correspond in part to the vision of the city as a space of abandonment, and relate to the situation of relegation suffered by the individuals. By emphasizing them, the social actors aim to show their realities, sometimes with critique and others with affection, so as to show in the reality that surrounds them what there is of more crude and ugly. This can point us to a very clear form of agency, where the social actors attempt to direct us to the reality in question.

The themes which appear in fifth (**youth identity marks** – Figure 13) more directly towards the ways in which youth experiences these cultures and their personalities echo this idea of an hybridism with imaginary peers. Fashion, in the form of clothing, shoewear (mostly snickers), jeans, various artifacts, as much as selfies, are ways to denote a collective identity of youth (as far as that is possible) and come off as a common theme in nearly all photos (Feixa, 1999). From here we pass into an understanding of the **lived space and the economic dynamism of the space** (Figure 14), more specifically, the images of (6) the **street commerce and economy, with neighbourhood grocery shops** and professional retail professions.

At the same time there appear images of (7) **neighbourhood sociability and leisure** (Figure 15), and even objects of entertainment or public decoration (plants, flowers). These themes serve as two aspects of the same reality: the relationship which the individual establishes with the neighbourhood life. As we can see, despite having today less importance than the "self", community ties of vicinity continue to be felt as important, and their traditions and practices are actively reproduced by the young residents. Whether in terms of the economic and commercial structures, or leisure practices, this tendency towards reproduction seems to us a very keen aspect of the social reality in question.

From here, the **three final themes** direct us to the city as a whole: (8) local, regional and national identities, in the form of symbols and spaces which bind the residents to Porto and Portugal (Figure 16); (9) images of immigration, multiculturalism, differences and new values, new clothes, new food, in short, the transition between a closed city culture and an openness towards globalized values; (10) and the images of tourism, of sightseeing, as well as the more naturalistic aspects of the city such as the river, the sky, clouds and distorted or onirically iconic images. Whereas the first point us to institutions such as the Porto Football Club, which bring together strong identities in the city, the second are better represented by ethnic stores which have started to appear in the historic centre of Porto, and which coexist with the autochthonous residents. The last thematic axis, perhaps the more elusive, are those which send us to a level which transcends the city, more accurately represented by fluxes and transition, change, and the "outside world" (Feixa, 2014).

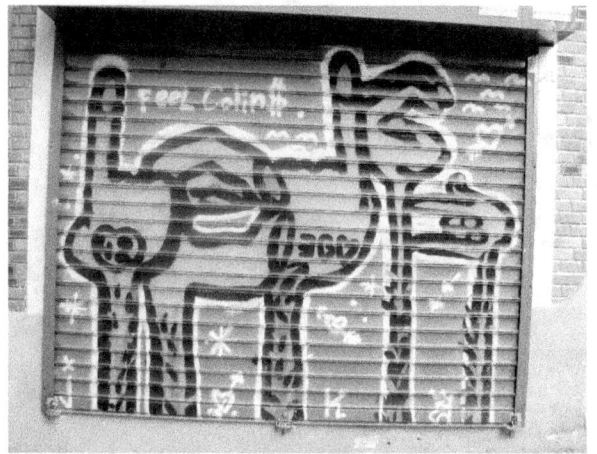
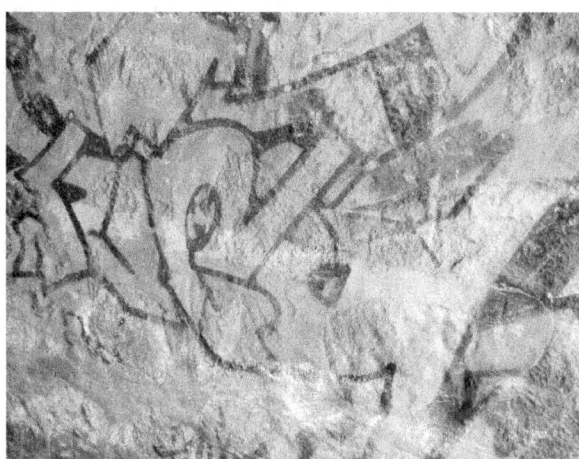
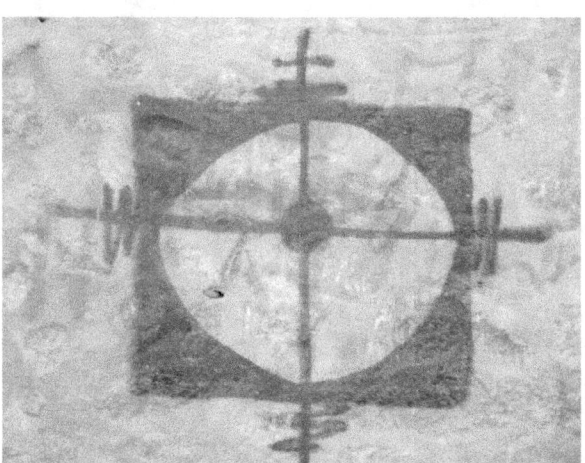
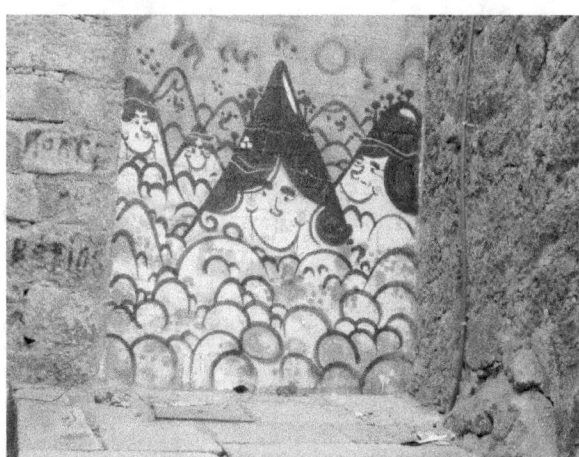

Figures 10 - Music, inscriptions in space, graffiti and tags, Source: ProPorto e trago um Porto em mim"[I *come from Porto and bring a Porto in me*] (FLUP/ INV3248) | 2012.

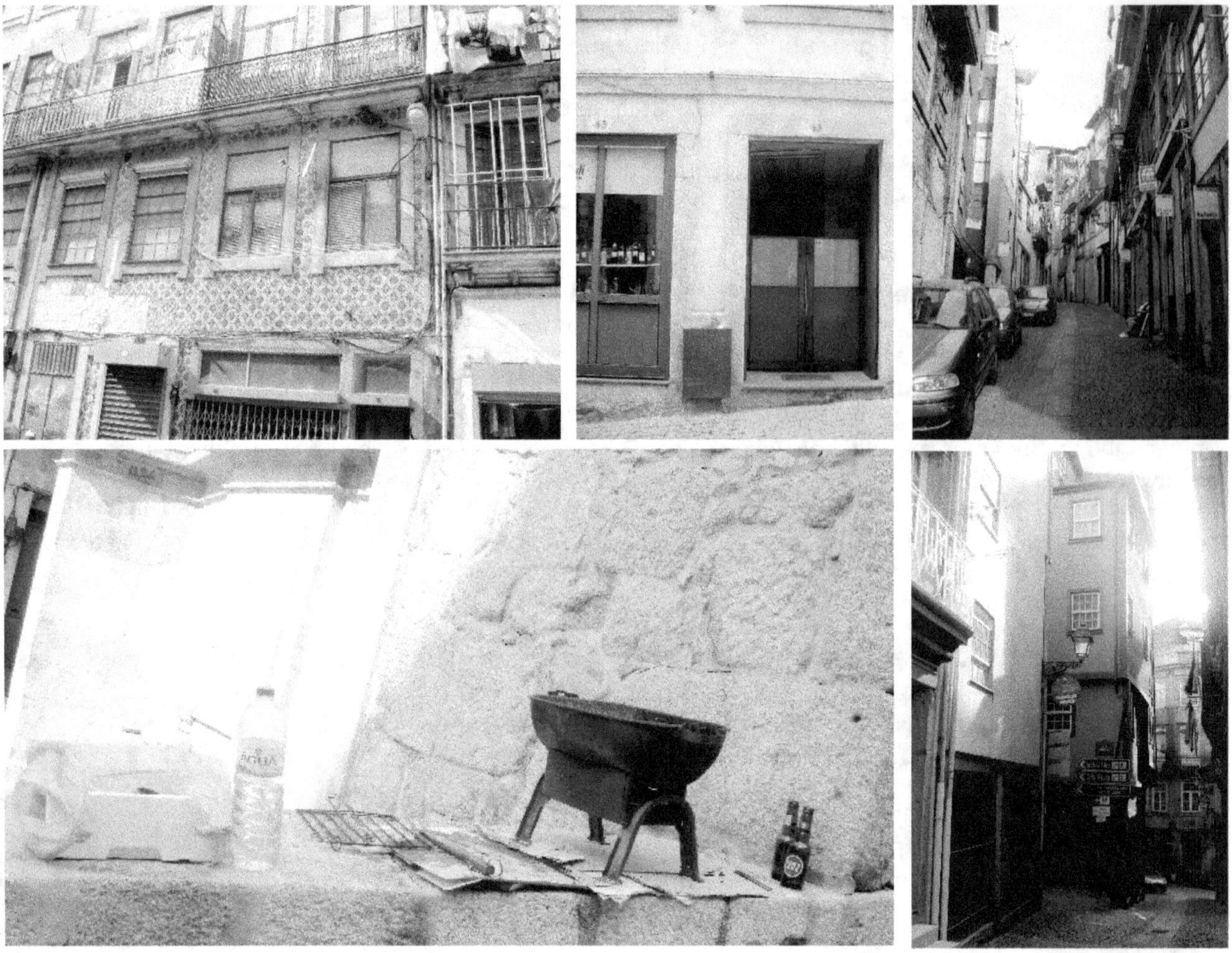

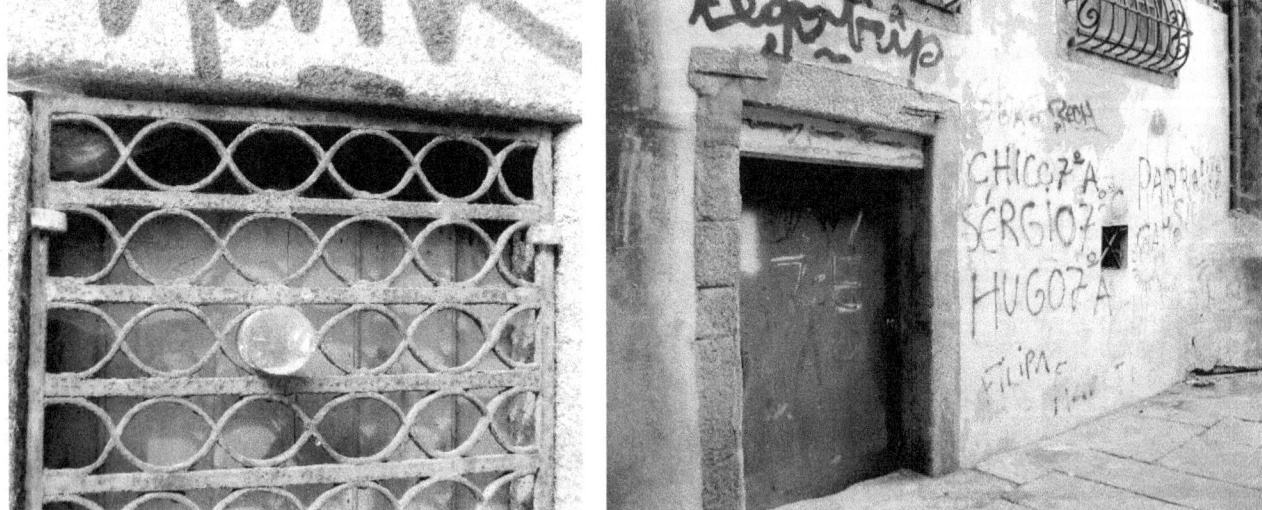

Figures 11 - **Localism and belongings,** Source: Project "Sou do Porto e trago um Porto em mim"[I *come from Porto and bring a Porto in me*] (FLUP/ INV3248) | 2012.

Figures 12 - **Periphery and city relegation,** Source: Project "Sou do Porto e trago um Porto em mim"[I *come from Porto and bring a Porto in me*] (FLUP/ INV3248) | 2012.

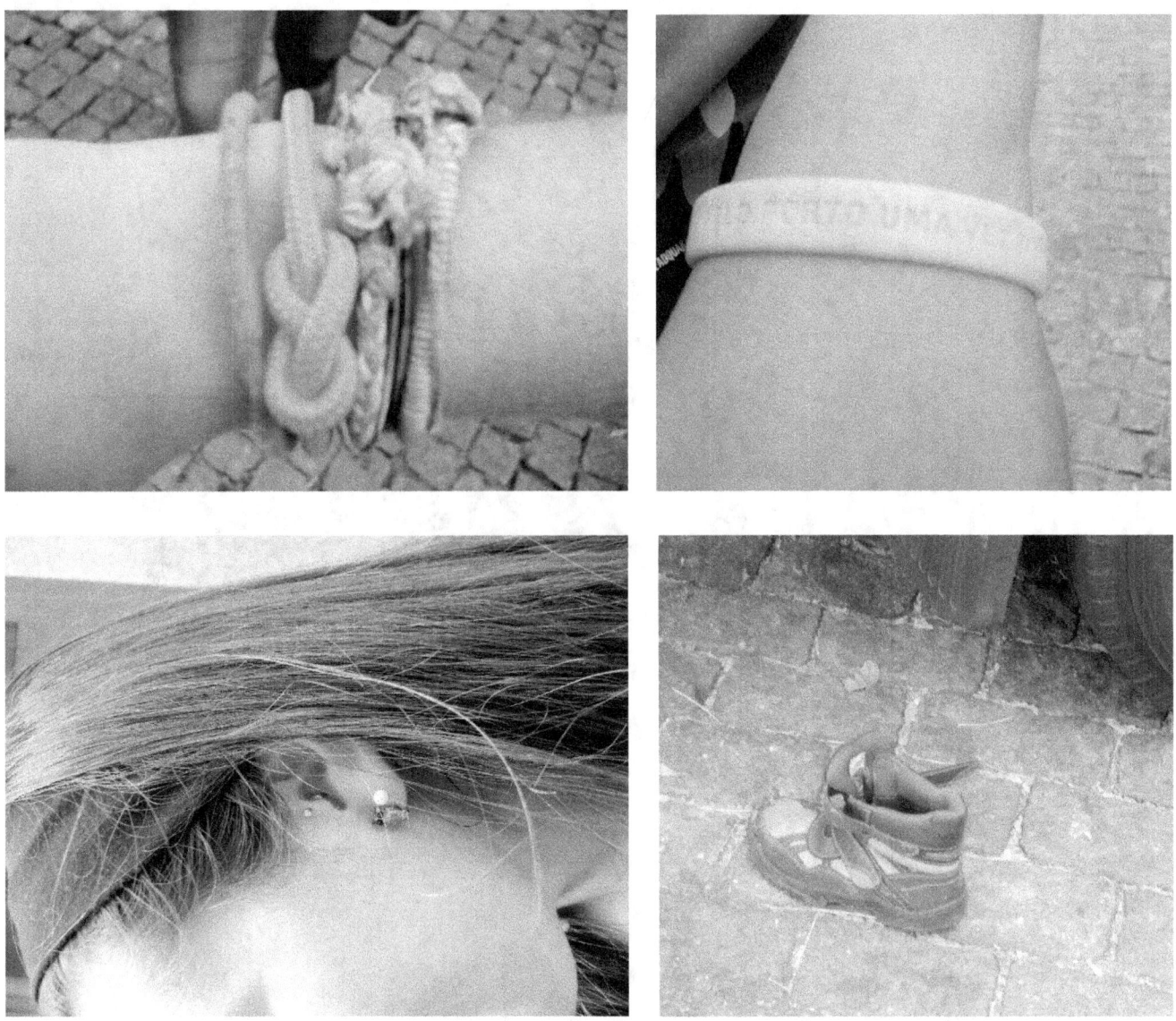

Figures 13 - Youth identity marks, Source: Project "Sou do Porto e trago um Porto em mim"[I *come from Porto and bring a Porto in me*] (FLUP/ INV3248) | 2012.

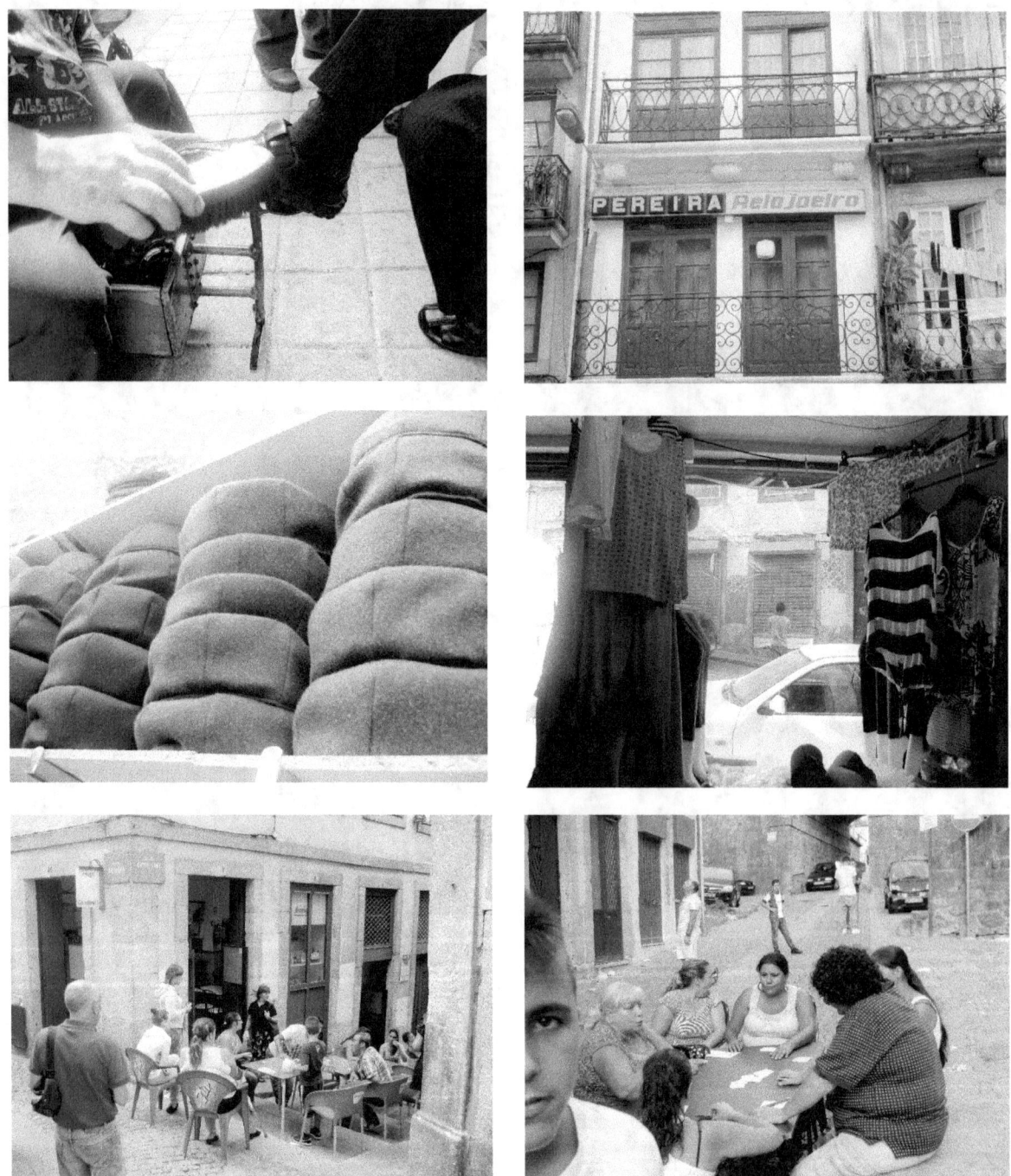

Figures 14 - Lived-space and economic dynamism, Source: Project "Sou do Porto e trago um Porto em mim"[I *come from Porto and bring a Porto in me*] (FLUP/ INV3248) | 2012.

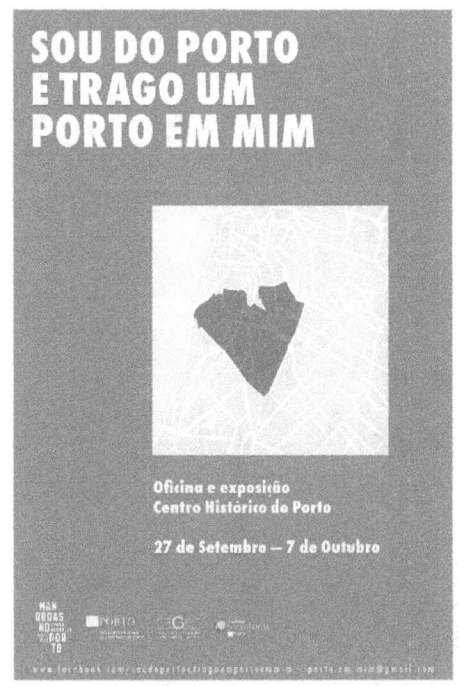

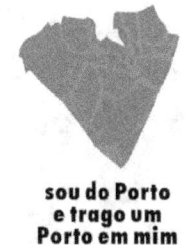

Figures 17 - Main poster for the project and exposition poster for the promotion of the soundtracks, Source: Project "Sou do Porto e trago um Porto em mim" [I come from Porto and bring a *Porto in me*] (FLUP/ INV3248) | 2012.

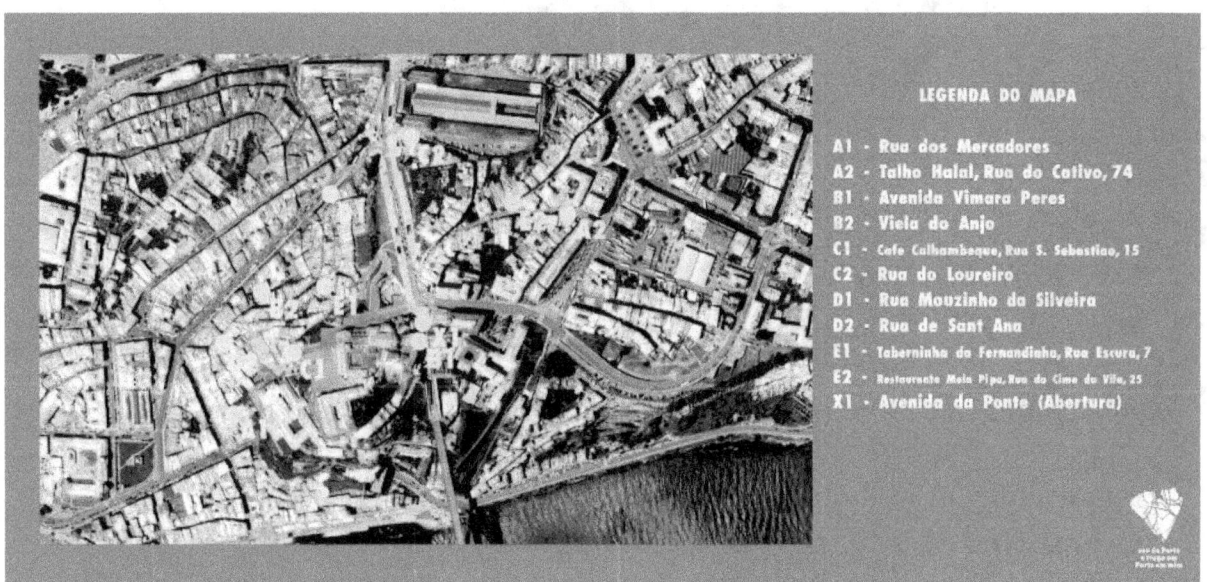

Figures 18 - Map of the location where the exposition took place, Source: Project "Sou do Porto e trago um Porto em mim" [*I come from Porto and bring a Porto in me*] (FLUP/ INV3248) | 2012.

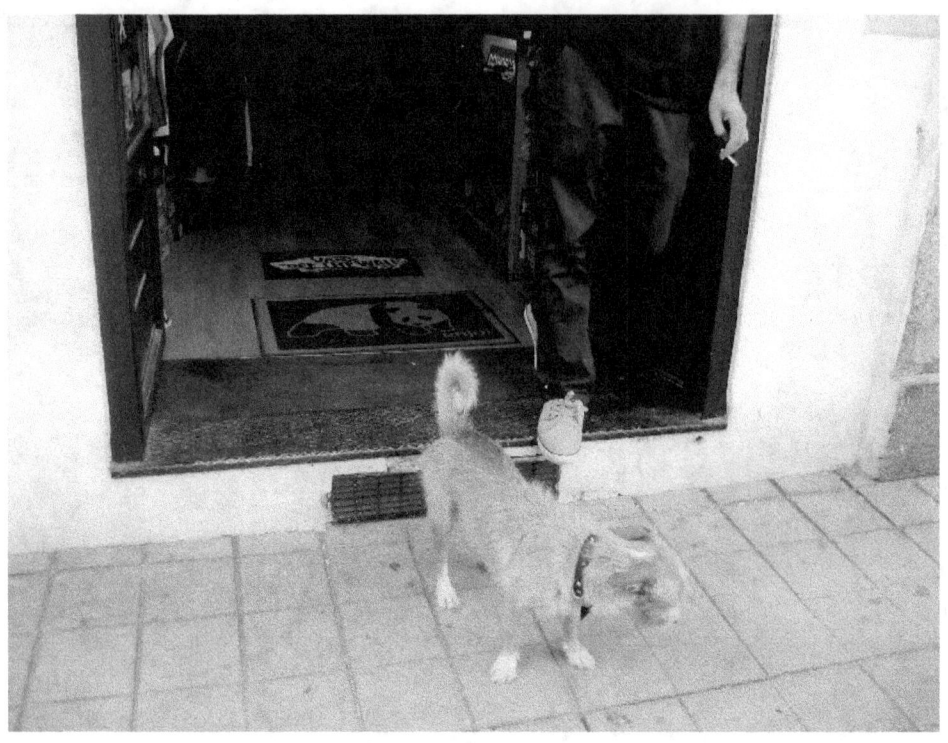

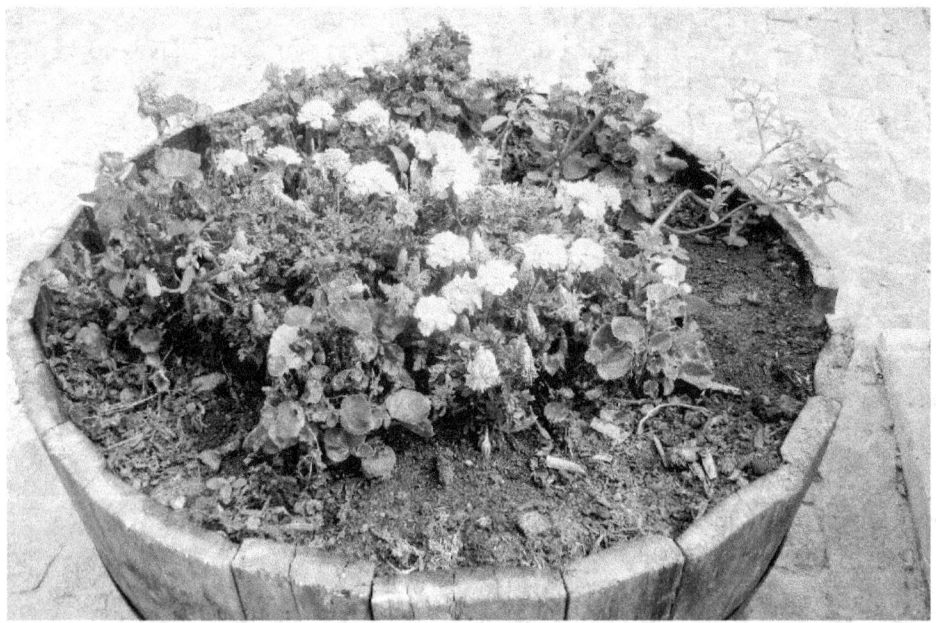

Figures 15 - Social space of the street and neighbourhood, Source: Project
"Sou do Porto e trago um Porto em mim"[I *come from Porto and bring a Porto in me*] (FLUP/ INV3248) | 2012.

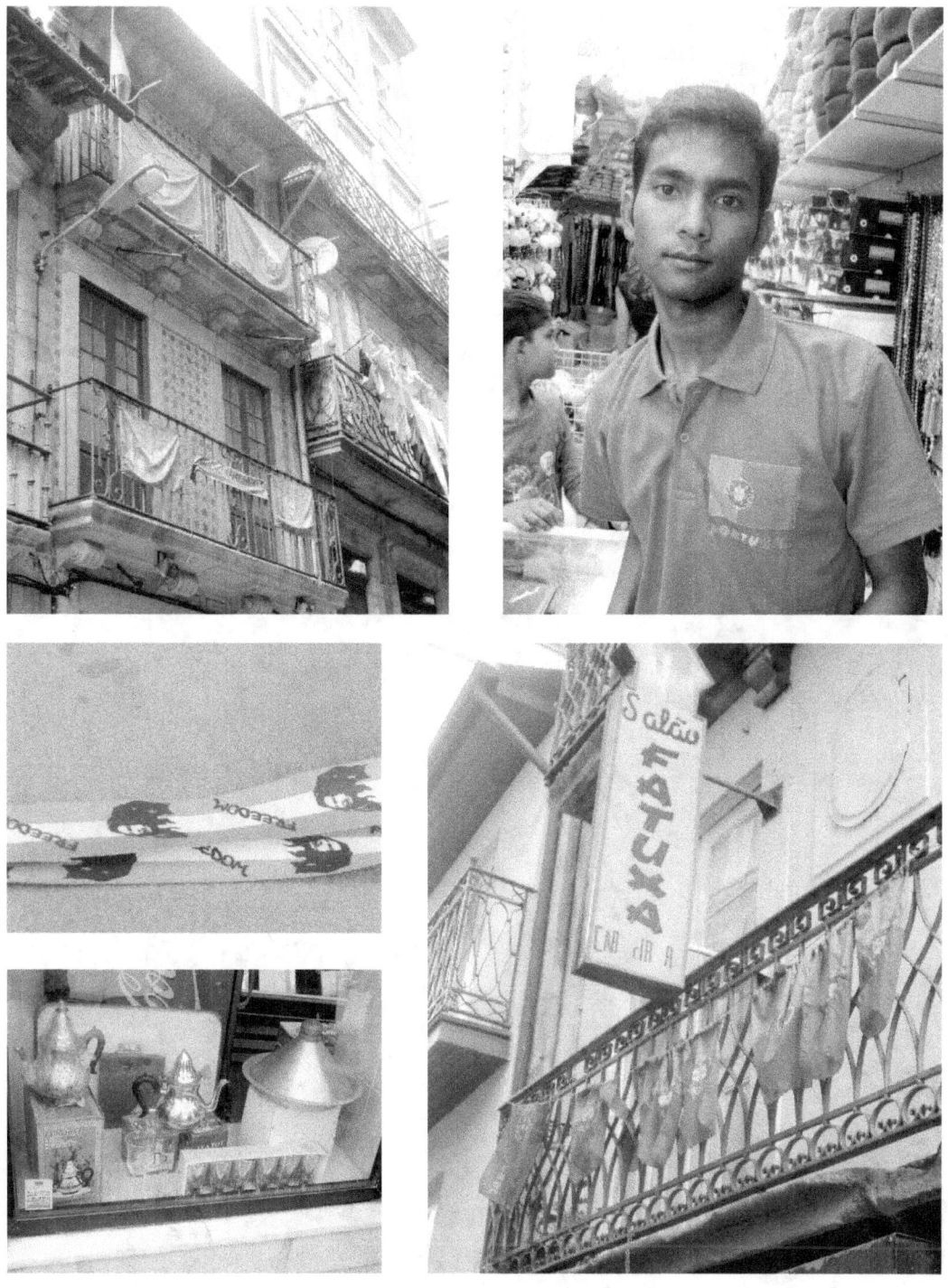

Figures 16 - Porto, Portugal, football and local, regional and national identities, Source: Project "Sou do Porto e trago um Porto em mim"[I *come from Porto and bring a Porto in me*] (FLUP/ INV3248) | 2012.

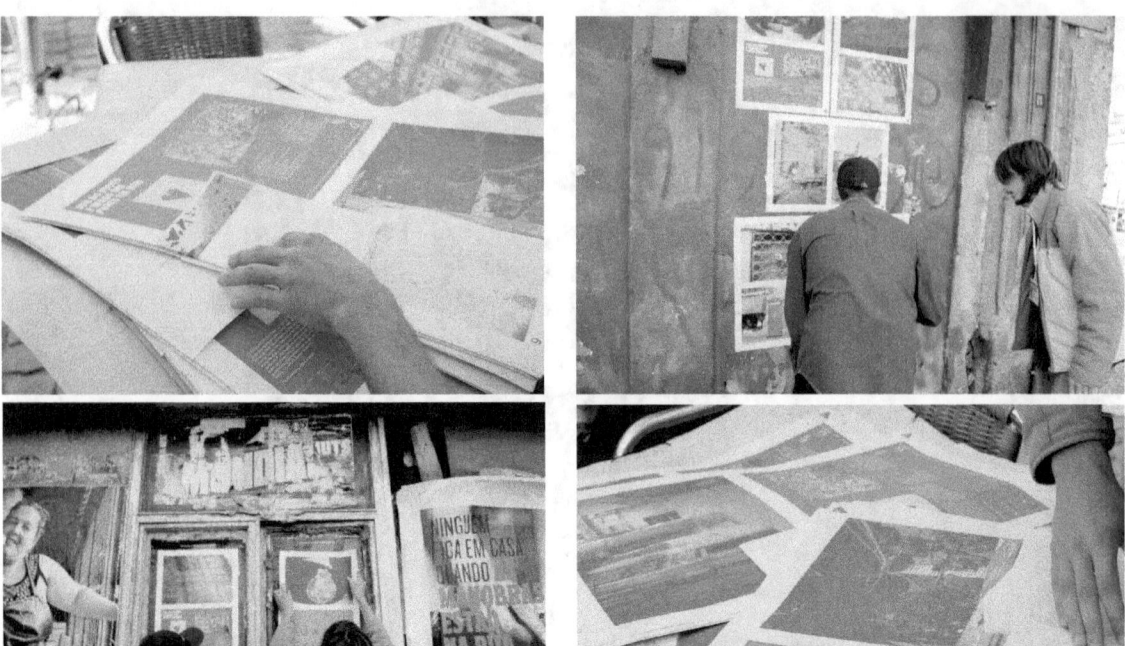

Figures 19 - Assembling the show, Source: Project "Sou do Porto e trago um Porto em mim" [*I come from Porto and bring a Porto in me*] (FLUP/ INV3248) | 2012.

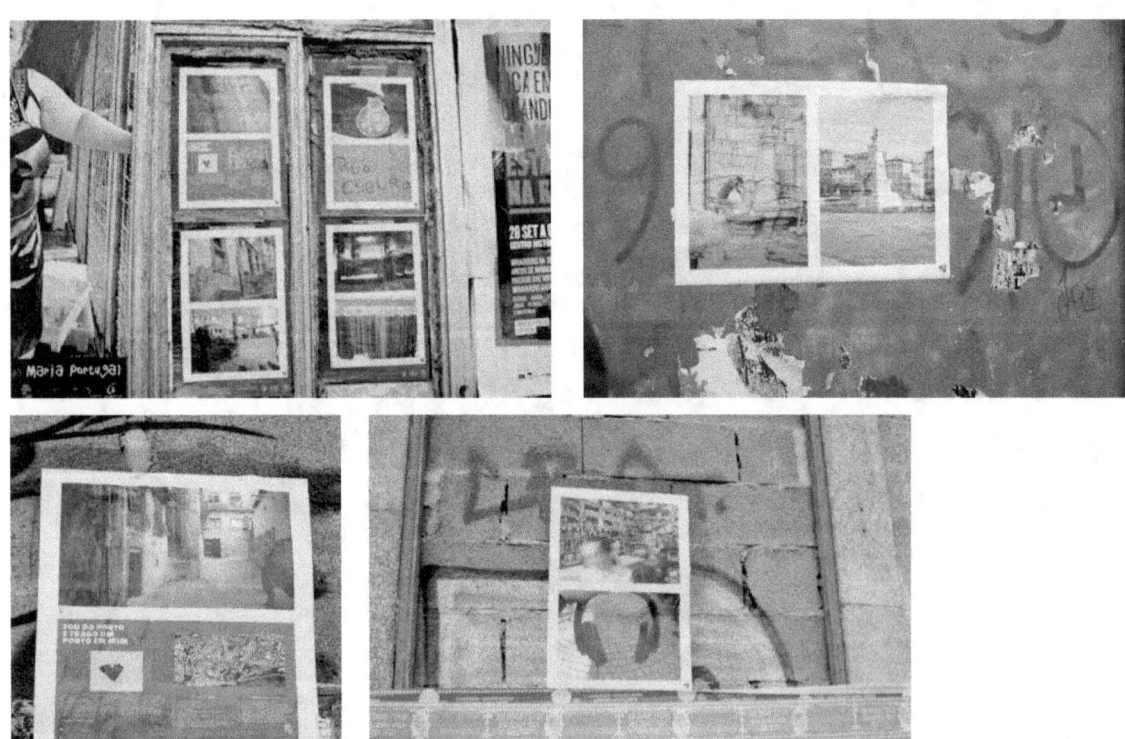

Figures 20 - The "I come from Porto and bring a Porto in me" in the walls, Source: Project "Sou do Porto e trago um Porto em mim" [*I come from Porto and bring a Porto in me*] (FLUP/ INV3248) | 2012.

A factor becomes, soon clear: the concerns of the individuals, shown in the number of appearances in youth portrayals, end up echoing our levels of analysis, as well as Schütz's notions, with some important nuances. The *ego* starts to understand social reality having himself and his conscience as an interpretative matrix, conceiving of his peer group (real or imagined), and then establishes relations with the immediate space, the neighbourhood, the city, and even with supra-city structures. This movement echoes the distinctions of *lebenswelten* made by the Austrian author when he speaks of the *umwelt* (the right-now world of fellow people), from the *mitwelt* of themes 5 and 10, that is, the world of contemporary people, ideas and places which are not geographically adjacent. Moreover, the crucial factor that tops their concerns relates to the two diachronic axes of his typology (the *vorwelt* in what concerns the past and the *folgewelt* in what concerns the future): the "Sé" cathedral, which serves as a unitary mark of their collective history, and a "glue" to their various experiences (Wagner, 1979).

It follows from what we have said here that we stand in front of an intersubjective object, constantly interpreted by the young residents of the Sé neighbourhood. If the construction of world begins with this taking of consciousness of an object – as Husserl would have it – then it is only through these individual worlds that we may seek to access each person's lifeworld, and through it, to give them a true right to the city (see Rogers, 2000)

5. The moments, the path and its people

> "Path: a patch of terrain over which you walk on foot. The road differs from the path not only because it is travelled by car, but also due to being only a line that connects a point to another. The road has no direction in itself; it has only the two point which it connects. The path is an homage to the space, however. Each part of it has a direction, and invites us to pause. The street is the devaluing of space, the latter which is seen today as nothing more than encumbrance of man and a waste of time." (Kundera, 2012, p. 167)

After identifying the paths, the moments, the people and the meaningful objects which the youth of our approach identified, we are dawning on a conclusion – forever left unfinished – of such a project as this. As we have previously mentioned, the project included a soundtrack collection which, for the purpose of this article we will not treat. Let us focus on the photographs – and in particular, in the exposition where they were shown from September 28th to October 7th in 2012, in the public space of the Porto Historic Centre and the Sé neighbourhood in particular (cf. Figure 17). Our focus was to show the photographs of the residents which we had contacted, producing an intervention which confronted real and representational space (or in Lefebvre's term, *le perçu* and *le vecu*), in the ways which we previously described.

This unraveling of paths in and through the city sought to address the objectives raised by Manobras Porto[7] which included, but were not limited to "taking back the city", to giving a voice to the citizens without discrimination, to recognize the economic, cultural, social and technical potential of the territories, and, conclusively, to "create conditions for the flourishment of an idea of a City as a work in progress, inclusive and unending" (Alvelos, 2013, p. 50). We cannot but recognize a good dose of goodwill and a certain excessive ambition in these objectives, in an intensive project which, after two years, completely vanished. However, noting the potential of these goals as guidelines towards which an individual should direct their beliefs, we can attest in our project the success of some of them. In fact, we can see in the discourse of the social actors the sort of filiation and belonging which the project sought to bring to life.

---

7 Cf. Among others, the Making of Call of Manobras Porto 2012 http://www.youtube.com/watch?v=yq7H7yd0rW8&feature=youtu.be; Their facebook page: https://www.facebook.com/manobrasporto; https://www.facebook.com/manobrasporto#!/radiomanobras; And the archive of the project http://www.museudoresgate.org/passa-pra-ca/

Tazul, 25 years old, Rua do Loureiro: "I like Portugal more than Porto or Spain and Italy"

Marcela, 14 years old, Travessa S.Sebastião: "I like everything about it here. I want to be here forever"

João, 16 years old, Rua da Banharia: "Banharia is my home, and some home"

Joana Cardoso, 24 years old, Rua da Banharia: "I like being here since it is where my family is"

Fabio, 25 years old, Rua Senhora das Verdades: "I like living here, I was accostumed to it, I don't know anywhere else, and here everyone knows each other"

Cristiano, 16 years old, Rua dos Pelames: "I really like living here. I have all my friends here."

Ana, 19 years old, Rua da Banharia: "It's a pretty and quiet zone. People all know each other, and they help one another"

Catarina, 15 years old, Rua da Ponte Nova: "I have all my friends here – it would be weird not to live here, I would feel odd"

Paulo, 15 years old, Rua Escura: "I really like living here, I don't want to go anywhere else. I'm proud to live in Sé. I'm happy here. The problem is that the houses are closed, they took people from here and now we have no one"

What did happen during the exposition? The young residents and their families went on a tour of the space which had their representations next to them. The presence of the media enhanced the importance of the moment, and in the complex everyday-lives of these youths, with their happiness and sadness, giving back to the Sé a normalcy which had long been missing. This singular moment, which sought to try and help mend the gap, both physical and socio-cultural, representational and practical, which put on one side the inhabitants of Porto and on the other the Inhabitants of Sé, was made smaller. The residents of Sé were given in part the tools to take back their right to the city, and despite their status as economic, cultural, habitational and symbolic dominated people, they were able to trace a path of their own: in short, to show inside the world, to catharsise the emotion of belonging to the city, to build their own Porto and to show it onto others (see Januchta-Szostak, 2010).

References

Alvelos, H. (Coord.) (2013). *Manobras no Porto*. Porto: Manobras no Porto.

Appadurai, A. (1990). Disjuncture and difference in the global cultural economy. In M. Featherstone (Ed.), *Global culture: Nationalism, globalization and modernity*. Londres: Sage.

Appadurai, A. (2004). *Dimensões culturais da globalização: a modernidade sem peias*. Lisboa: Teorema.

Appleyard, D. (1973). Notes on Urban Perception and Knowledge. In R. M. Downs & David Stea (Eds.), *Image and environment. Cognitive mapping and spatial behavior* (pp. 109-114). Chicago: Aldine Pub. Co.

Ascher, F. (1998). *Metapolis - acerca do futuro da cidade*. Oeiras: Celta Editora.

Augustine, Aurelius. (1913). The City of God, Vol.1. in The Works of Aurelius Augustine, Bishop of Hippo. Dods, Marcus (ed). Edinburgh : Morrison & Gibbs Limited. Retrieved from:https://ia902604.us.archive.org/25/items/cityofgodtransla01auguuoft/cityofgodtransla01auguuoft.pdf

Barthes, R. (2009). *Óbvio e obtuso*. Lisboa: Edições 70.

Bourdieu, P. (1999). *La Miseria Del Mundo*. Madrid: AKAL.

Campos, R. (2011a). Deambulações em torno do projeto da antropologia visual contemporânea: entre as imagens da cultura e a cultura das imagens. *Revista Digital Imagens da Cultura/Cultura das imagens*, 1, 28-44.

Campos, R. (2011b). Imagem e tecnologias visuais em pesquisa social: tendências e desafios. *Análise Social*, XLVI (199), 237-259.

Castel, R. (1995). *Les métamorphoses de la question social*. Paris: Ed. Fayard.

Certeau, M. (1980). *L`invention du quotidien. Arts de faire (vol.1)*. Paris: Union Générale d´Editions.

Chtcheglov, I. (1953). *Formulary for a new urbanism*. Retrieved from http://www.bopsecrets.org/SI/Chtcheglov.htm

Cohen, S. (1972). *Folk devils and moral panics: the creation of the Mods and Rockers*. Cambridge: Basil Blackwell Ed.

Cohen, S. (1993). Ethnography and popular music studies. *Popular Music*, 12(2), 123-138

Coverley, M. (2006). *Psychogeography*. London: Pocket Essentials.

Debord, G. (2003). *A critique of separation. in complete cinematic works*. AK Press.

Debord, G., & Wolman, G. (1956). *Mode d'emploi du détournement*. Retrieved from http://sami.is.free.fr/Oeuvres/debord_wolman_mode_emploi_detournement.html.

Durkheim, E. (1997). *The Division of Labor in Society*. New York: Free Press.

Eco, U. (1970). *Apocalípticos e integrados*. S. Paulo: Editora Perspectiva.

Eppler, M. J., & Burkhard, R. A. (2004). *Knowledge visualization*. Lugano: Università della Svizzera italiana.

Feixa, C. (1999). *De jóvenes, bandas e tribus*. Barcelona: Ariel.

Feixa, C. (2014). *De la Generación@ a la #Generación. La juventud en la era digital*. Barcelona: Ned Ediciones.

Ferreira, A. F. (1994). Habitação social: lições e prevenções para o PER. *Sociedade e Território*, 20, 8-10.

Fischer, C. (1975). Towards a subcultural theory of urbanism. *American Journal of Sociology*, 80(6), 1319-1341.

Fortuna, C. (2012). (Micro)territorialidades: Metáfora dissidente do social. *Terra Plural*, 6(2), 199-214.

Foucault, M. (1971). *The Order of Things*. New York: Vintage Books.

Geertz, C. (2008). *A interpretação das culturas*. Rio de Janeiro: Livros Técnicos e Científicos Editora S.A.

Goffman, E. (1982). *Estigma - notas sobre a manipulação da identidade social deteriorada*. Rio de Janeiro: Zahar Ed.

Grazian, D. (2004). Opportunities for ethnography in the sociology of music. *Poetics*, 32, 97-210

Guerra, P. (2002). O Bairro do Cerco do Porto: cenário de pertenças, de afectividade e de simbologias. *Sociologia, Revista da Faculdade de Letras da Universidade do Porto*, 12, 65-144.

Guerra, P. (2003). A cidade na encruzilhada do urbano: elementos para uma abordagem de um objecto complexo. *Sociologia, Revista da Faculdade de Letras da Universidade do Porto*, 13, 69-122.

Guerra, P. (2010). *A instável leveza do rock: génese, dinâmica e consolidação do rock alternativo em Portugal* (PhD Thesis in Sociology). Faculdade de Letras da Universidade do Porto, Porto.

Guerra, P. (2012a). A cidade inclusiva. In A. M. Figueiredo, J. M. P. Penabad, E. J. V. Álvarez (Coords.). *Retos de la Acción de Gobierno para las Ciudades del siglo XXI/Desafios da governação das cidades do século XXI* (351-383). Porto/Vigo: Eixo Atlântico do Noroeste Peninsular.

Guerra, P. (2012b). Da exclusão social à inclusão social: eixos de uma mudança paradigmática. *Revista Angolana de Sociologia*, 10, 91-110.

Guerra, P., & Quintela, P. (2014). *God Save the Portuguese Fanzines*. Porto: Faculdade de Letras da Universidade do Porto.

Hamnett, C. (1997). La polarisation sociale: déconstruction d'un concept chaotique?, In A. Martens & M. Vervaeke (Coords.), *La Polarisation Sociale des Villes Européenes* (pp. 111-123). Paris: Anthropos.

Harvey, D. (2008). The right to the city. *New Left Review*, 53, 23-40.

Hebdige, D. (1979). *Subculture: the meaning of style*. Londres: Methuen.

Januchta-Szostak, A. (2010). The Role of Public Visual Art in Urban Space Recognition. In K. Perusich (Ed.), *Cognitive maps* (pp. 74-100). Rijek, Crotia: InTech. Retrieved from http://www.intechopen.com/books/cognitive-maps/the-role-of-public-visual-art-in-urban-space-recognition.

Jenks, C. (1995), The centrality of the eye in western culture: an introduction. In C. Jenks (Ed.), *Visual Culture* (pp. 1-25). London & New York: Routledge.

Kundera, M. (2012). *A imortalidade* [translated by Miguel Serras Pereira]. Lisboa: Dom Quixote.

Ledrut, R. (1980). Espaces et sociétés. *Espaces et Sociétés*, 34/35.

Lefevbre, H. (1968 and 1972). *Le Droit à la Ville*. Paris: Éd. Anthropos.

Lefevbre, H. (1970). *Du Rural à l'Urbain*. Paris: Éd. Anthropos.

Lefevbre, H. (1981). *La Production de l'Espace*. Paris: Éd. Anthropos.

Löw, M. (2012). The Intrinsic Logic of Cities: Towards a New Theory on Urbanism. *Urban Research & Practice*, 5(3), 303-315.

Molz, J. (2011). Cosmopolitanism and Consumption. In M. Rovisco, & M. Nowicka (Eds.), *The Ashgate Research Companion to Cosmopolitanism* (pp. 33-52). London and New York: Ashgate.

Pais, J. M. (2002) – *Sociologia da vida quotidiana*. Lisboa: Imprensa de Ciências Sociais.

Pais, J. M. (2003). *Culturas juvenis*. Lisboa: Imprensa Nacional Casa da Moeda.

Pais, J. M., Carvalho, C., & Gusmão, N. M. (Org.) (2008). *O Visual e o quotidiano*. Lisboa: Imprensa de Ciências Sociais.

Paugam, S. (2003). *A desqualificação social. Ensaio sobre a nova pobreza*. Porto: Porto Editora

Pink, S. (2006). *The future of visual anthropology: engaging the senses*. Oxford: Routledge.

Redfield, R. (1954). *The role of cities in economic development and cultural change*. Chicago: University of Chicago Press.

Rogers, M. (2000). Alfred Schutz. In G. Ritzer (Ed.), *The Blackwell companion to major social theorists* (pp. 367-387). Oxford: Wiley-Blackwell.

Santos, H., Marques, T. S., & Guerra, P. (2014). Do 285 da Rua de Cedofeita à metrópole – vivências e representações urbanas. In J. R. Pinto (Coord.), *O 285 da Rua de Cedofeita* (pp. 218-242). Porto: Edições Afrontamento.

Schütz, A. (1996). *Collected papers. IV*. Dordrecht: Kluwer Academic Publishers.

Simmel, G. (1987). A metrópole e a vida mental. In O. G. Velho (Org.), *O fenómeno urbano*. Rio de Janeiro: Ed. Guanabara.

Soja, E. (1989). Postmodern geogaphies: the reassertion of space in critical social theory. London: Verso Press.

Soja, E. (1996). *Thirdspace: journeys to Los Angeles and other real-and-imagined places*. Oxford: Basil Blackwell.

Soja, E. (2000). *Postmetropolis: critical studies of cities and regions*. Oxford: Basil Blackwell.

Sorokin, P. (1969). *Principles of Rural-Urban Sociology*. [s.l.]: Periodical Service Co

Souza, M. L. (2010). Which Right to which city? In defence of political-strategic clarity. *Interface Journal*, 2(1), 315-333.

Tavares, G. M. (2011). *Uma Viagem à Índia, Canto IX*. Lisboa: Caminho.

Thomas, W., & Thomas, D. (1928). The child in America: behavior problems and programs. New York: Knopf.

Tonnies, F. (1957). *Community and society*. New York: Dover Publications Inc

Triggs, T. (2010). *Fanzines*. London: Thames & Hudson.

Urry, J. (2002). *The Tourist Gaze*. New York: Sage.

Wacquant, L. (1998). A Fleshpeddler at Work: Power, Pain, and Profit in the prizefighting Economy. *Theory and Society*, 27(1).

Wacquant, L. (2002). *Corpo e alma: notas etnográficas de um aprendiz de boxe*. Rio de Janeiro: Relume Dumará.

Wagner, H. R. (Org.) (1979). *Fenomenologia e relações sociais. Textos escolhidos de Alfred Schutz*. Rio de Janeiro: Zahar Editores.

Weber, M. (1966). *The City*. New York : Free Press

Wirth, L. (1938). Urbanism as a Way of Life. *American Journal of Sociology*, 44, 1-24.

Part III.
Urban interventions, representations, and the (re) production of urban space

Chapter 5

Ephemeral Art in Impermanent Spaces: The effects of street art in the social construction of public space

Ágata Dourado Sequeira

Abstract

This article sets out to show how the production and practices of street art in Lisbon have strong effects on what concerns the creation of images of the city – in its marketable consequences – and the promotion of discourses about the urban public space and its structures. Because street art displays a very particular relation with the urban space, the research on the dynamics that its practice and production create with the actors and institutions that shape the cities, show that street art has an active role in creating images of the city, as well as proposing discourses about its public space.

Addressing the topic of art worlds and their relation with the territory, this article results from a research on street art and its implications in the social construction of public space, from the urban context of Lisbon. Within this research, street art is conceived as an art world in formation, specific as it exists in-between an underground practice and a full participation in the contemporary art world and its markets.

The collection of street art images by the artists and street art enthusiasts, while a simple way to fight the inherent transience of this art form, perpetuating it through digital means and on internet's «virtual streets», allows the artists to showcase their work to a broader audience, with a conscience that many times precedes the street art piece itself, thought for its future virtual display rather than meeting the eye of the passer-by.

The new possibilities around the practices and projects of street art allow for new street art pieces to be created in a scale that, while illustrates the acceptance of this art form in the visual mainstream, also is effect of the role the powers that shape the cities consider street art can have in creating images that promote both a tourist and business destination as «modern» or «in tune with the times». On the other hand, many street artists and street art collective projects find that through street art and the possibility of intervening in larger scales and in legitimized contexts, they too can have a say in the fate of their cities, namely in the state of its buildings – many in derelict state or abandoned – and its relation to local communities and the unbalanced powers that shape the place they live and work. In this way street art can also be a visually compelling way of starting and promoting discourses about the public space of the cities, with several street art projects making questions and creating spaces for public intervention and citizen participation, in the continual process of production of meaning on the public space.

By showing how street art can both contribute to the creation of images of the city and the promotion of critical discourses on the urban public space and the powers that shape it, in a process that both connects with the crescent visibility of this art world and the new processes that involve a diversity of actors, from street artists to promoters, to the institutions, this article aims to be useful for researchers whose scientific inquisitiveness is directed to the urban space in general and its possible relations with an art world in development.

Keywords: street art, social construction of space, public space, urban sociology, art worlds.

1. Street art and images of the city

1.1. An ephemeral urban art

Street art is, genetically, ephemeral. Because they are outside, street art pieces are not only subject to the elements, as to human intervention, and therefore their disappearance or alteration is expected. The *habitat* for this art form, the street, characteristically enables the degradation of street art pieces, in what itself constitutes a dynamic relation between the intervention and the urban daily life.

The way artists deal with this predictable transience is diverse, and is connected to the diversity of their personal and artistic paths and the way they conceptualize the practice of artistically intervening in the public space. Therefore, when questioned[1] about the way they relate to their street art pieces after finishing them, their perceptions included both the *will to preserve* the pieces - protecting it from the elements and human intervention, even to the point of applying special protective coating -, and a certain *detachment* towards the fate of the piece, considering that once finished it is «no longer theirs». Within the tension between the will to preserve and the detachment towards the street art pieces, the artists' perceptions translate the way they conceive and frame their individual street art practice, in what constitutes, in fact, a process of socialization of the artist in face of that aparently inevitable condition.

On the other hand, the transience of the street art pieces can be positively valued as integral part of the intervention. As specific *habitat* of this artistic form, the street is also a dynamic environment. While continuing to explore the question of transcience in the creation of street art pieces, let's approach how photography comes forth as central element in relation to that ephemeral nature of street art, and also the possibilities it allows, together with the internet, in spreading the work of its artists.

1.2. Street art images

The will to preserve the ephemeral marks of expressive human intervention in the walls of the cities is not a recent phenomenon. It is worth mentioning the photographic collection of Parisian graffiti between the 1930s and the 1960s, by George Brassaï (2002). More recently, it is also essential the reference to the works of Martha Cooper and Henry Chalfant, who documented the subway graffiti art in the 1970s New York. The result of this compilation of images can be seen in the book *Subway Art* (Cooper e Chalfant, 2009). The photographic incursions in this graffiti world were made easy by the direct contact with the writers and their will to have a quality photographic record of their interventions, in what constitutes a way of «fighting» its inevitable transience.

In fact, photographing a piece is also to resist its predictable ephemeral nature, allowing that the work lives beyond its erosion. According to Ricardo Campos, there is a disjunction between the physical work and its image. This in the sense that, for a street practice that is so intimately connected to the physical space of the intervention – as is graffiti, but also street art -, being its localization, eventual erosion and inevitable transience, indissociable aspects of its definition, the collection of photographic images assumes the meaning of a rupture with that ontological condition (Campos, 2010:266).

Nowadays, the diffusion of street art images is enormous, receiving extensive projection through the internet, as well as print media. Street artists are fully aware of the potential of this diffusion, and so the photographing of their pieces, together with other technological resources, is frequently an essential part of their work, assuming the role of *memory technologies*, *communication technologies*, and *narrative and representative technologies* (Campos, 2010:270).

In what concerns the research project that originated this article, the way in which the street artists approached the role of photography in their work, during the interviews that were made, is also a relevant aspect. From their speech, photography appears as a way of preserving the street art intervention, as an image record that surpasses its ephemeral nature. Secondly, photography appears, for some street artists, as a key aspect of their street art practice, as way of learning and sharing new techniques. In this sense, it also allows for new sociabilities to take place between street artists, or between them and street art enthusiasts. Thirdly, photography constitutes itself as a way of observing the reactions of the passers-by, in the sense the act of someone casually finding a street art piece and then photographing it and putting it online can be a way of appreciating the artwork.

---

1 Within the set of interviews to Lisbon street artists that took part for the research project from which this article is a result.

Besides the relation between street artists and photography, also several photographers that are not related to making street art – both amateurs and professionals – dedicate their time to street art photography, which has as natural consequence the spreading of street art images throughout the internet. Johannes Stahl refers to the close relation between street art and visual culture in the following way: «(...) The new media have come to a sort of arrangement with the culture of *street art*. (...) Visual documentary has become an integral part of the action because it will most likely be all that remains of the work after a relatively short time.» (Stahl, 2009:221). Street art, its photography and the internet appear therefore in close relation, in recording pieces whose transience is a remarkable feature. As for the role of internet, it will be approached in the following section.

1.3. Virtual Streets

Reflecting on the role of the production of street art images poses questions, namely as to the street art that is made to expose itself to the eye of the passer-by correspond another one, made in regard to the eye of the photographer and the diffusion of images through the internet. Being the visibility factor of importance in the spreading of street art images by the artists, it is by some considered that the internet has a fundamental role, which might even take part of the creative planning of street art pieces. Therefore, the places of the interventions are frequently chosen besides their accessibility and visibility to passers-by, because the main intention is to make the pieces visible to a much larger set of people through pictures or films that show it on the internet. This way, the sharing street artists do of their work on the internet is an important part of their street art practice, giving much more visibility and replacing the experience of physical encounter of the public with the pieces, that so many times are located in secluded places.

Besides the effects that result from the encounter between the passer-by and the street art piece in the streets of the city, it is relevant to approach the effects of the diffusion of street art images in the «virtual streets» that a route through street art websites suggests. These «streets» expand through websites that include personal street artists' pages, blogs, online magazines, among others, namely those that are dedicated to concentrate and spread street art images at a global scale[2]. Another type of websites assume a city-oriented kind of structure, suggesting «virtual tours» to the street art they show[3].

Authors such as Stahl affirm that the presence of street art in the internet is almost equivalent to its presence in the physical world, which leads to assume that the will to document an ephemeral piece –which Campos designated as creating *digitalized memories* (Campos, 2010:271) – is just one of the many facets of a profusion of images that is also result of networking between the street artists, as well as street art enthusiasts (Stahl, 2009:223). The possibility that otherwise unknown street artists can show their work to the world, from a computer screen and through high-resolution images, is also noted by this author: «(...) today virtually unknown people can spread their message all over the internet. At the same time, this form of publication, whilst its individual successes are measurable by the number of hits, allows the originator to stay relatively anonymous if he wishes.» (Stahl, 2009:225).

However, with the spreading of street art images through the internet comes the risk of taking them out of context. There can be, on the other hand, an effort of providing spatial context, when these images are integrated in virtual routes, through the street art of a city, for instances. These efforts in giving spatial context to these street art images can constitute an approach to the concept of *circuit*, such as José Cantor Magnani defined it, within his analysis of juvenile groups (Magnani, 2010). This concept designates, in his words, «the uses of space and urban equipment – allowing (...) the exercise of sociability through encounters, communication, management of codes -, however in a more independent way in relation to space, without hanging on contiguity.» (Magnani, 2010:18).

From the perspective of Magnani and in the sense that there is something that identifies the location of the street art pieces, visual testimonies of the use of space, it can be said that a collection of such images can constitute a *virtual circuit*. However, seeing images of street art remains inherently different than the experience of finding street art in the city's streets, in the sense that in the first the surprise effect disappears, diluting the experience, as Anna Wacklawek referred (Wacklawek, 2010:179). In a picture of a street art piece, its location tends to be an accidental factor, that may or may not be identified.

---

2 Such as Wooster Collective (www.woostercollective.com) or Unurth (www.unurth.com).

3 Such as Google Street Art Project (https://streetart.withgoogle.com).

The emphasis of these images is the quality of the work itself, not the location. Even though the encounter with an image is always a mediated experience, as also is the observation of street art on the street, a street art image never allows for the same impact as finding a piece on the street: «(...) the record of the work exists, but in a sort of void where site and time are obsolete. This dislocation prevents a complete reading of the piece, since unless we actually experience the work live, we do not have access to its impact in or experience of a particular urban context.» (Wacklawek, 2010:178)

This observation raises further interrogations concerning the possibility of some street art being created specifically to be «seen» through a computer screen, on the internet, in pictures or film, instead of the encounter with the piece in the same physical place, due to the considerable media attention to the street art phenomenon, and consequent availability of means to some artists. And in such a case, in what way would it make sense to use the word «street», when recalling to this form of art, when the street is in fact virtual and the physical location of the piece is often unknown or difficult to find. At the same time, street art images in the internet can appear out of its specific context, proposing images of city in the general and unspecific sense of an urban contemporary imagery.

This mediated practice, with images of interventions making a strong presence on the internet, can be associated to the formation of new publics and practices, of people interested in following the work of street artists, be it virtually or through the urban streets. Dolores Hayden said that «along with new media come new definitions of public.» (Hayden, 1997:67), to which we can add that with new publics, also may appear new markets and new ways of exploiting these mediated street art images.

1.4. Images of street art in marketing and tourism

Presently, street art is subject to intense media attention. There is a certain hype of street art, manifest in the amount of hardcover books that show images of street art pieces, in the news about street artists and the amount of articles and websites that can be found online, as well as is the several street art initiatives that multiply all over the country and abroad – street art festivals, street artists' exhibitions, the emergence of street art tourism, and media images of street art that seem ubiquitous.

Concerning the effects of the use of street art images for tourism, I will now address what it can express about the construction of an image of the city for touristic consumption, as well as the relation between street art and marketing and publicity within the urban public space.

Economic and political issues dictate the importance of big cities, in a global context, distinguish themselves, in a movement towards competition that intends to attract both investment and visitors. This aspect is particularly appealing for contexts in which economic activity, in a broad sense, and apart from big corporations, appears underdeveloped or unstructured. Art in the cities – and also, with particular mediated relevance, street art – emerges as having a central role in its visibility at a global level: «No matter how restricted the definition of art is implied, or how few artists are included, or how little the benefits extend to other social groups outside certain segments of the middle class, the visibility and viability of a city's symbolic economy plays an important role in the creation of place.» (Zukin, 1996:82).

Such is the case of Lisbon, in which tourism emerges as unequivocal orientation of a considerable part of the decisions about the public space and the elements that constitute it, by the entities that have the power to decide about it. Whether this approach is sustainable in the long run, that would be a question to be developed in another context. However, it is surprising to note that the strategies through which cities intend to distinguish themselves, are on so many occasions, the same. Given this, street art images emerge as illustration of a contemporary and modern city, ideal for city breaks of visitors that are also contemporary and modern. No stranger to this transfiguration is the production of light discourses, for media use, profusely followed by images of colourful street art murals, that emphasize that contemporary dimension, so desirable for a competitive tourist destination.

Therefore, street art in the cities – and also Lisbon – appears to have a key role in several mediated constructions, in which the «rankings of the best cities to see street art» are example, while not saying anything, however, concerning the actual outline of the street art in these cities, on the projects that are taking place, or the conditions for the artists. Specifically, in terms of marketing of the cities, monumental street art interventions tend to constitute a valued source of images, which, taken out of context, present the city as an attractive, young and contemporary destination, while losing the diversity of discourses that these pieces, in fact, represent.

However, along with this imagery, a considerable set of business opportunities is created for small tourist businesses, which promote street art tours showing selected pieces in Lisbon, with the care to offer context and explanations on how they were made – which is not in itself a misrepresentation of street art, but an indirect way this art form can contribute to produce public space, in the sense it is the object of this kind of movements of the urban actors.

A distortion of an artistic object might, on the other hand, be present in marketing and publicity in a broader sense, in which brands that intend to associate with street art imagery do in three different ways: by appropriation of images of street art pieces, without asking for the consent of the artists; by hiring designers – connected or not to street art practices - to elaborate a kind of images that refer to street art; or by the participation of the brands in street art events, and in this sense representing an opportunity for paid work and visibility for the street artists, and even the possibility of not having their creativity compromised by a theme the brand might suggest.

Apart from the specific activity in the world of marketing that incorporates street art, it is relevant to approach the relation between publicity and artistic street practices as forms of occupation of public space. In its origin, graffiti and street art, in their most spontaneous forms, inevitably assume meanings of appropriation of public space, in the sense that who practices it intends to 'respond' to an urban ambient that is dominated by publicity and by architecture, both imposed, by making interventions in a particle of public space – a wall or other available structure – which becomes a canvas: «All graffiti and street art is a battle over public space: who controls it and what it is used for.» (Lewisohn, 2008:104). While the political consequences of street art are intimately connected to their specific context and the way they constitute an attempt to 'balance' the distribution of the powers that manage urban public space, the act of intervening in the public space is, in itself and beyond the message or image it conveys, a political act.

The billboard displays a symbolic element as evident as its physical dimension, in the sense it constitutes a legally authorized form of occupation of the public space, which is deeply intrusive of the everyday visuality of the city, by its inhabitants and passers-by. In a context such as Lisbon, in which street art interventions seems to increase its visibility and dimension, namely through the several initiatives that promote large scale muralist interventions, there seems to be a clear competition of the visual space of the city, at several levels. As Mário Caeiro indicates, there are pieces of art in the public space – street art or not – that compete with the city, the street furniture and structures, publicity, and even among each other (Caeiro, 2014:288), in a movement of complexification of urban public space, in its visuality.

2. Street art and the production of discourses about the urban space

2.1. Street art projects and local communities

While art in the public space can sometimes generate controversy, and other times consent, as it interferes directly with the delicate tissue of daily social interactions in urban context, let's now see how the experience of producing and organizing legal street art events can contribute to the intensification of a certain sense of community. The testimonies of the interviewed that dedicate themselves to these projects both illustrate and clarify their positions about that symbiotic potential that can be established between street art and communities.

The new contexts for the production of street art are articulated in distinct ways, as in what concerns the way they are organized, as their purposes. While, referring to the Portuguese context[4], Wool, Wool on Tour and Muraliza are street art festivals, project CRONO, on the other hand, developed under a project logic. Other events are promoted according to a different perspective, of incorporation within the work or associations or collectives, as is the case of the APAURB (Portuguese Street Art Association) and ÉBANOCollective street art initiatives.

As for Wool festival, which takes place in Covilhã, the relation with the local community is promoted through the very structure of the initiative, with sequential street art interventions, talks and workshops that stimulate the interaction between artists and the locals, along with a set of street art interventions that have a transformative effect of the public space, in permanent terms. On the other hand, project CRONO (Fig.1), which took place in Lisbon between 2010 and 2011 with several street art interventions, namely those in the facades of derelict buildings, assumed intents of urban rehabilitation and aesthetical qualification through the physical structures of the city – particularly, its derelict buildings – and the uses of its space.

---

4 Which were addressed in the research this article results from.

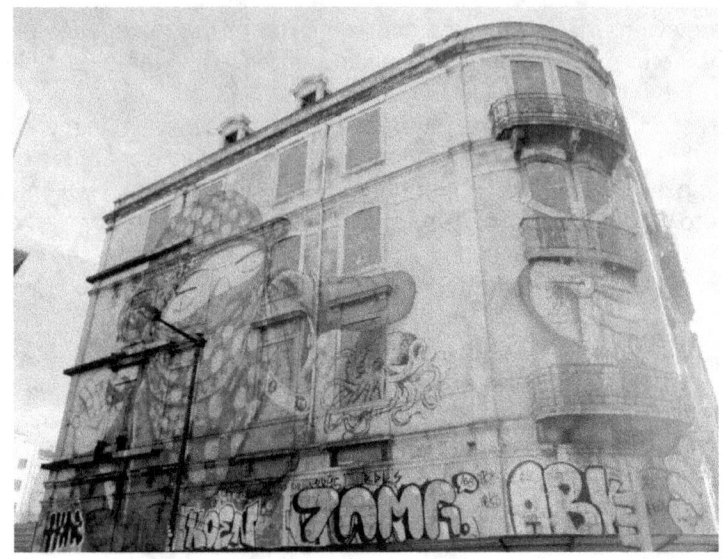

Figure 1 - Intervention in derelict facade, projecto CRONO, by Os Gêmeos. Foto by the author.

Therefore, it aimed to potentiate new relations between the city and its inhabitants, namely through the realization of the idea of public space as place for spontaneous action. In contrast, the projects connected with APAURB followed a different course of action, proposing voluntary collective action by all the interested citizens – not only street artists. The logic that underlies this course of action is the promotion of the involvement of the citizens in their city, through active participation in the betterment of public spaces for collective use. As for the institutional entity, through GAU (Urban Art Gallery – within a municipality department), the way their projects connect with community life has to do, on one hand, with the opening of calls for the participation of all the interested – specifically, in the initiative 'Recycle the Look', of painting of bottle banks – and, on the other hand and more significantly, the promotion of local rehabilitation through street art interventions that approach local aspects. This implies the selection of urban sensible projects, wherefore the importance of the active role the street artist can have in the process. An example would be the intervention in Junta de Freguesia da Penha de França (Fig.2), while another one, this time out of the institutional frame, would be the initiative «Passeios Literários da Graça», by ÉBANOCollective.

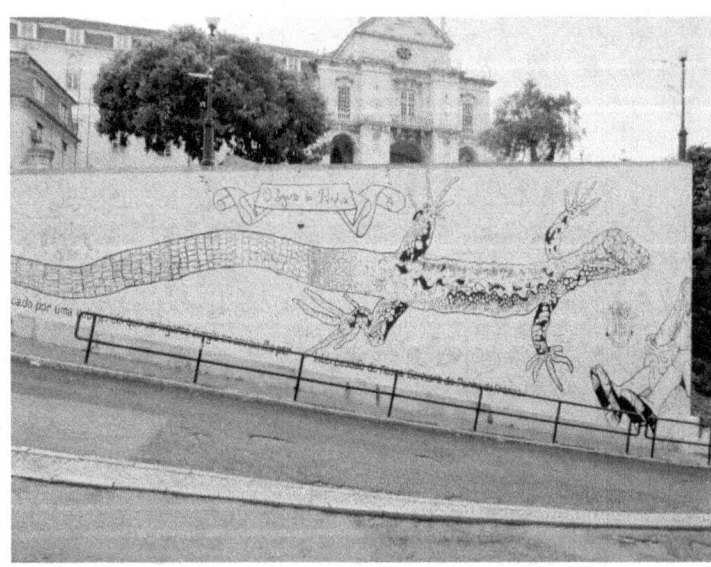

Figure 2 - Intervention by Leonor Brilha, in Penha de França, Lisbon. Foto by the author.

An important aspect in the incentive of local dynamics through street art is collective memory. The art intervention that opts to approach local histories consists of a crossing between immaterial culture and a specific material representation, in a tendency noted by Dolores Hayden (1997:67). Therefore, artists that incorporate that sensibility in their work can be contributing for the stimulation of local imagery within local communities, through works that might assume the quality of «memory artefacts», once «(…) the memory unravels as social and political act of construction and reconstruction of meaning (…)» (Andrade, in AAVV, 2010:16). Or, referencing Hayden: «Places trigger memories for insiders, who have shared a common past, and at the same time places often can represent shared pasts to outsiders who might be interested in knowing about them in the present.» (Hayden, 1997:46)

While public space, as we saw, is the place of encounter of individuals, the artistic interventions that approach aspects of the history and immaterial culture of a place assume the potential of allowing that the *place of encounter* becomes also the *place of sharing*, in the sense of belonging to a community and building discourses on the local specificities. Therefore, direct contact between those who organize street art initiatives, the street artists and the local communities where the interventions take place, is an important moment in the process of attribution of meanings to the actions and contributing that these can inclusively be associated with an emotional connection. In the words of Malcolm Miles: «But it is equally significant that such cultural work is carried out by individuals (...) whose contact with their public is direct (...). Human contact interrupts the blander realm of mass culture and advertising.» (Miles, in AAVV, 2010:41). Thus, human relations that establish within these projects among all the intervenients are a fundamental aspect in the construction of public space in urban contexts, in face of a hegemonic 'mass culture' and publicity.

2.2. Ruins and derelict buildings: Street art and abandoned structures

In large contemporary cities, the usage of certain urban structures corresponds to the apparent abandonment of others, which constitutes one of the most visible urban problems of the city of Lisbon: the amount of derelict buildings, of «expectant condition» (Ferreira, 2004:35), which configure a «cartography of sorrows» (Serrão, in Silva, 2014:17) of urban space. A walking incursion through the centre of the city is enough to assert this reality.

On the other hand, the vitality of cities and urban life can also manifest in these contexts, in the unused buildings that may risk ruin, that therefore resume their condition of places. Squats are an example, previously uninhabited houses that are occupied by young inhabitants, with the purpose of not only living but building a space for artistic and cultural expression, just as the artistic squats Elsa Vivant presented in her dissertation about Paris (Vivant, 2008). Street art also appears as recurrent presence in the decadent urban structures, abandoned or interrupted in their uses – structures that mark a «suspended social history» (Fortuna e Meneguello, 2013). According to Carlos Fortuna and Cristina Meneguello[5], these structures in ruins are consequence of a process they call «urbicide» (op.cit.), which frequently is, I'll add, the object of street art interventions. While attempting to build discourses on urban public space and their uses, these abandoned structures are used for street art initiatives, as canvas for interventions.

Such an example would be project CRONO, in what refers to the interventions that took place in the facades of derelict buildings in Lisbon, assuming the mission of signalling these expectant situations. This aspect also revealed itself as a visual element with important repercussions in what concerns the activation of reflections and discourses on the problem of derelict buildings in Lisbon. Another example is the street art interventions that took place in the Alcântara tunnel, promoted by APAURB, with the intention of improving an urban space of common use through voluntary and collective work. The initiative «Passeios Literários da Graça» by ÉBANOColective is also relevant in this matter, as its interventions in degraded facades expressed the aim of signalling the cultural singularity of a Lisbon neighbourhood, while commenting on the state of degradation of a significant part of its buildings. Institutionally-wise, the creation of a municipal organism, GAU, dedicated exclusively to the proposal and support of street art initiatives, can be interpreted as a sign of a process of urban public action with the intention of enhancing urban public spaces through street art, with the notion of the transient condition of this art form.

On the other hand, the individual initiatives of street artists also may express a discourse or commentary on the state of abandonment or degradation of urban structures. Street artist Tinta Crua, for instances, frequently glues his posters in the windows of empty stores (Fig.3), expressing the will to see them «filled» with something

---

5 In their research on two urban abandoned cine-theatres, in Portugal and Brazil.

that gives it the «life» that seems to be missing, while considering his interventions as a way of signalling this expectant condition of the structures of suspended use. Another street artist, Miguel Januário, from the project ±, frequently chooses derelict spaces for his interventions, as he considers these locations to enhance the message that underlies his point of view as an artist.

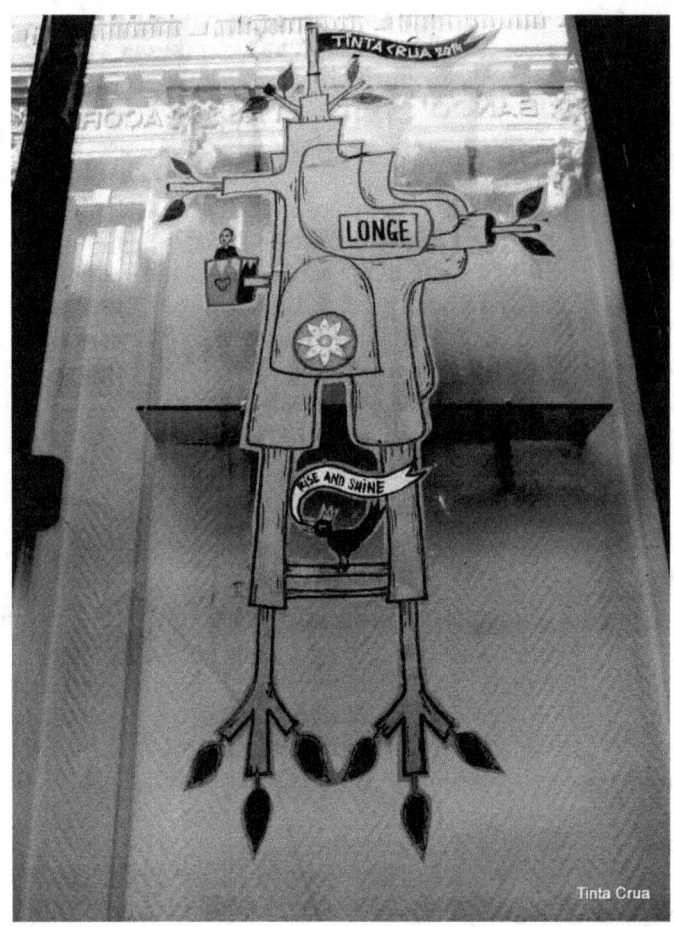

Figure 3 - Poster in abandoned store window, by Tinta Crua. Foto by the artist.

Returning to Fortuna and Meneguello, these authors consider that to stop the process of devitalization of the urban buildings involves «making democracy more democratic» (Fortuna e Meneguello, 2013:255). As we've seen, the art in public space can implicate the potential to encourage citizen participation, and therefore it can also be said that street art can have an active role in this matter, not only by signalling the situations of abandonment of buildings, but also by creating critical discourses about it. While public art participates in the construction of public space and sometimes appears as instrumental in the processes of reconfiguration of its uses, this can also happen with street art, through initiatives that, as integrated projects, can promote these mechanisms through artistic interventions, in a way that is as much effective as is the level of engagement with the local communities.

Urban art projects, in the public sense Hayden (1997) associates with the expression, indicate a way of conceiving public space that involves a considerable diversity of actors – promoters, artists, entities – and creative and expressive forms of approaching the urban issues. Presently, Lisbon constitutes an example, because for the first time a considerable set of interventions is made visible, with the aim of promoting dialogue and public discussion on the matters that concern urban buildings and their degradation and abandonment, while using this component of urban morphology as canvas for artistic intervention.

The diversity of these projects in which art operates in the public space – particularly street art – is expressive of how an expressive discourse can be created about the very place they operate, in a mechanism that brings street art closer to the languages of public art as promotor of citizen participation. According to Patricia

Phillips (1998), art in public space, appart from its form or duration, has the potential to create forums for dialogue: «A public art that truly explores the rich symbiotic topography of civic, social, and cultural forces can take place anywhere – and for any length of time. It would not have to conform to such formal parameters, for it would not find its meaning through its situation in a forum, but it would create the forum for the poignant and potent dialogue between obligation and desire, between being of a community and solitude.» (Phillips, 1998:98).

The element of transience is distinct, as inherent relation between street art and the physical space it occupies suggests questions about not only the lifecycle of the intervention, but, foremost, the place of the intervention, as Anna Wacklawek argues: «The experience of urban painting as a transitory process is inextricably tied to the work's meaning as an element of a city's changing composition.» (Wacklawek, 2011:91). Critical urban art, in which street art can be included namely through the individual or collective initiatives mentioned, therefore assumes a role of *construction of urban public space* (Low, 2014), inasmuch as the fluidity of its ephemeral condition contrasts with the rigidity the old monument paradigm intended to attribute to public space. Mário Caeiro (2014) states that that transience is particularly rich in the possibilities of creation and reception for an urbanely situated art.

From the street art projects in derelict buildings to the spontaneous interventions of street artists, a critical sense about the uses of public space stands out, as these constitute examples of critical urban art. To it underlies a critical and expressive discourse about the situations of abandonment of the buildings, not only by directly recreating artistically its memory in the public space it stands – encouraging therefore dialogue within the community – but also signalling these structures, using them as canvases for the interventions, in a visual appropriation that is never exempt of taking a stand. Artistic initiatives such as these allow to stimulate that «happening of the city and its citizens», that Mário Caeiro (op.cit.) referred to.

3. Conclusion: Images and Discourses about the urban public space

In this article I aimed to show how street art can both contribute to the creation of images of the city and the promotion of critical discourses on the urban public space and the powers that shape it, in a process that both connects with the crescent visibility of this art world and the new processes that involve a diversity of actors, from street artists to promoters, to the institutions.

The transience and degradation that are inevitable in street art pieces are central aspects in this practice, for which the street appears as dynamic habitat. Street artists deal with this ephemeral nature between the will to preserve their pieces or conforming with their erosion, with a certain detachment, considering each street art piece they create as a «gift» to the street. The photography of street art pieces assumes therefore a role of fighting this transience, while the dissemination of these pictures through the internet allows the artists to acquire bigger visibility and reach a broader audience.

The dissemination of street art images through the internet can lead to divergent experiences: on one hand, to observe street art through the internet, and on the other, to find street art pieces in their physical location, where they appear as surprise elements of the urban fabric. As for the relation between street artists and the potential that comes with the internet in their work, they assume the possibilities of a broader exposure of their work, with the consequent recognition and bigger audience. Some artists assume the street art they create as made specifically to be exhibited virtually, considering that to be an essential – and instrumental – part of their street art practice. The dissemination of street art images in the internet is therefore a central aspect in the construction of an artistic path in this specific art world.

On the other hand, this diffusion of virtual images is not without effects in what concerns the marketing of cities, since images of the street art the cities exhibit can contribute for the creation of a imagery of contemporary and modern city, made to attract visitors and investment.

Another aspect approached was the way in which the configuration of public space can expose the relationships of power that constitute it – particularly, in what concerns the disuse of physical urban structures. These, on the other hand, have the potential of proposing new ways of living the city, through the appropriation of these structures - be it by occupation, or by being subject to artistic interventions – and through their reconversion. Specifically, we've seen how the ephemeral nature of street art is connected with the impermanence of the urban buildings, and how this artistic practice can assume the role of promoting dialogue and discourses on the public space, in a specific urban context where the issues of degradation and abandonment of buildings is a distinct feature.

The way street art, within these legal contexts, results from the connection between the activities and the organizations that structure it was also addressed. Particularly, it was shown how a street art initiative can correspond to a direct and significant involvement with local communities, through local requalification as a collective process, with the stimulation of feelings of belonging to a community through the inclusion of the locals in the projects, or the creation and promotion of discourses about the projects and the way they refer to the community. These aspects include logics of action that underlie the different contexts of street art initiatives, in which the involvement with local communities is a factor privileged by the organizing entities.

Therefore, this is an artistic form that not only may bring itself closer to public art, as it may potentially maximize its effects, namely through the interdisciplinarity that underlies its planning, as well as in the net organization of several interventions.

References

Andrade, Pedro de (2010), «Arte Pública vs Arte Privada», in AAVV, *Arte Pública e Cidadania: Novas leituras daCidade Criativa*, Casal de Cambra, Caleidoscópio Edições, pp. 44-67.

Brassaï (2002), *Brassaï Graffiti*, Paris, Flammarion.

Caeiro, Mário (2014), *Arte na Cidade: História Contemporânea*, Lisboa, Temas e Debates/Círculo de Leitores.

Campos, Ricardo (2010), *Porque pintamos a cidade? Uma abordagem etnográfica do graffiti urbano*, Lisboa, Fim de século.

Cooper, Martha e Chalfant, Henry (2009), *Subway Art: 25th Anniversary Edition*, London, Thames & Hudson.

Ferreira, Vítor Matias (2004), *Fascínio da Cidade: Memória e projecto da urbanidade*, Lisboa, Ler Devagar.

Fortuna, Carlos e Meneguello, Cristina (2013), «Escombros da Cultura: O Cine-Éden e o Teatro Sousa Bastos», *in* Fortuna, Carlos e Leite, Rogério Proença (org.), *Diálogos Urbanos: Territórios, Culturas, Patrimónios*, Coimbra, Almedina / CES, pp.233-258.

Hayden, Dolores (1997), *The Power of Place*, Cambridge, The MIT Press.

Lewisohn, Cedar (2008), *Street art : The Graffiti Revolution*, New York, Abrams.

Low, Setha (2014), «Spatializing culture: An Engaged Anthropological Approach to Space and Place», in *People, Place, Space* #34, pp.34-38.

Magnani, José Guilherme Cantor (2010), «Os circuitos dos jovens urbanos», in *Sociologia: Revista do Departamento de Sociologia da FLUP*, Vol.XX, 2010, pp.13-38.

Miles, Malcolm (2010), «Clean City: Urbanism, Aesthetics and Dissent», in AAVV (2010), *Arte Pública e Cidadania: Novas leituras da Cidade Criativa*, Casal de Cambra, Caleidoscópio Edições, pp. 33-43.

Phillips, Patricia (1998), «Out of order: The public art machine», in Miles, Malcolm, Tim Hall e Lain Borden (eds.) (2000), *The Cities Cultures Reader*, London, Routledge, pp.96-102.

Silva, Gastão de Brito e (2014), *Portugal em Ruínas*, Lisboa, Fundação Francisco Manuel dos Santos.

Stahl, Johannes (2009), *Street Art*, s.n., Ullmann.

Vivant, Elsa (2008), *Le role des pratiques culturelles off dans les dynamiques urbaines*, Tese de doutoramento em Urbanisme, aménagement et Etudes Urbaines, Université Paris 8, Vincennes Saint –Denis.

Waclawek, Anna (2011), *Graffiti and Street art* , London, Thames & Hudson.

Zukin, Sharon (1996), «Space and symbols in an Age of Decline», in Miles, Malcolm, Tim Hall e Lain Borden (eds.) (2000), *The Cities Cultures Reader*, London, Routledge, pp.81-91.

Chapter 6

Between formal and informal practices to manage the city: the role of street art in the Old town of Palermo

Luisa Tuttolomondo

Abstract

The chapter presents the case study of Palermo in order to critically propose street art as an informal and destructured form of participation able to impact and modify urban space and to Foster new arenas of debate around the city. With this regard Palermo represents an interesting case and good field of observation. As a matter of fact, Palermo is a city that despite its location in the middle of the Mediterranean Sea and its huge natural and artistic heritage has always had many difficulties in enhancing local resources and Fostering local development. Moreover, this process has been always characterized by high levels of civil society engagement assuming very different forms, from highly institutionalized ones to more informal and fragmentary practices.

From this point of view the case of the old town is particularly interesting to observe. Starting from late 80's, after a period of abandon due to the ruins left by the Second World War, it begun to draw new attention from the municipal administration that operated in order to restore it. In this context, culture and civic participation played and still play a fundamental role in the process, without being able to radically change the situation so far. Today the old town still presents strong problems and obstacles to its total renewing, promotion of the art patrimony and improvement of its dwellers' quality of life. While at the governance level is possible to notice a continuous attempt to find durable solutions to the old town management, the urban space at stake is changing thanks to more informal and uncontrolled dynamics. Among these is street art that in the last five years started to spread in many areas of this part of the city, mainly thanks to the intervention of artists coming from outside the region. From the theoretical and methodological point of view this chapter aims to reconstruct the case study of Palermo by adopting a pragmatist sociological approach. The analysis will consider the complex dynamics of interaction between some formal and informal practice of urban management and civic participation taking place in the old town of Palermo. In particular, it will be analyzed the knowledge and discourse around some public problems regarding this part of the city and the actors involved, the public arenas and the practices of use of the urban space considered.

As a matter of fact, the phenomena of street art in the old town of Palermo has assumed very different forms: from random interventions in the underground squares of Vucciria a neighborhood that has now become the center of movida, to murals commissioned by local NGO's and aimed at transforming a dump in a square at Ballarò market. The impact of this phenomena on the public space is always different and span from the consolidation of some already existing dynamics, as the configuration of space as underground/bohemian space, to the promotion of a change in the use of urban spaces as in the case of Mediterraneo square at Ballarò.

1. The Old Town of Palermo

The Old Town of Palermo is one of the largest in Europe, with an extension of 250 hectares and a population of 23.382 inhabitants. Due to the bombing of the Second World War, a major part of its patrimony has been destroyed and the area has been abandoned both from the Municipal administration and by its inhabitants that moved towards the newest parts of the city (Cannarozzo, 2007). Starting from the 90's a new political season run by the center-left mayor Leoluca Orlando begins aimed at the renewal of the Old City. Thanks to European funding from the programme Urban many buildings have been restored, especially in the neighborhood of Kalsa. Besides, a strong cultural policy gave new centrality to the area and the city in general so opening up the city to dynamics of cosmopolitanism (Söderström, Fimiani, Giambalvo, & Lucido, 2009).

Nowadays the Old City has gained new centrality thanks to some factors of change: a progressive repopulation mostly by young people and immigrants, the new system of mobility and the pedestrianization of the some streets that Fostered the flourishing of new commercial and restoration activities, the raising of small art craft shops and cultural associations have raised, that enhanced the attractiveness of the area thanks to a variety of cultural activities. The old city so become not only the center of citizen cultural activities but also the center of movida.

Unless these signals of change the Old Town still presents a number of problems: the amount of public and private decaying buildings in need of restoration is still very high and some neighborhoods of the area are in a state of total abandon and poverty and are affected by illegal activities of control of the territory. In this context, the management of the Old Town and its renewing constitute a big issue of discussion both in the present public debate as in the city's public policy history.

2. Street art spread in the city

The phenomenon of writing arrives in Palermo in the 90's when it spreads in a rapid and significant way. Instead, street art take the field only in the last years and in a more discontinuous way thanks to the occasional arrival of artists coming from different parts of Europe. As a matter of fact, the city lacks a local scene whilst in other Sicilian cities as Catania there are many active groups and art collectives (Mondino, 2016).

The first significant street art interventions was carried out in 2009 in occasion of "Wallpapers", a festival organized during the Design Week in the neighborhood of Kalsa of the Old Town. The event brought in Palermo some of the most famous Italian street artists that intervened on the walls of the Convento della Speranza in the Magione Square. After this event street art interventions have been quite rare but in the last two years they increased significantly. Many murals and graffiti appeared in different parts of the city. In some cases they are the results of spontaneous initiatives, in some others they come from the request of inhabitants or local organizations.

Street art intervention spread not only in the Old City but also in some peripheral areas outside the city: in Borgo Vecchio, in Zen, at Cantieri Culturali in Zisa, at the Laboratorio Zeta, on the mountain Pizzo Sella. This happened thanks to a network of local enthusiasts, individuals or collective groups, involved in hospitality and networking activities between the local context and international street art scene.

After some early interventions of artists coming from the Center and North of Italy (Ema Jons, Hopnn, Collettivo Fx,), some others head to the city. After a first staying, they come back a second time, a third time and so on. They stop over for a short period of time or a longer staying. In this process every artists spread the word and encourage the arrival of other artists, or comes back together with other colleagues. The social relationships that the artists create with the local contexts (people, associations, informal groups, etc.) push and Foster the process of returning to the city and the realization of new art piece. The city ends up becoming a favorite destination not only for Italian artists but also for international ones (as for example the French street artist C215). Despite the high interest and mobilization of artists from outside, local artist only rarely dedicate themselves to street art interventions.

In general, artistic intervention in the public space of the city assume very different forms: they span from intervention commissioned by institutional subjects able to pay for the murals requested, to occasional and casual interventions coming from the need of individual self-expression. Between these two extremities there are hybrid practices as the one of murals requested by single inhabitants or by local association committed in the neighborhood, or coming from the militant initiatives of the single artists. In this process, the appearance of a mural and its meaning originate from the biography of places, the practices of use of citizens, and ends up producing unexpected effects as the resignifying of a space, and the promotion of a different use of it.

3. Why street art spread in the Old City of Palermo?

Three fundamental factors influence the spreading of the phenomenon and the choice of the place of intervention. The first one is the informality that affects some of the neighborhood of the Old City. Many researches on street art observe as dynamics of informality, conflicts and liminality constitutes a lever for the creative vitality of a place (Costa & Lopes, 2013).

These features can be easily found in the Old City where informal dynamics of management of the territory overlap official policies. This is a reason why institutions find many difficulties in the administration of the area. Despite the complex history of urban instruments and policies implemented by the municipal governs alternated in the last years (the plan of the Old City, the Master plan, the municipal office of the Old City, single interventions in the public sector) the management of the Old City remain a problematic issue. From mobility to nightlife, from the needs of its inhabitants to the poverty of many neighborhoods, the history of urban policies in the area is characterized by many attempts to solve such problems and consequent failures. Besides these efforts, dynamics of informal management still prevail, often coupled with illegal activities (illegal sales of food and alcoholics, racket, drugs dealing). For what regards the mobility one of the biggest issue is the presence of illegal driver parking that are distributed around the Old City according to pre-established logics of splitting up of the territory.

Concerning the quality of life of residents, night movida is one of the biggest issues and of difficult solution. Vucciria square, Magione square, Ballarò square are some of the main places of gathering of youngsters, characterized by the proliferation of pubs, restaurants and bars sale of alcoholics and food without proper license, occupation of public land without permission and music loud until late in the night. This situation often provoked the reaction/mobilization of those residents of high/middle class recently moved into the neighborhood, willing of a different management of the area and mainly based on criteria of tidiness, cleanliness and quietness. Another problem affecting the Old City regards the state of decay and risk of collapse of many private and public historical buildings. Despite the works of restoration carried put in the 90's thanks to the European Programme Urban, many buildings are still in need of restoration.

An other factor that influences the spread of the phenomena is the visibility that murals and graffiti in the Old City have. As a matter of fact, the walls of the Old City are an open air showcase for many artists that can circulate and let appreciate their art works to a wider public compared to the one of galleries.

Some neighborhood of the Old City perfectly fit these needs thanks to the partial renewal of the area occurred in the last 20 years. This process Fostered the happening of street art interventions always in search of visibility. At the same time the presence of murals and graffiti in urban spaces draws attention on the places where they are realized and increase the visibility of them by promoting their fruition o by let circulating through media of different type the pictures of the pieces.

Finally, it is possible to suppose that the spread of the phenomena in the city is a result of a general cosmopolization of the city (Söderström, Fimiani, Giambalvo, & Lucido, 2009), to which the city has opened up since many years. The permeability of the urban system to flows of people and trends of consumption coming from different places has certainly encouraged the development of the phenomena, allowing the access and transit of artists coming from different parts of the worlds, the word of mouth, circulation of art works and imaginaries linked to the city.

Albergheria

Mediterraneo Square it wasn't a square. Or it is to say, it was a dump until a group of young active citizens decided to clean it in order to transform it in a public space open to all citizens and inhabitants of the neighborhood in which it is placed.

The space of intervention corresponds to the perimeter of a building belonging to the curia and destroyed by the Second World War bombings. Of the previous building only the basement remained and its interior become a dump filled with any kind of garbage. This until a group of citizens under the name of "gardeners of Santa Rosalia" decides to clean up the space and transform it in a square (see figure 1).

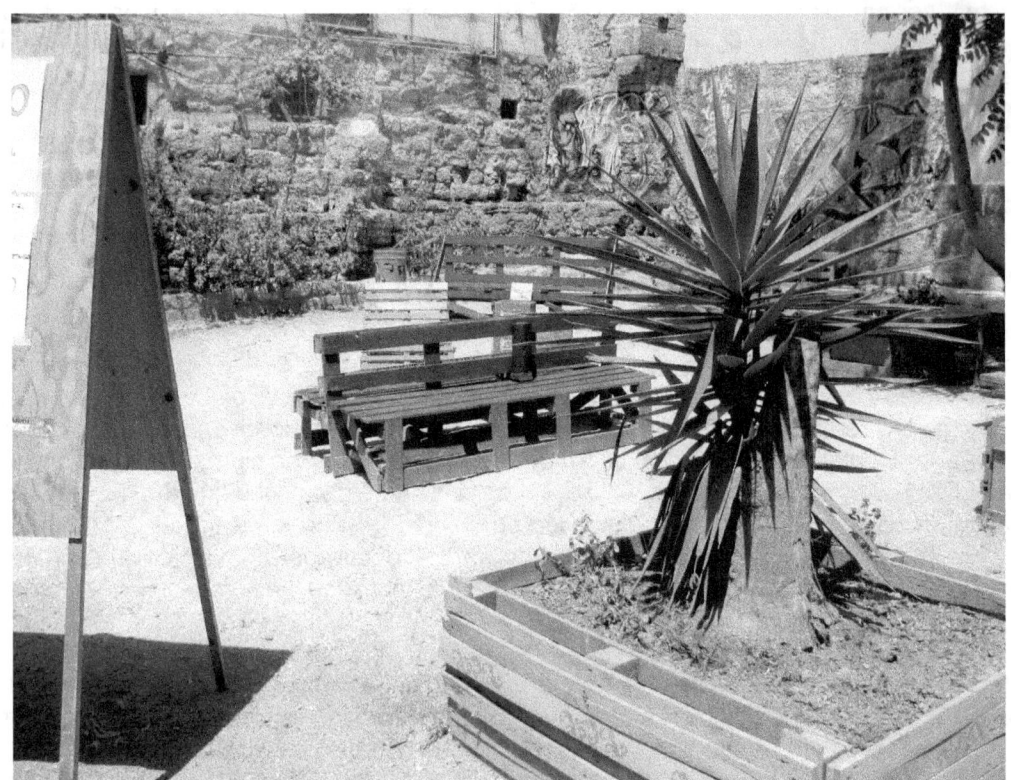

Figure - 1 Mediterraneo Square (photo:author)

The gardeners of Santa Rosalia are a group of young citizens that since 2010 try to bring some green in the neighborhood of Albergheria where they live and give it again the value of "sacrality", carrying out actions of guerrilla gardening, of caring of public spaces and territorial animation through theater performances and other activities.

During the period of the fest of Santa Rosalia in 2012 the gardeners decide to clean up all the area, placed at the cross between Paternostro street and Porta di Castro street. They took away the rubbish, they created flowerbeds and built urban fabrics with pallets. On one of the two walls surrounding the square the gardeners hung a billboard with the writing: "This square didn't exist before" (see figure 2).

At the beginning keeping the square clean turn out to be a difficult duty, because the majority of residents at first seems to be indifferent towards the new space. Only few families, involved in the initial intervention of arrangement, take on the duty of watering the plants and throw away the bottles left abandoned. To be steady in this enterprise turns out to be very difficult due to the extension of the space and the effort required.

But little by little the practices of use of the space begin to change. Initially, the square is used by the immigrant population of African origin. The majority of them are youngsters that attend the square during night and day to meet up with friends or simply to relax on the benches. The cleaning of the square keeps on being a problem, and so it is also for the maintenance of urban fabrics. At the same time some local associations starts organizing evening events. Among these is the sport competition "Mediaterraneo Antirazzista" (Antiracist Mediterraneo), whose linkage with the place is showed by the same name of the square. Later, the square starts to be used especially at night also by another typology of population: young middle class adolescents coming from different parts of the city. The use of the place is Fostered by the presence of a bar and a deli on the side of the square that serves food and beverages until late in the night. The increase in the number of users corresponds to a change in the management of the place. The square becomes cleaner, also thanks to shop owners' commitment. Their tables for customers now occupy both the square and the street.

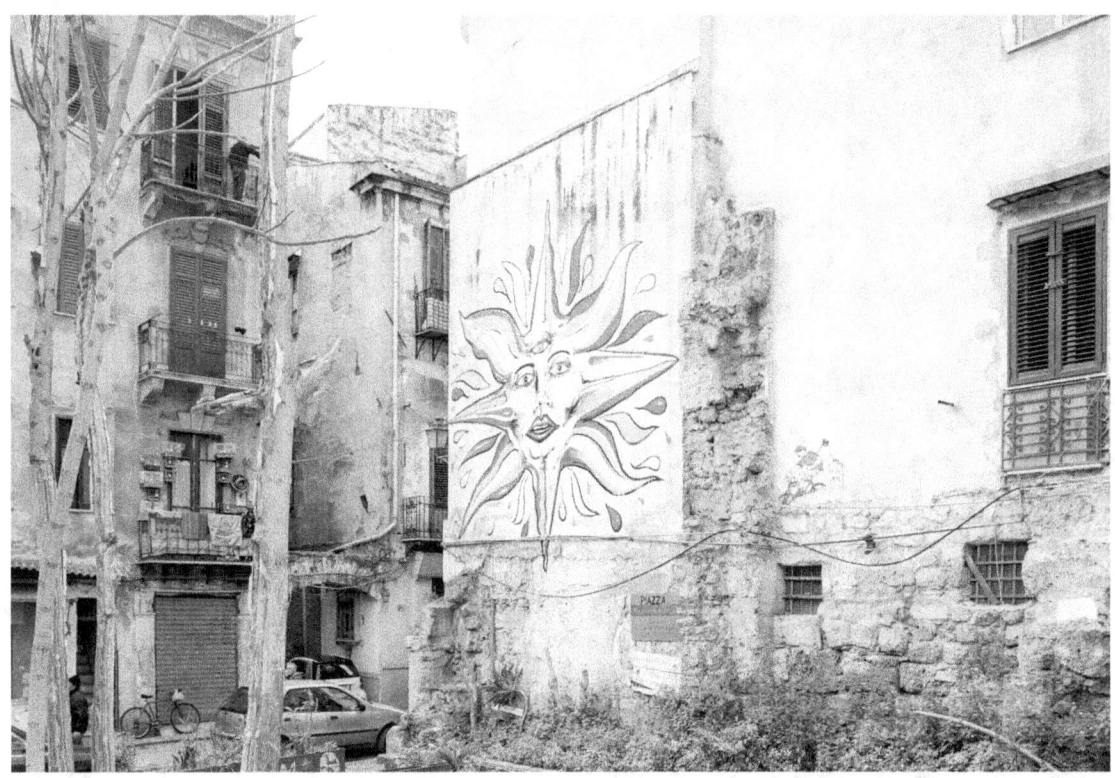

Figure 2 - Murals by Ema Jones (photo:author)

The history of change regarding the practices of use of Mediterraneo square is stressed by the realization of some murals. First one among these is a big sun (fig. 10) realized by the artist Ema Jones for the Palermitan rapper Christian Picciotto in occasion of the shooting of the video clip for the song "Sole", belonging to the musician's album "Piazza Connection"[1].

Always on the same wall there is a poster in tissue paper depicting a boy on a bicycle with a shirt in white and red lines. The poster was attached during a "baciattacchianata" (bike attaching) organized by an association of bicycle enthusiasts conducted with the company of Hopnn, a street artist from Marche. During biciattacchinate a group of citizens leaded by an artist (every time a different one) rides his bike through the city in search of spaces where to stick posters with drawings prepared by the guest. The posters (that always deal with the issue of sustainable mobility) are scattered throughout the city and are intended to raise awareness of the territory and promote the re-appropriation of the city by the participants.

Hopnn himself has later realized a small mural on the adjacent wall. Next to this is a larger mural by the Collective Fx entitled " Anti-Racist scorekeeper " (see figure 3.). This work comes from a request made to the artist from the association Handala in occasion of the Mediterranean Anti-Racism event held in 2014. This represents a marker, where on the one side are depicted the faces of historical figures who fought for human rights and racial integration, on the other one are those characters who have acted against.

---

1 See the video of Brano: https://www.youtube.com/watch?v=Cx6jHIWelaE

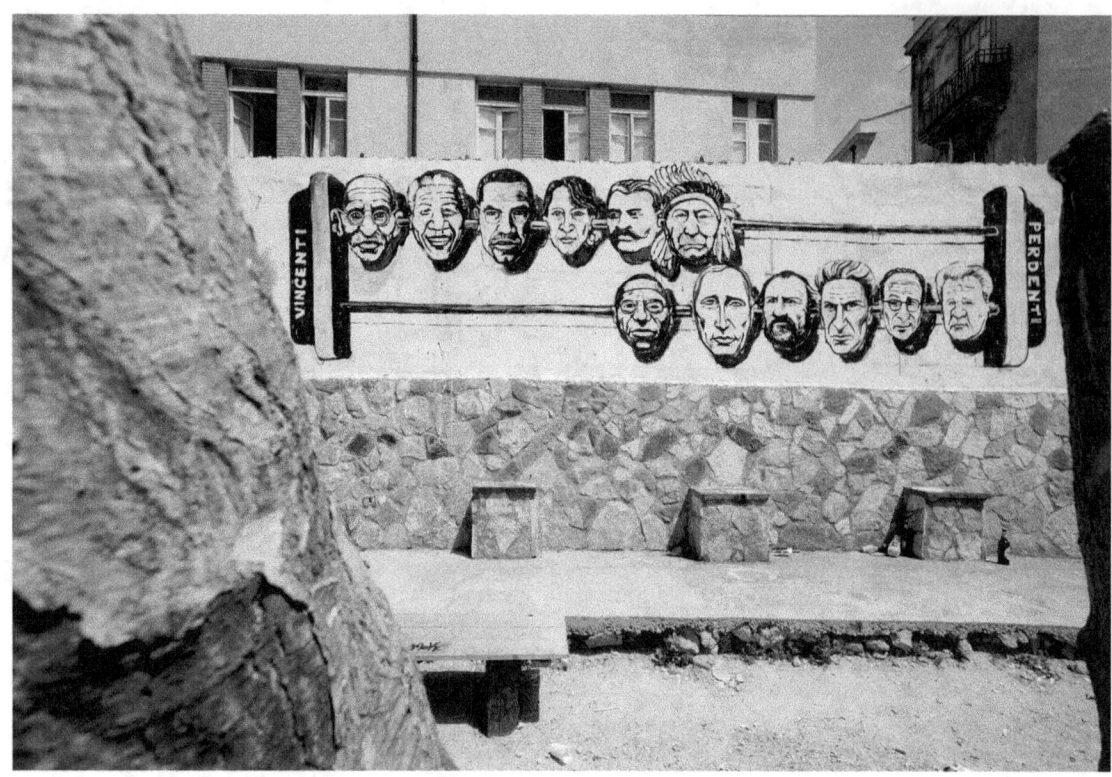

Figure 3 - Mural by Collettivo Fx (photo:Mauro Filippi)

The realization of these works is an event in itself. Far from being purely individual action of a single artist, painting on the wall often represent an event for meeting and socializing. The presence of an artist at work in the urban space produces a break in the everyday life routines. The event draws the attention of passers-by and residents that ends up participating in several ways: pretending indifference or simply observing, asking questions, making suggestions. The artist answers, by giving space to conversation and more or less extended exchanges of opinion. In some cases it is the artist himself to solicit questions. In the case of the work "Anti-Racist scorekeeper" for example the choice of the characters represented was the result of continuous dialogue with passersby, both young adolescents residents of the neighborhood and simple citizens passing by. The upper faces are the one of the winners : Gandhi, Nelson Mandela, Malcolm X, San Suu Kyi, Emiliano Zapata and Chief Joseph, the lower ones are those of losers: Milošević, Eichmann, Rodolfo Graziani, Chivington and Bagosora.

Today Mediterraneo Square is a place of gathering and meeting, as well as a symbol of the possibility of a bottom up renewal of the neighborhood. It is enjoyed by residents and associations that use it for meetings, events and concerts. One of the latest examples is the organization of social lunches in the framework of the activities of the collective "S.O.S. Ballarò" that was born in November 2015 thanks to the mobilization of some associations willing of implementing a coordinated plan for the redevelopment of the neighborhood (see figure 4).

Vucciria

The neighborhood of Vucciria is placed in the Mandamento Castello a Mare in the northern part of the Old City and takes its name from the popular market that used to be there in the past. Today the market has lost the prosperity it had once and only few stands remain selling vegetables and fish. As a matter of fact, the practices of use taking place in the space changed, so it has become the favorite place of youngsters for movida. The two major squares, piazza Caracciolo and piazza Garraffaello, and the small streets departing from it, are now full of bars, often illegal ones, that sells alcoholics and keep the music loud all the night long. Many of these activities are illegal, then lacking regular license both for selling alcohol and food and for occupying public land with tables and chairs.

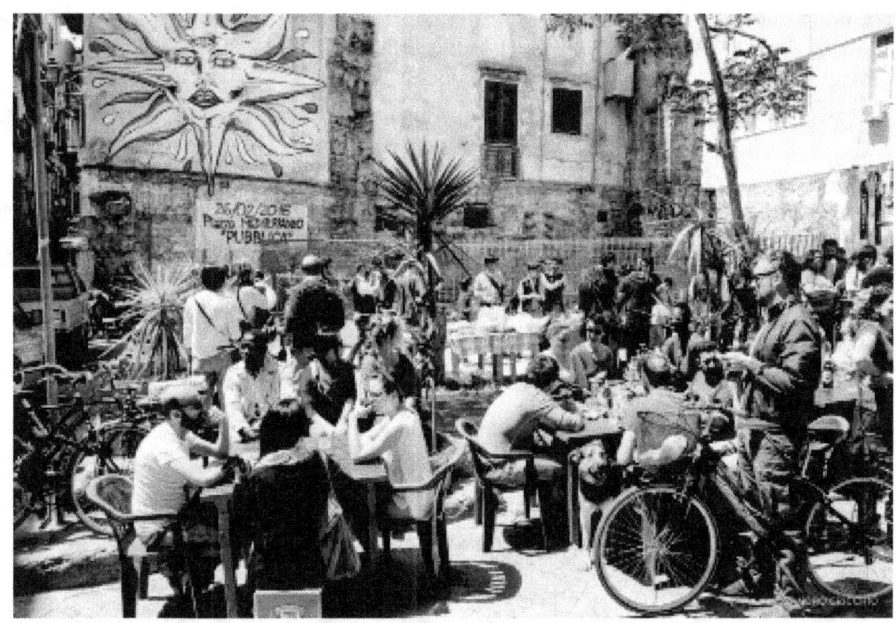

Figure 4 - Social lunch in Ballarò organized by the collective SOS Ballarò (photo:Mauro Filippi)

For who arrives from outside to the market the scene appears to be blurred by the smog exhaling from the stands cooking food. The main customers of the area are young people belonging to different social classes. The attractiveness of Vucciria also depends on the state of decay that affects it, due to the Second World War bombings. Many buildings of the squares are empty because precarious, half destroyed or in bad conditions. Between 2014 and 2015 two buildings collapsed due to the state of abandon of the area. Nevertheless, some of these buildings are inhabited, mainly by migrants or young students and workers.

On the walls and shutters of the Vucciria is possible to observe a great concentration of murals and graffiti. The density of street art interventions is so high that it is very difficult to distinguish a work art to another. The authors are many and of national and international origin. In particular, among the Italian artists we find: Ema Jones (Como), Bibbitò (Reggio Emilia), Collettivo Fx (Reggio Emilia), Hopnn (Ancona), Cyop&Kaf (Naples), Tilf (Como). Among the international ones: Pang (London), Julieta XLF (Valencia), Astro Naut (Madrid), Axel Void (Usa), C215 (Paris) , Knarf, Irga, Shiva, Frank e Max (Vien). Less numerous are the local artists: Sid, Trebel Art, Fare Ala art group, I Mangiatori di Patate e Bloom. The street art interventions in Vucciria originate in a total informal way. Some artists pass by the city for different reasons and decide to paint a wall. In some cases they come back many times (Collettivo fx) or they decide to spend a longer period in the city (Ema Jones). The single artist, both the one that pass by chance and the one who stays longer, often invite and persuade other artists belonging to their work and friendship to come.

Artists often come back and in so doing the murals in Vucciria rapidly increase. Their staying is facilitated by a network of support and friendship established with locals interested in the phenomenon for passion or for some connection with their profession. In some cases the artists arrives in the city because they are directly invited to participate to some events or initiatives.

When they paint informally in the neighborhood they can operate without any danger of police intervention because the area is controlled by informal dynamics and is resistant to institutional forms of control. Their art works solicit the enthusiasm of pub and bar's owners that in many cases promote the realization of a mural on the walls of their commercial activity. The creation of an artwork is always the result of an activity of intensive negotiation. Before starting to paint the artist ask to the wall's owner or to the neighborhood's residents for permission, or conversely is the owner itself or the resident that express the wish to see or to have a mural on its wall. In any case every artwork is originated by the establishment of a relationship, positive or some times conflicting between the artist and the locals. By painting artists get into the local dynamics and Foster informal networks of relationships that involve not only residents and pub owners but also city users. In so doing, street art interventions perfectly fit and adjust to informal dynamics and have the effect of strengthening the use of the area as a place for alternative young movida.

The murals' subjects play in different way with the surrounding space. They span from playful subjects (austronauts by Austronaut, men and animals with three eyes by Bibbitò) (see figure 5), to murals playing with symbols of Palermo (as the posters depicting Santa Rosalia with a suitcase by an anonimus, or Einstein proposed as the grandnephiew of Genius of Palermo by Collettivo Fx) (see figure 6), to graffiti that evoke to the commercial activities next to them (as the maritime themes of graffiti by Hopnn close to the fish sellers) (see figure 7). The effect of meaning coming from the whole of them is the strengthening of the underground and alternative connotation these places assume mainly in the night hours.

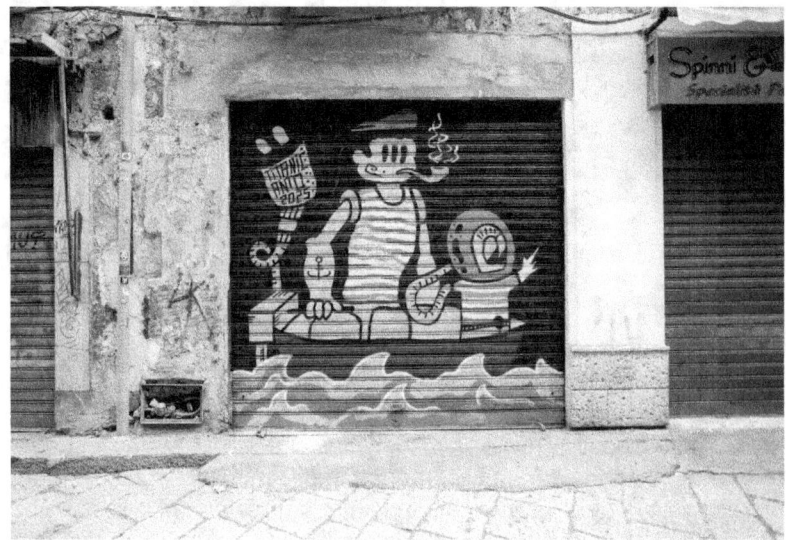

Figure 5 - Mural by Bibbitò and Astronaut (photo:Mauro Filippi)

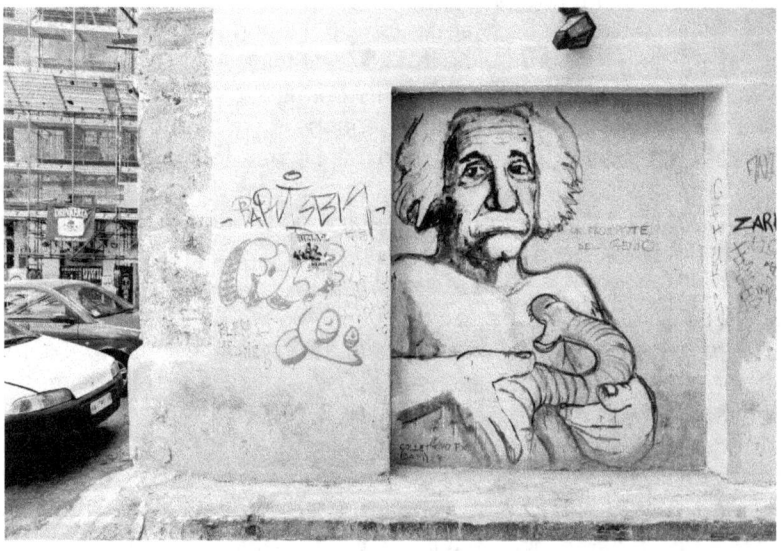

Figure 6 - Mural by Collettivo Fx (photo:Mauro Filippi)

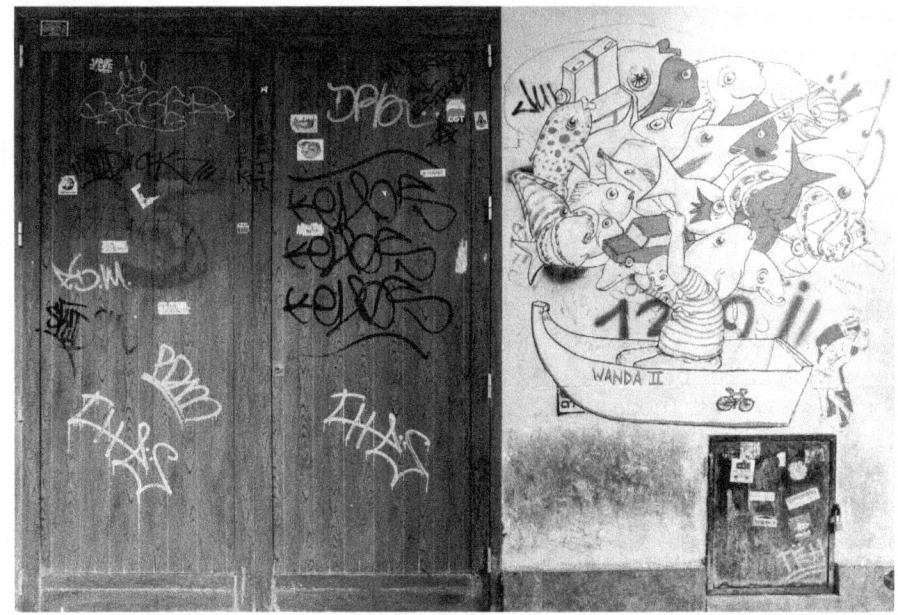

Figure 7 - Murals by Hopnn (photo:Mauro Filippi)

Moreover, in Vucciria it is possible to find not only street art interventions but also other artistic installation of urban art. The most significant example is the work of the Austrian artist Uwe Jaentsch, arrived in Palermo in 1999 and since then remained in the city because attracted by its places, especially piazza Garaffaello. This one has become its open air laboratory where he realized many art installations on the precarious buildings of the square like "la cattedrale die rifiuti" (the cathedral of garbage), made with garbage found in the neighborhood, and "Banca Nazion" (see figure 8), provocatively claiming for the raising of new alternative economy of Vucciaria. The last of these intervention is the red writing "on sale" made on the fountain of Garraffo aimed at denouncing once gain on the lack of attention and care towards the historical building of the square.

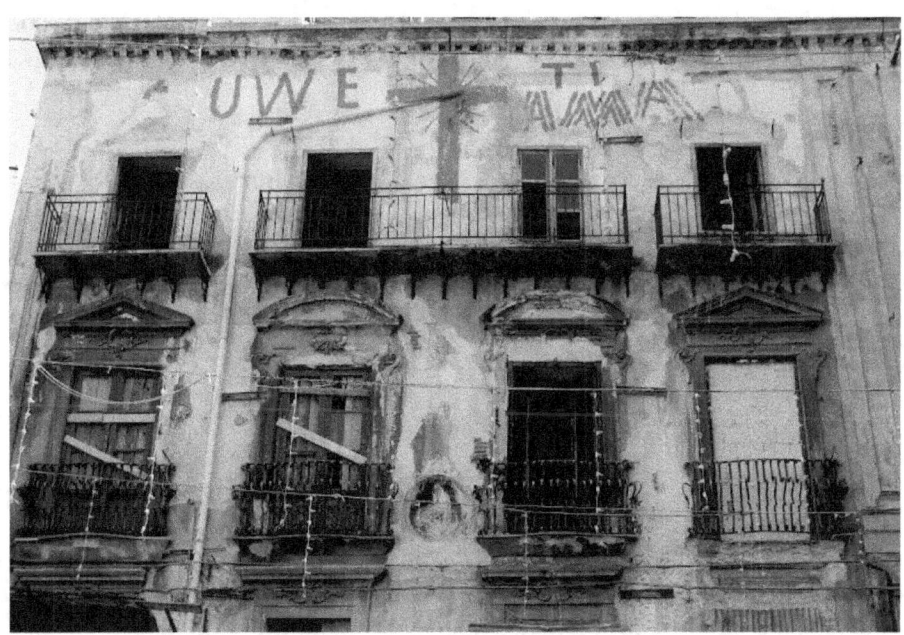

Figure 8 - Installation by Uwe in Garraffaello square (photo:author)

4. The practice of street art and the production of "public"

The cases reported presents different forms of interventions that produce specific impacts on the territory. In any of these it is possible to identify the activation of proper public arenas where the action is "proved" (Cefaï, 2007). As a matter of fact, the dynamics of activation and interaction draw attention and intervene on specific public problems. For example, the artworks realized in Albergheria contribute to signify a place previously used as a dump as a square, so intervening on the issue of the abandoned spaces of the city and on the lack of spaces for socialization.

The art interventions insert themselves in the mobilization strategies of a group of citizens and orientate the fruition of the space as a square. These are integrated in already existing fabric of relationships (those between active citizens, local associations and residents) and help to create some new ones, by capturing the attention of children from the neighborhood, of shopkeepers or simple residents.

In Vucciria, murals, tags and graffiti on the walls and shop shutters strengthen the connotation of space as a movida place so contributing to nurturing public debate and conflict around the practices of use and fruition of the Old City of Palermo.

At the same time the installations by Uwe propose the problem of the state of abandon of monuments and buildings raising on piazza Garraffaello and denounce the lack of sufficient public policies for the restoration of the Old City. These provoke the reactions of residents and citizens that state to be prone or adverse to artist's provocations. They claim for the intervention of the Municipality or ask for the sanction of the artist illegal occupation and defacement of public space, they mobilize media to report the news.

In all these cases even if street art (or in some cases public art) is based on the individual act of the artist (driven by ethical or playful aims, need of self-expression, etc.), this ends up to activate and strengthen networks and mechanisms of interactions between artists and locals, or artists and other artists. Networks are Fostered not only by relationships established among people on the place but also among local and foreign artists. Moreover the use of media amplify the process because allows to circulate images and contents at a local and international level.

So for example, the facebook page "Street art Palermo" report with pictures and texts the spreading of the phenomenon in the city, or local newspapers and magazines (Babbaluci news, Palermotoday), national ones (Repubblica), international ones specialized on art subjects (Artribune, il Gorgo) write news on recent interventions and their effect on the city public debate. Moreover, professionals, enthusiasts and artists as well publish on Youtube video commenting on their art works (as French street artists C215).

In these cases public arenas arise (Cefaï, 2002), functioning as theatrical devices where every art intervention constitutes a performance that activate other new reactions. The street becomes a stage where artworks are visible to a wide public. By the act of painting and by the murals' contents street art so produces rifts (Mondino, 2016), breaks rules and norms of behaving in public. Every intervention produce a "moral shock" that active process of interaction, so producing "public" (Cefaï, Carrel, Talpin, Eliasoph, & Lichterman , 2012). In this process, the effect of proximity (proche) between the artist and the space, between the artist and inhabitants plays a fundamental role. Apart from the physical act of painting, it is the workart in itself that bear inscribed the body that realized it so anyway producing a sense of public activation.

5. Street art as practice of active citizenship

The phenomenon of street art has been widely studied in the framework of social science mainly from the anthropological and sociological point of view and from the art critic perspective as a movement made of well-defined practices, rituals and codes. More recently some studies highlighted the meaning of these practices also as exercise of citizenship. For example Iannelli (2015) focuses on the aspect of political participation implied by public art. It represents a communicative process able to Foster knowledge, opinions, attitudes and orientate citizens' behavior. With this regard the author notices the strict connection between art and political participation by pointing out as the first one is often used as a rhetorical and communicative tool as in any mobilization practice. In this frame, artists and their art practices are addressed as:

"actors of the contentious politics on their own, which activate collective actions in order to obtain social and political change: art is considered mainly as one of the repertories that activists choose among others". (Iannelli, 2015, p. 235)

In particular Iannelli refers to that branch of public art defined as "relational" because it aims to involve citizens within this kind of art intervention. Public art can thus be a catalyst of active citizenship not only from the point of view of the artist, but also from the point view of the citizens directly or indirectly involved in the art intervention. Street art and writing, if meant as "texts" (speaking in semiotic terms), turn out to be a practice of reappropriation of urban space that operate a continuous writing and re-writing of its meaning. It represents a practice of active citizenship that produces interactions by proximity or conflict with other actors of the public space as institutions, citizens, community (Mastroianni, 2013):

> "The textual metaphor show up in all its epistemological and cognitive strength and show as a practice of urban writing and re-writing can be carried out together with the involvement of institutions, of citizenship and subcultural communities in a process of appropriation of urban texture, that assumes the feature s of a from of active citizenship. A form of active citizenship "artistically orientated", that find in the metropolitan sign a form of expression and participation, that aims to take the floor in the public sphere, in the muralism an activity of urban regeneration" (Ibidem, p.60).

In this sense these practices produce public space thanks to the interaction of heterogeneous voices and actors according to different modalities and strategy actions. The sign on the wall represents a taking of the floor that together with other acts of speech (as seen in the previous paragraph) contributes to create proper public arenas on specific issues. Street art, for its being practiced in the street, for the whole of interactions and modalities by through it shows up, represents an interesting laboratory to observe the functioning of public space, its meaning and the modalities by which it is produced (Dourado Sequeira, 2015).

Even though a specific aim or political intention is not always present, street art can anyway be meant as a form of action able to create political subjectivity (Murray, 2015). If, as Murray suggests (ibidem), we focus more on the actions by which this practice operates than on the artist itself, it is possible to observe as it can produce a break in predetermined routines, habits and norms so allowing the insurgence of new forms of citizenship.

This interpretation also draws on Isin's work (Isin, 2012) that in her research on new forms of citizenship distinguishes between actions and acts. The first one regards forms of citizenship that in some ways are compliant or agreed with the govern authority, the second ones instead produces a break, overcome physical and symbolic borders and in so doing create new forms of citizenship. In this last case, aspects as creativity, autonomy and inventiveness are not curb in predefined rules but lead the research of innovative practices of participation. Street art and writing seems to carry out this kind of operation (Murray, 2015):

> "These creative, inventive and autonomous acts of citizenship enacted by these writers and artists have provided the possibilities or potentialities to break not only their static and habitual modes of everyday behavioral activity but those of others. In doing so they are both involved in actively critiquing the dominant institutional order and contributing to the repertoire of collective activism and memory, even if they are left unresolved and are ignored by the authorities they are meant to critique" (Ibidem, p.63).

Even where there is not an explicit reference to political intention, street art can produce citizenship and mobilization, by involving a wide amount of people that is not limited to professionals but include the simple citizen as well. Unless its ephemeral and spontaneous nature, and maybe because of this, these artistic practices produce activation by involving inhabitants, professionals, activists and Fostering new strategies of action.

This feature clearly emerges in the cases explored within the city of Palermo, where the forms of active citizenship and public debate are many: from the cleaning up of a square before used as a dump, to the critic of the state of decay of the buildings of Old City, to the connotation of a neighborhood as a favorite place for movida.

6. What impact on the city?

Beside the capacity of producing new forms of citizenship, the phenomenon of street art can be analyzed by focusing on the impact of this practice produce on the urban fabric, especially for what concerning its relation with urban public policies.

With this regard, Costa (2014) observes as the reaction of institutions to the phenomenon can vary considerably from attitudes of total disinterest to tolerance to repressive interventions or to forms of promotion through institutionalized initiatives. In some cases, in the same context it is possible to find the presence of opposite political attitudes as in the case of Lisbon wherein some places are applied repressive policies, but in some others street art and writing are promoted through specific institutions.

The institutionalization of street art, recognizable in many Italian cities, derives from the idea that creativity and therefore artistic practices that generate it can represent a fundamental asset for the development of the city. Urban creativity can be seen as a set of processes able to promote urban development. Therefore, the trend in urban policies is to promote it through specific policy orientations, mostly inspired to models of urban governance (Costa, Seixas, & Roldão, 2009):

> "Creativity, a key factor for the development and creation of value in contemporary economies, transversal to all activities and social practices (from the cultural and more "creative" through to all others) has a potential that may be explored at local level, within a logic of promoting urban vitality and competitivity, which may prove highly relevant to sustainably boosting various facets of urban development (economic efficiency, social equity, environmental quality, civic participation and identity and cultural expression), and replacing more reductive logics of action, frequently centered on the mere exploitation of short term competitive advantages (Ibidem, p.26)

The recent institutionalization of street art and urban art in general find its justification on these assumptions. According to them many festival and interventions of regeneration with famous international artists have been organized in the last years, able to attract a wide public.

With reference to the case of Palermo it is possible to observe a substantial disinterest of the public authorities towards the spread of street art in the city during last years. As it has been observed, the informality affecting many of the neighborhoods of the city has Fostered and allowed the development of this artistic practice in very different ways. The analysis of the above mentioned cases permits to observe a significant impact on the practices of use of the city, on the transformation of spaces and on the public debate.

As we have noticed, the case of Mediterraneo square in Albergheria demonstrates how street art interventions can contribute to transform and promote the use of space as a square in a quite difficult neighborhood affected by decay and lack of spaces of socialization.

The patchwork of murals, tags and stencils on the walls and shutters of the market of Vucciria fully get into the debate regarding the modalities of fruition of the space, the rules that are supposed to regulate it, and the conflict between youngsters and residents about the bowing down of movida until late in the night. The connotation of the space of the market as "underground" and "alternative" thanks to the many murals and graffiti Foster the use of it as favorite place for movida and encourage youngster to attend bars and pubs of the area. The installations by Uwe draw public attention on the issue of the restoration of many historical buildings of the Old City so forcing the Municipality to state its purposes about the issue and the citizens to rake position.

In the cases reported it is possible to observe specific impacts on policies and practices of management of the city. These sometimes turn out to be clear and durable, some others more temporary but in any case they are significant for their payload especially if we look at the spontaneity, casualty and informality by which these kind of interventions occur.

References

Cannarozzo, T. (2007). Centri storici come periferie: il caso del centro storico di Palermo, tra eccellenza e marginalità. Conferenza INU "Territori e città del Mezzogiorno: "Quali periferie? Quali politiche di governo del territorio?". Napoli.

Cefaï, D. (2007). Il quartiere come contesto, risorsa, posta in gioco e prodotto dell'azione collettiva. In T. Vitale, In nome di chi? Partecipazione e rappresentanza nelle mobilitazioni locali. Milano: Franco Angeli.

Cefaï, D. (2002). Qu'est-ce qu'une arène publique?Quelques pistes pur une approche pragmatiste. In D. Cefaï, & I. Joseph, L'heritage du pragmatisme. Conflits d'urbanité et éprouves de civisme (p. 51-58). La Tour d'Aigues: Editions de l'Aube.

Cefaï, D., Carrel, M., Talpin, J., Eliasoph, N., & Lichterman , P. (2012). Ethnographies de la participation. Participations (4), 7-48.

Costa, P. & Lopes, R. (2014). Is street art institutionalizable? Challenges to an alternative urban policy in Lisbon. DINÂMIA'CET – IUL, Centro de Estudos sobre a Mudança Socioeconómica e o Território, Lisbon.

Costa, P., & Lopes, R. (2013). Artistic intervention in public sphere, conflict and urban informality: an international comparative approach to informal dynamics in cultural districts. Resourcefull cities: 29-31 August. Berlin: Paper presented at the International RC21 Conference 2013.

Costa, P., Seixas, J., & Roldão, A. (2009, Dezemblro). From 'Creative Cities' to 'Urban Creativity'? Space, Creativity and Governance in the Contemporary City. Working Paper (80).

Dal Lago, A., & Giordano, S. (2008). Fuori cornice. L'arte oltre l'arte. Torino: Einaudi.

Dourado Sequeira, A. (2015). Out in the Streets: the possibilities and implications of making art in the city's public space. In D. De Freitas Simões, & P. Soares Neves (A cura di), Lisbon Street Art & Urban Creativity 2014 International Conference. Lisbon.

Giambalvo, M., & Lucido, S. (2011). Flussi globali e sviluppi locali. Trasformazioni urbane ed economie della cultura a Palermo. Tafter Journal (32).

Guarrasi, E. (1978). La condizione marginale. Palermo: Sellerio.

Iannelli, L. (2015). To govern artfully. Linking public art to political participation towards new forms of urban governance. In L. S. Conference, D. V. De Freitas Simões, & P. Soares Neves (A cura di). Lisbon.

Isin, E. (2012). Citizens without frontiers. London: Bloomsbury.

Mastroianni, R. (2013). Dal segno metropolitano al muralismo artistico. In R. Mastroianni, Writing the city Scrivere la città Graffitismo, immaginario urbano e Street Art . Roma: Aracne.

Mondino, M. (2016). Immaginario urbano e street art: percorsi ed esplorazioni tra le vie di Palermo. In S. Borvitz, Metabolismo e spazio simbolico. Macerta: Quodlibet.

Murray, K. (2015). Rethinking political subjectivity in the urban context through the lens of graffity and street art. In D. V. De Freitas Simões, & P. Soares Neves, Lisbon Street Art & Urban Creativity 2014 International Conference. Lisbom.

Ruiz, L. M. (2015). Street art and urban space: a problem or an opportunity for local governments? Barcelona as a Case Study. In P. S. Neves, Lisbon Street Art & Urban Creativity: 2014 International Conference. Lisbom: Daniela Simões.

Söderström, O., Fimiani, D., Giambalvo, M., & Lucido, S. (2009). Urban cosmographies. Roma: Meltemi.

Tumminelli, G. (2010). Sovrapposti. Processi di trasformazione degli spazi ad opera degli stranieri. Milano: Franco Angeli.

Zenteno, E. (2015). Vivere quotidianamente la relegazione: I casi del quartiere ZEN di Palermo e della favela Paraisopolis de São Paulo. Roma: Tesi di Dottorato in Teoria e Ricerca sociale - Sapienza -Università di Roma.

Chapter 7

Camilla Watson photography and its impact in the social production of public space in a neighbourhood (Mouraria) in the inner city of Lisbon

Madalena Corte-Real; Maria João Monteiro Gomes

Abstract

This research analyses the extent to which the photographic work of Camilla Watson has affected the social production of space in a district of the historical part of Lisbon. This particular public-art-in-place exhibits the elderly residents through pictures displayed in the neighbourhood's public spaces. In a context of transformations that the territory is undergoing, the analysis aims to understand how far it contributes to change the way the area is socially produced in terms of spatial practice, representational space and representation of space.

Two kinds of experiences were considered; that of the resident and the visitor, meaning two groups that perceive, conceive and live the place in very different ways. Based on the information from outside the neighbourhood as well as from residents involved in the project, the intention is to capture two different constructed realities and to compare the way the work is understood and felt in those contexts.

For the residents the artistic work has been accepted, approved and appropriated because it became part of their daily routine environment. From an external point of view, the analysed art project binds the old quarter with the new one. By being part of the new creative scene it links the new visitors with the longstanding residents, helping to redefine the way locals are perceived and how the area is experienced.

Keywords: space production, experience, public-art-in-place

1. Introduction

This chapter focuses on the eventual impact of art in the social production of space, considering as a case study Camilla Watson's photographs in Mouraria. It is public artwork developed with the community in an inner city neighbourhood of Lisbon.

Our hypothesis, considering this case study, is that the cultural production of urban space, intentionally or not, contributes to the transformation of the urban environment which affects how it is experienced and ultimately generates new practices.

In this sense the research question, based on Lefebvre's theory, addresses *how far Camilla Watson's photography contributes to the production of space.* Under this analysis it is important to understand the external perception of the territory, considering in what way this work became an intrinsic element of it, and to acknowledge the local population's perception of being part of this project.

The research starts with a brief description of Mouraria and the socio-spatial changes that have been taken place, followed by a description of the photographic interventions.

Theoretically, three interrelated concepts were considered that frame the analysis: *public art* under the context of the *social production of space* and the way it is *experienced*.

The applied methodology aims to characterize and assess the potential contribution of this artistic intervention on the different perceptions of space. An analysis of the way this artistic project is referred to on the internet intends to capture the representation of the work. In parallel two different interactions to the place are analysed, that of the people who live and use this area on a daily basis and the visitor's experience.

2. Mouraria in a Context of Socio-Spatial Transformation

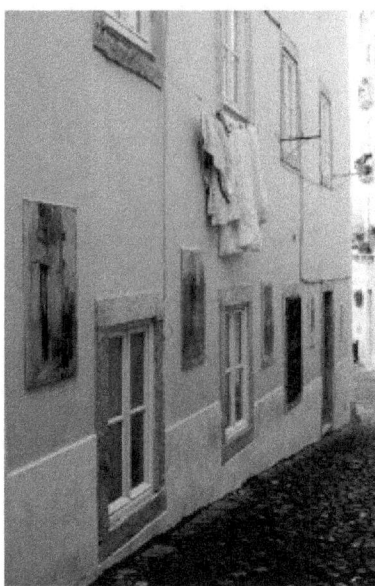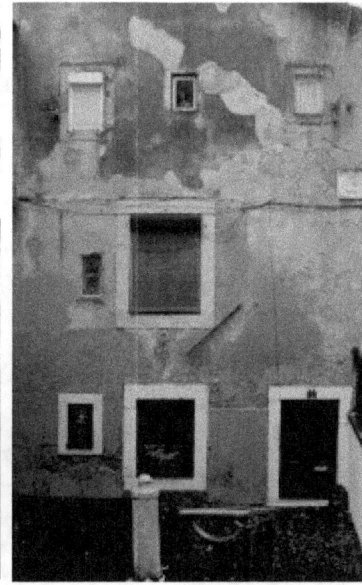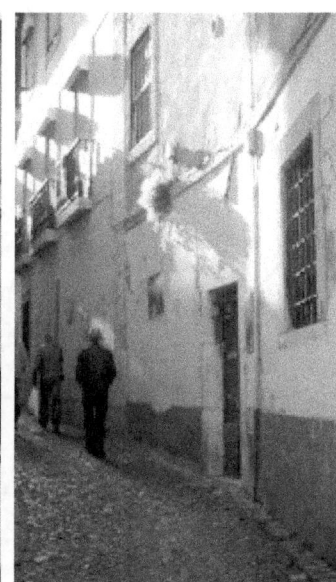

The area that is being studied is a neighbourhood on a downhill slope with narrow and labyrinthine streets that has about 5,800 inhabitants. The territory received people from rural areas that came to Lisbon to work. They contributed to the development of a particular urban popular culture (Costa, 1999) that can be identified in the inner city neighbourhoods in Lisbon marked by practices like Fado music, the festivities to celebrate the day of the municipality, rivalry among different historic neighbourhoods, the religious procession, its narrow morphological layout, the traditional trade and the local organizations. These are all elements that nurture a strong connection between the locals.

Especially in the last decades, the territory has been receiving an immigrant population that has introduced a multicultural atmosphere that identifies this area in particular with people from south Asia and China who have opened stores and warehouses, restaurants, grocery shops and supermarkets.

Currently the area is becoming attractive for new residents, including students and young people with high qualifications and artists, namely (European) foreigners, who are attracted to this environment in the historical part of the city.

Since 2011 a transformation process has been initiated, largely triggered by the municipality in financial and strategic terms. A multi-targeted program is being implemented because the territory was identified as a run-down area, affected by the deterioration of the public realm and buildings, as well as social problems that had to be addressed including many elderly residents, a local population with low qualifications and high unemployment, prostitution, as well as drug trafficking and consumption.

Fado, a music genre, developed during the nineteenth century in the popular neighbourhoods of Lisbon, is invariably part of Mouraria and as a central element of local identity, it was considered an important lever in the promotion of the territory.

Mouraria is being used to market the image of a multi-cultural, open and tolerant cosmopolitan city. Several events are being held such as the Festival for Everyone (*Festival Todos*) initiative - Walk of the Cultures, which has taken place every year since 2009 and, as stated by the city council, aims to define Lisbon as a city committed to the dialogue between cultures, between religions and between people of diverse backgrounds and generations. According to the municipality it has contributed to the destruction of territorial ghettos associated with immigration, opening up the city. (http://festivaltodos.com/intro/home).

Apart from the key actors undertaking socio-cultural interventions like local charities, numerous players were attracted to the territory due to a sudden recognition of its potential. An area that was previously not recommended to walk through is now becoming trendy and causing a ripple effect in the surrounding area. These newcomers are creating new spaces for leisure and consumption attracting new residents and visitors as well as devolving a new sense of security to the territory. There is an increasing presence of guided walks and other tourists that wander around in the area.

3. The Empirical Object - A tribute to the People of Mouraria

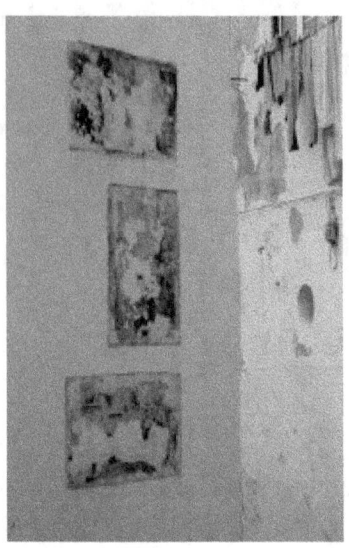 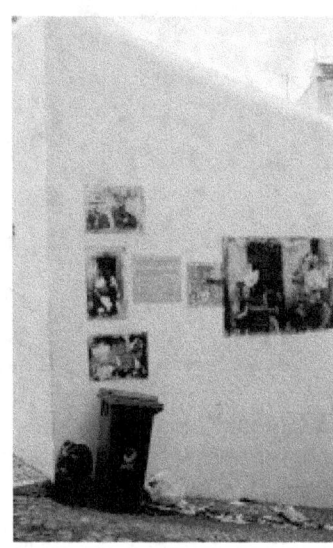 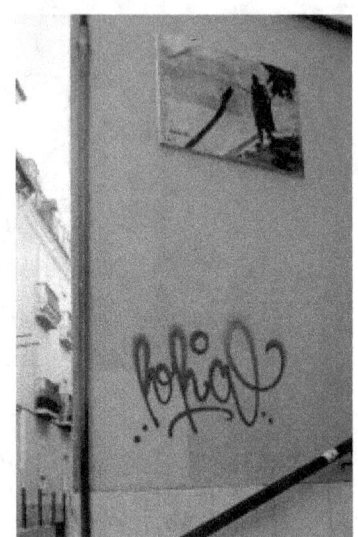

Camilla Watson settled in Mouraria by chance in 2007. On her way to São Tomé e Principe the photographer made a stop in Lisbon. She became enchanted with the area where she bought an apartment and has her workplace. She began to establish a relationship with her neighbours who passed by her studio, which is always open. In 2009 she had the idea of putting pictures on the street's walls, either directly or on wood.

One of the projects, financed by the multicultural *Festival Todos* is called *Tribute*: a way of thanking the hospitality received since moving to Portugal and honouring her neighbours. Based on the same technique, the photographer also did two other projects. One was called *Inside Out* and does not exist anymore. The aim was to document the renovation of a building as well as to photograph the people in the area. The other project was about *Fado* done in 2013, both were commissioned by the city council.

According to the artist the intention of all these works, apart from its aesthetic concern, is the collaboration with the local community. It was a cooperative process in which those involved accepted to be part of it and chose the images that went on the walls. In the case of the Fado project the people in the borough, the families that have been there for generations, all have some link with Fado. About eight of the people in the exhibition have already died so the photographer worked with the relatives to find old images. The twenty-six exhibited musicians and singers have some link to Mouraria and in this sense it is a project about the community, its history and its music. Watson's photographic work *Tribute* consists of prints of elderly people from the community displayed on the rough textured walls, reflecting the people that have themselves been marked by their tough lives. The aesthetic quality of time is reflected in her work, merging real people and real buildings, reinforcing the image of its unity and dependency.

This photographic work is an example of art created and generated in and for the public realm of Mouraria. Her material is the ordinary people and buildings; the images capture an imprisoned reality of the daily lives of its residents enhancing perceptions and meanings of this particular neighbourhood.

There is a continuity between the experience of the work of art and the everyday lives of the residents. It gives an introduction to the neighbourhood, an unexpected insider's perspective for the visitor of the community's atmosphere, revealing the lives of the local residents and getting closer to them. The photographer states that the feedback has been very positive:

> They really like it and the people on the walls they loved it, they wanted to be on the walls so it's a success in terms of a collaboration (...) Their response would be I was born here, I lived here, and all my family is here so I think it gives a sense of territory which I think it is really good when so much is changing. We have a lot of new people moving, it gives them a sense of their history. These people are the ones who made the area what it is. (...) some people think it is negative but interestingly not the people who have been here a long-time, they [the newcomers] don't like the tourists that come and see the pictures (....) There are three or four people that I know who complain about tourists all the time but it is not the people who have been here for generations (...) I think they mind [the longstanding residents] when the prices go up, that's the down side, there is no control over the rents, that's the only down side I think. That's how cities change unfortunately.

People are celebrated on the old walls of the neighbourhood that are comprised of successive sediments of centuries of the city of Lisbon, printing onto them an additional memory. The work has a humanizing character in a territory that has been successively forgotten and neglected. It depicts neighbours who seem to have been caught up in their daily lives in ordinary clothes without make-up or staged scenarios. Ordinary people become part of the urban fabric establishing a connection between the photographed and the walls.

Interestingly nobody tried to destroy or vandalize the work. Once someone wrote on a picture and then somebody from the area cleaned it and it all came off.

Although commissioned for a particular event, Watson considers *Tribute* to be a hobby and the project as being part of her community. For the photographer this is an ongoing project. The artwork will stay alive so long as people keep requesting new photographs to be displayed.

But it is also an ephemeral project. In a context of change, in which many transformations have been occurring in the area, this could seem like a form of eternalizing the longstanding residents and to preserve the past, but as stated by the photographer the pictures only have a limited durability and then they will fade.

4. Three Main interrelated Concepts

4.1 Public-Art-In-Place

Public art is considered to be art that takes place outside conventional spaces like museums and galleries, put in the physical public domain intended to be accessible to everyone and in this sense it has to consider the relation between the artistic object and the public context (Miles, 1997, p. 1; Finkelpearl, 2001, p. 5; Januchta-Szostak, 2010, p. 80). It invariably affects the urban space, individualizing it, building a new identity of place and contributing to the creation of spaces (Sharp, Pollock & Paddison, 2005, p. 1004; Januchta-Szostak, 2010, pp. 81-82). The latter refers to the way that the unique form of artworks makes them stand out from the surroundings. Art provides spatial tags helping with orientation and navigation and also as anchor-points on mental maps of the inhabitants and tourists.

The act of placing art in a certain space tends to give meaning to the object and the space itself. For Remesar (2005, p. 134), there is a clear distinction between spaces for art and public art in place with the latter, in its global sense, being a process with three phases: *recreation, approval* and *appropriation* by the user of the place.

Public art works as a symbol, generating and enhancing cognitive and/or abstract meanings of space. In addition to an aesthetic perspective, public art has an urban component that establishes a reciprocal relationship with the surrounding socio-spatial context. It occurs between two poles in view of public space: on the one hand it is art regarded as a public object (a subject of beautification detached from the environment), on the other it is art within the city (art as reciprocally connected to its surrounding dynamics).

Currently, urban artistic interventions are a recurrent instrument of territorial requalification. By redefining the urban environment, it triggers or emphasizes the social transformation of urban spaces. Miles (1997, p. 2) refers to its significance in the context of the convivial city and related strategies of place making and the redefinition of public space. Sharp, Pollock & Paddison (2005, p. 1004); Hall and Roberson (2001, p. 5, 10) critique the use of public art in urban regeneration and question the extent to which they really help communities in run-down inner city areas.

In the present case study, the focus is on the relationship between public art and the place making, particularly in the context of physical up-grading of a territory and how far it has contributed to the way the territory is characterised.

4.2 The production of Space

The social production of space, is a socially produced reality in the context of a particular society. Its spatial production, according to Henri Lefebvre (1991 [1974], pp. 33, 38, 39) arises from the interconnection of three processes:

- *Spatial practice*, meaning the material and social dimension of an activity. Closely associated with the perceived space;
- *Representations of space,* as the dimension of spatial conception and description, connecting perception and lived space, becoming an organizing factor or framework with impact on spatial practice;
- *Representational space,* concerns the meanings and the relationships established with the lived space. It overlays physical space, making symbolic use of its objects.

In this article we intend to approach the neighbourhood and the experience of the public realm where the intervention stands through the re-appropriation of these processes, analysing it as a social production process. The production of space exists as a complex and multidimensional reality. So, in the same way Lefebvre addresses three moments of social space with a phenomenological character centred in the body's experience: the *perceived*, the *conceived* and the *lived*. The three dimensions of the production of space are auto-productive of the individual and society (Lefebvre, 1991 [1974], p. 40).

4.3 The Experience

Access to the artistic intervention is not restricted to a specific materiality but to a reality felt and thought as an experience. Quoting Yi-Fu Tang (2007 [1977], p. 8) "experience is a cover-all term for the various modes through which a person knows and constructs a reality".

This study concerns two types of experience, the resident or quotidian experience and the visitor experience. They represent two distinct ways of constructing realities and the production of space. As Rapoport (1990 [1982], p. 15) states, the activity's components or the details of the activity (proper, way of doing it, associated activities and meaning), are determining factors when sharing the perceived attributes and meanings associated to them. The daily experience of residents has a prevailing functional aim, which results in them having a more *operational perception* of place (Appleyardd, 1973, p. 109). This condition is dominated by a body-memory and the cognitive abstraction from the environment granted by the repetition of routines. There is a physical and emotional stability, a reliable connection with the environment, which allows a state of *obliviousness* (Seamon, 1979, pp. 103-105). The visitor's experience is focused around leisure activities and is therefore dominated by a *responsive* and *inferential perception of place.* The visitor gazes the public realm with an open and active attitude, watching it and comparing it with their expectations (Appleyardd, 1973, p. 109). The perceptive attitude of *watching* is an active external attention (Seamon, 1979, pp. 103-105).

Another important distinction between the quotidian and leisurely experience of the environment is that, as Yi-Fu Tang (1990 [1974]:64-65) states, the visitors evaluation, the view from the outsider, is essentially aesthetic. The outsider judges by appearance, by some formal canon of beauty. Although superficial, it is a fresh view often able to perceive merits and defects in an environment that are no longer visible to the resident.

5. The Method

This chapter presents the methodology used to determine how far the cultural production of urban space, deliberately or not, contributes to the transformation of the urban environment.
Based on the premise sustained by the theoretical approach, it is considered that the experience of the public realm is determined not only by the socio-spatial dimension and the individual characteristics of the walker, but also by the specificities of the experience.

To take into account external references, different online reports (from the national and international press, blogs, city guides) were considered as they provide a huge amount of current and up to date information. The intention was to capture the symbolic representations projected in the last few years about the territory and the particular photography projects, through an exploratory research and content analysis. This sought to answer the following questions: how often are the pictures referred to? What is transmitted about these projects and by whom?

Visitors were questioned about characteristics of the neighbourhood in the past, how it has changed, as well as the aspects that have persisted. Within this framework the respondents were also asked how the artist's work is perceived. Socio-demographic information like the age, gender, nationality, profession and level of education of the interviewees was also taken into account.

Some of the photographed were interviewed in order to understand how they dealt with the process of being exposed and becoming, materially speaking, part of the neighbourhood buildings. The aim was to understand how their lived experience of the streets had changed. In this context the questions addressed whether they photographic portraits were recognized by their neighbours and the visitors and how they felt about it. Locals were also asked about what has changed and what has stayed the same in the area.

6. Data Analysis

6.1 Camilla's Work on the Web

Online travel articles from newspapers and magazines, travel sites and personal blogs, offer an enormous amount of insight about Mouraria and Camilla Watson's work. The analysis of this online material reflects the evolution of a territory in transformation, from a run-down area to an area increasingly themed around leisure and travel. Her work is an example of someone who breaks the stigma that still affects this historic neighbourhood of Lisbon, claims a website in 2011. (https://vimeo.com/23090337).

"Walks in the inside" written by an inhabitant of Lisbon, reveals the use of the street as a stage by making the photographic production an outdoor installation, in a natural environment. The relation with the local community is enhanced. It explains that during the work, the photographer contacts and links with the inhabitants, rebounding the "local soul": "Mouraria with open arms". The art is reincarnated in the urban landscape. The artist's technique is also exposed: the photographs are developed in a prefabricated atelier, a darkroom with black plastic using a handmade process (http://myguide.iol.pt/profiles/blogs/passeios-ca-dentro-camilla).

Also in 2011 the *Guardian* writes about street art in Lisbon saying that "Her exhibits have proved popular with locals and visitors, and will remain in place indefinitely, funding permitting"(http://www.theguardian.com/travel/2011/jan/29/graffiti-street-art-lisbon-portugal).

Some online accounts of her work refer to the fact that it immortalizes local inhabitants and preserves local identities. A blog in 2012 talks about "the historic, sleepy district of Mouraria (…) it's rare to find older ordinary folk given the limelight in works of art. I hope that these pieces will leave the legacy they intended to create and that they will be preserved and treasured by the community and tourists alike". (http://www.foodandthefabulous.com/recipes/cheddar-cheese-parsley-beer-bread-exploring-the-birthplace-of-Fado-mouraria/#sthash.e0DF21jm.dpuf).

In the following years Mouraria has increasingly become a reference in the context of the city of Lisbon. So have Camilla Watson's pictures, in particular the work with the elderly residents. In a French article from 2013 "Lisbonne, ça bouge, mais où?" this street art was called urban poetry (http://www.lxfactory.com/ficheiros/noticias/imprensa_pdf_5148b424d3bd6.pdf).

An article from 2013 recognizes the duality of Mouraria where "Some of the white walls were peeling while others had fresh paint". Beyond the interpretation of the pictures, interviews with the photographer were also undertaken where she gives her own understanding of the connection between the elderly and the walls and the wish to break the barriers of a gallery: "Here, everyone's a part of it. Everyone appreciates it because it's outdoors". In her opinion the visitors like it very much because the expression in the photos is between the subjects and her, and in this sense it is a form of getting closer to the community (http://matadornetwork.com/notebook/lisbons-walls-an-interview-with-photographer-camilla-watson/). Considering how Watson approached the people that were photographed, she says that the locals were open to being photographed. When the idea of putting the pictures on the walls came up, the first person that was asked was someone whom everyone liked. Using liquid emulsion she tried to the print images directly onto the walls which failed completely, so she decided to print on wood and kept on developing her technique. (http://www.tasteoflisboa.com/eng/blog/facebook/article/72#.VqDNnvmLRdg). In 2015 most of the buildings in the square where she has her studio were regenerated and tourism became a constant presence. A visitor that stayed there in an apartment wrote: "Each building on the street has a portrait of the elderly residents who live there, a series called 'A Tribute to Mouraria' by the photographer Camilla Watson. And even though there are a lot of tourists, and every now and again a walking tour goes through our square, there's a sense of community and a laid-back way of life here that's so appealing" (http://peekingduck.co/welcome-to-mouraria-lisbon/).

6.2 The Visitors

People who had recently been in Mouraria, that were living in the Lisbon Metropolitan Area, were asked to answer a questionnaire. Many said that although they live in Lisbon, they had never visited the area or only did so when they were very young.

We received 22 questionnaires of people that visited Mouraria recently, 14 women and 9 men. The ages were within 50-34 years old. All of them have at least a college degree.

In terms of nationality, the majority are Portuguese and four were foreigners. When asked about the first trip to the neighbourhood the answers were very diverse, and as for the last time they visited, everybody answered 2015 or even 2016.
As mentioned by most of our visitors, Mouraria was seen as a closed, 'no-go' area; a kind of ghetto, an inaccessible location (narrow streets and no parking facilities with very bad access), unknown, and intriguing; not visitor friendly and definitely not a touristic place. The image they have does not come from a personal experience but from a shared public image of this territory.
The visitors' answers about what the neighbourhood was like in the past, were dominantly descriptions of its social-cultural and economic character. Three related images of the neighbourhood stand out:
- The run-down Mouraria, related to drug trafficking and consumption as well as prostitution; old and poor residents living in dilapidated buildings as well as dirty and dark streets.

-The authentic Mouraria, the old neighbourhood, the cradle of Fado, with genuine Lisbon residents. A non-touristic area with local shops and small restaurants.

- The *multicultural Mouraria*, with its migrants mainly from Africa and Asia, living in this affordable part of the city. When asked about the present characteristics of this neighbourhood, the Mouraria that was described was the one currently experienced and perceived. Nevertheless, this perception has probably been influenced by the new users and the media. An evolutionary process is evident where the three images persist but with a different importance:

-The *authentic Mouraria*, the neighbourhood of the old residents and strong community relations, is now accessible and valued as the main characteristic of the area. The perceived atmosphere of the old traditional neighbourhood, the typical small restaurants (*tascas*) and the Fado are all highlighted. The old buildings now became the reflection of the authenticity of the neighbourhood, not yet affected by the tourist industry and main commercial brands.

-The *multicultural Mouraria* stands out now as a tolerant ambience and culturally rich with new restaurants and events associated to the different communities.

-The *run-down Mouraria* that still exists and is actually reinterpreted. Although problems with crime are still identified by the local population, it does not seem to have a big impact on the visitors not only because it is probably less visible in the areas where the visitors move, but also because their attitude enhances the positive features.

Mouraria, as it is revealed to the outside, is undergoing a process of change: as underlined by the visitors, new people come because it is cheap, there is a new vitality, a new kind of public and tourists, there are more social and cultural events like dinners, concerts, open air cinema, exhibitions and commodities. Restaurants and cafes of a higher quality and price range are now on offer. Those interviewed also mentioned the fact that now there was more diversity and more young people. It became safer both by day and night, which brought more people in from outside. It is becoming a trendy area where people go for leisure.

When the visitors were asked what they thought about the photographs, some did not pay much attention, did not notice, or had no opinion, either because they usually go by night or the photos do not represent a reference for them. Most respondents were quite positive and clear about the purpose of this art intervention and three main characteristics were mentioned:

1. The opinions enhanced the social meaning of exhibiting residents, with an important significance for residents and visitors. According to the statements, this is a form of presenting the neighbourhood from within, honouring the longstanding residents, showing that they matter and making them feel proud of their history and thus preserving as much as possible their authenticity by strengthening and increasing their identity. As underlined by this statement "I Like them because they show us the neighbourhood from within, the people that really live there; and it's good for those people, to see that they matter and that each neighbourhood is made of the people that live there, they are the most important thing, whoever they are, age, gender...". Another testimony says "It is important for residents and for visitors. Actually when we were there some residents proudly showed us the photos. Clearly it is strengthening and increasing their identity."

2. Respondents frequently mentioned the way the work contributed to the perception of public place, for instance enjoyment (lively, stimulating, and interesting) as well as pleasantness (attractive, beautiful, pleasant, and inviting) were enhanced. Interestingly, it was felt that the work transmits a sense of intimacy and awakens a curiosity to find more photographs.

3. When asked if they felt that this art was an anchor-point for Mouraria, although not everybody agreed, the ones who gave a positive answer made not only a spatial reference but also a temporal one.
 The photos were seen as a spatial reference in the area, becoming part of the street and of the neighbourhood landscape. An interviewee said that this work represents something which makes Mouraria stand out from other neighbourhoods. For the passer-by it feels like entering a community with familiar faces, which can be reassuring. In view of the temporal dimension it was pointed out that, "they act like a bridge between knew and old, acting as a way of communication between different cultures and between different generations." It is interesting that the ephemeral character of this work is not perceived or is often forgotten by the observer who refers to this work as a form of suspending a certain time on the walls, "a legacy to be preserved and treasured", "it crystallizes moments in time that soon will disappear, taking into account the age of the photographed" and that "they will always be a historical and cultural reference".

6.3 The Residents

Five residents were interviewed, four residents that participated in the artistic work and finally someone, that approached us. She was pleased to provide information about the photographer, the people who were photographed and about the neighbourhood. When asked if she was represented on the walls, the old lady stated that she was invited to participate but did not want to. Although living there for a long time, she likes to keep a certain distance. As she explains, "I do not like to spend my time in the streets and in the cafés, chattering about each other, and exposing my life." The other four interviewees all have in common the fact they have worked in local commerce (tavern, shoemaker, drugstore and restaurant).

When questioned about the evolution of Mouraria in recent years, it is interesting to note that although some start by saying that everything has changed and one states it all remains the same, by the end there is an overall concordance in their points of view.

The character of the old quarter, the human relations and the lack of parking areas are aspects that according to these longstanding residents remain. Although there have been some improvements, the lack of security and continuing problems associated with drug trafficking were also referred to.

According to the interviewees, the prevailing feature of the new neighbourhood is the existence of a temporary population. Bearing in mind that the respondents work in local trade, tourism is generally seen as positive, but they think that the proliferation of apartments for temporary use by tourists may affect the community. Traditional commerce has been substituted by restaurants as well as other types of outlets or is being run by immigrant communities that are present in the area. Another mentioned aspect was the rise of rents.

From these interviews, and taking into account the fact that that all the contacted people were elderly with a longstanding relationship with the neighbourhood, it is interesting to note that when talking about the past, different periods are referred to. This can be seen in the following quotation from a resident that has lived in Mouraria for forty years and has worked there for seventeen:

> Practically everything has changed. There was the traditional trade, most of these houses closed. A few years ago it had a lot of life, then it died, everyone was stuck in their homes. Now we have customers who are here until midnight, the styles are different than before. I hope there will be no bars, it is a pity if that comes to this area with everything it brings – here there is still a little bit of security - I don't mind more trade, more restaurants…

When asked about the photographic intervention they all consider to be positive, highlighting its importance for the people visiting the neighbourhood. As time goes by the inhabitants seem to have got used to the pictures on the walls.The two men interviewed stated that to be exhibited had no great significance for them, and according to one of them it is something that only people from outside the neighbourhood value. The female residents interviewed appeared, in a rather discreet way, to be pleased about being part of the photographic work. One admitted that the suggestion of putting an image of her on the wall came from herself: "I do not like to see my photos but I found the idea of having our photograph on the wall funny. I really like seeing the dispersed photographs, I think it's nice… Some of the people have passed away…"

One of the interviewees stated that she likes to show the photographic work to people, in particular her picture to family or friends who visit her. She also stated that she likes the photos, the interest that the tourists show and the fact of being recognised by them.

Given that over time the pictures will disappear, this is viewed with pity but accepted as normal. When asked if it would bother her if the photographs would no longer exist, one of the interviewees stated, in a pragmatic way, that nothing lasts forever. Focusing on the importance to the character of the street, another resident said that it would be a shame to let the photos "die" because they give a certain interest to the streets, something that awakens the attention to the people passing by.

7. Discussion: Does Watson's Work have an Impact on the Production of Space?

The present analysis of an artwork in the public realm happens in a context where the place which hosts the projects, the neighbourhood of Mouraria, is undergoing socio-spatial transformations. The city itself is going through profound changes, becoming fashionable and increasingly noticed in the international context as a tourist destination, enhancing its traditional and historical character but at the same time the creative and trendy scene. In this context old neighbourhoods have continued to gain prominence as territories for consumption where the whole landscape is to be gazed upon and where visitors search for the "picturesque", the "authentic" and the "typical".

The same space is practiced in different spatial and social realities that often overlap but do not coincide. The Mouraria practiced by the residents is predominantly during the daytime routines rooted within the space and the social surroundings. The Mouraria practiced by the visitor is shallower but fresher and frequently occurs by night. The way the intervention of Camilla Watson affects the experience of space in terms of how it is perceived, conceived and lived is connected above all with the relationship that is established with the neighbourhood, for some it takes place within the routine spaces of their daily lives, for others in their places of leisure.

7.1 The visitor's Experience

The artistic intervention, by its particular characteristics and by the way it merges with the space, interferes with the visitor's *representational* dimension of space. For the visitor they gain visibility, by the unusual act of having pictures exposed outdoors or by the disclosure given to this work. Whether for its artistic or social interest, this photographic work undeniably participates in the new image of the neighbourhood.

The spatial concentration of the intervention within a particular part of Mouraria overlaps with one of the zones with more restaurants and new outlets (art galleries, ceramic shop, vintage shop), regenerated houses and renewed public spaces, defining a welcoming and safe part of the neighbourhood.

The images released by the media combined with leisure experiences of space, confirm the quarter as more open, authentic, multicultural and creative. The art participates in the space cohesion, linking the area within the neighbourhood and in the identification of the genuine but secure space.

7.2 The Resident's Experience

The artistic intervention in this study appears to be clearly integrated in a particular setting, which more than hosting this particular art project, is the element of its production. As we were able to capture from the interviewed residents, it does not seem to affect the way they perceive and practice space in their daily lives.

It is interesting that before the presence of people from the outside, the images gain value as an element of pride, representing a narrative about the neighbourhood, affecting the meaning given to that space (representational space) and the way the space is described (representation of space).

The photographs apparently end up having a similar function to family portrait in a living room of a home, exposing moments with visitors, giving clues about the identity of those who live there and also those who have left.

7.3 Conclusion

Watson's photographs seem to be inevitably part of the way the neighbourhood is presently experienced, since her work is seen as something which makes Mouraria stand out. The work is an intrinsic element of the past, by exposing the longstanding residents, creating an empathy with this community, and the new representation associated with a trendy scene. Her work, particularly the one dedicated to the elderly, became invariably a reference point in the area and is often referred to in the touristic circuit as one of the main points of interest in the territory.

This artwork is experienced by visitors in an emotional way, firstly by breaking the image of a run-down area, and secondly by creating a level of proximity with the older residents. In this way it fulfils its imaginary of being closely connected to the local identity of Mouraria.

Over the course of this neighbourhood's transformation, the artistic intervention of Camilla Watson participates in the different dimensions of the production of space by being part of how this continuous process of neighbourhood change is experienced. In this way it has generated new narratives, creating images that validate and ultimately consolidate the social representation of space.

References

Appleyard, D. (1973). Notes on Urban Perception and Knowledge. In R. M. Downs & David Stea (Eds), *Image and environment. Cognitive mapping and spatial behavior* (pp. 109-114). Chicago: Aldine Pub. Co.

Costa, A. F. (1999). *Sociedade de Bairro – Dinâmicas Sociais de Identidade Cultural*. Oeiras: Celta.

Finkelpearl, T. (2001). *Dialogues in public art*. Cambridge, Mass.: MIT Press.

Hall, T., & Robertson, I. (2001). Public Art and Urban Regeneration: Advocacy, claims and critical debates. *Landscape Research,* 26(1), 5-26. http://dx.doi.org/10.1080/01426390120024457

Januchta-Szostak, A. (2010). The Role of Public Visual Art in Urban Space Recognition. In K. Perusich (Ed.), *Cognitive maps* (pp. 74-100). Rijek, Crotia: InTech. Retrieved from http://www.intechopen.com/books/cognitive-maps/the-role-of-public-visual-art-in-urban-space-recognition.

Lefebvre, H. (1991 [1974]). *The Production of Space*, trans. Steven Nicholson-Lord, Oxford: Blackwell.

Miles, M. (1997). *Art, space and the city*. London: Routledge.

Rapoport, A. 1990 [1982]. *The meaning of the built environment - a non-verbal communication approach.* University Arizona Press.

Remesar, A. (1997). Public Art: Towards a Theoretical Framework. In A. Remesar (Ed.), *Urban regeneration* (128-140). [Barcelona]: Universitat de Barcelona.

Seamon, D. (1979). *A geography of the lifeworld. Movement, Rest, Encounter.* London: Croom Helm.

Sharp, J., Pollock, V., & Paddison, R. (2005). Just art for a just city: Public art and social inclusion in urban regeneration. *CURS*, 42(5), 1001-1023. http://dx.doi.org/10.1080/00420980500106963

Tuan, Y. (1990 [1974]). *Topophilia. A study of Environmental, Perception, Attitudes and Values.* New York: Columbia University Press.

Tuan, Y. (2007 [1977]). *Space and place.* Minneapolis: University of Minnesota Press.

Part IV.
Public art and
the resignification
of public space

Chapter 8

Street art in Yogyakarta, Indonesia: Messages of the streets

Polona Lupinšek

Abstract:

The chapter attempts to illuminate street art in the city of Yogyakarta, located on the island of Java, Indonesia. Author represents the social-cultural reality of works that reflect problems of the city, as well as of the entire contemporary Indonesian society. The main focus is in the processes of creativity, placed in the historical context of the country and the local atmosphere of the city itself.

These processes reveal the praxis of street artists based on data gathered through field work. Artists' social engagement is reflected in their cooperation with the communities and in their works themselves. The presence of street art contributes to different levels of living in the city: visual, socio-political, cultural and economic. It can be concluded that its presence strengthens the identity of the city, shapes social awareness and gives voice to the people. Nonetheless, it remains one of the few critical factors in the city.

Keywords: street art, processes of creation, urban communication, Jogjakarta, Indonesia

1. Introduction

In Yogyakarta, the city of culture, traditional art is available at every step whereas contemporary art is less exposed and promoted. Street art actions stimulate the importance of contemporary art, which is slowly coming to the fore and, therefore, provides contributions to the city in different manners.

The sides of the streets of Yogyakarta are used as parking lots during the day and as improvised restaurants at night. Streets are places of demonstrations, music, art performances and installations that are all omitted in the following chapter where merely art forms on the walls are being analysed.

Through insight into the art world of street artists, I have got an overall image of social reality of Yogyakarta, its culture and problematics. The phenomenon shows that street art is a medium through which those problematics are expressed and such approach makes street artists of the city severely socially engaged. Using anthropological methodologies such as (participant) observation and interviews (mostly relaxed discussions), I was searching for information of art practices.

Living in the city most of the time for the past two years gives me an opportunity to see a development of street art and its impact. However, the chapter is mostly based upon the intensive field work conducted from May until September 2014.

2. Invisibility of street art

Using Alfred Gell's perspective, I put focus on the creation processes of street art rather than solely on artworks as final products. In addition, it made the research elaborate on social networks within which art production is conducted. Gell placed art into social context. He was emphasizing that anthropological approach to art should study social relationships within which artworks are being produced. The stress is on the art nexus: circulation, acceptance and consumption of the artwork. Embedded in such network, artwork exerts its particular variety of agency and act as social agent (Gell, 1998).

Such approach allows us to understand creative processes on levels of the individual, social groups and society. It is revealing cognitive systems; conceptualization of everyday life, representation of the worlds and forms of particular social praxis and identities (Repič, 2012).

In the following text I am presenting the construction of art through its direct message (denotation level) which is reachable by anyone, as well as through indirect message (connotation level) which is inscribed into local communication and social codes. Through the analysis of street art in Yogyakarta, I was trying to grasp the invisibility in the visuality of street art while considering various factors influencing street art production from the beginning until the end, focusing on the agency of street artists.

The invisibility is hidden in the processes of making art, namely in the activism of the artists which stimulates social change. On the field, I have noticed that street artists are in constant contact with people whose perspectives are often incorporated into their artworks. Firstly, when they use ethnographic methods gathering information in the field as the material for their creations. Secondly, when they are out on the streets creating on the walls. Anthropological approaches within street art praxis in Yogyakarta are bridging the disciplines. Being engaged in such social art actions, the artists usually use anthropological methodologies, mostly subconsciously.

Anthropologists and artists are gradually becoming interested in each other. Both disciplines share interest in ethnographic fieldwork and they are both socially engaged. Moreover, they are both studying politics of identity and representation as well as political economy of contemporary world. The intentions of artists are nowadays more important than the artwork itself and the artwork may be the interaction with community which produces sociability rather than tangible result (Laine, 2009). The art of public space is not only physically present, but is also establishing the relationship with its environment, mostly during the art process itself. One of the purposes of street art projects is to contribute to communities "to consolidate its identity through promotion of local culture" (Andres). Being severely socially engaged in social and political activism, street artists in Yogyakarta fit in the below described perception of contribution of artist itself. In this way, they are justifying art which represents social relationships in the vicinity of objects that serve as social agents (Gell, 1998).

Indonesian artists' perception of Copyright Law (as well as Intellectual Property issue) is revealing attitude of Indonesian artists towards their own artistic contribution which is being seen mainly as social and intergenerational and never individualistic (Aragon & Leach, 2008). Art production is not perceived as an intellectual property: most artists do not claim authorship and copying is not seen as an ethical problem. During the process of production they share their knowledge; moreover, they perceive their collaborative productions and sharing as a lore without recourse to formal law. The essence of production lies in social relationships and not in the (final) product of it. Furthermore, artists mostly present themselves as mere followers of their traditions and even attribute their accomplishments to traditions, forebears, or God (Aragon, 2014).

We might call street art activities *artivism* as it converges activism and art production. The term itself is a hybrid neologism that signifies work created by individuals who use a creative expression for activism and self-empowerment. Such work stimulates social dialogues, amplifies and disseminates social consciousness of various groups addressed as well as it makes a critical intervention in the public space (Sandoval & Latorre, 2008).

The activist character of street art in Yogyakarta is spread by its direct or indirect messages. Only by claiming expressive surface a (graffiti) artist already challenges social rules and problematizes commercialization of public space and monopoly of advertising (Milkovič-Biloslav, 2008). Therefore, every street art creation not being conducted according to precedent agreement with the owner of the wall can be labelled as political. Nonetheless, in the context of Yogyakarta, it is most probably made illegally which expresses its anti-system tendency. Not all street creations hold a direct message and are political only in their act (process of making art) while their visuals are purely decorative. On the other hand, many of street art works are direct with loquacious images as well as slogans, or both, and the indirect message of it (usually) has a shock effect.

No matter whether art on the walls is being made on the basis of previous agreement with the owner (mostly art works made under umbrella of street art projects) or not, it is bearing critical note. According to Nenad Jelesijević, the adjective critical is the synonym of public, as he argues that public must be understood as something that is at the same time active-political articulated, e.g. critical. Political and artistic activism must be interwoven in synergy and as such, represent the active critical position of the individual towards his social environment of contemporary post-neoliberal society (Jelesijević, 2008).

3. Contextual outline

The most exposed street art features are: the anonymity of the author, criticism of their work and illegality (Jakob, 2008; Velikonja, 2008). These features ascribed to street art within western context are not completely applicable to the phenomenon of street art in Yogyakarta. Nevertheless, street art in Indonesia, state of control and censorship, call out for discussion about messages of its streets.

3.1 - From repression to democracy of Indonesia

The thirty-year-long period of dictatorship began with Indonesian independence, when Sukarno was named as first Indonesian president. The governance mode from 1945s until 1967s was called "guided democracy". In that time, political force was military supported, anti-colonial movements threw out former Dutch colonialists and the national pride was implanted into consciousness of the people (Brown, 2003).

The economic development of Indonesia began with Sukarno's successor, Suharto. He took over in 1967 at the transition from Old to New Order, when another period of dictatorship based on depoliticization of population, strict censorship and rapid removal of political opponents began (Brown, 2003).

However, the rebellion toward the regime which was stimulating ignorance started in the era of New Indonesia when mostly students started to take actions. Radical student movements have long history in modern Indonesia. In 1945 students were the backbone of independence movement directed against the Dutch colonial authorities. They were helping to initiate political change most dramatically in 1965-66, when they spearheaded the movement which resulted in the downfall of Sukarno and the rise to power of then-General Suharto. Student activism in Jakarta in 1997-98 was intense and their political tradition of opposing authorities ended with troops shooting down and killing four students at Trisakti University in West Jakarta in May 1998. On 21 May 1998, Suharto formally resigned the Presidency (Brown, 2003).

Indonesian government used art for promotion of reinforcement of national politics. Sukarno promoted a vision of common Indonesian culture while Suharto thoughtfully melded these unity-in-diversity approaches by admitting regional traditions, but put them into the frame of province divisions or other nationally administered political units (Aragon & Leach, 2008).

In the post-New Order period, Indonesia slowly started to create new political parties as well as giving more freedom to media and giving more acknowledgement to Chinese-Indonesian identities. Consequently, it created good conditions for the development of a democratic republic which gave the opportunity for cultural and political redefinition after the long period of repression (Dirgantoro, 2010).

The governance mode did evidently influence the development of Indonesian art, which needed long time to become critical. Radical changes of Indonesian art originating in postmodern thought started to emerge around year 1998. During the so called "heat of contemporary art" period many young artist at the time used art as an instrument for social changes and emancipation (N/A, 2013). The latter is being confirmed by the following statement: "Indonesian art became truly critical only after Suharto resigned." (Ucup).

3.2 - Javanese centre of culture and its symbolism

To better understand what motivates street artists at the local city level, let me below introduce Yogyakarta's atmosphere and its features.

The city is located in the southern part of the island of Java, where it borders the Indian Ocean. Having the status of a province, it is called Yogyakarta Special Region. The city covers around three thousand square kilometres. Its population has more than three million souls (according to data from the year 2010; Pradoto, 2012).

Tourism is the leading sector, which contributes to economic development and is a major contributor to gross domestic product. People living on the outskirts of the city work in agriculture sector which is being rapidly reduced and replaced with other non-agricultural economies (Pradoto, 2012).

Yogyakarta is the centre of Javanese culture and the city of abundant cultural heritage. Regional, national and global influences which are setting up cultural dynamics of the city are accepted open-handedly (Adaby Darban, 2004).

There are two kinds of symbolism present: the religious symbols and the symbols of colonialism replaced with symbols of nationalism. Urban imagery, e.g. urban symbols are reflecting social-cultural situation of urban community which was historically established. Symbols are practically disclosing an urban culture (Nas, 1993a).Yogyakarta is a relatively new but traditional city (Nas, de Groot & Schut, 2011). It was established in 1755 as a result of the Mataram kingdom having been split into two political entities: Yogyakarta and Surakarta. Urbanism of Yogyakarta is rooted in Javanese pre-colonial spatial distribution based on the centrality of the royal palace. Until today, the city is being governed by pre-independence monarchy or sultanate. The role of the sultanate is obviously reflected in the urban development of the city (De Giosa, 2011).

The complexity and power of Javanese spiritual life and the intertwinement of politics and social integration with religion was emphasised by Clifford Geertz in his work The religion of Java. He ascribed great complexity to Javanese syncretism. Animism was the most common belief until Hinduism was brought to the island in 400 AD, followed by Islam in the fifteenth century. Thus, it can be said that integration of various mentioned elements created folk tradition of the island and basic foundation of its civilization (Geertz, 1964).

The city was founded based on principles of a sacred geography common in Southeast Asian kingdoms: the centrality of the royal palace mirrors the essential part of a mandala (De Giosa, 2011). The core of the city follows an imaginary cosmic line which links the sacred mountain located north of the city (Merapi volcano) and the Indian ocean south of the city (Ford, 1993).

Some years after the independence of Indonesia (1945-1949), Yogyakarta was the capital city of the new established nation due to the chaotic situation in Jakarta. The centrality of the sultan was in this period replaced by national centralized ideology focused on the figure of the republic's president (De Giosa, 2011).

The symbol of post-independence era is represented by the first state university, University of Gadjah Mada (UGM) built in 1949. It made Yogyakarta a national educational city, creating a new urban centre north of the palace-centred spatial distribution. Nowadays, this Javanese city has more than sixty universities and other institutions of higher education (De Giosa, 2011). One of them is the Institute of Indonesian Art (ISI), located in the south, which gives Yogyakarta's artistic reputation. Yogyakarta is namely known as a city full of underground artists of any genres, a great part of the city's identity (Setiawan, 2010).

Tensions between kampung[1] communities and capitalist-oriented urban development are slowly eroding the cultural unity of the city. The state, capitalist enterprises and the municipal government have tried to modernize the city through private housing, luxurious condominiums and shopping mall constructions. Meanwhile, hand crime, squatting, prostitution, uncontrolled expansion, water and air pollution, and low hygienic standards are occurring in more and more marginalized kampung areas (De Giosa, 2011). Modernization of the traditional city creates a new cosmos of the place, where the high and middle class lead the way and are consequently creating a new phase of symbolism (Nas, 1993b).

A symbolic dualism is represented by a tension between globalization and localization within Yogyakarta. The former is being represented by modern constructions that are taking over urban landscape, while the latter is being represented by open spaces of traditional markets and food stalls as the persisting symbols of local identity (De Giosa, 2011). The problematics of dualistic urban development is being reflected in the street art of Yogyakarta where the artists are advocating interests of kampung communities which are being influenced by considerably negative effects of modernization.

In the 1970s, Bali was the primary tourist destination, while Yogyakarta was the second region of touristic development. At first, the city attracted solely local tourists. International tourism started to emerge in the 1980s when hotels and restaurants started to be built rapidly (Hampton, 2003). A decade ago, Yogyakarta's tourism development was "bottom-up" oriented: "pro-poor" tourism was contributing to local economic development. Tourists were

---

1 Both, *kampung* or *desa*, are the names for villages throughout Indonesia. In the context of Yogyakarta they are the smallest administrative category of the city. *Kampung* is mostly used for areas within city centre and *desa* for the periphery, outside of the ring road (Anita).

mostly backpackers who had modest requirements which could be fulfilled by locals without large investments. However, the current government is encouraging "top-down" mass tourism (Hampton, 2003).

On the one hand, tourism stimulates development, but on the other hand, especially for local people, it often means destruction. Rapid growth of hotels "is changing the city's atmosphere, which is becoming counterproductive to the city's concept based on education and culture - both of them being significant elements of Yogyakarta's identity" (Digie Sigit). A local street artist, Andres, is at the same time concerned about Yogyakarta openness: "Yogyakarta receives all guests open-handedly and it does the same with foreign investors. Local people sell the land and consequently abandon farming. Yogyakarta is changing."

There are many propaganda campaigns taking actions against such phenomena. One of them is the slogan which is being included into many street art creations: "Jogja ora didol" or "Jogja not for sale". (Anita)

4. Walls and artists of Yogyakarta

It took some time for street art in Yogyakarta to start developing in the sense of street art as it appeared in New York in the 1970s. Street art in Yogyakarta is a recent phenomenon present only about for a decade. First occurrences on the walls of Yogyakarta were "vandal in their character". Those were random signs without messages, usually unreadable. Those signs were mostly tags on private surfaces and represented as an absolute contrast to today's "beautiful" murals. Afterward, graffiti started to emerge and only after graffiti did murals show up (Anita).
The beginning of street art was marked by the exhibition of murals in the garden named Suwung in 1997. The mural project was called Apotik Komik (Farhansiki). The group of comic and visual artists took over the name and started to create on the streets (Setiawan, 2010).
Street art in the city became popular after project Sama-sama. Together, a project of international exchange between artists of Yogyakarta and San Francisco was conducted in 2001. Mutual cooperation of artists in Yogyakarta brought exchange of ideas and, therefore, street art in Yogyakarta became more complex. The messages of the street art creations started to fill in primary decorative character of it (Farhansiki). The group's intention was to use art media such as mural, graffiti and comic to show their creativity on the public surfaces of the city. Their aim was to encourage the dialogue and interactions between people in urban environment (Setiawan, 2010).
Along the mentioned project, the political atmosphere of the state influenced the progress of street art. Big walls of creations talking about social-political problems started to emerge in Yogyakarta in 1998 (Lee, 2003). However, Megan Wilson, the coordinator of the above mentioned project, stated that at the time of her arrival in 2001, she could hardly find any street art (murals; Wilson, 2003).

Instead of the term mural, at the time still unknown for artist in Yogyakarta, they used the phrase *komik untuk wall* or comic for wall (Merdikaningtyas, 2006) or simply *coretan-coretan* (Farhansiki). They wanted to embellish unused and abandoned places of the city by decorating public walls. Artist and leader of Apotik Komik, Bambang Witjaksono, stated that at first the works were not considered as visual art but were solely perceived as decoration of the city (Merdikaningtyas, 2006). According to findings of Hendri Wiyanto, street art in Yogyakarta derived from comics present in Yogyakarta since the 1970s as a rebellion against high art which was including solely paintings exhibited in indoor spaces. Early street artists took the essence of comic, namely visual and story, transforming it to different variants of street art and overcoming divisions of low and high art (Wiyanto, 2015).
Since the present writing is not about categorizing street art, I should briefly mention that I have noticed two streams of movements in Yogyakarta during my field work. Firstly, the individuals with their own artist names who are following their inner inspirations based on current or past events. They go out on the streets in the middle of the night; alone or sometimes accompanied by their friends. Secondly, groups, often formed by previously mentioned individuals, whose aim is to create community based street art.
Profiles of street artists do differentiate enormously by education as well as by age. Even though, deriving from different backgrounds, the majority of them are former ISI students. Streets artists are young men; although, I was meeting female artists as well but none of them were active individually as street artist. Artists in Yogyakarta are mainly freelancers, taking temporary jobs (sometimes those come in form of street art projects). The majority of street artists are also active within music scenes, usually hardcore, metal or punk. But the art is always in the first

place, while music is treated only as a hobby. Their artist names (Anti-tank) and styles of clothing are often influenced by punk philosophy of anti-capitalism, anti-racism, and others.

Anagard, the artist-name of Andres, derives from avant-garde. He is the one who introduced Yogyakarta street art to me. He is an ISI graduate who is now constantly in contact with foreign students and takes them to places of encounters where members of street art movement are gathering: exhibitions, concerts, discussions or to his home. He took on the role of mentor to young ISI students who help him execute street art projects.
With some I associated directly, as well as with others while attending forums, discussions and other kind of gatherings. All street artists that influenced my research are predominantly socially engaged. There are two active groups which I met in the field and use street art as a medium of expression, as a part of their activities.

Firstly, Taring Padi group, which was established in 1998 when groups of young people, mostly artists, gathered with a goal to perform and increase awareness through art. The aim was to "destroy moral and social values of those in power" (Fitri). They are a group engaged in "collective art" (Ucup) whose wide range activities include music, discussions, workshops and art brought onto the streets. The group is known for its woodcut posters which are being made "while we put music on and walk barefoot on coloured woodcut to print the image on the paper" (Fitri).

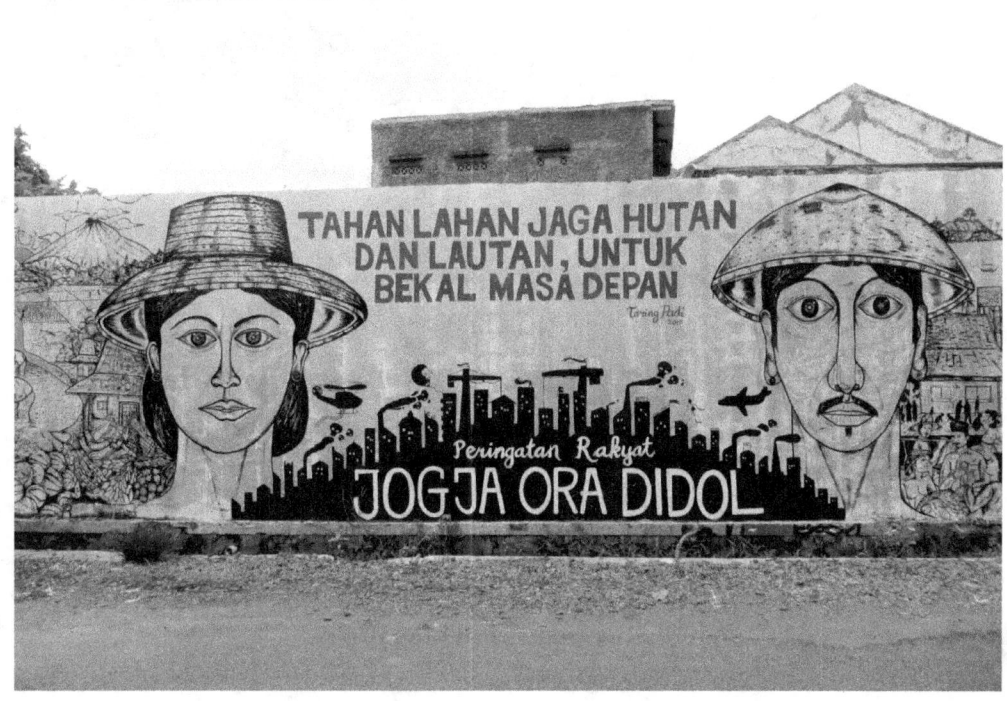

Figure 1 - Taring Padi mural: "Jogja is not for sale."
Yogyakarta, December 2015. Author: Polona Lupinšek.

Secondly, Ruang Kelas SD crew is a group of artists comprised mostly of current and former ISI students formed in 2011. They organize various street art projects; in last three years, each year they organized the community based project called Geneng street art project which involved local, *kampung* problematics, mainly abandoning agriculture. During the last project in October 2015, members of Taring Padi group painted a mural with a slogan: "The land, forest and ocean should be protected for the sake of future. Jogja is not for sale. Reminder to people." (see figure 1). The goal of such activity is "to reach the understanding of visual art, especially street art, and to stress out its criticism as well as stimulate collaboration of communities within which we live and work." (Andres). Street art is an ever changing phenomenon and its techniques are almost countless. The most common in Yogyakarta are posters, stencils and murals. The first two are widely popular because once created, they can be reproduced immediately. Posters of thin paper are being glued on the walls, previously created whether as digital design or as digitalization of photography, painting or woodcut. Stencils are cut outs being sprayed on the surface. On the other hand, it takes more time to create murals; contemporary frescoes.

I mostly followed the street artworks along the main roads near the Indonesian Institute of Arts (hereinafter ISI) in the south to the centre of the city, up to monument Tugu. Most critical and communicative street art can be found in the city centre, inside of ring road. It is concentrated along main roads, most of them at big crossroads where hot walls or *tembok panas* (Isrol) are located. Vandal signs or *coretan-coretan* in local Javanese language are present all over the city. However, the main focus stays on exposed public surfaces where the thoughts of the artist can reach wide audience.

The shift from decorative street art to the politically inspired artworks on the walls was a logical move in the grip of neoliberal economy and social turmoil of the state after the period of reformation. As an alternative communication option, street art offers a democratic arena for people (Lee, 2013).

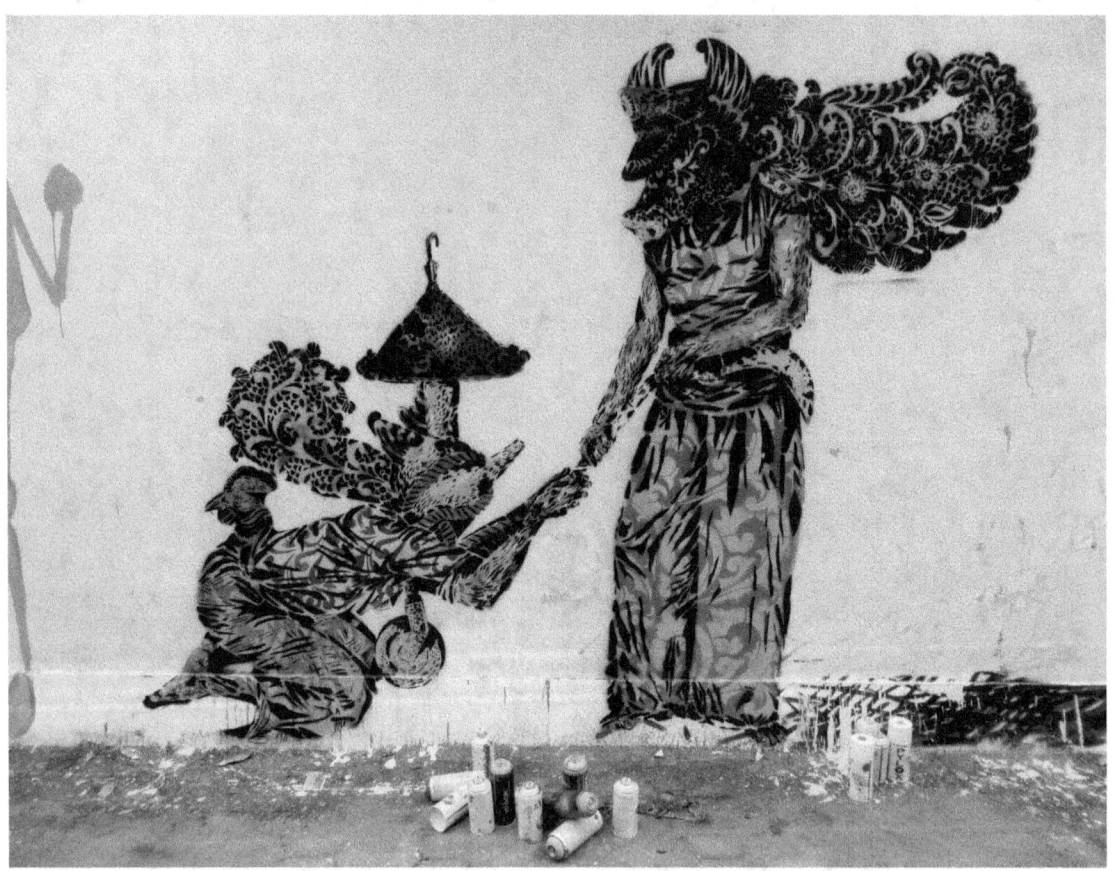

Figure 2 - Anagard's pig mouthed policeman and figure of farmer.
Yogyakarta, December 2015. Author: Polona Lupinšek.

5. Variety of messages

Sometimes messages are wrapped into decorative patterns which make the message indirect, but still stimulating critical thinking of the audience. In his distinctive style, Anagard captures animal figures in sort of batik motifs. Animalization of the figures is frequent: dogs, pigs and rats are representing symbols of avarice, greed, crime, filth and obscenity (Kiswondo, 2010). Anagard most recent creation was made at the request of the owner of Kebun Bibi art space, whose wall is now having a stencil of pig mouthed policeman who tied farmer's figure, estranging farmer's attributes through rope. The complex stencil draws attention to the decrease of agriculture on the periphery of the city (see figure 2).

Other significant messages were distributed during the parliamentary elections of 9th April 2014 and presidential elections of 9th July 2014. Politics was the main topic of conversation for more than half a year. Street artists responded greatly to the uproarious events occupying the streets of Yogyakarta in that time. Foreplays of various campaigns were trying to harangue people into voting, moreover election days were full of euphoria. Indonesian political behaviour is intense and it consists of a mass rallies, marches full of symbols of political parties accompanied by encouraging speeches resembling revolution atmosphere. The latter has little to do with tradition and derives from western political practices. Sukarno was achieving national consciousness by encouraging massive participation of citizens in political marches and parades (Anderson, 1972). This way of promotion stayed popular until this very day. Activities taking place on the streets were extremely vibrant that time: noisy motorbike parades, posters with faces of political candidates and flags in colours of political parties on the one side and critical street art works on the other.

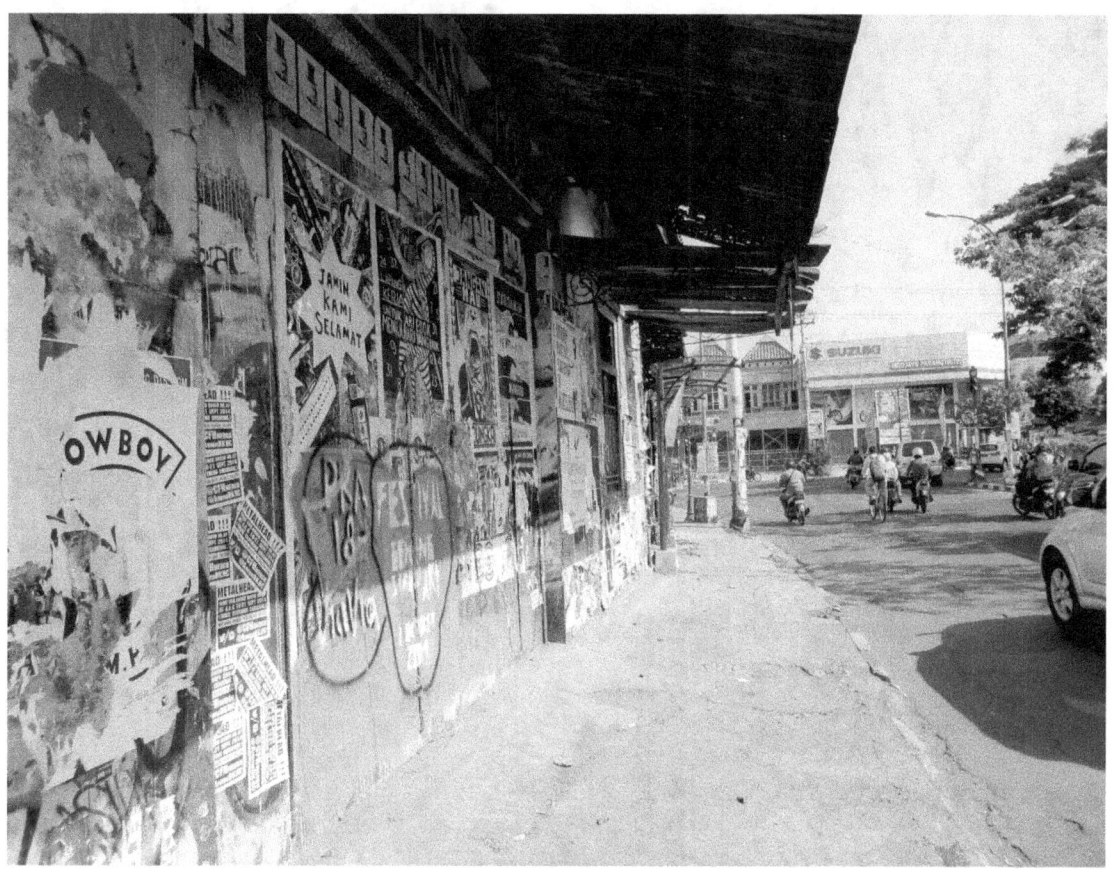

Figure 3: Hot wall Pojok Beteng Wetan full of posters.
Yogyakarta, September 2014. Author: Polona Lupinšek.

The Pojok Beteng Wetan hot wall was flooded mostly by Taring Padi posters (see figure 3). Those were reproduced woodcut prints from 2009, when the posters were initially made for educational purposes in the time of elections (Ucup). Each poster had a different slogan, one among them: "We do not need the photo of your face but a good and explicit working plan which will benefit the people, not only as a promise!!!", and another: "Natural resources are the right for all of us. Not our debt, but responsibility. Do not continue democracy which might pledge the country." (see figure 4).

Messages of street art are eminently direct when anthropological as well as artivism approaches are used. Such methodologies were used in "Jogja ora didol" street art initiative when people of different backgrounds gathered at iCAN gallery: local street artists, American high school students having an excursion and a representative of Indonesian heritage organization. They were discussing shortage of water due to rapid development of tourist infrastructure of Yogyakarta. According to the debate and previously gathered information in the affected communities they created collage street art presenting the problem. The part of it was Anti-tank's poster with motifs of mountain Merapi and monument Tugu Golong-giling which represents Javanese unity, accompanied with slogan: "Jogja speciality – hotels." (see figure 5). The poster is still being distributed to different parts of the city.

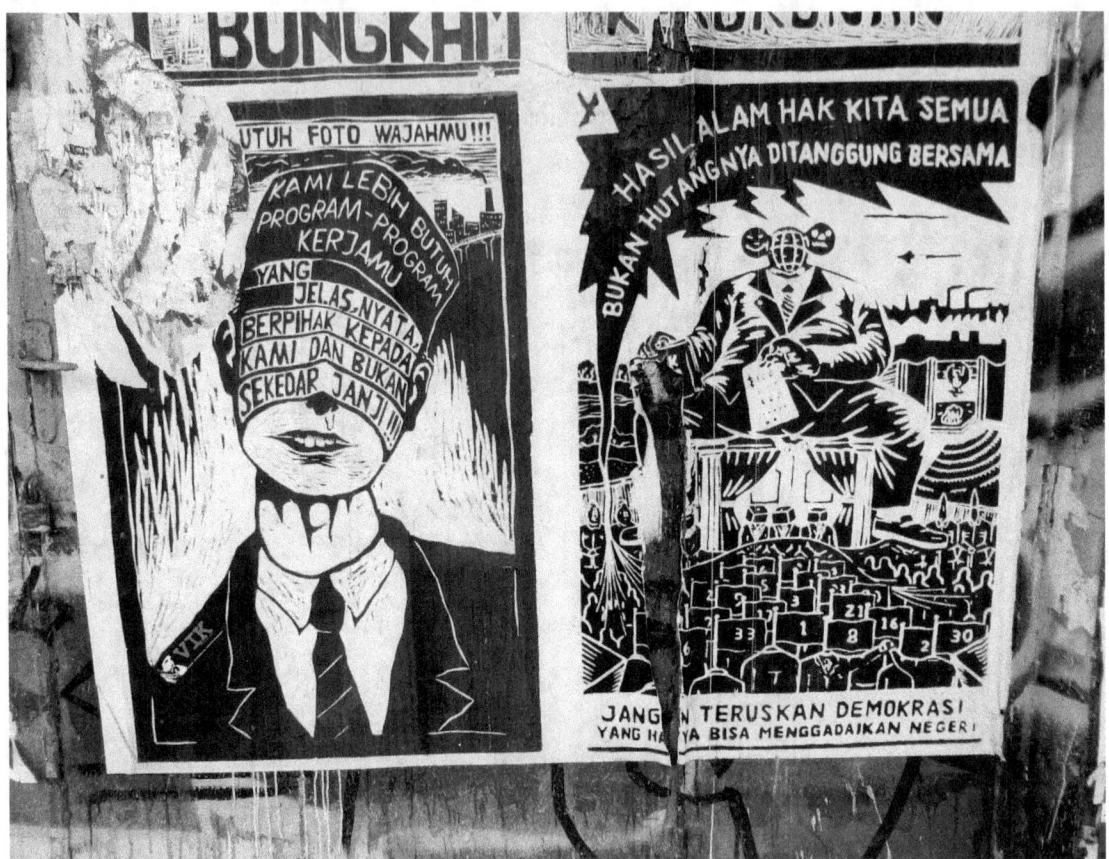

Figure 4 - Black and white Taring Padi posters. Yogyakarta, July 2014. Author: Polona Lupinšek.

On field the street artist meet the reality of everyday life. Given that they are working on a local level they are easily accepted by people, furthermore, sometimes they are part of these communities. The latter makes them even more engaged: "Because of the city's bad governance, people fight over basic life needs. Before, water was something that connected poor and rich, but now it represents a luxury available only to the rich and an unreachable commodity for the poor. I wish people would became aware of this problem. I want to expose it in order to speed-up the search for solutions." (Digie Sigit)

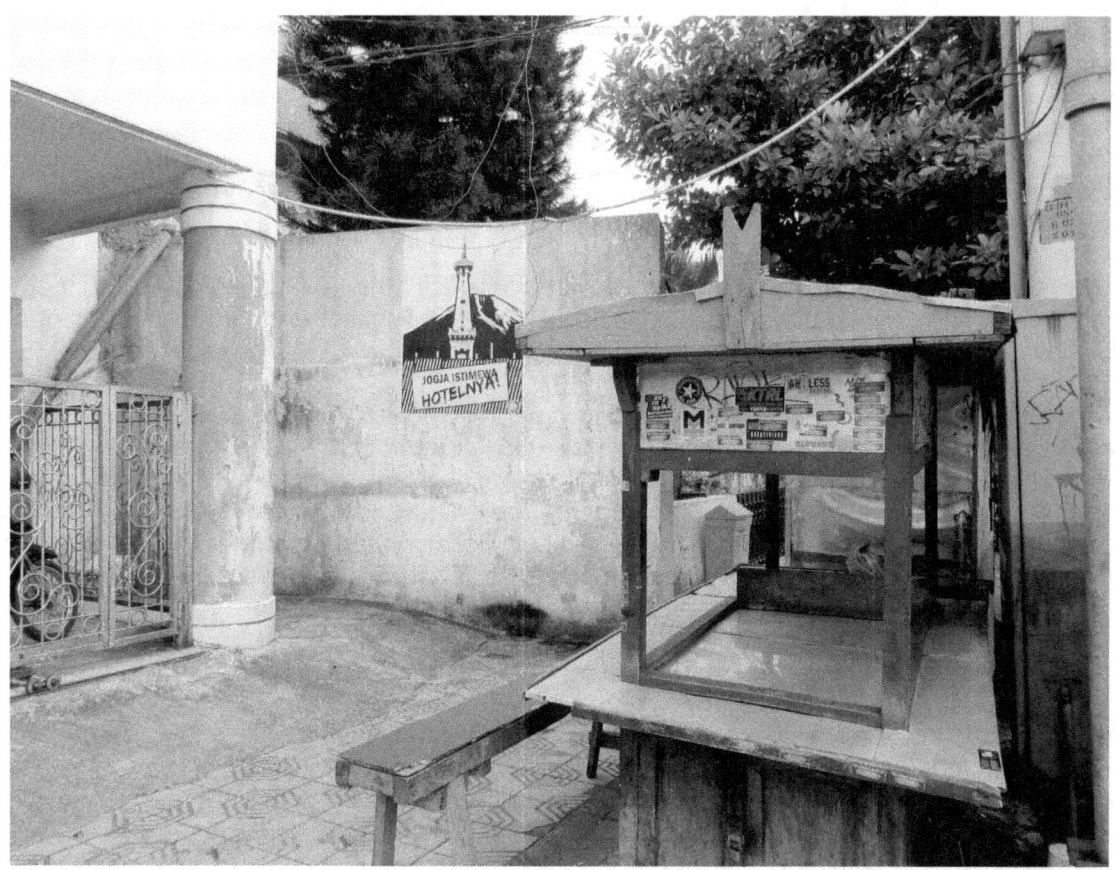

Figure 5 - Anti-tank poster. Yogyakarta, December 2015. Author: Polona Lupinšek.

6. Conclusion: From people to people

Based on the research of development of mural art within local communities in Durban, South African Sabine Marschall concludes that mural occasionally works as an initiator of social and political changes. At the same time, she emphasizes that actual changes happen rarely. She notifies that the presence of street art along with the collaboration of artists with local communities is resulting in various benefits such as providing social awareness and social criticism, strengthening the identity of community, encouraging social actions. It works as a medium of expression for a particular community and contributes to the development of artistic and creative skills of people involved, through which they can potentially improve the quality of their lives. It also empowers socially neglected groups and reduces violence (Marschall, 1999).

Benefits of street art are visible at different mutually interlinked levels. Those are visual, social-political, cultural and economic benefits deriving from street art activities that contribute to the people of the city, even though, all of them are not equally represented.

The most prominent benefits in Yogyakarta are social-political ones, which mainly occurred as an aftermath of street art projects that could be called collective art projects. They were undertaken in certain parts of the city, usually within one *kampung* or *desa*.
Within the framework of these projects, various local communities were involved in the process of artwork creation. While some participated in technical implementation such as contacting people and acquiring permissions, others were participating in the creation of the artwork itself (contributing ideas as well as at the application of the work on the wall).

At this point, I want to expose the achievement of recruiting a young generation of ISI students into street art circles by Andres, who thinks they should spend their free time more creatively. During the process of creation they were somehow forced to think about society that surrounds them, as well as they were collaborating with seniors of street art movement in Yogyakarta. This is collaborative art, which is also the essence of Taring Padi activities that include not only artists but also people without artistic background and skills. The latter is not important; the process of creating art is at stake here while the final product is put aside.

During creative process people are being confronted with problems of their everyday life to which they might not give constructive criticism nor do they search for solutions. Creating forces them to think about it, although, only for the duration of the project or until the visualization does not fade away.

The involvement of people in the process of creating along with the street artists "mentorship" contribution offers new perspectives to the artwork interpretation. Often the slogans accompanying images are written in English, thus, incomprehensible to the people. Besides they often do not go into details of artwork and they see it solely as decorative or vandal intervention. It can be concluded that Yogyakarta street art members mostly offer awareness through the process of art creation and less awareness solely through artworks themselves. Particularly, street art creations in the time of elections were expressing strong social criticism and pressure people to take actions. Interestingly, not much response was given and works stayed uncensored.

Collaborative art creation offers people a new way of communication through which they can express their problems as well as expose their advantages, their local traits and values. Such expression strengthens the pride in their own culture which is often being scorned when compared with the West. The latter is clearly a great contribution to the cultural level: the identity of the communities and consequently, the identity of the city is being strengthened. Furthermore, it can be said that street art stimulates *genius loci* of the city. In Yogyakarta, where the preference is given to traditional art, street art is a promotion of contemporary visual art.
To a visual level, street art contributes with vividness, which makes the urban landscape of Yogyakarta interesting and attractive. Particularly due to decorative visualizations, physical environment is becoming more human-friendly and beautifies the neighbourhoods through creative processes.

Yogyakarta is getting an artistic image which is being used as one of the leading elements in the development of the city. This is the contribution in terms of strengthening Yogyakarta's "brand" of artistic city which contributes to the development of tourism. To some extent this is an indirect economic contribution of street art. Likewise, the economic benefit is also partial financial income of the artists. Those are gained by selling their merchandise or raising funds for their projects. Nevertheless, economic benefits are not strongly represented especially due to the lack of dialogue between artists and urban developers such as architects, landscapists, and others. No concrete collaboration has been noticed.

It seems that economic benefits are the effects of others: social-political, cultural and visual. While in other western cities public art policies have been implemented, Yogyakarta has not come to that point yet. This might be because street art in the city is a relatively recent phenomenon and, therefore, authorities have not recognized it as a vital element of the city so far. For this reason street art stays "illegal-free" and as such, the significant element of urban landscape. Using participatory approaches, the interactions between artists and their environment has been stimulated. Through such street art activities, local, national and global problems are being recognized. In conclusion, street art stays one of the rarest critical factors which publicly speaks about the issues of the city as well as of the whole country nowadays. Ultimately, art is being used as a vehicle and a tool for messaging about social, economic and political injustices.

References

Adaby Darban, A. *et al.* (2004). *Kraton Yogyakarta: The history and cultural heritage.* Jakarta: Karaton Ngayogya-karta Hadiningrat in Indonesia Marketing Association.

Anderson, B. R. O'G (1972). The idea of power in Javanese culture. In C. Holt (Ed.), *Culture and politics in Indonesia* (pp.1-70). Ithaca in London: Cornell University Press.

Aragon, V. L. (2014). Law Versus Lore: Copyright and Conflicting Claims about Culture and Property in Indonesia. *Anthropology Today, 30*(5), 15-19.
doi: 10.1111/1467-8322.12132

Aragon, V. L. & Leach, J. (2008). Arts and Owners: Intellectual Property Law and the Politics of Scale in Indonesian Arts. *American Ethnologist, 35*(4), 607-631.
doi: 10.1111/j.1548-1425.2008.00101.x

Brown, C. (2003). *A short history of Indonesia: The unlikely nation?* Australia: Allen and Unwin.

De Giosa, P. (2011). Urban symbolism in Yogyakarta: In search of lost symbol. In P. Nas (Ed.), *Cities full of symbols: A theory of urban space and culture* (pp. 85-106). Leiden: Leiden University Press.

Ford, R. L. (1993). Model of Indonesian City Structure. *Geographical Review, 83*(4), 374-396.
doi: 10.2307/215821

Gell, A. (1998). *Art and agency: An anthropological theory.* Oxford: Oxford University Press.

Geertz, C. (1964). *The religion of Java.* New York: Free Press of Glencoe; London: Collier-Macmillan.

Hampton, P. M. (2003). Entry Points for Local Tourism in Developing Countries: Evidence from Yogyakarta, Indonesia. *Geografiska Annaler. Series B, Human Geography, 85*(2), 85–101.
doi: 10.1111/1468-0467.00133

Hilal, A., Wardhani, F. (Producer) & Merdikaningtyas, Y. A. (Director) (2006). *Yogyakarta berhati mural.* Yogyakarta-Indonesia: Indonesian Visual Art Archive.

Jakob, K. (2008). *Street art in Berlin.* Berlin: Jaron Verlag GmbH.

Jelesijević, N. (2008). Javna umetnost pod represijo: Je javna umetnost sploh možna? *Časopis za kritiko znanosti, domišljijo in novo antropologijo, 16*(233), 201–207.

Kiswondo (2011). Half-Man-Half-Dog iconography: Antimilitarism campaign in the artworks of Taring Padi. In A. Yunanto & Hae, Z. (Eds.), *Taring Padi: Art Smashing Tyranny* (pp. 41-76).Yogyakarta: Lumbung Press.

Laine, A. (2009). Complementarity between Art and Anthropology: Experiences among Kolam Markers in South India. *Suomen Antropologi: Journal of the Finnish Anthropological Society*, 34(2), 58–69.

Lee, D. (2013). "Anybody Can Do It": Aesthetic Empowerment, Urban Citizenship, and the Naturalization of Indonesian Graffiti and Street Art. *City & Society*, 25(3), 304–327.
doi: 10.1111/ciso.12024

Lunn, M. J. (2006). *Street art uncut.* Singapore: Craftsman House

Marschall, S. (1999). A Critical Investigation into the Impact of Community Mural Art. *Transformation,* (40), 54–86.

Morphy, H. & Perkins, M. (2006). The anthropology of art: A reflection on its history and contemporary practice. In H. Morphy & M. Perkins (Eds.), *The anthropology of art: A reader* (pp. 1-32). Oxford: Blackwell Publishing Ltd.

Milkovič-Biloslav, G. (2008). Kriminalizacija grafitov v tujini in doma. *Časopis za kritiko znanosti, domišljijo in novo antropologijo*, 36(321–232), 241–250.

Nas, P. J. M. (1993a). Introduction. In P. J. M. Nas (Ed.), *Urban symbolism* (pp.1-12). Leiden; New York; Köln: Brill.

Nas, P. J. M. (1993b). Jakarta, city full of symbols: An essay in symbolic ecology. In P. J. M. Nas (Ed.), *Urban symbolism* (pp.13-37). Leiden; New York; Köln: Brill.

Nas, P. J. M., de Groot, M. & Schut, M. (2011). Introduction: Variety of symbols. In P. J. M. Nas (Ed.), *Cities full of symbols: A theory of urban space and culture* (pp. 7-26). Leiden: Leiden University Press.

Repič, J. (2012). Umetnost, urbanost in diaspora: Kulturni center Museo conventillo Marjan Grum v Buenos Airesu. In J. Repič & J. Hudales, J. (Eds.), *Antropološki vidiki načinov življenja v mestih* (pp. 211-230). Ljubljana: Znanstvena založba Filozofske fakultete.

Velikonja, M. (2008). Politika z zidov: Zagate z ideologijo v grafitih in street artu. *Časopis za kritiko znanosti,* 36(231–232), 25–32.

Sandoval, C. & Latorre, G. (2008). Chicana/o artivism: Judy Baca's digital work with youth of color. In A. Everett (Ed.), *Learning race and ethnicity: Youth and digital media* (pp.81-108). Cambridge, MA: The MIT Press.

Setiawan, T. (2010). *Role of public art in urban environment: A case study of mural art in Yogyakarta city* (Unpublished master's thesis.) International institute of urban management of Erasmus University Rotterdam, Rotterdam, The Netherlands.

Wilson, M. (2003). Two communities and beyond. In A. Noble (Ed.), *Sama sama/Together: An international exchange project between Yogyakarta - San Francisco* (pp.4-10). Yogyakarta: Jam Karet Press.

Wiyanto, H. (2015). Yogyakarta Agropop, culture & identity. In F. Oktanio (Ed.), *Look out below* (pp. 58-97). Yogyakarta-Indonesia: Srisasanti Syndicate.

N/A (2013). *Seeing Paintings: Conversations Before the End of History* (Text at exhibition of contemporary art at Art Space – Yogyakarta).

Chapter 9

Urban Visuality through Stencil

Rachel Souza

Abstract

This article examines common understandings of the aesthetic elements that arise in the execution of stenciling as a public art form. In this way, the article investigates the aesthetics and semiotic dynamics of stenciling within the public environment. The text uses urban visuality as an entry point to further explore the city as collage and the stencil artist as a bricoleur. Furthermore, the text identifies two sign-like elements of the stencil's insertion in the city: symbolic overloads, and the resignification of symbolic aggregations.

Keywords: Stencil; Aesthetics; Public Art; Semiotics.

1. Urban Visuality

Layers of information – materialized in graffiti, stencils, posters, stickers, and tagging – overlap on boundary walls, public walls, and private walls. These objects, and these surfaces, are disposed to circulate through the city, infuriating those who cry out for the courts, for the police, for the right to property, and for "cleanliness." All of these elements are components of an urban visual structure: they define the appearance of a city, along with advertisement campaigns, street signs, ever more vertical buildings, passersby, streets, cars, and all other kinds of vehicles. The production of images takes place through this dynamic of interaction, contextualizing the society into which the images insert themselves.

"The images disseminated in our cities are bound to our reality – whether the reality is that we are consumers (advertisements), we have laws (road signs) or that we rebel (graffiti)." (Waclawek, 2011: p158). In other words, urban visuality is composed of passersby, of the intermittent flow of people in a quotidian ballet, both in terms of this ballet itself, and in terms of what effects it causes. Understanding the visuality of the city, therefore, means understanding this conjuncture: the urban dynamic.

We can say that urban flow produces a visuality like that of an ephemeral and unstoppable collage, in that it allows for the occasional joining together of people within the constant transit of the fabric of urban life. Stenciling both inserts itself into and arises from this dynamic. The ambience of the city dictates the ephemeral and anonymous structure of stenciling, in which information – despite being affixed to the city's walls – does not remain, or else does not maintain its original meaning. The city is a space of dislocation and communication, a place in which layers of information overlap, and in which the anonymous makes itself structurally present. The Brazilian anthropologist Janice Caiafa examines relationship dynamics and the transmission of knowledge in cities in her article "Comunicação e Diferença nas Cidades" ("Communication and Difference in Cities"). On the experience of urban life, Caiafa writes:

> Urban recodification [occurs through] the marks that form (and that present, delimit, and arrange hierarchically), [and that are] are constantly redistributed, because the city does not stop receiving other flows that modify its social and physical space. Therefore, the city continuously transforms and reproduces itself through these marks. (Caiafa, 2003: 92).

The constant transit of people generally unknown to each other within the fabric of the city – with a degree of absolutely trivial contact – is the principal characteristic of urban life. This flow presents these unknown identities with the opportunity to establish some sort of social relationship through their experiences on the street. The street, therefore, is a space for contact between strange subjectivities, and for connections between distinct worlds. It allows for brief contact between people who, were it not for the random chance typical of urban encounters, might never meet. Caiafa refers to this public contact as the agency of "strange worlds." She writes:

> The possibility of being affected by strangers is a mark of urban life, an imposition or an opportunity in the spaces of big cities. Communication always involves differentiation, and always brings together or creates strange worlds…[Thus,] the experience of the strange and unexpected is a mark of cities: it is what characterizes cities as singular universes of circulation and communication. (*Ibid*: p91)

However, Caiafa notes, "cities also promote integration (they are not only dispersed)." (*Ibid*: p92).

Urban visuality is the product of this relationship made possible by urban life, a relationship in which subjective exchanges take place through superficiality and through a degree of anonymity in a space of dislocation and communication with constantly overlapping layers of information (as mentioned in the beginning of the chapter). This visuality presents a characteristic of molding the encounters between "strange worlds." It, in and of itself, is the product of the articulation of strange elements. In this sense, we can compare urban visuality to the artistic practice of collage, in which integration occurs not through similitude, but rather through difference: through the grouping and arrangement of heterogeneous elements.

2. Collage

In considering stenciling within the context of urban visuality, it seems pertinent to present central aspects of collage as an artistic practice, so as to understand more amply certain characteristics of collage, and to allow for a study of the aesthetic of stenciling.

Vitor Iwasso attributes our contemporary relationship with images to technology and democratization; he sees collage and the use of technology as multifaceted, interconnected ways of living. In his introduction to an article about collage, Iwasso describes a scene from *Artaud Double Bill,* a 2007 film by the Canadian filmmaker Atom Egoyan. In the scene, a woman enters a cinema in which Godard's *My Life to Live* is about to begin screening. The woman sits and begins to send messages on her smartphone, while a second woman in the next projection room watches another film. There is a cut to a third projection room in which a third woman watches a third film. The first woman plugs in her phone, films the projection, and sends it to the second woman. In the following shot, the images being filmed on the second woman's phone appear, overlapping with images from the other film . According to Iwasso,

…the banal character of the actions seen throughout the short film show how a series of procedures that were previously restricted to a specialized universe have been amply integrated into our everyday life with the advent of new technologies, thereby significantly transforming our perception. (Iwasso, 2010: p40).

The historical rise of collage reflected a new subjectivity, itself the product of an era of industry and mass culture. The technique, like others throughout the history of art, was a reflection of cultural changes such as the acceleration of time, the mass production of objects, and the necessity of transporting these objects in what was then an incipient industrial society. The acceleration and flow of information through images in this vaunted era of technological reproduction also extends to mass-produced images, since "the development of collage as an artistic process establishes, since its beginnings, a narrow link to the industrial universe; and, in a more profound way, to the graphic arts, the category responsible for the production of visual information." (*Ibid*: p43). Artists work with this excess by reprocessing available printed material, and by appropriating parts of existing images so as to construct new ones.

Collage, in the most ample sense of the term, is not only a technique and a formal solution; it is also a process, a mode of operating through selection, appropriation, and recontextualization. Iwasso aims to redefine the term; he writes:

> I risk defining a first possible path toward "updating" collage in today's art. Here, I refer to works of art constructed through large-scale bricolage, [works] that extrapolate the shuffling categories that *Combine Paintings* evoked by creating physical and affective characteristics of objects in space. (*Ibid*: p47).

Sérgio Lima says that collage corresponds to the "exploration of a new syntax through the cutting of previously known images. As Max Ernst says, it is not the glue [*cola*] that makes the collage." (Lima, 1984: p29). Lima offers several examples of the use of collage in visual arts, including collage "as graphics: the graffiti scrawled in certain public bathroom; the sayings of May 1968 scribbled in sentences and images on the walls of Paris, etc." (*ibid*: p22-23). We can deduce that Lima understands collage as the juxtaposition of elements in an ample way. He applies collage to an expanded field, or as he would put it, an expanded visual language.

> Visual language extends itself in a way that, by definition, is loving: it understands its object and its transformation. In other words, it understands the dialectic of the thing itself, in and of itself, of its identity and invocation (as image). This allows for its symbolic reproduction, the production of the imaginary and, through this impassioned choice, its recognition. The gaze establishes the cut as a dialogic dynamic that articulates its expression, in which one element comments on, criticizes, and completes the other, rather than as a potentially linear reading of its materials transformed –by definition – into elements. (*Ibid*: p280).

Although the historical aspect referred to by Lima is not necessary to our discussion here, it is worth noting that, historically, collage is an old technique, but also that it took on more importance in the visual arts through the Cubist movement.

> It is an undisputed point, regardless of one's analysis, to declare the invention of collage in the first decade of the twentieth century as a fundamental step in the history of Western art. It is catalyzing action for infinite other investigations that, with their diverse propositions, permeate the modern avant-garde. (Iwasso, 2010: p40).

Stenciling is not a collage technique: it is a technique of graphic reproduction, with a master image and copies derived from that master. What brings stenciling close to collage is the result of the practice of stenciling as public art. Collage is implicit to the practice and visuality of stenciling on the street, where stencils are juxtaposed with other elements. Posters; other artworks; visual debris; and the material wearing down of surfaces, among other elements, form a cut-up and fragmented visuality. Stencils have the potential to adhere to a "neutral" place, but there are two reasons why this generally does not occur:

Finding a surface in the city without any other visual information or other vestiges is a very difficult task, given that the city itself is a system of information.

Urban artists work on the principle of communicating with and appropriating signs in order to construct their own signs. This dialogue is constructed with whatever these artists find on the surfaces where they choose to create work. Collage is therefore implicit to the choice of space.

3. The Stencil Artist as Bricoleur

Collage is similar to the stenciling as public art both because of its related aesthetic results and also because of the implications that it raises, as well as the characteristics of its emergence. Collage emerged in response to the excessive industrial super-production of images; it brings together material and information that have already been produced, instead of producing material and information in order to bring them together. For its part, the practice of street stenciling takes place through the sum of available visual productions. In choosing a place that best serves the information to be presented – according to the criteria that each artist establishes individually – stencil artists adds another layer of information to those that already exist. This occurs not only in terms of the material elements of a given wall, but also in terms of the urban visual structure composed of buildings, passersby, and advertisements.

All of the experiences that take place within a city – and those that the city causes to take place – produce images. Therefore, they also produce an aesthetic result. On the basis of this relationship, which forms urban visuality – and which is formed of heterogeneous fragments of images, of which the art produced in urban contexts is one – one can see bricolage as a form of understanding urban settings and their complexities. Social bricolage is defined as an arrangement of heterogeneous fragments, with the aim of creating synthetic unity, such as in the creation of work based on a diversified gamut of objects. It is an ample concept, coined by Claude Lévi-Strauss, and it is through his work that the concept of bricolage first took on theoretical relevance.

Lévi-Strauss differentiates mythical thought (which he refers to as "the savage mind") from scientific thought, thereby establishing a discussion about the perception and organization of forms of thought. Mythical – or mytho-poetic – thought is constructed through narratives and metaphors, while scientific thought is that which works through relationships conceptually. Lévi-Strauss contrasts these two forms of thought and identifies a structure in mythic thinking that he calls bricolage. This term emerges as a designation for "spontaneous action" based on a form of thought linked to action without abstraction; it is a method of organizing thought paved with metaphors and mythologies. The object of scientific thought is conceptual: the systemization of sensitive data with epistemic ends. In contrast, mythic thought concerns itself with practical order; it groups sensitive data empirically, based on experience. Here, "mythic" thought can be understood as "common knowledge" that organizes information without analytical concerns. However, Lévi-Strauss also identifies a organizing structure for these empirical forms of knowledge when he states that "[m]agical thought is not to be regarded as a beginning, a rudiment, a sketch, a part of a whole which has not yet materialized. It forms a well-articulated system, and is in this respect independent of that other system which constitutes science." (Lévi-Strauss, 1966: p13) Bricolage takes place by chance, through chance encounters between different forms of information:

because what [the "savage" set of tools] contains bears no relation to the current project, or indeed to any particular project, but is the contingent result of all the occasions there have been to enrich or renew the stock or to maintain it with the remains of previous constructions or destructions. (*ibid*: p17)

Bricolage refers, as well, to the juncture of various elements towards the formation of a unique and individualized whole. When Lévi-Strauss appropriates the term, he explains that the French verb *bricoler* is traditionally used when talking about "billiards…hunting, shooting, and riding," as it refers to "some extraneous movement: a ball rebounding, a dog straying or a horse swerving from its direct course to avoid an obstacle." (*ibid*, 16)

Bricolage, like the dynamic of urban visual structure, brings together previously produced information and materials, rather than producing them to later bring them together intentionally. It is also like artists who, by choosing a place that best expresses their information according to their own criteria, add a layer of information to pre-existing information. Artists' thinking is not only oriented towards choices regarding the place that best dialogues with the concept of their work, but also with the aesthetic results of this choice. An artist whose choices are based on visuality reflects back on urban bricolage. The bricoleur as Lévi-Strauss original Brazilian translators, Almir de Oliveira Aguiar and Maria Celeste de Costa e Souza explain:

> is someone who carries out a work using means and expedients that denounce the absence of a preconceived plan, and that remove themselves from the processes and norms of a given technique. A bricoleur is characterized especially by the fact of working with fragmentary materials that have already been elaborated. (Lévi-Strauss 1989: p32).

By analogy, and following this line of reasoning, we can say that stencil artists are bricoleurs, given that they do not define precisely what they will find in the places where they work, or which elements they will utilize in order to compose a complete work. Improvising and working with the unforeseen play significant roles in stencil artists' ephemeral dynamic, and in the lack of a guarantee for their works' maintenance. Urban artists work with overlapping, with the spontaneous juxtaposition of works of art, as well as with the works' disposal within a dynamic in which many artists erase the work of others.

The improvisation related to the creative use of available resources and materials is a method, a structure of thought through which the visuality of the artistic object makes itself manifest. Public art must necessarily relate to questions of locality in dealing with an environment that is not a white cube, but rather a street where the walls are already replete with meanings. There are aesthetic questions that apply specifically to this condition of public art, of which the role of bricolage as a method inherent to public art is especially noteworthy. As I have already discussed, stencils are instruments in consonance with contemporary urban ways of life; therefore, stenciling proposes a dialogic relationship grounded in urban time and in the speed of contemporary urban connections. This form of dialogue finds its aesthetic materialization in bricolage. The relationships constructed in the space-time of the streets are similarly based in material and visual bricolage. The information that streets carry with them may be reorganized through public art. There is no doubt that when artists bring their work to the streets, they are not proposing signs, but rather rearticulating the signs that surround their work. This process occurs even without the artists' intent, by the simple fact of inserting new signs into an urban system of information, signs that enter into dialogue with the place.

4. Stencil Aesthetics

A work of art conceived for traditional means of circulation ought to be determined by its chosen limits of physical support. But for stencils, and for urban art in general, the artist's references are not based only on this physical support. Instead, stencil artists must carry out a re-articulation of signs, completing their work with whatever is available in the area that surrounds its execution. This re-articulation can take two forms: it may occur through symbolic overload, or through the resignification of symbolic conjunctures.

4.1. Symbolic Overload

"Symbolic overload" refers here to the aesthetic result composed by a work of art in dialogue with the space onto which it has been superimposed. In symbolic overload, layers of signs accumulate and affirm the fragmentation of prepared elements while clashing among themselves. All of the stencils featured here are bricolages, in that they are overloaded with symbols of everyday visuality.

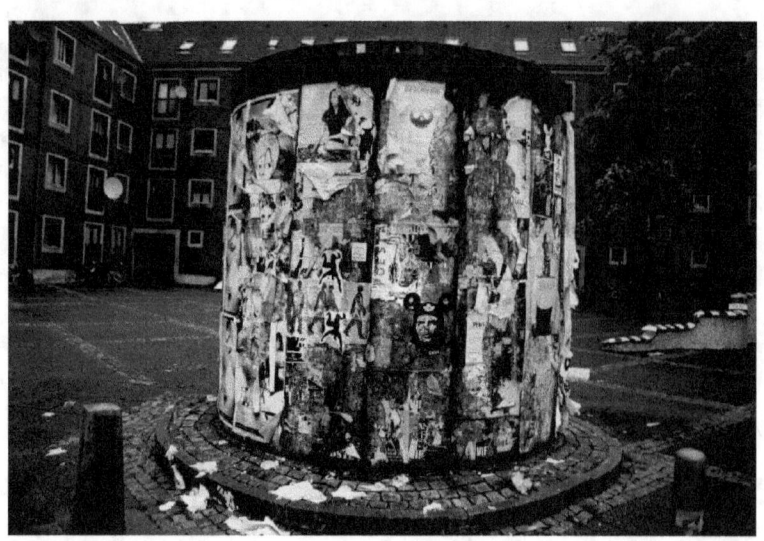

Figure 1 - **Ozi Duarte** e **Celso Gitahy**'s work featured among other urban works.

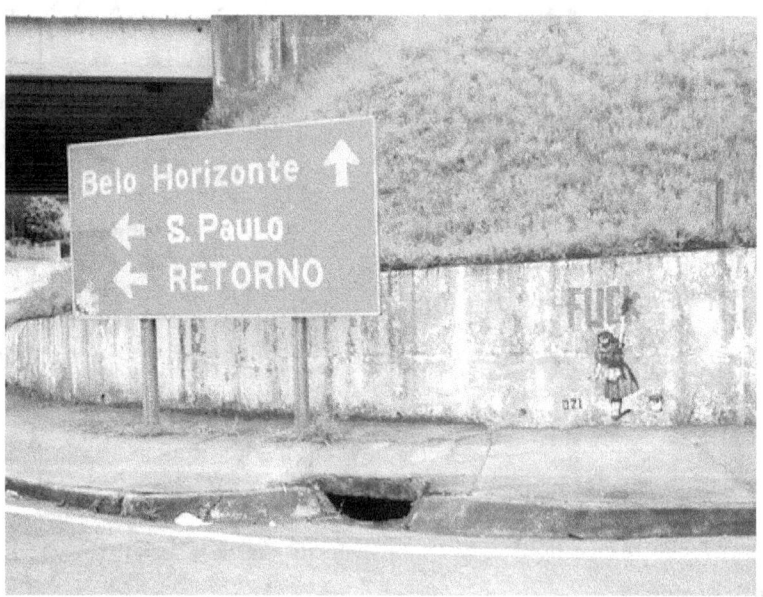

Figure 2 - **Ozi**, *Vandalice*, São Paulo, Brazil.

Artistic practice in the streets, as I have already mentioned, involves joining images together on a surface so as to establish dialogue. At times, this takes place not only through the location of a given work, or through the fact of a work being placed on the street, but also through the juxtaposition of different elements. In the first image above, many different aesthetic elements join to compose a consonant visuality: a stencil of a fragile girl in a situation of apparent danger; the remnants of an advertisement for a reggae festival; the shreds of various surrounding papers; as well as surrounding phrases and tags. Even though each element may well have been placed separately, in a distinct moment, the results of these placements compose a visual unity, since the visual elements – in shades of black and white – are practically duotone. In the next image, the work of the artists Celso Gitahy and Ozi Duarte mix with the vestiges of other materials. We can perceive that the above images are juxtaposed because various layers of visual information compose the meaning and visuality of the stencil. This aesthetic is marked by the composition of the work in relation to its environment, a junction that takes place chaotically: it presents a symbolic overload, the effect of which affirms its fragmentation. Ozi's *Vandalice* – a subversive parody of Lewis Carroll's *Alice's Adventures in Wonderland* – is inserted near a sign that shows the possible routes available to

118

those passing through by car. Meanwhile, a girl – symbolizing sweetness and innocence – writes, at the edge of a highway sign, a message that clashes with these adjectives; she proposes an idea of nihilism and disillusion, as though the direction to be chosen had no importance. It is an image that counteracts the childlike universe of the character of Alice, as well as the meaning of an everyday, utilitarian symbol. The dialogic possibilities that stencils carry as public art materialize in these artworks, as well as in those shown below:

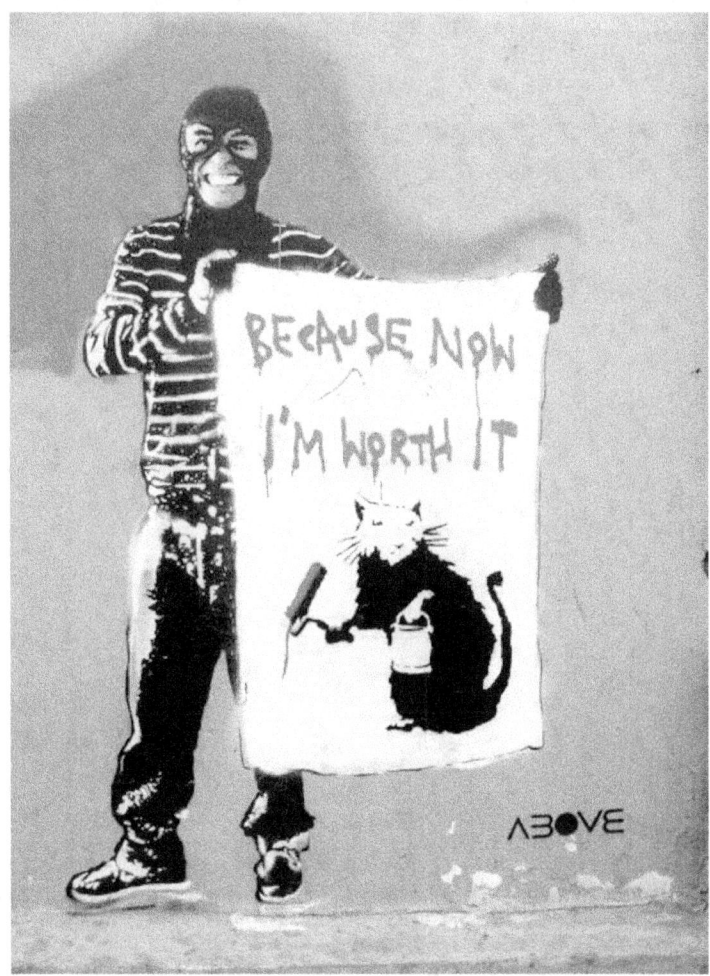

Figure 3 - **Above**, *Because Now I'm Worth It,* Paris, France, 2010

The principal aspect of this artwork is to satirize the commodification and valorization of urban art, and to comment on the dynamic of validation within the art market. In the stencil, a thief steals a public work made by Bansky, the famous English artist. The phrase "Because Now, I'm Worth It" is clearly an ironic commentary on the tension that Banksy represents: namely, the inclusion of graffiti in the art market, and the values attaches to such works. Here, stenciling in and of itself serves as symbolic overload, as it groups together disparate information in order to form semiotic unity, based on the strange interplay between the diverse elements it presents. These elements include one of Banksy's public artworks, featuring his iconic mouse and a sentence – supposedly written by Banksy himself – symbolizing the recognition of his artistic and financial value; a thief using gloves and a mask that impede his identification, smiling in commemoration of his success in stealing a valuable art work; and the wall of the urban environment. The work itself presents meaningful symbolic layers and, when it is shown on the street, these layers are not only subject to the addition of other elements; they also contextualize, semiotically, the environment in which they originated. The situation that the stencil proposes runs counter to the universe of public art. The irony it presents stems from the image of the thief, from the mouse's consciousness of its value as an object of art, and from the sentence that explains the meaning of the work.

The graffiti artist Blek Le Rat made a stencil (**Blek le Rat,** *Florence Aubenas*, Paris, France, 2005) in response to the kidnapping of Florence Aubenas, a French journalist, in Baghdad. During the 151 days that Aubenas was missing in Iraq, the artist Blek Le Rat spread images of her in strategic points throughout Paris, both as an appeal and, paradoxically, as a form of marking her absence. This stencil is located directly under a street sign; it is therefore guaranteed to draw attention. The stencil, like the fountain in the center of the photograph, the wall on which the work is placed, and the people and the cars passing by, inserts itself as another object composing urban visuality. Here, there is no semiotic resignification, but rather one more data point in a system of information.

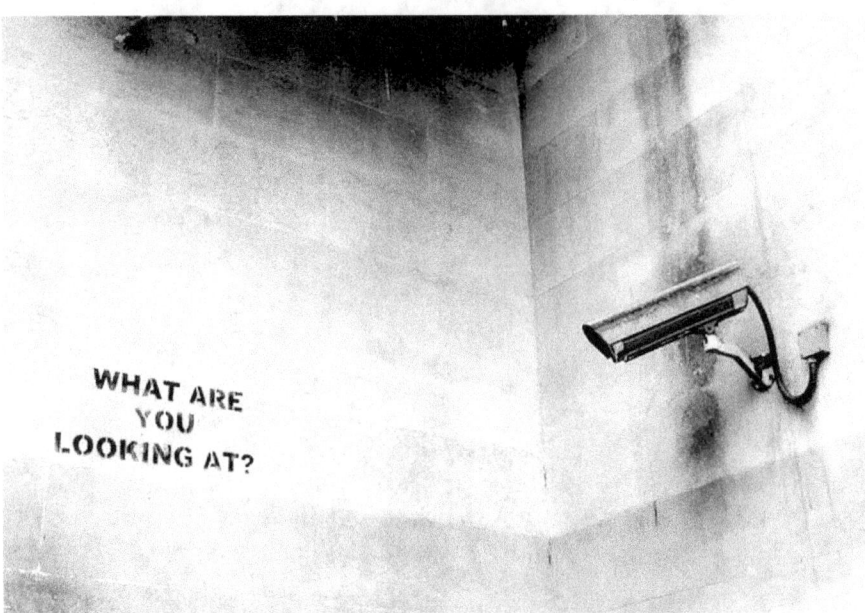

Figure 4 - **Bansky**. *"What Are You Looking At?"* London, UK, 2005

Here, Banksy places the question "What Are You Looking At?" in front of a security camera, commenting on the contemporary excess of vigilance and monitoring. Proportionally, the United Kingdom is the country with the greatest number of security cameras in the world; in London alone, there are close to 10,000 cameras installed in public areas. Under the pretext of policing the city so as to reduce and prevent criminality, this vigilance becomes a tool of indiscriminate social control that hinders citizens from exercising their freedom. This security instrument observes local social dynamics so as to control them more thoroughly. Yet here, instead of carrying out its objective, the camera serves to contextualize Banksy's protest. Therefore, different layers overlap, different signs that seem strange taken together, given that Banksy's addition opposes and confronts the element of governmental order. The symbolism of the camera at work is juxtaposed with the addition of the stencil that directly questions its social function. The scene is composed of symbolic overloads, juxtaposing the elements of camera, wall, stencil, and the passersby who motivate all of the movement. Banksy's sentence is an element that deconstructs the camera by questioning it.

4.2. The Resignification of Symbolic Conjunctures
A stencil can insert itself into the urban environment as one more sign, causing existing signs to overflow (as we have seen above); or it can be inserted in a manner that resignifies existing signs. This second type of stencil symbolizes the insertion of elements that rearticulate the meaning of an original sign. The new sign that a stencil proposes enters into a direct dialogue with its environment, highlighting the meaning that is already imposed on its locale. It does not add another layer of information beyond what has already been established; instead, it resignifies the existing context. In this sense, it is like an extra electrical plug imposed on a highway, emphasizing

the character of connection that the highway already possesses, or like a passerby who occasionally encounters another, as occurs every day in a city.

Figure 5 - **Roadsworth,** *Male Plug,* Canada

Figure 6 - **Roadsworth**, *Female Plug*, Montreal, Canada.

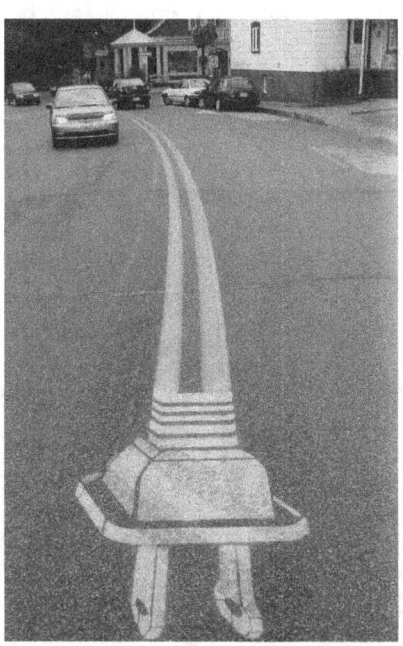

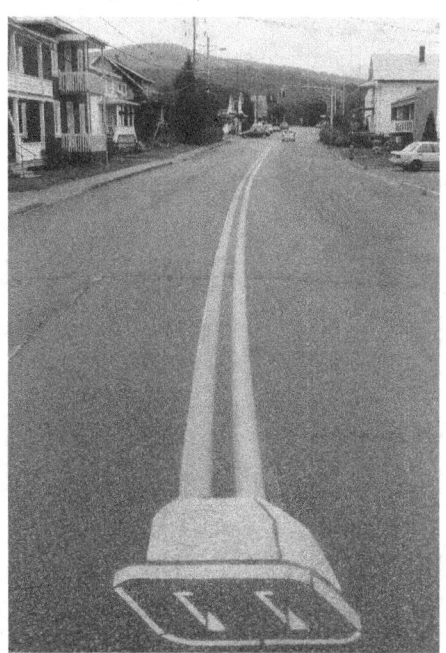

Figure 7 - **Tobias Starke,** *Dialogue*, Pripyat, Ukraine.

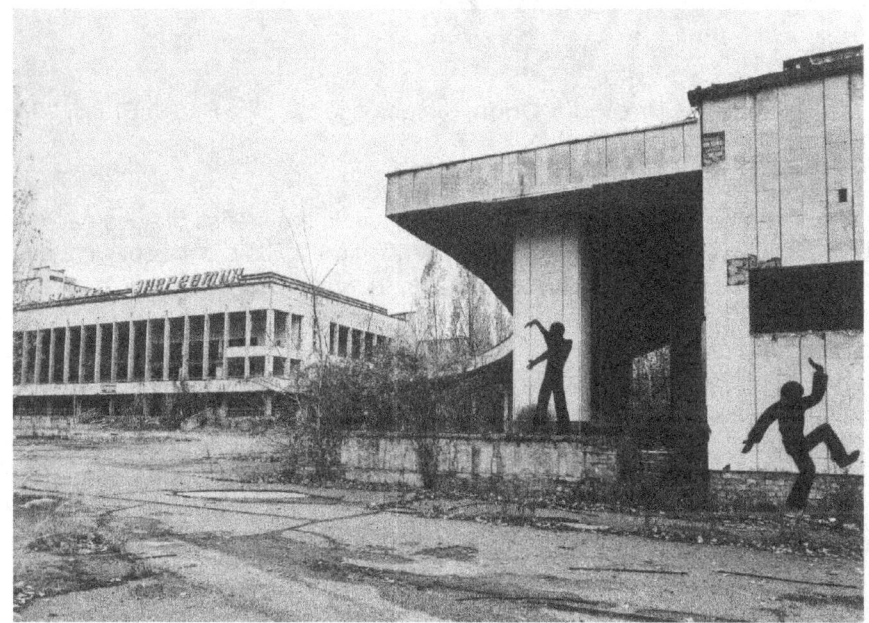

The three images above re-articulate signs established by the city. The artist Roadsworth works with the idea of highways as elements that organize and integrate a city. Because a highway is extremely functional, in the sense of having a determined function to carry out – namely, transporting vehicles – it is not bound to a single possibility of artistic expression. Roadsworth's plugs intervene in the visual, urban vocabulary and propose new meanings for utilitarian symbols.

The third image, placed in the city of Pripyat, refers to the disaster that took place in April 1986, when a nuclear explosion at the Chernobyl nuclear reactor caused an escape of radioactive material. The intensity of the accident, which released 400 times more radiation than the atomic bomb dropped on Hiroshima, made the city uninhabitable. The deaths caused by the accident, as well as the subsequent exodus from the city, caused Pripyat – situated in northern Ukraine – to become known as a ghost town. It is exactly this imaginary that the artist approaches with the above stencil. These are works of bricolage because of their resignification of symbolic conjunctures, and because their insertion into the environment does not offer us a chaotic aesthetic result of disparate information, but rather something new and homogeneous. A sense of strangeness occurs through this symbolic unity through the harmonious juxtaposition of visual elements.

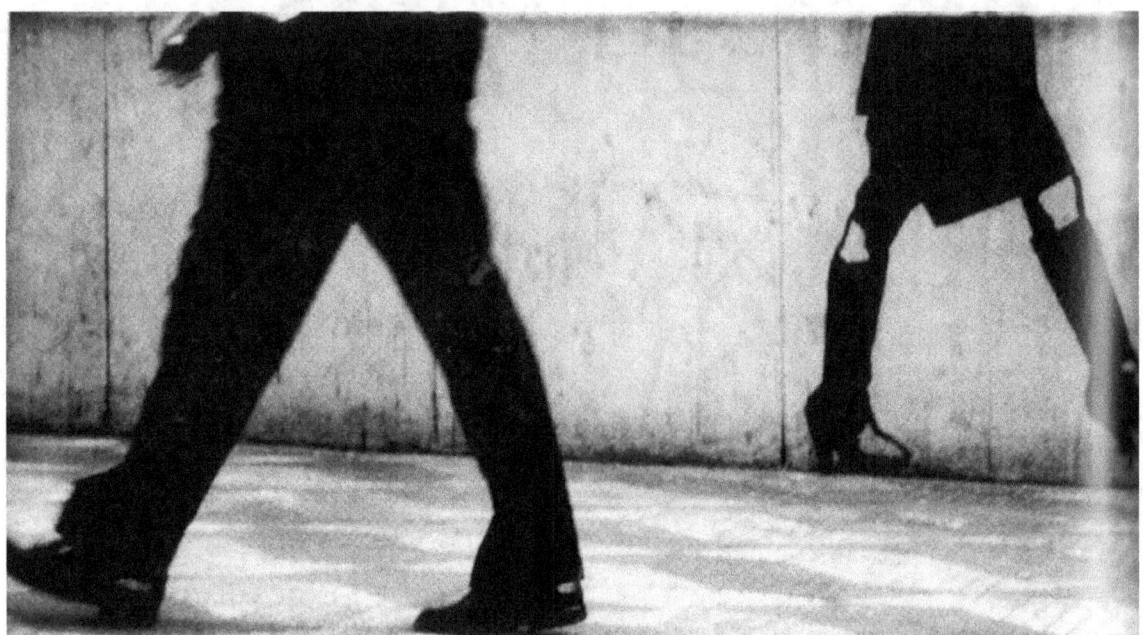

Figure 8 - **Alexandre Órion**, *Metabiótica 05*, São Paulo, Brasil, 2003

Alexandre Órion's photograph proposes a relation between the stencil of a woman walking in the opposite direction of an actual passerby, thereby calling attention to the flow of people in a city. It also suggest the impersonal nature inherent to major urban centers, in which the intense flow of people and information makes anonymity a structural characteristic of the city and, therefore, of stencils as public art. The aesthetic result is harmonious; it does not clash with our expectations of a city. It is only by looking closely at the photograph that we can tell that the person walking in the opposite direction is, in fact, a stencil. The representation of a woman walking refers to the casual nature of public urban contact. The project of which this specific work is part brings together urban stencil and photographs to compose the sense of the artwork. It is a scenic work in which photographic registry is the final component. The project depends on the context of the city to create works that reach their conclusion only through documented interactions with passersby. Structurally, the above stencil relies on its surroundings for its meaning.

References

Aguiar, Almir de Oliveira and Maria Celeste de Costa e Souza, (1989), In LÉVI-STRAUSS, Claude. O Pensamento Selvagem. Campinas, Brazil: Papirus.

Caiafa, Janice, (2003), "Comunicação e diferença nas cidades". Lugar Comum - Estudos de Mídia, Cultura e Democracia, n.18.

Iwasso, Victor, (2010), "Copy/Paste: algumas considerações sobre a colagem na produção artística contemporânea. ARS, vol.8, n.15.

Lévi-Strauss, Claude, (1966), The Savage Mind. Trans. George Weidenfeld and Nicolson Ltd. London: Weidenfeld and Nicolson. Online: http://monoskop.org/images/9/91/Levi-Strauss_Claude_The_Savage_Mind.pdf

Lima, Sergio, (1984), Collage em nova superfície. São Paulo: Massao Ohno; Parma: Raul di Pace.

Prou, Sybille e ADZ, King, (2008), Blek le Rat: Getting through the walls. London: Thames & Hudson.

Waclawek, Anna, (2011), Graffiti and Street Art. New York: Thames & Hudson.

Images Information

All images used here are in the public domain on the Internet, published on blogs and websites.

Above, Because Now I'm Worth It, Paris, France, 2010 (http://www.unurth.com/ABOVE-Because-Now-I-m-Worth-It-Paris)

Alexandre Órion, Metabiótica 05, São Paulo, Brasil, 2003 (https://br.pinterest.com/amiau0097/alexandre-orion-metabiotica/)

Bansky. "What Are You Looking At?" London, UK, 2005 (http://www.elmundoenmimaleta.com/wp-content/uploads/2014/01/banksy-08.jpg)

Ozi, Vandalice, São Paulo, Brazil. (http://flickrhivemind.net/Tags/est%C3%AAncil,ozi/Interesting)

Roadsworth, Male Plug/Female Plug, Montreal, Canada. (http://www.ufunk.net/artistes/roadsworth-street-art/)

Tobias Starke, Dialogue, Pripyat, Ukraine. (https://br.pinterest.com/pin/136656169913013198/)

Chapter 10

The Writing on the Wall: Embraced or Despised

Voica Puşcaşiu

Abstract

Due to the fact that for some researchers the difference between the "Graffiti" and "Street Art" is irrelevant for their methodology, there seems to be no clear consensus upon the usage of these terms, and they are interchangeable even within the artistic community. However, studies concerning the history of these practices make a clear distinction between the two, and the very existence of separate terms, begs the explanation that even though it derived from Graffiti, Street Art has become something that Graffiti is not. The differences are substantial and on many levels, and they are particularly important for this study since they can explain the way Graffiti and Street Art are perceived by the public.

"Graffiti" originates from the Greek word graphien, meaning "to write", and it is actually very appropriate for the contemporary practice because these works literally consist of a signature, or "tag", where the author's nickname is written on a wall. The author is generally not considered an artist, but is almost exclusively referred to as a "writer" or "tagger". The letters used for tagging are highly stylized, rendering the piece largely unreadable for an inexperienced viewer, and their only intended audience is the writers' community. Because only other taggers are competent in determining the value of a piece, the aesthetics of Graffiti becomes inaccessible to the regular people that encounter it on the streets. Not understanding its rules, not being able to see any sort of beauty or purpose it's more than likely it will be thought of as property damage and vandalism. In the context of the taggers fighting each other for "territories", Graffiti also became associated with street gang behavior, which further distanced the general public from wanting to understand and appreciate this art form. Much like other forms of contemporary art, accessible to only the educated few, Graffiti receives the same sort of hostile response, but while Contemporary Art is largely constricted to museums or galleries, Graffiti is somehow forced upon the public, it exists in the public domain but at the same time it makes no effort to reach out to its large audience.

Street Art on the other hand, has the clear advantage of being directed at everyone it comes into contact with and its wide array of styles, techniques, and messages has gathered an enormous fan base all around the world. More often than not Street Art is seen as an improvement upon the bare city walls and through surprise, wittiness, and humor it managed to become not only accepted, but also protected as an art form. It is not to say the Graffiti is dismissible as an artistic practice, but if we take into consideration the role affect and emotional connection play in the success of art in the public space it is easy to see why it is still frowned upon.

1. The Writing on the Wall: Embraced or Despised

"If it takes longer than five minutes, it's not Graffiti." (Mint&Serf, 2015)

The sustained rise in popularity of the Street Art and Graffiti movements, largely prompted by the massive dissemination through the means of the Internet, also meant an increase in the number of articles written on this subject by journalists and scholars alike (DeNotto, 2014) and this volume further proves the validity and the interest for research on these topics. Despite the increasing number of articles there it is quite easily noticed that there still seems to be a lack of terminological consensus when it comes to the usage of the terms Graffiti and Street Art, which can cause misdirection. Most often the terms are used interchangeably and what is more interesting is that this is practiced even by some of the artists themselves, which only adds to the perpetuation of this confusion.

In the case of some researchers the terminological difference is rendered irrelevant by their methodology and that is understandable, however studied concerned with the history of these artistic movements do make a clear difference between these two terms (Wacławek, 2011). While it can be argued that since the distinction is not always made or even known, there may not be an actual need for it, the opposite is actually true, because it is instrumental in explaining why some of these works are considered vandalism and are removed, yet others are beloved and even become iconic. The very existence of two distinct names, begs the explanation that they are in fact different art forms, and yet despite that interest has been shown for clearing up the differences between them, the articles are inconstant and often underline the superficial analysis that focuses on the secondary characteristics while ignoring the more important ones.

An example of this is the fact that there seems to be a consensus on the fact that Graffiti is quick and gritty, like an illicit activity should be, but it should be clear that speediness onto itself is not a sufficient characteristic in order to distinguish between this and Street Art. Another mistake comes from applying very site-specific guidelines which will no longer be standing when considering a different location (Bartlett, 2015), besides the fact that this is not proper practice, it also fails to successfully clarify things. For the sake of this clarity, it must be mentioned that throughout this paper the terms will be used in accordance to Wacławek's work where it is underlined that even though it derived from Graffiti sometime in the last 30 years (DeNotto, 2014; Wacławek, 2011, p. 12), Street Art, or post-Graffiti art as she sometimes calls it (Wacławek, 2011, p. 12), has ended up becoming something altogether different.

For some a valid distinction seemed to be the medium in which the works were created (Linton, 2012), but the evolution of both art forms made this an inconclusive criteria. Although spray pain was mostly used for Graffiti, we can now see Graffiti artists using stickers (Weisberg, 2015), which was predominantly a Street Art practice. In the same time Street Art has reached such a wide array of mediums that it basically can be made out of everything from moss, ready-mades, tiles, and of course spray-paint. Actually one of the first and most widespread Street Art techniques besides stickers was stenciling which was often done with sprays.

The most common distinction comes from the fact that Graffiti is concentrated on letters while Street Art is distinguished through its use of logos (Wacławek, 2011, p. 32). This is undeniably a good starting point, but it also proves insufficient since there are some Graffiti works that incorporate characters from popular culture (Thompson, 2009, p. 41) and at the same time there is also a lot of Street Art centered on letters and lacking any other imagery. Thus further important distinctions must also be made, they concern the subject of the works, their aesthetics, and last but not least, the audience towards which they are directed. This being said, Graffiti's subject is almost exclusively the author's nickname, an exception is that it can sometimes be accompanied by a dedication, such as "to Mom" (Thompson, 2009, p. 41), while Street Art has an incredibly wide variety of subjects and messages.

This is one of the golden rules when establishing if something belongs to Graffiti or Street Art, but from here the distinctions can be developed further especially when considering their audiences. While Graffiti is largely unreadable for people outside its artistic community and its aesthetics and value are judged solely by peer members, Street Art is distinctly directed at everyone it happens to come into contact with. Its aesthetic is also much more relatable and open to judgment and analysis, while its message is usually clear, even if it is just funny or whimsical. While the motivations stem from the same desire to reclaim public space, their choice of practice points towards different directions through which to accomplish this and Graffiti's exclusivist attitude and closed aesthetics renders it hostile in front of the audiences.

The crossovers do exist, but are rather limited and they include the aforementioned inclusion of a character in Graffiti. Also the so-called Graffiti murals could belong to this crossover category if one takes into consideration they are painted by Graffiti artists but legally and usually on commission, they don't include the artist's signature or at least that's not the main subject, which places them closer to Street Art practices. It must be noted that the Graffiti murals are cited to be the most successful determent against Graffiti itself (Lombard, 2013, p. 99), by occupying an otherwise blank wall. Of course there are artists that engage in both art forms, usually starting with Graffiti and moving on to Street Art, but both are sometimes practiced simultaneously, and while this is not an issue, the works themselves inevitably fall in one of the two categories depending on the style used in each particular case.

When considering in which of the two categories the many images and words that exist unsanctioned in the public space fall, it is important to also recognize the existence and tradition of latrinalia (Dundes, 1966), or restroom graffiti, which has a much longer tradition than the contemporary Graffiti practice. Despite its name, this belongs into a category onto itself, but which is in truth much closer to what we would call Street Art mainly because of their various subjects, and styles which include drawings, political comments, advice, and poetry. Even though the artistic intention behind them is debatable, they are interesting especially because of the written dialogue they prompt (Molloy, 2013; Trahan, 2011) and the fact that they're largely enriched by the replies.

2. Graffiti and vandalism

Graffiti as a word originates from the Greek word *graphien* meaning "to write" and afterwards it was used in Italian as *graffito*, meaning "to scratch" (mostly referring to words) (DeNotto, 2014) and it was in this sense translated to the English language where it has been in use since the 19th century, however nowadays it seems to be a dirty word (Jechow) with an undesirable connotation. Contemporary Graffiti refers to a very specific practice that took off in the 1960s in Philadelphia, with Cornbread and Earl being the earliest examples (Wacławek, 2011, p. 10), and which spread to other cities in the United States, most notably New York. There, it quickly turned into a massive phenomenon in the hands of the youth that wanted to make their presence known and claim the city as their own. It is for this reason that most of it was done on subway cars by the means of which the works could travel "all-city" (Masilamani, 2008, p. 5).

In accordance to the etymology of the word, and Graffiti artists are most often referred to as "writers" and their practice is actually just that, an often highly stylized form of writing their nicknames, as if the entire work consisted actually of the artist's signature. This gesture of proclaiming "I was here" was done through several types of works, the simplest and generally the smallest one was the *tag*, it was just the outline of the letters and generally a single color was used, but there are also the larger, more intricate *pieces*, short for "masterpieces", which themselves can be seen in a wide variety of styles depending on the lettering that was used. At first, these travelling *tags* often included a geographical indication next to the nickname (Thompson, 2009, p. 41; Wacławek, 2011, p. 14), which served in identifying their authors with a neighborhood, and also helped them engage in a city-wide dialogue with writes from different parts of the city. Proliferation was key, as the one with the largest number of tags was deemed "king" of a certain train line and thus commanded the respect that came with the title.

This better helps to understand why such a dynamic might be appealing to gangs that in their territorial battles began to use tags in order to establish an entirely different kind of hierarchy and respect, based not on playful competition and respect from the writers' peers, but on real-life, physical violence, which were a far cry from the Graffiti rivalries and battles that basically went only as far as a writer covering up another one's *piece* (Chalfant, Habib & Silver, 1983). Because the writers were organized in "crews" (Thompson, 2009, p. 36) the public's opinion on them being involved in gang behavior was only consolidated, despite the fact that other than cultivation a mentor – apprentice relationship, the Graffiti crews were not in any way related to gangs, even back in those early days and much less now (Trajtenberg, 2014, p. 174-5). In reality crews facilitated both competition and collaboration and writing was seen as a thoroughly social activity (Thompson, 2009, p. 32), an alternative to gang membership they were not concerned with protecting a territory but with self-expression (Wacławek, 2011, p. 43) and so the writer's network was an important part of establishing a reputation.

In one of the earliest pieces written about Graffiti, it is quite clear that the first writers came from all over New York and from a variety of socio-economic, and ethnic backgrounds (N/A, 1971), thus it is very important to specify that while gang-related Graffiti stopped at simple and often legible tags which served a different purpose (Wacławek, 2011, p. 12). Graffiti as an artistic expression evolved into *pieces* that were large, colorful and close to abstraction, the social aspect of writing is again underlined, by the fact that these works were judged by their fellow peers and it was in this way a certain writer reached respect within the community. Of course the illegal aspect was important in judging the pieces as it was quite a feat to have a clear line and no drips (Witten & White as cited in Thompson, 2009, p. 46) all the while working under pressure and undercover, but it was this set of skills and precise movements that made a writer famous.

Ever since its appearance Graffiti was seen as a threat, both for the authorities and from the outsiders of the culture. For the commuters using the trains it spoke of violence, of a city no longer under control, Graffiti was associated with poverty and urban decay, but also thought off as gateway crime (Wilson & Kelling as cited in Wooters Yip,

2010). Neighborhoods where it flourished became even more undesirable because they showcased authorities' lack of interest or power in the area. Even the fact that spray paint cans were sometimes stolen by kids and teens who couldn't afford to buy them created a connection among this culture and shoplifting (Rahn as cited in Masilamani, 2008, p. 5). These may seem as prejudices, and they were for the most part, but they prove very hard to combat, and the reason for that may just lie in the intrinsic characteristics of Graffiti, namely its closed aesthetics.

The majority of the people that encountered the works did not understand them, nor were they meant too, and thus it was increasingly hard to defend or like something that is intended to keep you out instead of drawing you in. It made the commuters on the trains feel so uncomfortable by not belonging to their own environment that when the "meaningless tags" that held no message for them were taken down by the authorities, they applauded this effort, despite the enormous amounts of money that were spent and the fact that it actually made the trains to run slower (Masilamani, 2008, p. 9). This goes to show just how little sympathy there really was for the Graffiti writers and their craft, a feeling which has not changed much all this time, probably because Graffiti has for the most part remained just as cryptic, and it is thus more than likely to be considered vandalism.

Even in the early years of Graffiti some effort was made to reach out to the larger public, in order to make them connect to the culture, this was done either by making the *pieces* more readable (Miller as cited in Thompson, 2009, p. 42) or by including characters from popular culture alongside their nicknames, and the first one to do so was the ever-present BLADE, who in 1974 included a snowman on a Christmas-themed train car (Stewart as cited in Thompson, 2009, p. 46). It is important to realize that these writers understood what it took for their works to survive in the public space and what was needed most of all, was for the public to approve of them. These efforts were however undermined by the sheer number of abstract *pieces* and *tags* which were by far a majority and have already settled the score in favor of removing everything, but they were nevertheless a lesson for younger generation of Graffiti artists, who have since led this art form on its way to commodification by making their signatures more readable (Lombard, 2013, p. 98).

The wars against Graffiti almost drove it to extinction, and now it's certain to be found almost everywhere except for the trains (Gonzales, 2010). However the art form still continues to evolve and spread, largely due to the help of the Internet which brought old-school Graffiti to audiences which had previously no contact to speak off with this culture. In Europe especially, it was precisely this lack of former context that was in Graffiti's advantage, since there was no real biased on racial urban segregation. Nowadays Graffiti, though still very much a crime, is being analyzed as part of a widespread youth culture whose members thrive on the low-level risk is provides, while feeling creative at the same time. The culture's members are not limited to any social class or education level and they don't consider their behavior to be in any way anti-social (Light, Griffiths, & Lincoln, 2012, p. 351) or linked to gang activity.

Ever since the early 1970s when the Graffiti craze was at its highest in NY, the writers started to get noticed by the art galleries and even though there was a number of shows and reviews in important magazines such as *Artforum* and *Art in America* (Thompson, 2009), their artistic careers never really took off, and neither did their very specific art form. Translating tags to canvas didn't feel authentic (Danto as cited in Riggle, 2010, p. 248) and when giving up the tags in favor of other subjects, their interpretations were often accused of being overly sentimental (Thompson, 2009, p. 207-10). All in all Graffiti had a hard time being considered art and the only two artists to break onto the high-art scene were arguably not writers to begin with (Wacławek, 2011, p. 63). There is pretty established confusion in calling Keith Harring a Graffiti artist for example, while after a brief analysis he was proves to belong to Street Art, before it was even a movement.

Once again one might notice that the critical reception on Graffiti was much more favorable in Europe where it was compared to Blues and Jazz and where its unmistakable working-class American attitude was praised as art (Thompson, 2009, p. 69), but this did not help things much back on the home front. Even today, despite existing and evolving all around the world, Graffiti is still haunted by its original misunderstanding and this is proven by the cases in which it was taken down despite being done legally (Turco, 2014). In order to further expand their fan base, artists are now choosing to do legible works, especially in really visible spaces precisely because they want their audience to experience a better connection to their art (Amuck as cited in Lombard, 2013, p. 98). It is also this tamer side of Graffiti which has been co-opted by several brands marketed at teens in order to make them look just edgy enough to be considered cool (Manco, 2011).

Of course this commodification also had a lot to do with hip-hop becoming more and more mainstream, and Graffiti is and has always been related to this music genre (Wacławek, 2011, p. 55-6). However this should not be view as if true Graffiti has perished, because this clearly still and takes on a variety of forms. It is hard to say when, if ever Graffiti will lose its bad reputation, but it is clear that this was partly achieved by trying to play an exclusivist game in the public space and that it did not sit well with the audience. The case against Graffiti was built in a similar manner to the one against Serra's *Titled Arc*, on the principles of "we don't like it, it has to go" (Winn, 2005). Chances are that unless massively educated in this particular direction, the public's opinion is not going to change, and just like Serra's conceptualism, Graffiti will remain a niche art movement whose existence on public domain will always be subject to contestation.

3. Street Art and urban visual culture

With Graffiti's situation being what it is, it would be of little wonder if Street Art, which started off as an extension that evolved from Graffiti and is also illegal, would be in the same situation, but in reality things couldn't be more different. While the motivation behind Street Art was initially the same as the one of Graffiti, and the artists' dream was to achieve notoriety through their art, this movement quickly distanced itself and wanted to stand out. No other words are more appropriate in expressing this feeling than those of Erosie: "When you have 17 tags on a wall, why add an 18th when you can add a symbol that sucks up all the attention?" (as cited in Manco, 2005, p. 113) The distance grows even more when one starts to consider the specific way some Street Art is connected and involved with the larger community through their messages and aesthetics, which is something that cannot be easily said of Graffiti.

In some ways Street Art is all about reclaiming public space and is very similar to Graffiti especially when considering artists that place their logos and characters in great abundance, much like taggers, but it can also go in several other, very different directions, which is what really makes it stand out. Of course some Street Art has a simply decorative function that does not go deeper than eye-candy, but even in this situations people still seem to appreciate the skill that went into creating the works, especially since many are conscious of the challenges of working at a large scale or in a precarious environment (Trajtenberg, 2014). The message may be simple, but this is secondary, which is why Street Art is considered as being able to beautify an otherwise gray area, which is something one never hears about Graffiti even though it too is bright and colorful (Visconti, Sherry, Borghini & Anderson, 2010). The explanation is again found in the fact that the skill needed to create a Graffiti piece, even though it takes plenty of it, is less apparent for an untrained eye.

We can see how in the case of Street Art, even though it is illegal, the authorities usually take into account the public's opinion and chose to preserve some of the artworks that have become iconic for a certain city or area, this is true even for unexpected cities that have little tolerance of Street Art (Zaporozhets, Riise & Kolesnik, 2014), which only proves that a well, placed work has the potential to go over virtually any barrier. This creates a paradoxical situation because they are still technically, and legally vandalism, but now the taxpayers' money could just as well go towards protection and renovation or for removal (CHD, 2013, p. 43). This situation however also gives way to interpretation and hypocrisy on behalf of the authorities since of course no one will even dream of taking down the David Bowie mural in Brixton that has become a pilgrimage site since the artist's death (Proto, 2016), but authorities can, and have removed a certain work, despite being done by Banksy, one of the most well-know Street Artist. They argued that the work in question, regarding the treatment of immigrants in the United Kingdom was racist, and cordially invited the artist to make another "more acceptable" piece, which would, of course be an honor to keep (Johnston, 2014).

Street Art as we have seen can be political, some in more obvious ways than others, depending on the artist. Projects like those of JR (McCarthy, 2015) are quietly political, raising awareness on certain social issues but not through the use of slogans, but more subtly through heavily emphatic visuals. His black and white photo portraits inevitably seem classic and universal, thus commanding a certain power and when humor is also involved they lose sentimentality perhaps, but become even more relatable. Some of the most beloved examples of Street Art rely on wittiness, humor, and surprise, those are the ones that make people look twice, and thus they notice their environment in an unexpected way, and at the same these works engage in a dialogue with both their audiences and their surroundings.

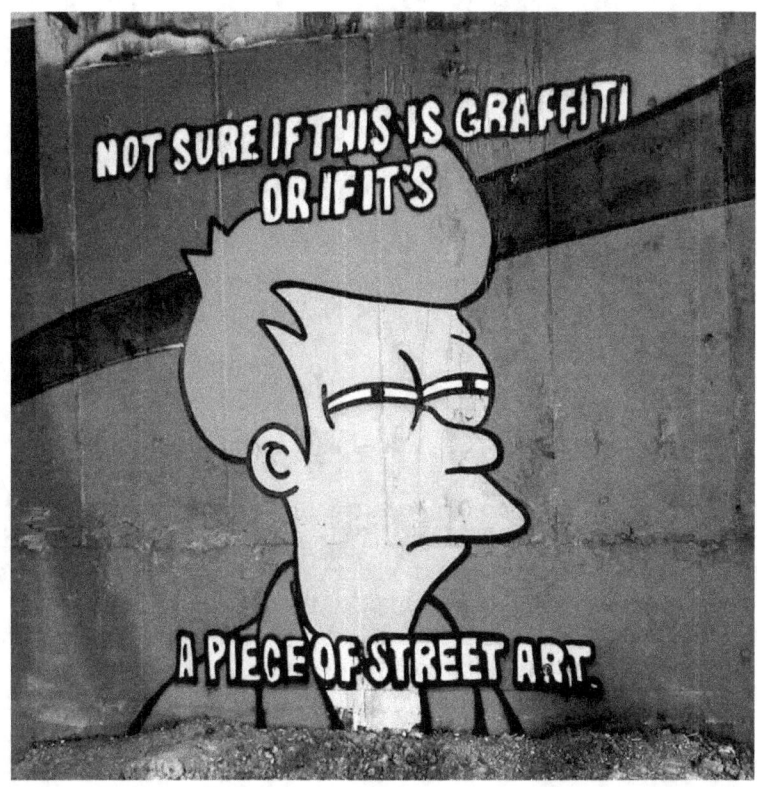

Figure 1 – Artwork by LUSH, Melbourne, Australia. Courtesy of the artist.

Surprise and humor have been proven to be successful strategies when creating a visual identity or even a product (Ludden, Schifferstein & Hekkert, 2008, p. 30) and if we view artists working in public spaces as self promoters, which both Graffiti and Street Artists claim to be (LADY PINK as cited in Thompson, 2009, pg. 26), then the analogy is feasible. Success is considered to have been reached when a positive and durable connection is established with the consumers (Norman, 2004), in this case the viewers, and thus a loyal fan base is formed. By using an instantly recognizable style, logo, or character, Street Artists create a strong visual identity, much like a brand. This is true for the taggers as well whose brand is their own nickname, but this proved much weaker in establishing a lasting affective connection, as opposed to the ones Street Artists seem to be able to make.

Some artists have reached a level of fame which seems incompatible to their anonymity and illegal nature of their works, and from this another apparent paradox has emerged, namely the fact that their works which are supposed to be free for all and unsalable are starting to fetch record sums in art auctions. Much like the old-school Graffiti artists who entered the galleried because of their illegal art (Thompson, 2009, p. 164), more and more Street artists are also having gallery shows, and even the world's most reputable museums are starting to get in on the Street Art action. This does not seem to detract from their original works which are still appreciated and hunted down by tourists with cameras and *aficionados* more than ever. What institutional affiliation or even just acceptance does however, is boosting the scale on which the artist can work, for example JR's portraits adorned the cupola of the Pantheon in Paris while it was being renovated (N/A, 2014), and thus attracted an even flow of tourist at the monument, and in another, even more impressive example, the work of Space Invader made it to the International Space Station (N/A, 2015a), as well as on several buildings belonging to the European Space Agency (N/A, 2015b). He used his signature tiles to create space, and alien themed mosaics, which shows just how much this artist has evolved from his Atari inspired aliens, without losing his edge or his humor.

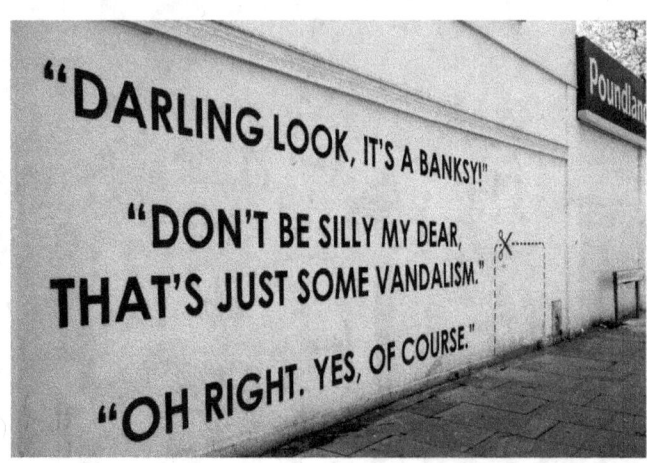

Figure 2 – Artwork by MOBSTR, London, United Kingdom. Courtesy of the artist.

The larger implication of the authorities in giving consent to Street Art has prompted some serious worries about this art form's connection to the process of gentrification (Schacter, 2015). Most artists deny that there is a conspiracy towards this (Rushmore, 2015), so one should objectively look for explanations elsewhere. While a neighborhood with Graffiti paints an unsafe picture, it is quite clear that one with Street Art is not only desirable to live it, but it can also bring new people to an area, which only proves just how much of an impact Street Art has and also the level of information and interest that is currently manifested towards this art form. Only in the last year two large (and legal) projects of this sort were started in opposite corners of the world, showing that it is a global phenomenon, and no longer even constrained to urban environments it is also quite clear from the case of these projects that the intent is not always directed towards a gentrification of the said areas. The best example of this is *Djerbahood* (Harmel, 2015) that was meant to boost the tourist attraction in a small Tunisian village by inviting a large number of world-renowned Street Artist who had the particularly difficult task to harmonize their works to the specific architecture of the location. The second one is the L.I.S.A. (Little Italy Street Art) Project (Turco, 2014) that takes place in the very heart of New York, and it is its stated goal to boost the locals' economy by bringing more people to this part of town through Street Art, which had already been proven as a successful strategy in other boroughs. Street Art is not however without its faults on its critics and as it becomes noticeable that more and more Street Art is now done on commission or at least with permission these faults are increasingly discussed. Working in accordance with the wishes of the landlord or those of the community, ensures by and large the longevity of the works, and also an artist's occasion to work under less pressure and create a larger project, but it is exactly this evolution that has spurred some of the greatest critics against Street Art, namely that it is becoming less radical. While it is true that mass popularization advances the most popular forms of artistic expression (CHD, 2013, p. 42) it must also be accepted that in the public space, the public might just be right in deciding what to choose for itself, even if that does not include the highest form of art. Generalization is unfair in any direction, some Street Art was and always will be purely decorative, which has not lessened the value of any of the other forms it takes. And while for various reasons not all works survive on the streets it is this particular dynamic that makes Street Art so spectacular. In the meantime, instead of unnecessarily mourning the death of political Street Art we should consider that Banksy has just place a work that once again criticizes the treatment of immigrants in an even more prominent location (Ellis-Petersen, 2015).

4. Conclusions and implications

As we can see the need for a proper terminological distinction is more than justified when analyzing the effects and possible consequences of two very different art forms that just happen to share a stage. Some have even said that a distinction is necessary *because* Graffiti has a bad reputation and it unjustly drags Street Art down with it (Almendrala, 2011), thus reinforcing the prejudices that surround Graffiti as practice. Without aiming to detract any value from what is a legitimate, if not legal, visual form of expression, the social realities must not be denied, and while both of them continue to share the public urban scene, it must be recognized that despite Graffiti's complexities and intricacies, it seems not to do so well. This however is far from being due to Street Art intentionally collaborating with the system, and rather because of the voice of the people. Graffiti's fan base is still restricted to its insider community and to youngsters that don't with little to no influence, while Street Art's clearer message and more diverse "anything goes" attitude simply reaches a wider audience and festivals dedicated to it have reached never-before-seen numbers. The benefits of public art are also being studied more frequently (Smedly, 2013) and the initial conclusions indicate that good public art manages to bind a community around an artwork and make it feel proud. The examples of public art that is indifferent to its viewers abound, but research suggests that Graffiti does leave people indifferent, but goes at the opposite end of the spectrum and even manages to bother people. Simultaneously, Street Art's strategies, especially its playfulness are now being used in sanctioned public art after their success was noticed. On the other hand, it has been observed that while Graffiti usually lessens the market value of a property, Street Art offers a unique opportunity to sell a house as something attached to a work of art (N/A, 2007). The greatest promise both of these art forms have to offer is to challenge the existing power system (CHD, 2013, p. 41), and by successfully infiltrating the established gallery system, they managed to do just that. Although it is never sure how long the interest is going to last, on a scale larger than Graffiti, Street Art still proves to be a valid alternative of becoming an artist that lives off its trade, all the while bypassing the usual rules for doing so, and it is in this way that it is truly able to challenge the establishment.

References

Almendrala, A. (2011, February,2). Street Art vs. Graffiti in Los Angeles. Huffington Post [online]. Retrieved from http://www.huffingtonpost.com/2011/02/02/los-angeles-street-art-vs-graffiti_n_816625.html

Bartlett, L. (2015, August 13). Ten ways to tell the difference between Street Art and Graffiti. *Westword*. Retrieved from http://www.westword.com/arts/ten-ways-to-tell-the-difference-between-street-art-and-graffiti-6961170

Chalfant, H., Habib, L., Silver, T. (Producers) & Silver, T. (Director). (1983). *Style Wars* [TV Movie]. United States of America: Public Art Films.

CHD. (2013). Notes on the commodification of Street Art. *Art Monthly Australia*, 263: 42-44.

DeNotto, M. (2014). Street Art&Graffiti: Resources for online study. *College and Research Libraries News*, 75(4), 208-211. Retrieved from http://crln.acrl.org/content/75/4/208.full

Dundes, A. (1966). Here I Sit: A Study of American Latrinalia. *Kroeber Anthropoligical Society Paper*, 34, 91-105.

Ellis-Petersen, H. (2015, January 24). Banksy's new artwork criticizes use of teargas in Calais refugee camp. *The Guardian* [online]. Retrieved from http://www.theguardian.com/artanddesign/2016/jan/24/banksy-uses-new-artwork-to-criticise-use-of-teargas-in-calais-refugee-camp

Gonzalez, D. (2010, February 4). Graffiti's story, from vandalism to art to nostalgia. *The New York Times* [online] Retrieved from http://www.nytimes.com/2010/02/05/nyregion/05graffiti.html?pagewanted=all&_r=2

Harmel, A. (2015). Art in the Arab Street: An Innovative and Ambitious Festival Bring Street Artists to Tunisia, *Public Art Review*, 26(2), 34-37.

Jechow, E. Public art, public statements: An opinion on Graffiti. [online]. Retrieved from http://musedialogue.org/articles-by-genre/visual-arts/street-art/public-art-public-statements-an-opinion-on-graffiti/

Johnston, C. (2014, October 1). Council removes Banksy artwork after complaints of racism. The Guardian [online]. Retrieved from http://www.theguardian.com/artanddesign/2014/oct/01/banksy-mural-clacton-racist

Light, B., Griffiths, M., Lincoln, S. (2012). 'Connect and Create': Young people, YouTube and Graffiti communities. *Continuum: Journal of Media & Cultural Studies*, 26(3), 343-355.

Linton, G. (2012). Street Art vs Graffiti on the streets of Los Angeles. *Global Graffiti Magazine*, 6 [online]. Retrieved from https://globalgraffmag.wordpress.com/2012/02/15/street-art-versus-graffiti/

Lombard, K.J. (2013). From Subways to Product Labels: The Commercial Incorporation of Hip-Hop Graffiti. *Visual Communication Quarterly*, 20, 91-103.

Ludden, G.D.S., Schifferstein, H.N.J., Hekkert P. (2008). Surprise as design strategy. *Design Issues*, 24(2) 28-38.

Manco, T. (2005). *Street Logos™*. London and New York: Thames&Hudson.

Manco, T. (2011). The Fundamentals of Street Art. *Huck Magazine*, 30, 100-102 [online]. Retrieved from http://issuu.com/huck-magazine/docs/huck30?mode=window&printButtonEnabled=false&backgroundColor=%23222222

Masilamani, R. (2008). Documenting illegal art: Collaborative software, online environments and New York City's 1970s and 1980s Graffiti Art movement", *Art Documentation*, 27(2), 4-14.

McCarthy, J. (2015). The work of art in the age of spectacular reproduction. *The Nation* [online]. Retrieved from http://www.thenation.com/article/the-work-of-art-in-the-age-of-spectacular-reproduction/

Molloy, C. (2013). "Curiosity won't kill you cat": A meditation on bathroom graffiti as underlife public writing. *Writing on the Edge*, 24(1), 17-24.

N/A (1971, July 21). "TAKI 183" spawns pen pals. *The New York Times*. p. 37.

N/A (2015). Photos: 'Space Invaders' on the International Space Station [online]. Retrieved from http://www.space.com/28888-space-invaders-art-esa-photos.html

N/A (2015). Space Invader Schematics [online]. Retrieved from http://www.esa.int/spaceinimages/Images/2015/10/Space_Invader_schematic

N/A. (2007). Buy Banksy's mural and get free house attached, *Reuters* [online]. Retrieved from http://www.reuters.com/article/us-arts-mural-idUSL0739817620070207

N/A. (2014). Au Pantheon! Thousand of faces inside and outside the monument! [online]. Retrieved from http://www.jr-art.net/news/au-pantheon-thousands-of-faces-inside-and-outside-the-monument

Norman, D. (2004). *Emotional Design: Why we love (or hate) everyday things*. New York: Basic Books.
onetime4yourmind. (2015). *Throw-up ABCs – A is for...* [online]. Retrieved from http://www.12ozprophet.com/news/throw-abcs/

Proto, L. (2016, January 12). David Bowie fans leave a sea of flowers at Brixton mural. Evening Standard [online]. Retrieved from http://www.standard.co.uk/news/london/david-bowie-fans-leave-a-sea-of-flowers-at-brixton-mural-a3154036.html

Riggle, N.A. (2010). Street Art: The transfiguration of the commonplaces, *The Journal of Aesthetics and Art Criticism*, 68(3), 243-257.

Rushmore, RJ. (2015). Has Street Art "Sold Out and Gentrified Our Cities"? [online]Retrieved from https://blog.vandalog.com/2015/11/has-street-art-sold-out-and-gentrified-our-cities/

Schacter, R. (2015). From Dissident to Decorative: Why Street Art Sold Out and Gentrified Our Cities [online]. Retrieved from https://theconversation.com/from-dissident-to-decorative-why-street-art-sold-out-and-gentrified-our-cities-46030

Smedly, T. (2013). Banksy, Gormley or Hirst, Is Public Art Good for the Nation's Wellbeing?, *The Guardian* [online]. Retrieved from http://www.theguardian.com/sustainable-business/banksy-gormley-hirst-public-art-wellbeing

Thompson, M. (2009). *American Graffiti*. New York: Parkstone Press International.

Trahan, A. (2011). Identity and ideology: The dialogic nature of latrinalia. *Internet Journal of Criminology*. Retrieved from http://www.internetjournalofcriminology.com/Trahan_Identity_and_Ideology_The%20Dialogic_Nature_of_Latrinalia_IJC_September_2011.pdf

Trajtenberg, G. (2014). The intricacies of Street Art learning: A sociological explanation. In Zembylas, T. (ed.) *Artistic Practices: Social interactions and cultural dynamics* (pp. 166-179). Abingdon: Tylor & Frances Books.

Turco, B. (2014). Graffiti mural deemed too graffiti, gets buffed [online]. Retrieved from http://animalnewyork.com/2014/graffiti-mural-deemed-graffiti-gets-buffed/

Visconti, L., Sherry, J.F., Borghini, S., Anderson, L. (2010). Street Art, sweet art? reclaiming the "public" in public place. *Journal of Consumer Research*, 37, 511-529.

Wacławek, A. (2011). *Graffiti and Street Art*. London and New York: Thames&Hudson.

Weisberg, J. C. (2015). The difference between Street Art and Graffiti [online]. Retrieved from http://schriftfarbe.com/the-difference-between-street-art-and-graffiti.

Winn, S. (2005, March 8). Vandalism or art? /Part two: The public space belongs to everyone and no one. Caught in the middle are those who treasure public art and those who would paint over it. *SF Gate* [online]. Retrieved from http://www.sfgate.com/entertainment/article/VANDALISM-OR-ART-Part-Two-The-public-space-2724748.php

Wooters Yip, E. (2010, January 21). What is Street Art? Vandalism, Graffiti or Public Art Part I. Art Radar [online]. Retrieved from http://artradarjournal.com/2010/01/21/what-is-street-art-vandalism-graffiti-or-public-art-part-i/

Zaporozhets, O., Riise, E., Kolesnik, A. (2014). The permanence of ephemeral: Tsoi Wall 23 years after. *Coactivity: Philosophy, Communication*, 22(1), 38-52.

**Part V.
Research action
in practice: urban
interventions and
knowledge co-creation**

Chapter 11

Graffitti, street, delirium: arts defiances

Elenise Cristina Pires de Andrade, Edivan Carneiro de Almeida, Milena Santos Rodrigues

Abstract

To provoke with art the experiences developed for three events that occurred simultaneously in September-2014 at Feira de Santana, BA. To call the sensations - not only the explanations - as an attempt to deflect, subvert with photographic images that we'd had been produced from these events. To seek the Deleuzian concepts of "sign" and "diagram". Instead of explanations and coherence, the three authors of this text and their photos aims to proliferate connections and provoke the invention of new ways of looking and experiment the world, the city, the production of knowledge, the cultural expression of artists. What can the images do when they don't want to explain, to illustrate, to remember the cities?

We will explore the images of a graffiti event in a public school wall; another event about street art in a museum and, finally, an academic meeting sponsored by the "Trace", a research group (at Universidade Estadual de Feira de Santana, Bahia, Brasil), that wished to provide a 'multi-alogue' (no only a di-alogue) between different knowledges, expressions, everyday students, teachers and artists in connection with the plurality of directions and places in the city. Events that proposed to amplify the risks and the powers of the encounters.

Our proposal is not to explain or speak directly about the events, but speak about how these interconnections can provoke us to think about the field of research and university extension programs on education in / with the city. To provoke (in art, life, writing, education, anywhere) chaos outbursts, slights to the ratings and moral judgments and... de-focus. Arts defiances...delirious... drowns... lines... To provoke with art and the art. To let it go through by becoming experimentations. Delirium power of life... of cities.

To (un)frame in an attempt to empty the representational connections of lines and colors in the graffiti's movement. The point is not just to be in contact with this movement in order to understand and uncover the meanings of the drawings on the walls but also, and above all, to fade into these lines of flight, in the movement of passing by the street, in the thoughts - that have not been designed yet - transit.

Keywords: Photographies, cultures, philosophy of difference

Graffiti: Art Instigates

Provoke with art experiences developed during three coexisting events. Meetings, resonances, happening colors. The 2nd Graffiti Meeting, an initiative of Youth Group Coletivo H2F[1], aimed to maximize and empower graffiti

---

1 There were many artists from several parts of the country and some from abroad. (For more information http://www.facebook.com/2encon trodegrafittifsa?fref=ts). The youth Group Coletivo H2F aims to widen relationship within cultural actions that transforme the city and reach other youngster through hip-hop and mainly having a social contribution for the local communities in order to bring up discussions around population social reality.

2 The city is 100 km away from Salvador, Bahia, population of 556 mil inhabitants and it is the second largest city of the State. (Source: http://www.cidades.ibge.gov.br).

art in the city and set the event at the Cultural Schedule of Feira de Santana[2] and roundabouts, concentrating the activities at Jose Ferreira Pinto Public State School's walls. The Museum of Contemporary Art Raimundo de Oliveira (MAC) has held the Fair-Art (FeirArte) which consisted in local artists exhibitions of urban expressions (see figure 2), workshop and the Opening of *TRACEjando by Feira de Santana: expressive drives* - an academic event by Trace Research Group, Department of Education of Feira de Santana State University (Uefs), focusing actions on a round-table interface[3] with Street Art Scholars, mainly graffiti and artists (see figure 1). Also, in this event, there were two workshops for Senior High School students from that school which has offered its walls to the graffiti's artits: one about poetry and one another about how to make a video.

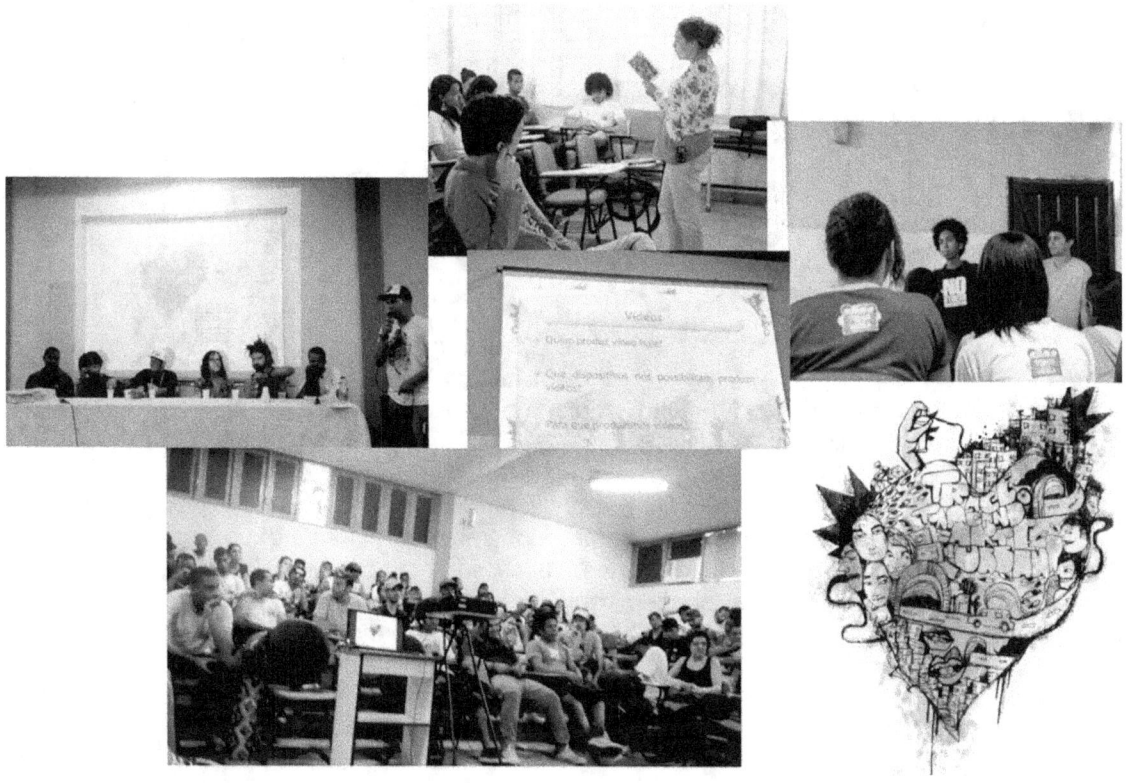

Figure 1 - The Event *TRACEjando Meeting at Feira de Santana: expressive pulsation.* Rould-table TRACEjando, Uefs (on the left). Poetry Workshops and video production at school Colégio Estadual José Ferreira Pinto. Source: Trace group research personal file. Poster by Kbça Grafitti.

Instigating by using those events, shocking in terms of boundary-type for the disclosure and discussion of opinions and ideas. Desires that go through a multi-dialog among multiple knowledge, expressions and students, teachers and artists daily routine in connection with plurality of senses and places at the town. Scientific knowledge, artistic artifacts that are understood and spread across museums, streets, schools, walls, notebooks and university.

---

3 Round-table "The Art is in the Streets" in 26 September 2014, composed by: Leandro Lima (on behalf of Youth Group Coletivo H2F), Evanilton Gonçalves Gois da Cruz (master degree student from Bahia Federal University), Professor Dra. Roselene Cássia de Alencar Silva (Departament of anthropology and ethnology at Bahia Federal University), André Kaja Man (artista do graffiti artist from Rio de Janeiro), Júlio Costa (graffiti artist from Bahia) and Sinho (graffiti artist and MC from Aracaju, SE).

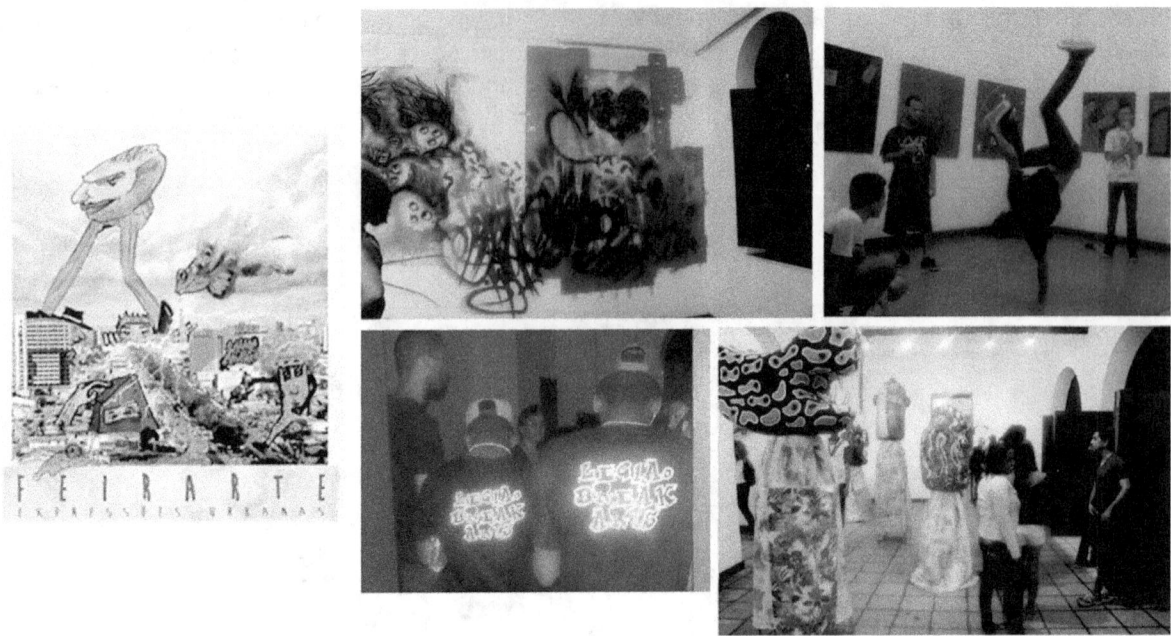

Figure 2 - *FeirARTE Poster: urban expressions* (on the left). Contemporary Art Raimundo de Oliveira (MAC). Source: Trace group research personal file. Poster by Don Guto.

Provoking by arousing a multiplication of meanings in our research with images and sounds, blurring the fixity of representation, register and verdity. Instead of explanations and coherence, proliferating connections, awaking the creating of new ways to see and live up to the world. Lines, traces, scratching, colorful drawing and colors in order to take risks, experiencing by reaching tones, shades, lights, sensations with and about the town. By asking ourselves, having at hand the intercessors of sigh concepts and Gilles Deleuze diagram: What can gestures and encounters/meetings do with the images when they do not aim to explain, illustrate or register the cities? What gestures would work as intensive signs to provoke and force us to feel the difference, to experience time and its multiple truths, as proposed by Nascimento (2013)? Questions and desires to move around images and videos made by this article actors, during and after the 2nd Graffiti Meeting, charting images of the event and participants opinions (artists, teachers and students), enabling to understand them as intensive contemporary character to go beyond the means of communication and/ or data for the research. Not agreeing that images and words/ideas in/from the voices in a text that simply show us and explains ideas, representations, knowledge, thoughts about something or someone, on the contrary, seek the way, the gesture between them and something within us that match up with them. Intensity of the instant. Pulsating and intensities to bother thoughts.

Risking, along with that perturbation, is another way to propose something through scratches/sketches on the wall, using graffiti. Experiment by dislocating views. Breaking through streets, walls, surfaces in significant shifts/ turn around. Everyday's spin and flow images and voices that were produced were in those events. Our wishes echoed by the attempt of deconstruction, the deviation of subversion, calling the feelings, not just the explanations with discussions on this article.

Signals to emanate gestures. Body-Gesture at risk. Connections, contacts, contamination in intense movements, as proposed by Ricardo Basbaum (2006, p. 67) "We can consider that a diagram will always be generated as a device related to the maximum proximity to the site of the experience [...]", materialization of becoming when the viewer is captured by a work/artwork into a field intensities. Risking ourselves with Deleuze and the diagram functions, when the philosopher, the going through the work of Francis Bacon, proposes that the painter in his paintings/images, challenges figuration and narration. Aspects that, for Deleuze, effects are insisting on invading the pictures (not only of Bacon). It challenges untied-nots, lines and forces - the diagram.

Bringing 'thinking the art' with Deleuze and moving around articulations with aesthetic experience, building a research-in-experimentation that is contaminated by the virulence of thoughtless in the thought. It is to find out how this concept of diagram hinder us to exploit this gesture-hand-drive images to experience the encounter with graffiti artists on the occasion of the 2nd Graffiti Meeting of Feira de Santana (see figure 3).

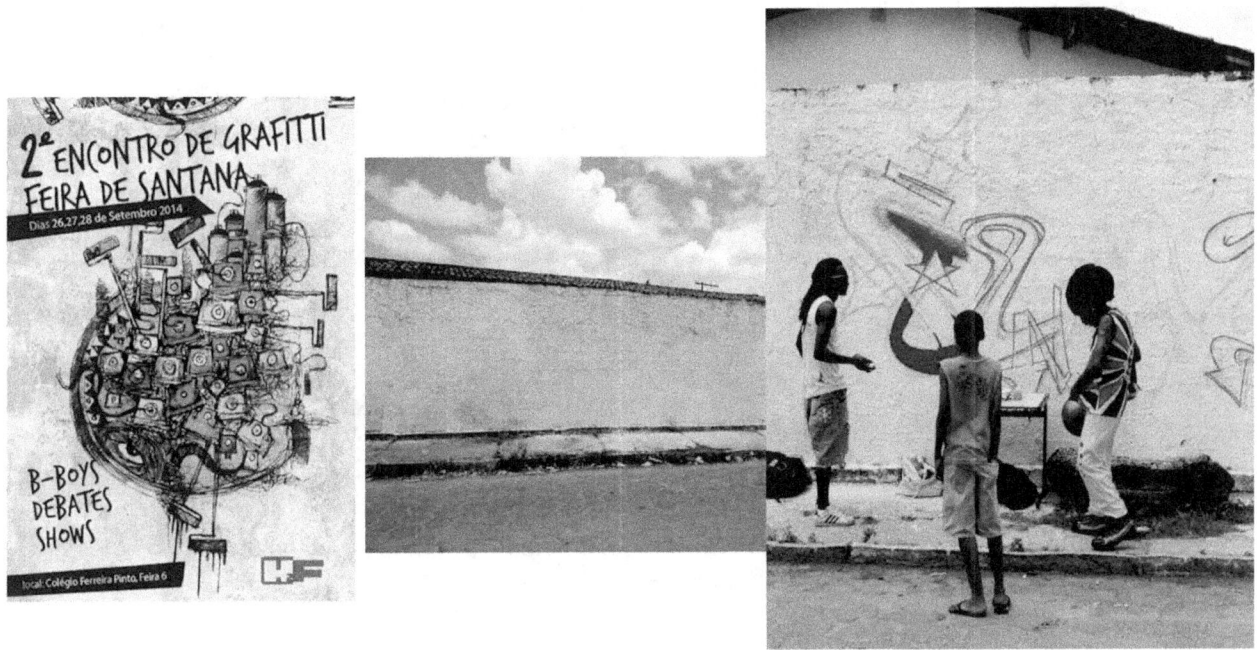

Figure 3 – *2nd Graffiti Meeting* (on the left). Public School Colégio Estadual José Ferreira Pinto (on the right). Source: photos by de Marcos Barata, personal file. Poster by Kbça Grafitti.

Meetings, cities, streets and walls in order to instigate two project-research[4]. Throughout 2013, projects actions enabled a group of youngsters from the town (in 2014) to develop some activities to produce and express knowledge along with images and sounds from the city. Experimenting/ trying out versed at risk/scratch. Risking... Trying unframed images (see figure 4). Wanderings through the ideas and words with the signal conception, with Deleuze, it was the strongest inspiration to cause a third research project "Cities (un)framed within images: experimentations crossing the conception of signs" bringing the desire of tensioning: what are images able to do when they do not intend to explains, illustrate, register the cities?

---

4 Both ongoing projects since 2012, they aim to better understand ways of expression, participation and social belonging from youngster in different production, consuming environment and cultural diffusion in Feira de Santana-BA.

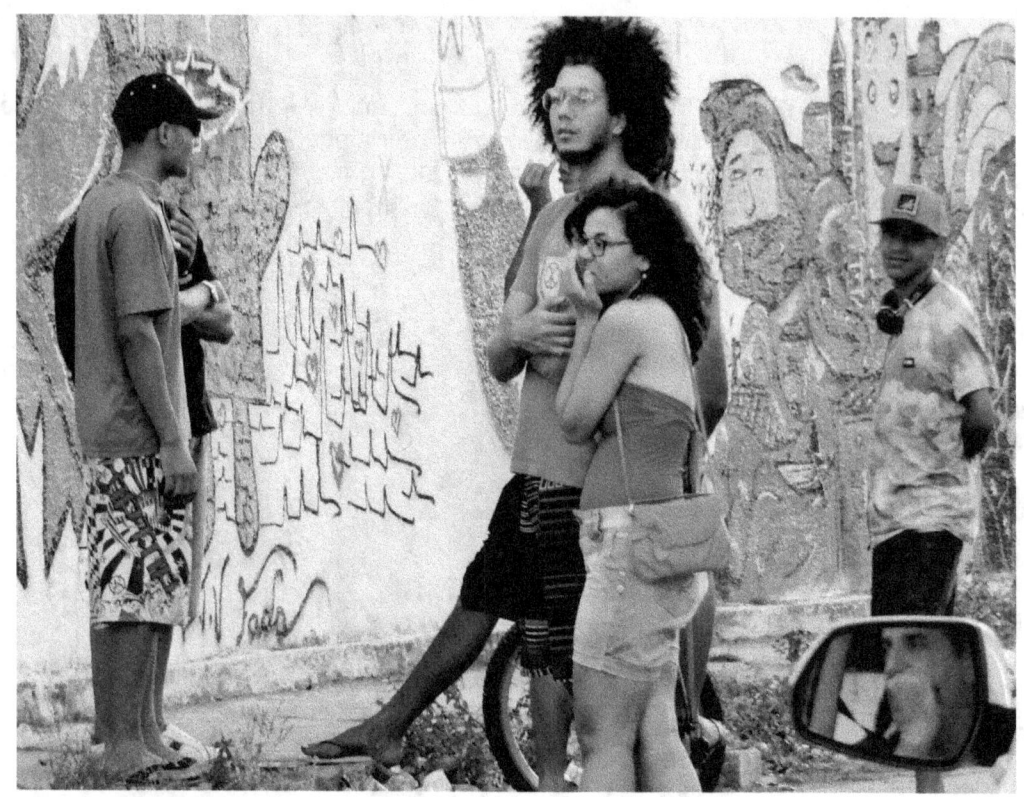

Figure 4 – Public School Colégio Estadual José Ferreira Pinto outside wall photo while the 2nd *Graffiti Meeting*.
Source: Edivan Carneiro de Almeida photo, 27 September 2014, personal file.

Streets Spin

Integrating the Youth Group, MAC's desire, our research in reverberation, and a Public School. Meetings, chatting, setbacks, invitations. Streets took over and allowed us of being invaded by uncertain lines, walls of the city. Artists marked the school, university, the museum, streets, souls, eyes, walls' skin. Inventing (un)frameworks in an attempt to empty the representational connections of lines and colors in the graffiti's movement. The question would be not only to contact this movement in order to understand and uncover the meanings of the drawings on the walls, but also fading away through these lines while passing along the street in the transit of the thoughts that have not even been thought yet. Bother, dislodge, move...

Work with tiny particles released from the spray, moving gestures that "[...] violate the expectations of the culture that predetermines, in a context like the city, it is how and when the space and time can be used" (Ramos, 1994, p. 44). Graffiti, most of the cases, sets up in a posture of opposition to a standard urban sense, "[...] that subverts the meaning of the place and the established patterns of communication in the public space [...] The *bombing of the city*, a metaphorical figure that reveals the destructive nature, massiveness, tentacular of an action that aims categorically to mark the city's visibility space" (Campos, 2009, p. 20, emphasis added).

Although, in accordance with the approach of Ricardo Campos, it is not the understanding and comprehension that he does about graffiti that we exposed here. Campos takes anthropology assumptions of visual communication to make his analytical readings of urban movement. For the author, "In this context, the city is taken as a visible product of a set of individual and collective desires, expressive resource that is collectively celebrated as material for human communication." By taking the photos and the concepts of Deleuze, it is not intended that the city is capable of reading comprehension, but it produces temporal spacing, space widened from the expressive intensity of signs that emerge gestures. Not only with them but through them...

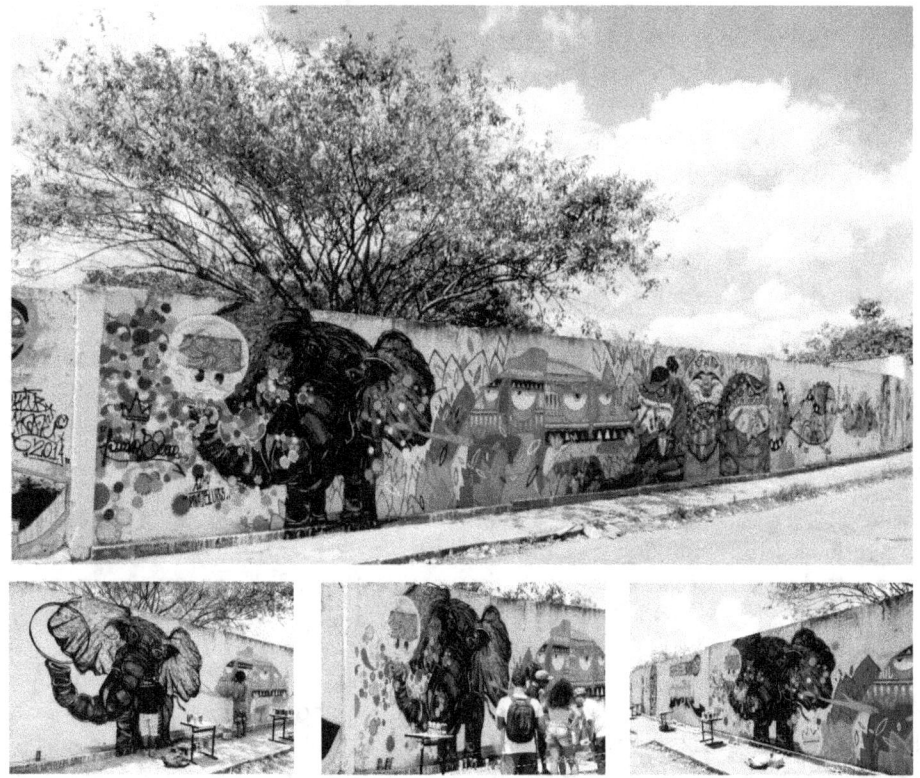

Figure 5 – Public School Colégio Estadual José Ferreira Pinto outside wall photo while the 2nd *Graffiti Meeting*
Source: Marcos Barata photo, 27 and 28 September 2014, personal file.

Spins, involutions, dizziness. Drafts, scratches, risks, colors, bubbles, frogs, elephants. Skepticism, classifications, rankings (see figure 5). How many possibilities of creating city inventions could exist through graffiti art on a school wall?

Paulo Roberto, who is the vice principal of the Public school, describes the strangeness caused by graffiti art:

"What we have seen at one or another spot at the city are images that ... we have even suggested for viaducts, dead business concrete space. We suggested that they [the artists] could go to those place to vandalize "pichar" [literally spoken in quotation marks], and make their art out there. For instance, authorities say it is vandalism, but for them, it is art. For Ferreira Pinto's community, it is another understanding." Daily scribbles/scratches on walls build up and make up cities. Color gray in slow or fast motion, not necessarily apparent, visible, but sensitive. Political and aesthetic mobilizations questioning us about how to get away of the representation plan and create landscapes-sensations from a cliché image, in a mechanic movement of signs. Basbaum (2009) presents an interesting reflection of diagram concept that emerges in relation to his artistic work with the public, indicating a "[...] double movement of forces of thought and concrete, as a device to produce changes" (Basbaum, 2006, p. 73).

Lately I've been working with diagram as a tool - using it to open and occupy a kind of intermediate space between speeches and artwork. There is a building process to obtain this space, bringing words altogether and weaving/interlacing a dynamic space with lines and several visual elements. Above all there is the desire to establish in the picture, rhythm and pace: without a proper rhythmic model, the diagram does not work *per si*. Indeed, pulse, producing resonance, rhythmic vibration - they are what ensure the diagram movement and production to the necessary registration, otherwise it would become an abstraction that does not intervene, it does not move any space and it does not occupy any area. (Basbaum, 2010, p. 2, our translation).

Taking risk and daring the colors, rhythm, likely the graffiti artists and the local communicate has done, as also observed at the vice principal's speech. Escape from a common sense/thought. "It is needed to understand affection and so, in accordance to an update procedure which puts away outside forces, a different feeling" (Nascimento, 2013, p. 68). Graffiti artists clearing out colors-flow that is spread along the public school walls in a nearby or distant borough, once that the university is located far from the city center, the street Fair VI. According to Kbça Grafitti, one of the organizers artists: "The street Fair VI is like a bridge between two worlds: University and several suburbs that are out there around". The interesting school location was the main reason for the event: "An opening in Uefs *lance*[5], we have never managed to do something within Uefs, so we thought it would be feasible during Ferreira Pinto street Fair VI, because only then they would like and open students' and any other people's eyes".

Andréa Pinheiro, the school head master, and her team and teachers, not only has made available a huge white screen, the school walls, but also has sheltered them throughout September 2014 weekend, becoming feasible the 2nd Graffiti Meeting, promoting street-wall-school chain process. Student-wall-headmasters. Colors-wall-scratches-graffiti. Andrea's own words:

"When we mentioned about graffiti meeting, many people had the idea that, who would be here, would be people to spray everything in black. This is the first idea that someone thinks of graffiti. However, as the artists proceeded with the workshops, creating art, coloring the wall, they saw that graffiti is an art. An urban art, right? It is not placed in an art gallery, it is priceless. So the real price is the beauty we have here at our school today".
Risks/scribbles that makes up the walls beauty, graffiti's traces to dare the streets. Chaotic twists and spraying colors fragments, drawings, gestures, signs. Diagram. Rhythms shifted from one organi-city (organicity) to pulsate in other thoughts regarding the movement of production and dissemination of knowledge, articulating itself as a questioning of aesthetic-political statement of what we call representational politics, manifested in so many repetitive researches which prioritize one hierarchical model of communication, recognition, providing few opportunities of meaning multiplication and expansion for the phenomenon, objects, images, research, cities.

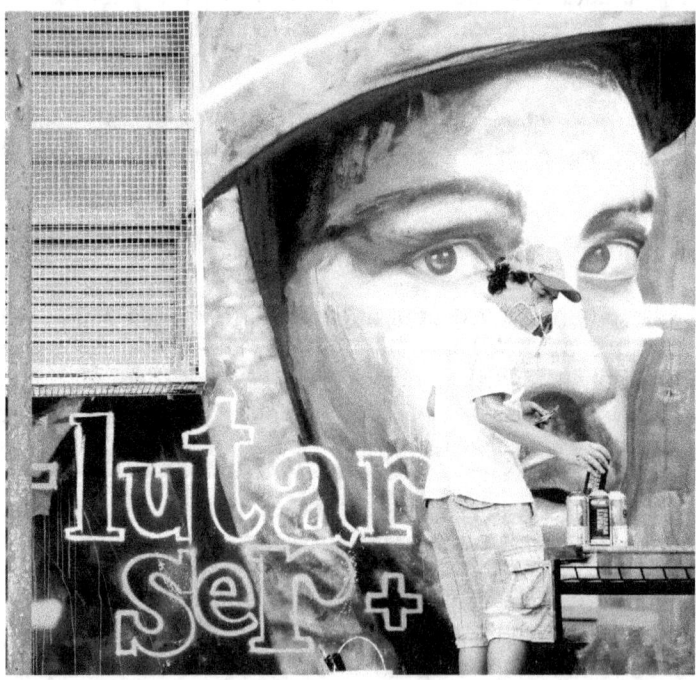

Figure 6 – Carlos Bobi and his art at the *2nd Graffiti Meeting*. Public Shool Colégio Estadual José Ferreira Pinto inside wall.Source: Milena Rodrigues photo, 27/Aug/2014, personal file.

5 Some expressions used by the Gaffiti artists were original kept due to the fact they are in their own way of living and resisting against aggression and prejudice.

The colors roam over the cities and awake, kill. Unblock streets, feelings, thoughts. "What interests me is how, tracing lines, offering words or dividing surfaces also are drawn on shared places" (Rancière, 2012, p. 101). Ways of sharing that involve amplitude "[...] sensitive for the community, forms of their own visibility and their disposal" where "[...] the question arises of aesthetic relationship/policy" (Rancière, 2009 , p 26) - understanding the aesthetic as a way to articulate ways of doing, means of visibility and thinking of ways and their relation, implying an idea of the effectiveness of thought, concluded the French philosopher.

In the following, a school teacher states, likewise Rancière:
"Now only they pass by and get delighted. [...] students, community. I saw a father standing still, staring at the wall and said 'Wow! I wanted to have these photos! Come close to see better' - he did not even know I was a teacher - 'Look at the work on that wall! How perfect this soldier is! [see figure 6] I have been looking here and there non-stopping, I wish I could have seen those artists doing that.' Concluding, the wall has been made up and became more beautiful!"

Passing by, looking at and commenting. Contemplate. Risk? Thus, we have provoked a questioning between the conceptual proposal of the risky operation of the diagram with the intensity of the signs, which, as mentioned by Nascimento (2013), in Deleuze takes a sensitive nature, [...] we are open for the sign to the power of active creative forces" (Nascimento, 2013, p. 67). Forces that activate unthinkable and so subversive, verses that explode and spread a desire for power. Proliferations in spins of sensation seeking a thought with immersed images in the current movements of visual arts in a group action to unbalance fixed boundaries among image, fiction and reality. Plus, among knowledge, memory and explanation, and street politics, art and creation. Ana Godoy (2013), commenting on a Klossowski article, in which the author discusses some criteria present in Nietzsche's work, focusing on what current movements that are *Earth management*[6], pointing out another movement not observed by the French author.
[...] That [movement] of wandering lines undo the incessant references [...]. Lines whose movements express another policy that does not recognize borders, dispenses what it should be, do, think and feel, betraying the significance of systems, referentiality, saying other and surprising practices, clearing flows, creating other streams, undoing the machineries control and submission (Godoy, 2013, p. 130).

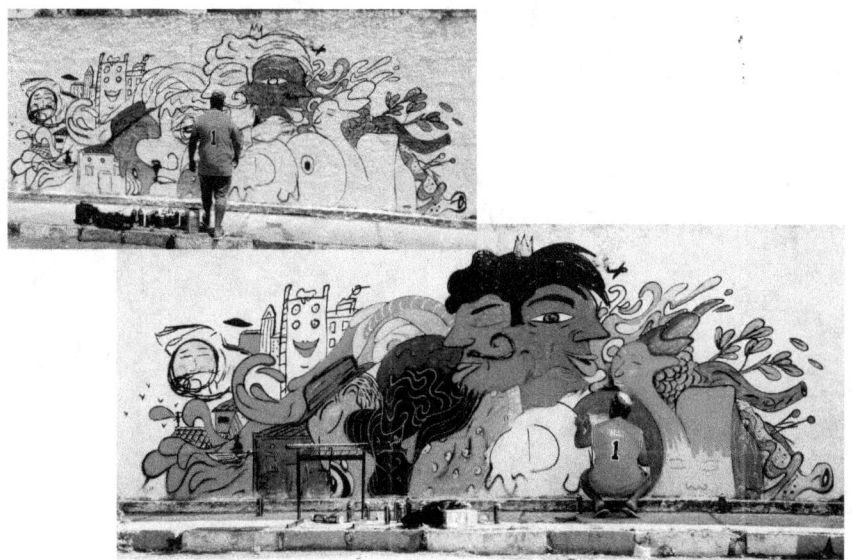

Figure 7 – Public School Colégio Estadual José Ferreira Pinto outside wall during the *2nd Graffiti Meeting.* Don

---

6 "Klossowski, 1972, in an article about some criteria presented in Nietzsche work, states that the total Earth management and the existing planetary plan obey an irreversible economical movement, that one that takes everything due to establishing – goals, paths, itinerary, calculated actions, on behalf of statistical future that consolidate roughness of the mankind and its mediocrity that would demand another movement" (Godoy, 2013, p. 130).

Guto while making art. Source: Milena Rodrigues photo, 27 September 2014, personal file.

Initial scribbles on the wall that not necessarily will be a graffiti image. Breakdowns in wandering lines to another political tension with the world. How many times, we wondered by the initial scribbles what it would happen with that screen-wall. After lots of wrong guessing, we gave up and kept an eye at the invention. Encounters, unthinkable meetings popping up with the artists movements. Don Guto, an artist, risk, took risks and reddened the plot with open-closed eyes to spy (see figure 7). It is exactly our own wish in order to control what we see, know, think about what we intend to subvert in tiny particles in order to invade our wishes for the research. Resistance to the betrayal of the systems of meaning.

The eye that does (not) speak. The mouth that does (not) see. Redness... According Ana Godinho (2013, p. 136), "In *Lógica da Sensação*, the problem is about having an impossible eye. Thinking while feeling, indeed, but getting the impossible eyes and ears." We must disturb... Are not the acts of an everyday living nuisances and/in experience? Streets, walls, color, *in-ventaded* cities, *out-ventaded*, at risk for the expelling the need of explanation and (re)cognition of eye-touch-ears-walls-thoughts boundery. Be open to small and delicate gestures, almost (in) visible. "It was a very enjoyable time to paint that empty wall out there. Out of the blue, three [artists] has arrived and started building up and something came out, everyone was here waiting for: how is it going to end up? And suddenly it draws our attention" mentioned the local teacher Nayara. Breaking up and putting our sensations at risk.

Occupying and invading the wall through the affection. Ephemeral art grooving the walls and invading the apple of the eye, bothering the haptic eyes. Splitting up in thoughts a feeling, creation. The wall is not just a wall, nor the hand is only an eye neither the eye is only the city, and "[...] the diagram is not a relative zone of uncertain optical, but it is an absolute zone of indiscernibility or objective indeterminacy, which opposes to the view of a manual power as foreign power" (Deleuze, 2007, p 137).

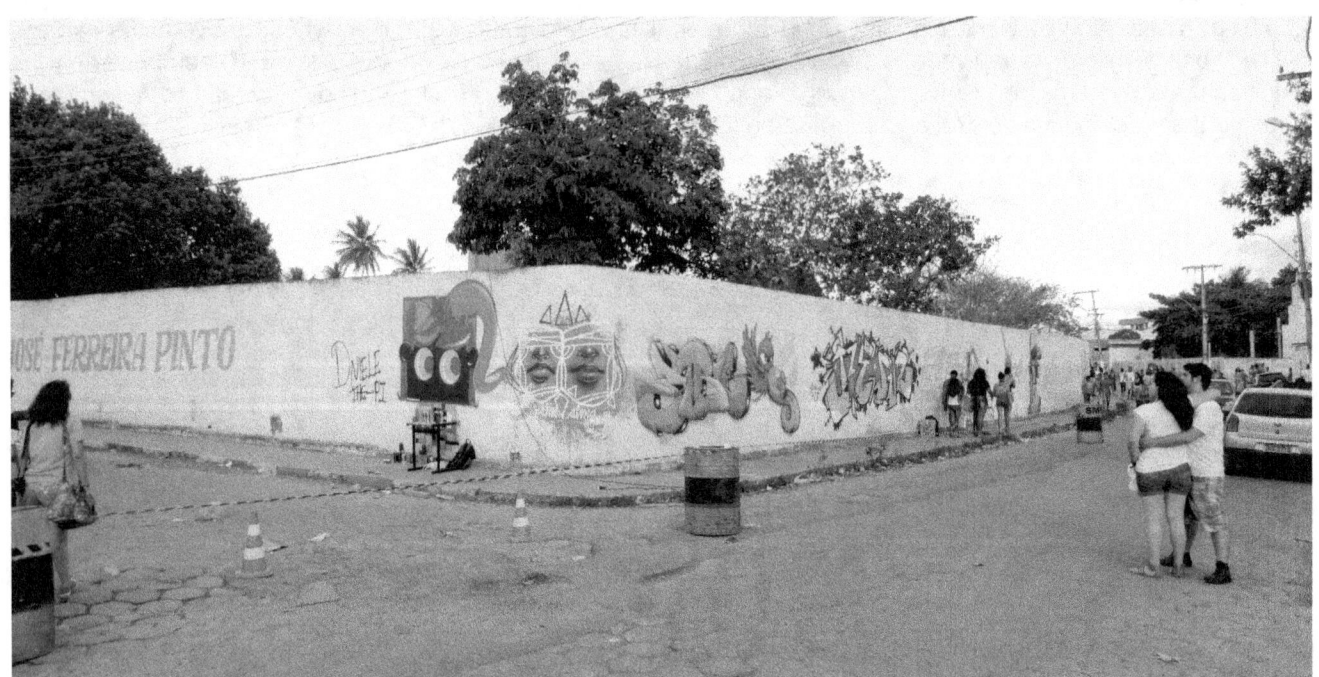

Figure 8 – *2nd Graffiti Meeting* various pieces of art. Public School Colégio Estadual José Ferreira Pinto outside wall. Source: Edivan Carneiro de Almeida photo, 27 September 2014, personal file.

The streets, eyes, cars, cameras, sprays, colors, walls. Walls that move before our eyes and freeze us, contemplative... walls that fold before the eyes (from whom?) and invite us to madness... (see figure 8) Throughout the weekend, artists flooded with their lines, their jets multiple colors and contours of the walls of the school. Sharing. Graffiti as an art, tells us Kbça, "You have the power to dialog with people, with the place", hence the main goal of the event according to the artist - is to move the city scene, politicizing. Through a politicization of colors, sprays, gesture scratching, risks, sensibilities not only on the retina...

"From now one, students want to do the same on their own because they believe it is possible to do so, right? [...] And they want it to be kept for good. Few days ago they asked teachers if it would be there or not, whether someone would erase it. The answers was 'No, it would not disappear. It would last according to the time it resists on the walls. Here it will not take it away, right?'" (Maria Manoela, history teacher).

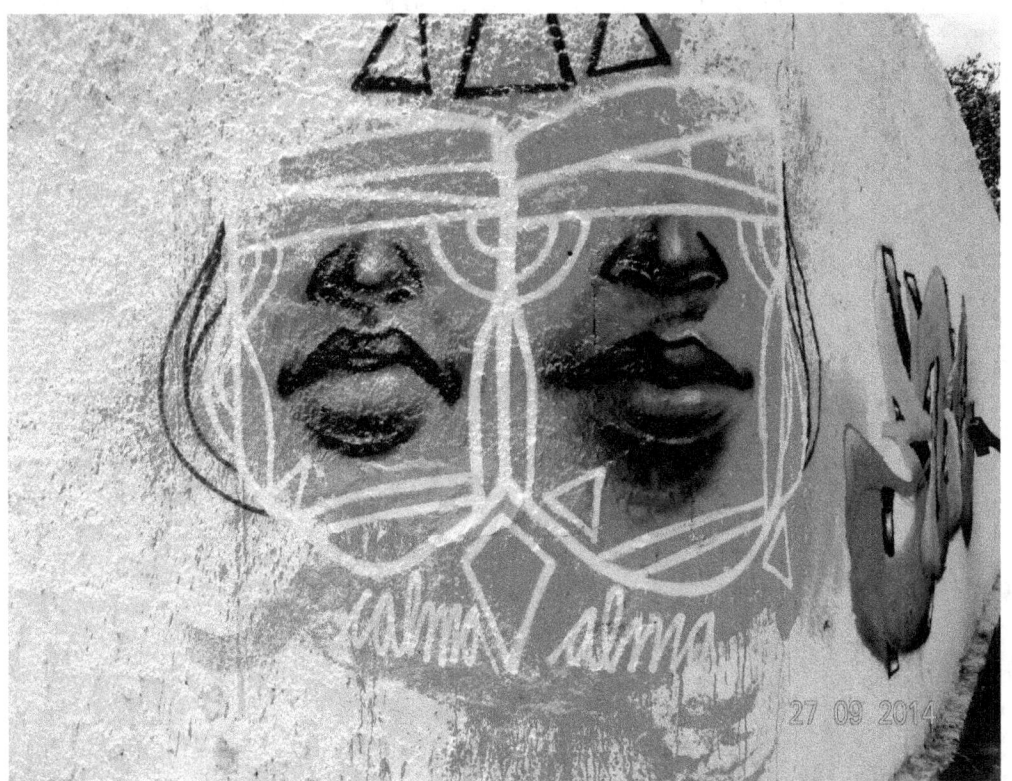

Figure 9 – In detail, *2nd Graffiti Meeting* photo. Jose Ferreira Pinto Public School's outside wall. Source: Edivan Carneiro de Almeida photo, 27 September 2014, personal file.

Sensibility displayed over the rough walls, in the tact of the eye, in view of the skin, allowing us to slip all through the new image plots that outlines with the vibration of spray cans on the graffiti men's hands (see figure 9). Students words in admiration, residents, invitation to graffiti wall... Movement thought and felt by the artists who promoted the meeting in transforming... the image on the rough world invite us to look with hands, touch with eyes these shadows, all the (im)possibilities to decode the meaning, (dis)connections among the drawings. Acting in craziness. Vital event through the gesture-body. Charles Mendes, also one of the graffiti artist highlighted: "My painting is a fair image, which decides nothing. It's a real graffiti, urban art, vandalism, genuine graffiti, all those aspects moving altogether." Delirium power of life... of cities.

Delirium Voices: The City Twists
Waging images of walls-worlds, multiplicities of knowledge, pluralities expressions clustered in order to set up everyday scenario, streets, cities in which here they are all resonances in sensations plan to proliferate thoughts before being analytical categories represented and identified as images. Provoking (in art, life, writing or nowhere) chaotic outbursts, not assumptions nor moral judgments and... blur, dim, e.g., centers that no longer need to *be obliged to see*.

Blurring what is intended to be consistent to the fields of (re)cognition, especially when we put ourselves through walls, streets, risks/sketches and colors from/with/in the cities. Dismiss the obviousness of explanations (whether conceptual, sensory, communicational).

For us, from *Levante*[7] was a great happening, a legacy that has been written on the walls! It is out there at Ferreira Pinto school, on its walls, beauty that remains. Mainly, it is remarkable for people who walk by! There were people who has never heard about graffiti and has known it for the first time due to the meeting! There were also ones who has deconstructed that graffiti's negative point of view! That's awesome! The environment was terrific. For us, it was an absolute success!" (Bruno Galego)

Experimentation that invites to escape from the fixed/rigid representations and from exercises of recognition on a narrative imagery that is to be felt (in Deleuze's expression of meaning) for the feel-fragment of a place scratched. «Scratching places. Making these foreign places from themselves: what is forced to be also the unplaced, the gap between that place and itself [...]" (Oliveira Jr, p 207, 2013.). Shifts in delimitation of the political resistances, markings and boundaries when discussing the supremacy of memories-remember-forgetfulness, images of *reality* and visual *experimentations*. Street and graffiti.

Therefore, we believe in an action of the images, presenting them as active spaces of creation, thought and knowledge, willing to escape from linearity/flatness that organizes *the before/previous* - the moment when the image is produced - and after - when it is seen. Moreover, this organizational movement wants to occur within a logic of continuation and a controlled and stable communication. What we aim is escapes from a political representation, is "[...] to 'distinguish' image representation' (object or content) from 'image as a creator" (Buci-Glucksmann, 2007, p. 70), questioning to what extent an image can/requires quantity of analogies...

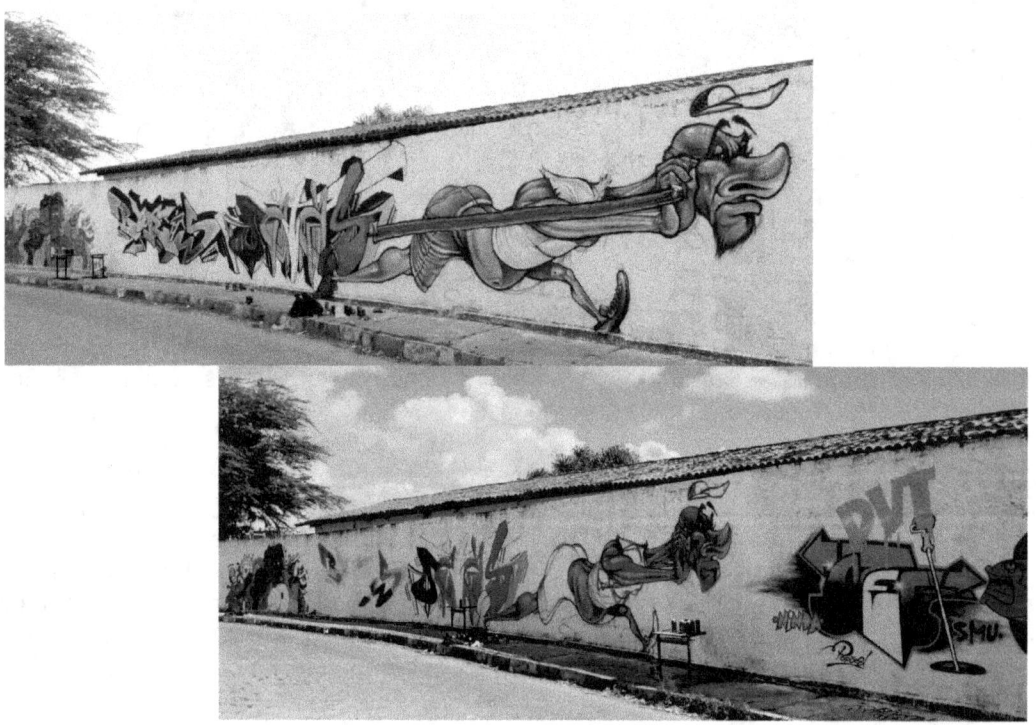

Figure 11 – Public School Colégio Estadual José Ferreira Pinto outside wall during the *2nd Graffiti Meeting.*
Source: Edivan Carneiro de Almeida photo, 27 September 2014, personal file.

---

7 Levante Youth Popular Movement became national in 2012, originally from Porto Alegre-RS in 2006 by rural citizens, people from Homeless and Land Movement (MST) and Small Agriculture Representatives (MPA). The main motto is the dialog and urban youngster organization, specially the poorest ones coming from big cities outskirts - once, recently, a large amount of popular movements do not want to be settled down in slams, denying the possibility of organizational and political fight to a huge amount of Brazilian people. In a day-by-day, young people promote actions about education in a public school, health system in a neighborhood, leisure, art and culture. As the ovine the acts on local and youth questions, it is possible to see a huge diversity such as from hip-hop groups to undergraduate courses. However, the only platform able to unit Levante Movement is by a Popular Project for Brazil, a group of structural modifications, rights acquisition - Agrarian reform program to democratization of media associate with social fight and people claim on streets.

"But I have something to look at and even after thousands times, we are not able to get all the details, nor decode everything that the artist wants to say. So, graffiti is a popular art, it is a street art and it has to be valued, I like it a lot. I do not understand as much art but this image... blue, white, seems to be eyes that stare at us and at the same time are not eyes so it calls... [see figure 10] It draws a lot of attention. I live here, walk by here every day, so this picture remains" (Jaci, school teacher).

Image that remains or let us portray/depict the observation of the world, in a sense of inviting other traits, shapes, actions of aesthetic under other angles, right? Images in wandering worlds, multiplicities of knowledge, pluralities expressions clustered in order to set up everyday scenario, here they are considered resonances in sensations plan to proliferate thoughts before being analytical categories represented and identified by images. An eye that is not the eye but sees. Blue and white that proliferate in feelings and expressions, no rush, when out there someone goes to school. Becoming *ex-pressed* by the world. Letting it go through the trial of acting.
Rhythms, cities, bodies, gestures in a mechanism that requires gap in the recognition and representation. Fragments that do not wish to be collected for (im)probable configuration of an image, thought, wall, city, education... A piece of graffiti or three? How many artists? Which (im)possibilities of linearity the image causes (see figure 11)? Objects, things, streets, lines... "What we call a 'map' or even a 'diagram', is a set of several lines running at the same time" (Deleuze, 1992, p. 47). Two Brazilian artists and a Swede, who did not speak or understand Portuguese, performed this image expression. Touching each other, and simultaneously looking each other, particles that spray to sparkle and slips - just like the wheels and the driver's feet of the vehicle, the cap, a feeling "Because on the moving street, it is experienced above all a strange moving of things" (Godoy, 2013, p. 2). Awkward. Contamination. Affections. Friction. Rubbing forces. Affect thoughts. Intensive experience of the body-matter-gesture. Sign as affection that makes us follow the lines.

It is the line that is between two points, but the point that is the intersection of several lines. The line is not regular, the point is just line inflection. [...] It is like a deviation of movement that occupies the space in a whirlwind way which is likely to to arise at any point. (Deleuze, 1992, p. 200).

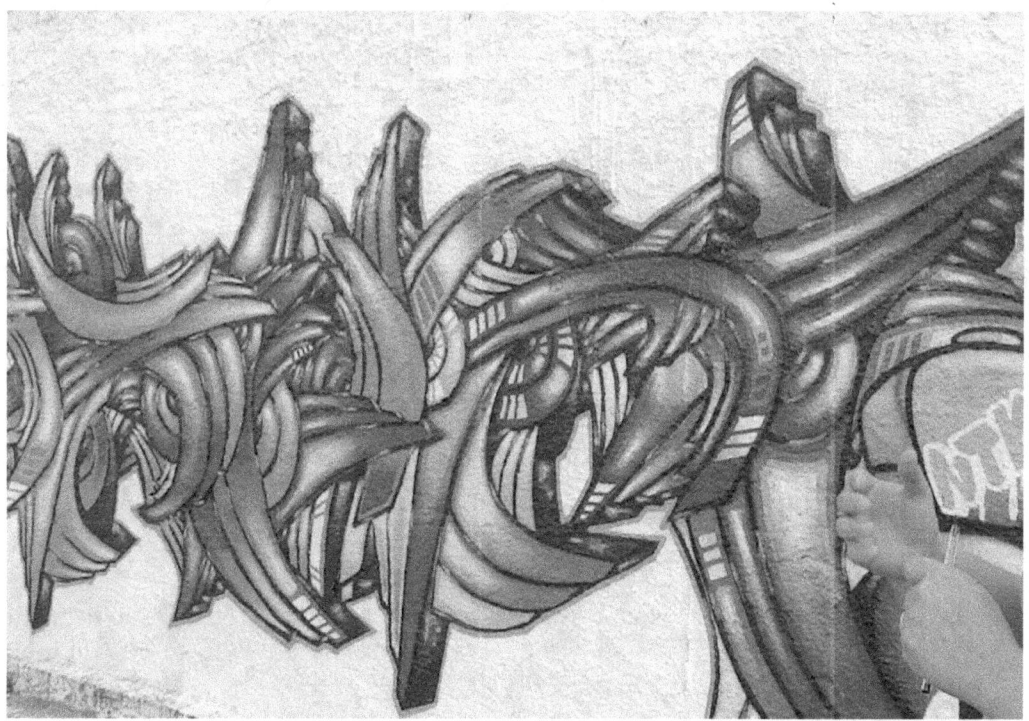

Figure 10 – in detail, 2nd Graffiti Meeting photo. Public School Colégio Estadual José Ferreira Pinto outside wall. Source: Scene plot with Prof. Jaci, made by Edivan Carneiro de Almeida, 30 October 2014, personal file.

Dispersion-intersection-composition points of sprawling paints on turbulent streets, walls, schools, education of delusional direction because in this way "[...] the city exists in a field forces correlation that is constantly in friction" (Galvão, 2008, p. 42). Shifts to the outside which is also inside, once school is off of the unique spacetime relation, choreographing artists, students, researchers, residents, colors, winds, trees in other rhythms. Choreography that involves chaos, contours that sing by deformities, cities invented by movements. Spatial surfaces leaving the crystallized dimensions and invites time to delirium...

References:

Basbaum, R. (2006). Diagramação e processos de transformação. In: Cruz, J. (Orgs.). *Gilles Deleuze: sentidos e expressões*. Rio de Janeiro:Ciência Moderna. (2010).

Sur, Sur, Sur, Sur... comme diagramme: carte + marque *Multitudes*, (n. 43), [on line] (p. 24-27). Retrieved from http://www.cairn.info/revue-multitudes-2010-4-page-24.htm. Accessed in 17 March 2015.

Buci-Glucksmann, C. (2007). Variações sobre a imagem: estética e política. In: Lins, D. (Org.). *Nietzsche/Deleuze: imagem, literatura e educação*. Simpósio Internacional de Filosofia. Rio de Janeiro/Fortaleza:Forense Universitária/Fundação de Cultura, Esporte e Turismo.

Campos, R. M. O. (2009). "all city" – graffiti europeu. *Revista de Antropologia, v. 52,* (n. 1), [on line], (p.11-46). Available in: Retrieved from http://http://www.revistas.usp.br/ra/article/view/27330. Accessed in 17 March de 2015.

Deleuze, G. (1992). *Conversações*. Trad. Peter Pál Perbart. São Paulo:Ed. 34. (2007). *Francis Bacon: lógica da sensação*. Trad. Roberto Machado (coord.) Rio de Janeiro:Jorge Zahar.

Galvão, D. G. (2008). *A Fabricação de Teresinas: subjetividades e imagens fotográficas na experiência teresinense do Salão Municipal de Fotografias (1995-2005)*. (Unpublished master's thesis). Universidade Federal do Piauí – UFPI. Centro de Ciências Humanas e Letras - CCHL. Programa de Pós-Graduação em História. History MD in Brasil. Piauí, Brasil.

Godinho, A. (2013). Diagramas para pensar/diagramas de sensação. In: Gallo, S.; Novaes, M. & Guarienti, L. B. O. (Orgs). *Conexões: Deleuze e políticas e resistências e...* Petrópolis, RJ: DP&A; Campinas, SP: ALB; Brasília, DF: Capes.

Godoy, A. (2013). TransKafka: uma experimentação. In: Grupo Transversal (Org.). *Educação menor: conceitos e experimentações*. Curitiba:Prismas.

Nascimento, R. (2013). Dimensões políticas da teoria deleuziana dos signos. In: Gallo, S.; Novaes, M. & Guarienti, L. B. O. (Orgs). *Conexões: Deleuze e políticas e resistências e...* Petrópolis, RJ: DP&A; Campinas, SP: ALB; Brasília, DF:Capes.

Oliveira Júnior, W. M. (2013). A rasura dos lugares – fragmentos espaciais re-existentes em vídeos. In: Gallo, S.; Novaes, M. & Guarienti, L. B. O. (Orgs). *Conexões: Deleuze e políticas e resistências e...* Petrópolis, RJ: DP&A; Campinas, SP: ALB; Brasília, DF:Capes.

Ramos, C. (1994). *Grafite, Pichação & Cia*. São Paulo:Annablume.

Rancière, J. (2009). *A partilha do sensível: estética e política*. Trad. Mônica Costa Netto. São Paulo:Ed. 34. (2012). *O destino das imagens*. Trad. Mônica Costa Netto. Rio de Janeiro:Contraponto.

Chapter 12

Beyond the visible on decoding the layers of a cultural quarter: photo-essay on a reflexive urban intervention

Pedro Costa and Ricardo Lopes (PT)

Abstract:

Drawing on a research-action based methodology the authors developed three experiences of urban interventions, linked to a scientific research program, in three consecutive years, in informal urban contexts in Bairro Alto, the main cultural quarter of Lisbon. In this paper we explore some of the results of one of these urban interventions, the happening "Beyond Visible", which was particularly directed to explore the reflexivity on this neighborhood's users and to promote the discussion on the codification layers of a cultural quarter and its inherent conflicts. Through the confront of its users with their perceptions and representations about Bairro Alto area, this intervention brought us interesting results which enable us to explore the different layers of (in)visibility in the informal urban contexts that are present in a cultural district such as this one, as well as in many creative milieus.

Keywords: Creative Milieus; Conflict; Informality; Cultural Quarters; Public Sphere; Artistic Urban Interventions; Photo-essay: Bairro Alto

1. Introduction[1]

Cultural quarters have been widely studied in recent years as they embody broader structural transformations associated with urban change, but also as they are privileged arenas for tension and conflict, manifested both in spatial terms and in people's lived experiences. The wide variety of gentrified residential city enclaves, ghettos, glbt villages, ethnic quarters, red light districts and creative quarters can be seen as a commonplace feature of contemporary urban landscape (Bell and Jayne, 2004), which often brings vitality and vibrancy for many ancient or abandoned areas of cities, but also as an arena for frequent conflicts between residents and users, gentrifiers and traditional residents, new activities and traditional activities, night users and day users, and so on (Costa, 2008; Costa et al, 2010, Costa and Lopes, 2012, 2015). Public space is often the privileged sphere for these tensions and conflicts, with the expression of multiple power relations at the levels of the physical space, the experiences it provides and the symbolic field. In parallel, these are also frequently liminal spaces, marked by transgression and social and individual expression of the self, in contexts where social control is mitigated and openness and tolerance to diversity increase.

---

1 This paper, developed through the particular format of a photo essay, draws upon an urban intervention and a research process which was previously explored in two other parallel papers, now under publishing process, which were devoted to the analysis of a set of 3 urban interventions conducted in the Bairro Alto area by the authors between 2010 and 2012 (Costa and Lopes, 2016a, 2016b). Parts of the short text that is presented here in this visual essay are tributary of those two texts, which themselves draws upon two previous versions, which were presented at several international conferences: "Artistic intervention in public sphere, conflict and urban informality: an international comparative approach to informal dynamics in cultural districts", Paper presented at the International RC21 Conference 2013, Resourceful Cities, Berlin (Germany), 29th-31th August 2013; and "Artistic Urban Interventions, Informality and Public Sphere: Research Insights from Ephemeral Urban Appropriations on a Cultural District", paper presented at XVIII ISA World Congress of Sociology "Facing an Unequal World: Challenges for Global Sociology", Pacifico Yokohama, Yokohama, Japan, 13th-19th July 2014 and at European Sociological Association Research Network 37 "Urban Sociology" Mid-Term Conference "Public spaces and private lives in the contemporary city", Lisbon, FCSH-UNL, 19th-21th November 2014. The authors acknowledge all the comments and suggestions made by the reviewers and participants on those sessions.

Drawing upon a research-action based methodology the authors developed three experiences[2] of urban interventions linked to a scientific research program, in three consecutive years, in Bairro Alto, the main cultural quarter of Lisbon, Portugal (see Costa and Lopes 2016a, 2016b for details). In this paper we explore some of the results of the third of these urban interventions, the happening "Beyond Visible", held on December 2012. This event was particularly directed to explore the reflexivity on this quarter's users and to promote the discussion on the codification layers of a cultural district and its inherent conflicts, expressed both on material and symbolic arenas. The photo-essay that is here presented is based on some the results this intervention brought us, aiming to explore the different *layers* (in)visible in the informal urban contexts of Bairro Alto.

Artistic intervention was for us a particularly interesting way of looking at these neighborhoods and to understand the multiple layers of uses and segregations that bring vitality in everyday life to these parts of the complex organisms that cities are (see Costa and Lopes 2016a, 2016b on this)..Our previous research on several cultural quarters in diverse contexts (Costa and Lopes, 2013, 2015), based on desk research, observation and visual ethnographic approaches, providing a comparative perspective of their public sphere, enabled us to question and to bring to discussion the characteristics of each of these districts, concerning their morphology, creative dynamics and informality, trying to understand the main features that can contribute to the development and vitality in these cultural quarters as well as their specificities.

With these interventions, taking as empirical context the Bairro Alto district in Lisbon, we tried to in-depth this analysis, in several directions (cf Costa and Lopes, 2016a, 2016b), and in this particular case we focused on the issues related to the multiple codification layers reflected in the practices and representations of this quarter's users.

2. The "Beyond Visible" *happening* (Bairro Alto, 2012)

In December 2012, we tried to explore this kind of ephemeral intervention promoting in Bairro Alto an *happening* entitled *Beyond Visible*[3]. The *happening* intended to introduce in the quarter a "new living room" for one night in an expectant space of Rua da Barroca. Its main concept was to explore the idea of the several layers of codifications that compose the creative milieus, particularizing for the case of this quarter and the way people "represent" (and "read") it. Thus, along that night, the people that passed by on the street were invited to enter in a "dark space" and to build their own exhibition, through their own course through those rooms, without segregation of any kind people or practices.

The happening was visually announced with a projection of several photos overlapping in the opposite façade of the intervened building. The projection drew a diffuse image of Bairro Alto (composed by those overlapped layers) which suggested that something different was happening on that space. Closer to the venue, people started to see one door, where it was possible to enter in a "dark space", and another one, where there were people going out on the rhythm of photographic camera's flashes.

The intervention suggested an inverted route of exhibition. It started with images of people that had already been photographed projected on the wall of a "waiting room", where visitors received "UV light" lamps which they were invited to use in the subsequent rooms, at the interior of the *happening*. After people were invited to enter to that "dark space", they started to unveil phrases that were written with "transparent ink" on the interior walls of the building (the sentences were previously collected through interviews made with people in Bairro Alto in different periods of the day and represented the opinions and image of those citizens about it). The variety of sentences written and the technique used allowed each visitor to discover different things and to interpret them from different points of view. Along the exhibition, the visitors were surprised by other complementary artistic interventions: in a small performing space two actors (Nuno Antunes and Beatriz Henriques) talked with the visitors (one at a time)

2 *Espaços Liminares*, in 2010 (http://espacosliminares.blogspot.pt/); *Bairros como nós*, in 2011 (http://bairroscomonos.blogspot.pt/); and *Beyond Visible*, in 2012 (http://beyondvisibleba2012.blogspot.pt/).

3 More info at http://beyondvisibleba2012.blogspot.pt/

about Bairro Alto; during all the visit, the "background noise" constructed with sounds collected in the quarter (musicians: JPShelaq / Geraldes / João) accompanied the visit. At the end, the visitors were surprised by four photographers (Thiago Feitosa / Carolina Mota / Alexandre Abreu / Mariana Cortes) that had prepared a replica of a professional studio to photograph them and, in this way, being "formally" photographed they become also part of the artistic intervention - not just as spectators and participative elements, but also as an object exhibited (and actively performing for it…).

Naturally, besides exploring artistic and research aspects, the exhibition tried also to create one critical sense in audience who had been tempt to think about the quarter and its happenings from a different perspective, enhancing a reflexive process about the quarter, individually and collectively.

3. A photographic approach to the multiple (de)codification layers of a cultural quarter

In this visual essay we focus on the evidence provided by our subjects on the multiple layers of visibility and importance that were brought to discussion about Bairro Alto in the intervention that we have developed. Being cultural quarters marked by liminality and multiple layers of codification, mostly in the cases where gentrification and massification processes take place, as this one (cf. Costa and Lopes, 2013, 2015, Costa 2013), these aspects are particularly relevant.

As preparatory process to this intervention we asked to its users' two simple questions: one was about what Bairro Alto meant to each one of the persons inquired; the other one was to name a place in Bairro Alto which would be important or somehow representative for that person. The answers to these questions were obtained through a brief fieldwork, conducted on two complementary ways: through direct short interviews on brief strolls around the neighborhood during daytime and nighttime, and also by an simple e-mail survey forwarded on a snowball methodology.

The display in the intervention presented the results achieved on a way which aimed to be able to promote reflexivity, confront and discussion among participants' contrasting views. Most of the space of exhibition was covered by the sentences obtained to the first question, which people would discover, with their lamp in their hands, un-hiding it from darkness, through their individual course, wherever they pointed out their lights. In a specific small space, near the end of the trail (a small bathroom with its door open) were the answers to the second question, with the names of places mentioned by people… In parallel, another small bathroom gave the opportunity to people to express themselves (with a microphone recording what people would be willing to leave), in front of a wall where the word "Fala" (speak), provoked the visitor (although the results of this last device were a little bit disappointing, and were not explored in this paper).

In our presentation, we opt to let the photos talk, and just highlight some of the phrases and expressions collected on each legend, trying to make a little more evident the main topics that are significant in the several divides that cross the difference layers and segregations which characterize contemporary Bairro Alto (older and traditional residents, newcomers; cultural activities; new "creative" activities; nightlife activities; traditional commerce; nightlife users; artists; gentrifiers; etc).

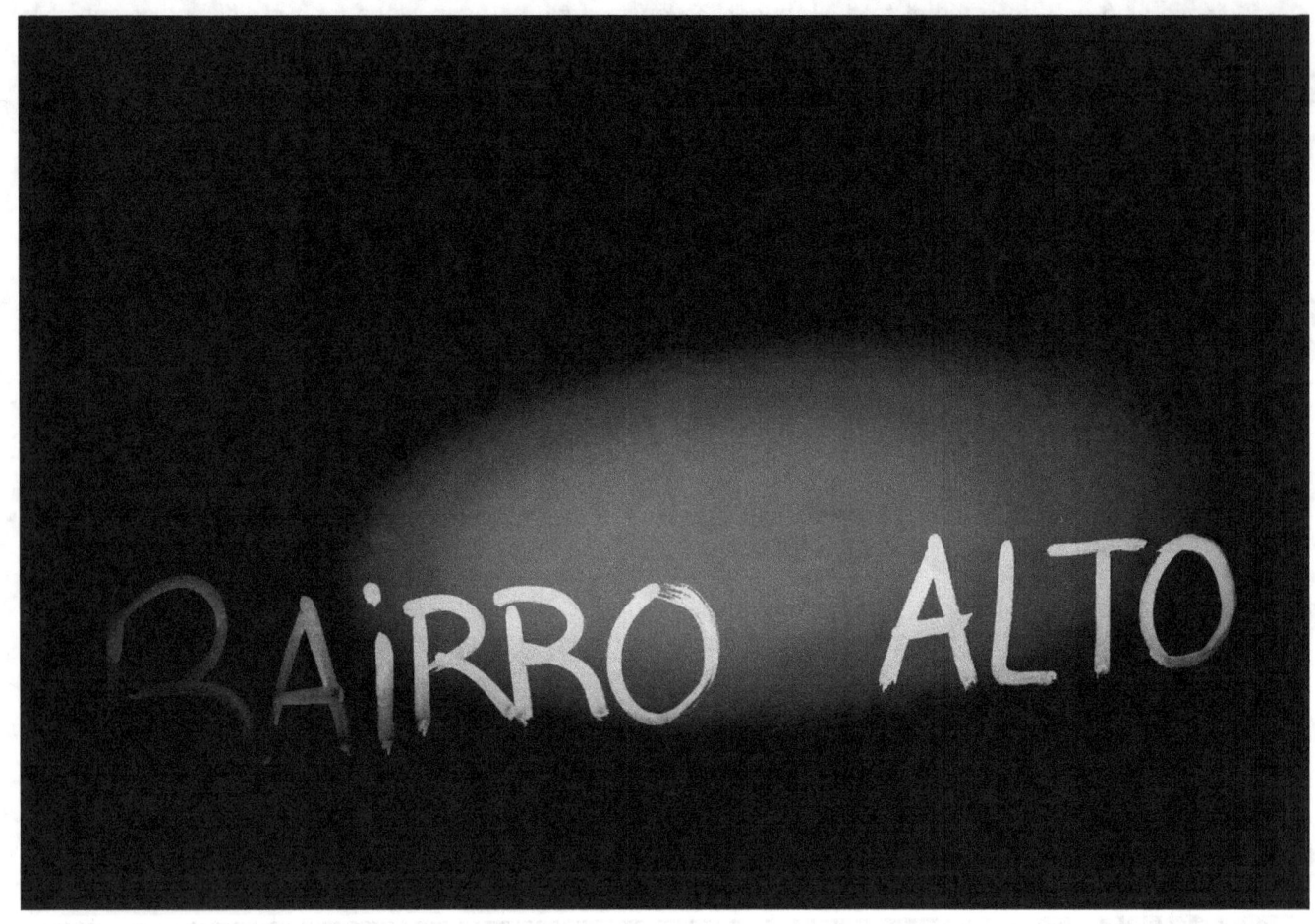

Figure 1 - The intervention: previously collected expressions about 'Bairro Alto' were displayed on the walls, written with an ink which was just sensible to UV lights. Each person would make visible a particular "vision" of Bairro Alto through the path which would be constructed by each one, pointing his lamp to the wall and unveiling certain phrases, through the several rooms of the exhibition. "Bairro Alto"

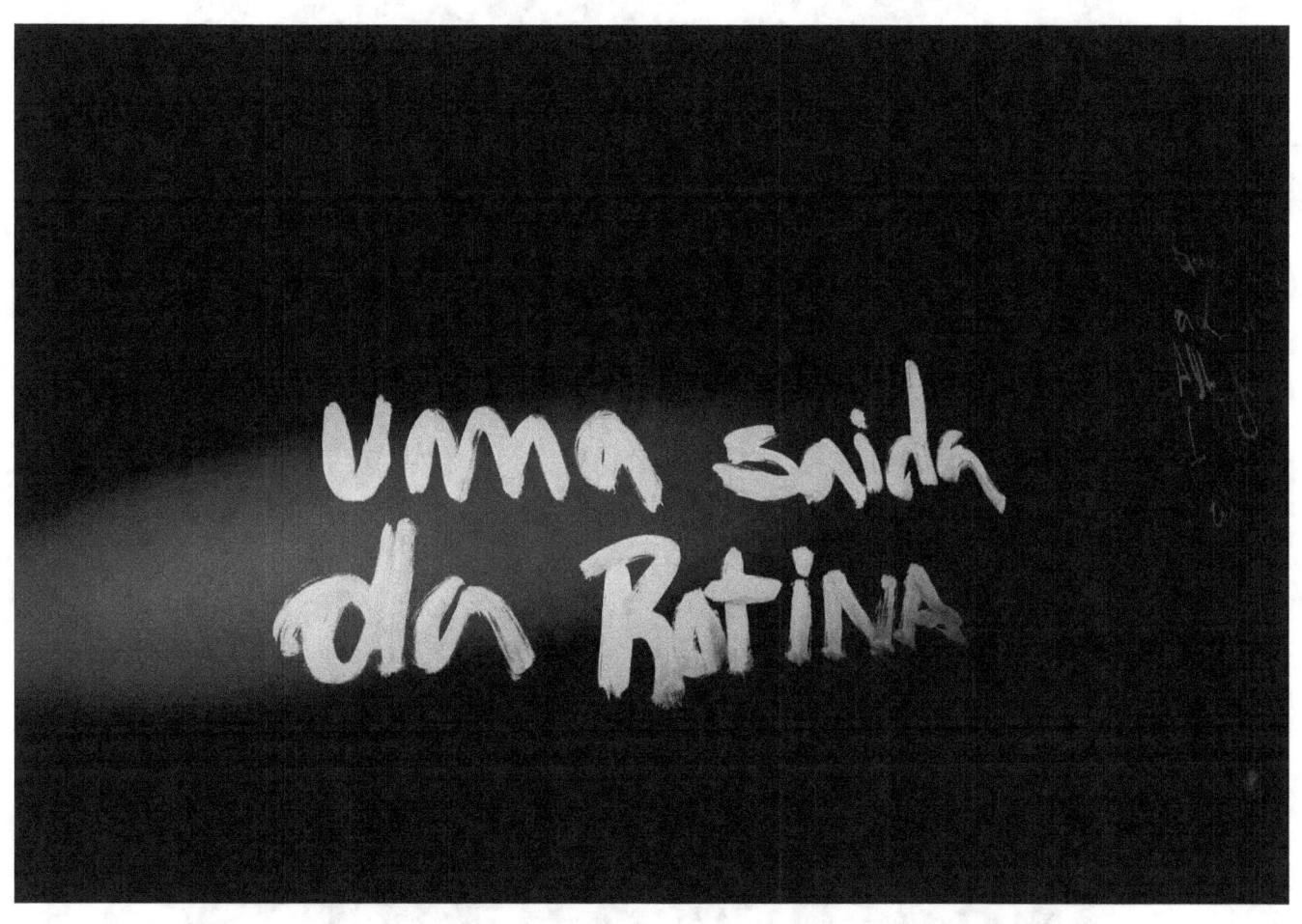

Figure 2 - What is, for you, the Bairro Alto?
"A way out from everyday life"

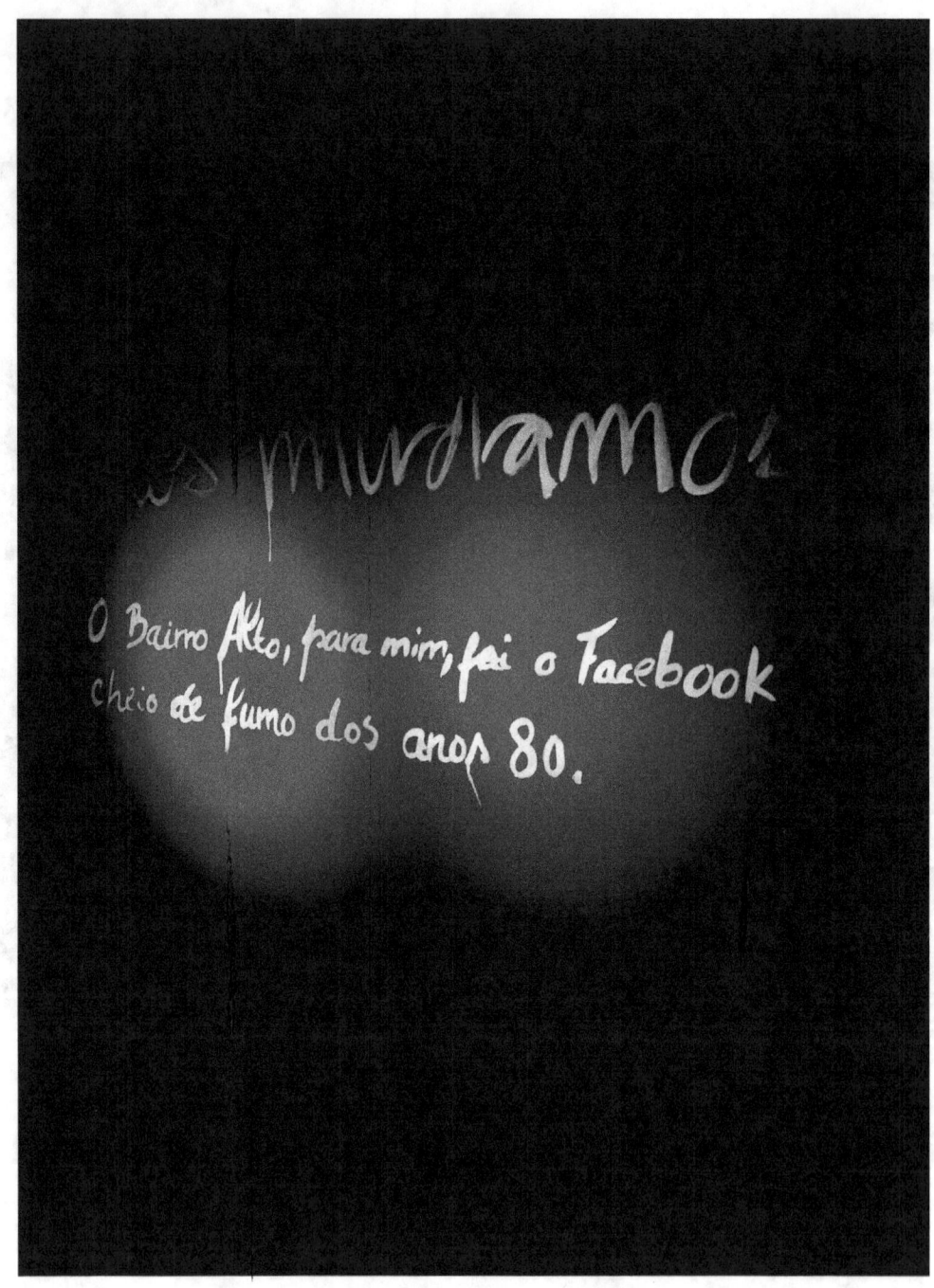

Figure 3 – What is, for you, the Bairro Alto?
"We change [with the neighborhood]"
"Bairro Alto, to me, was the smoky Facebook of the 80's"

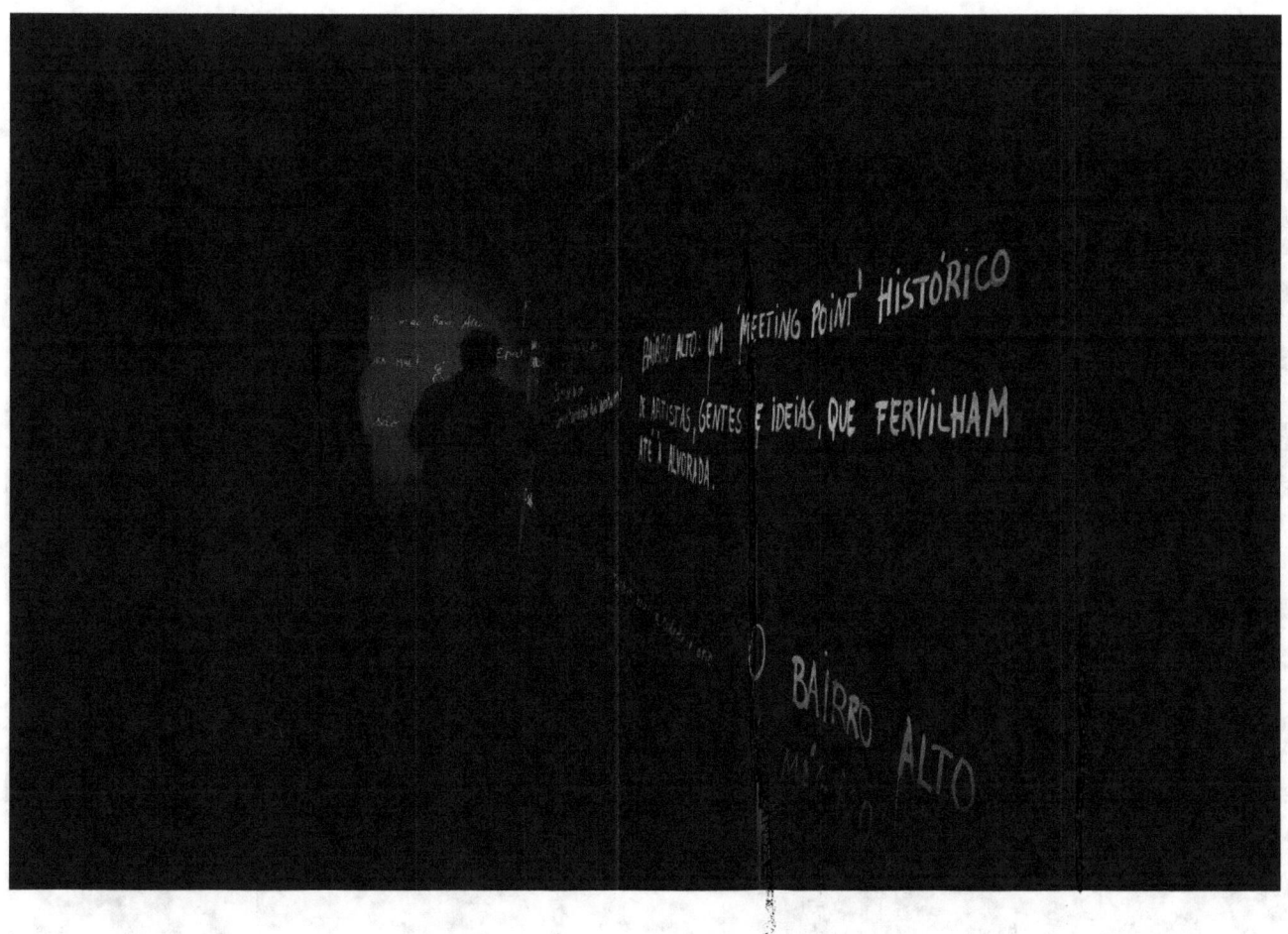

Figure 4 - What is, for you, the Bairro Alto?
"...an historical 'meeting point' of artists, people and ideas, which simmer till dawn"

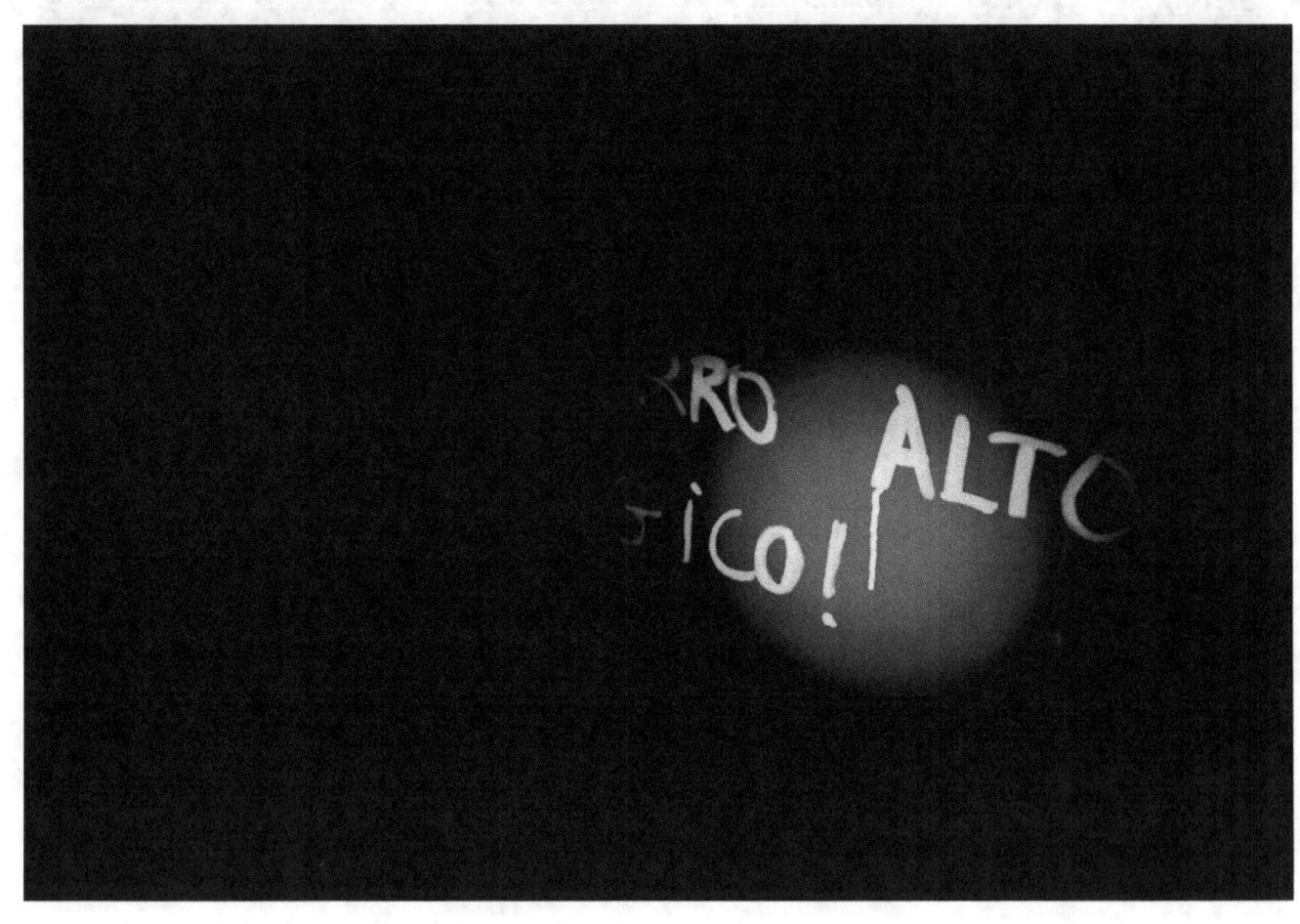

Figure 5 - What is, for you, the Bairro Alto?
"… Bairro Alto is magic!"

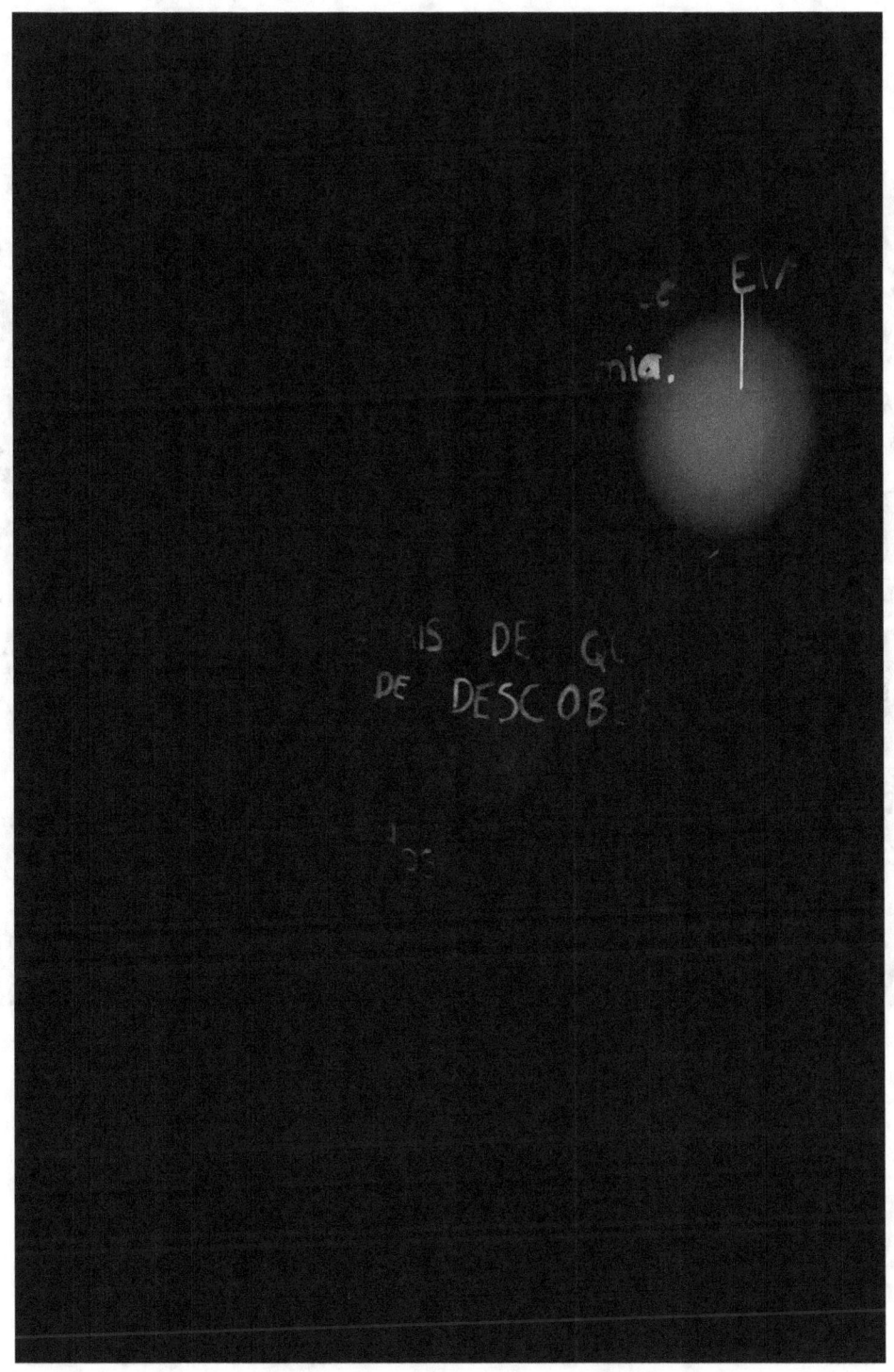

Figure 6 – What is, for you, the Bairro Alto?
"…evasion… bohemia … contact… places…discovery … all…"

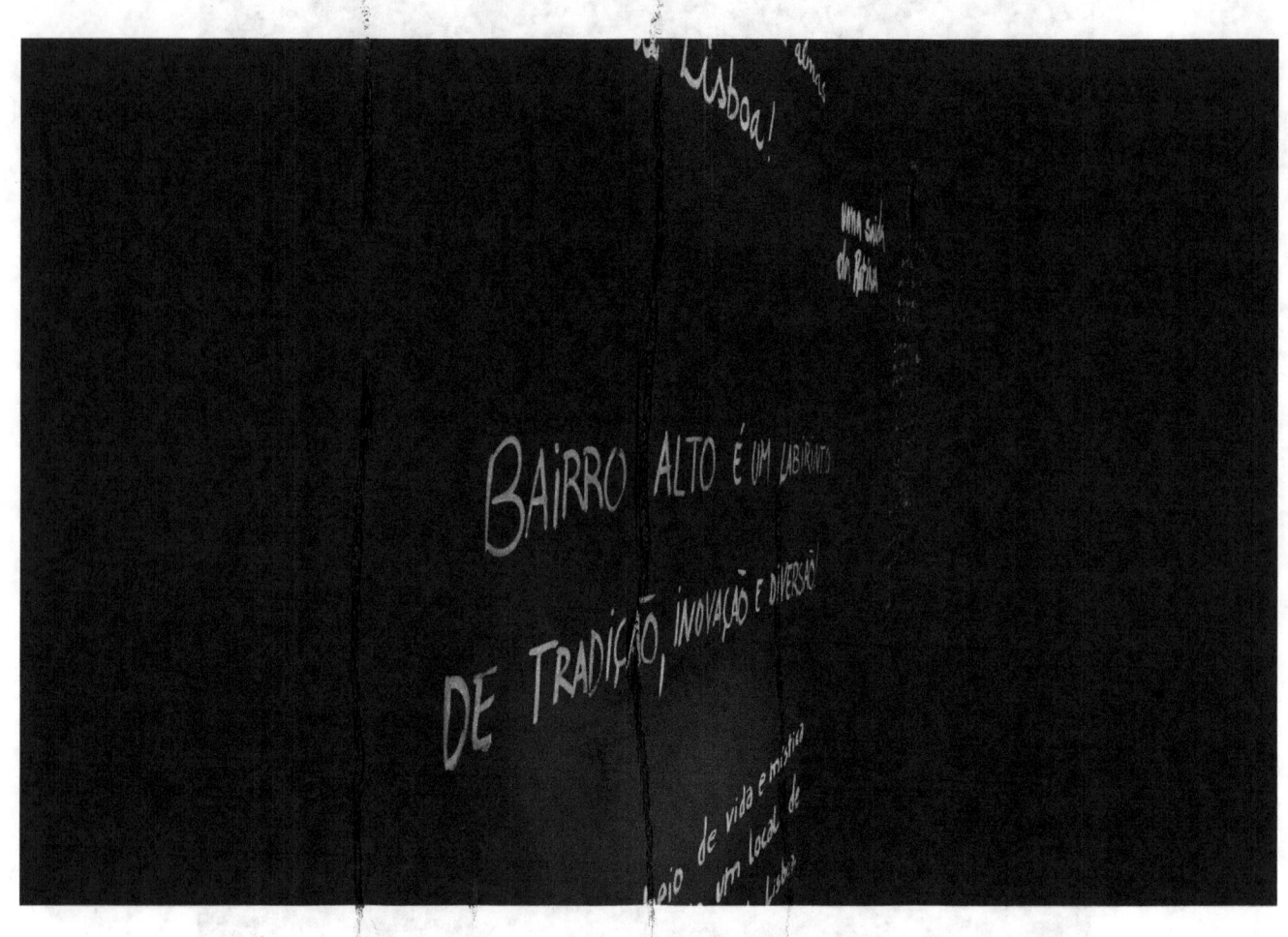

Figure 7 – What is, for you, the Bairro Alto?
"Bairro Alto is a labyrinth of tradition, innovation and fun"

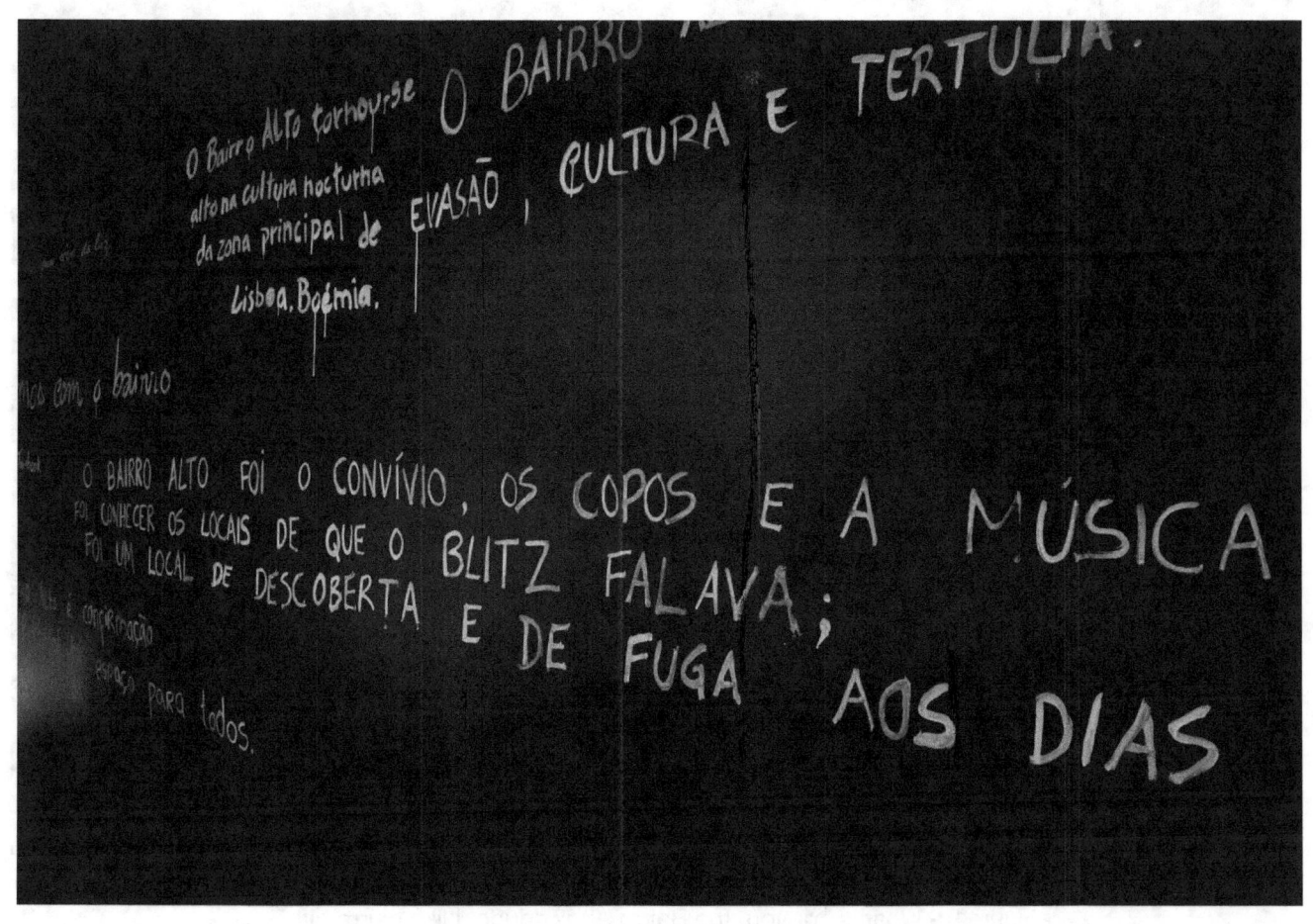

Figure 8 – What is, for you, the Bairro Alto?
"Bairro Alto got high on nightlife culture",
"…main area of bohemian Lisbon";
"…Bairro [Alto is] evasion, culture and *tertúlia*" [Portuguese expression for intellectual chatting and debate]
"Bairro Alto was the meetings, the glasse and the music;
It was to know the places whose Blitz [portuguese music journal] talked;
It was a place of find and escape the days…"
"…space for all"

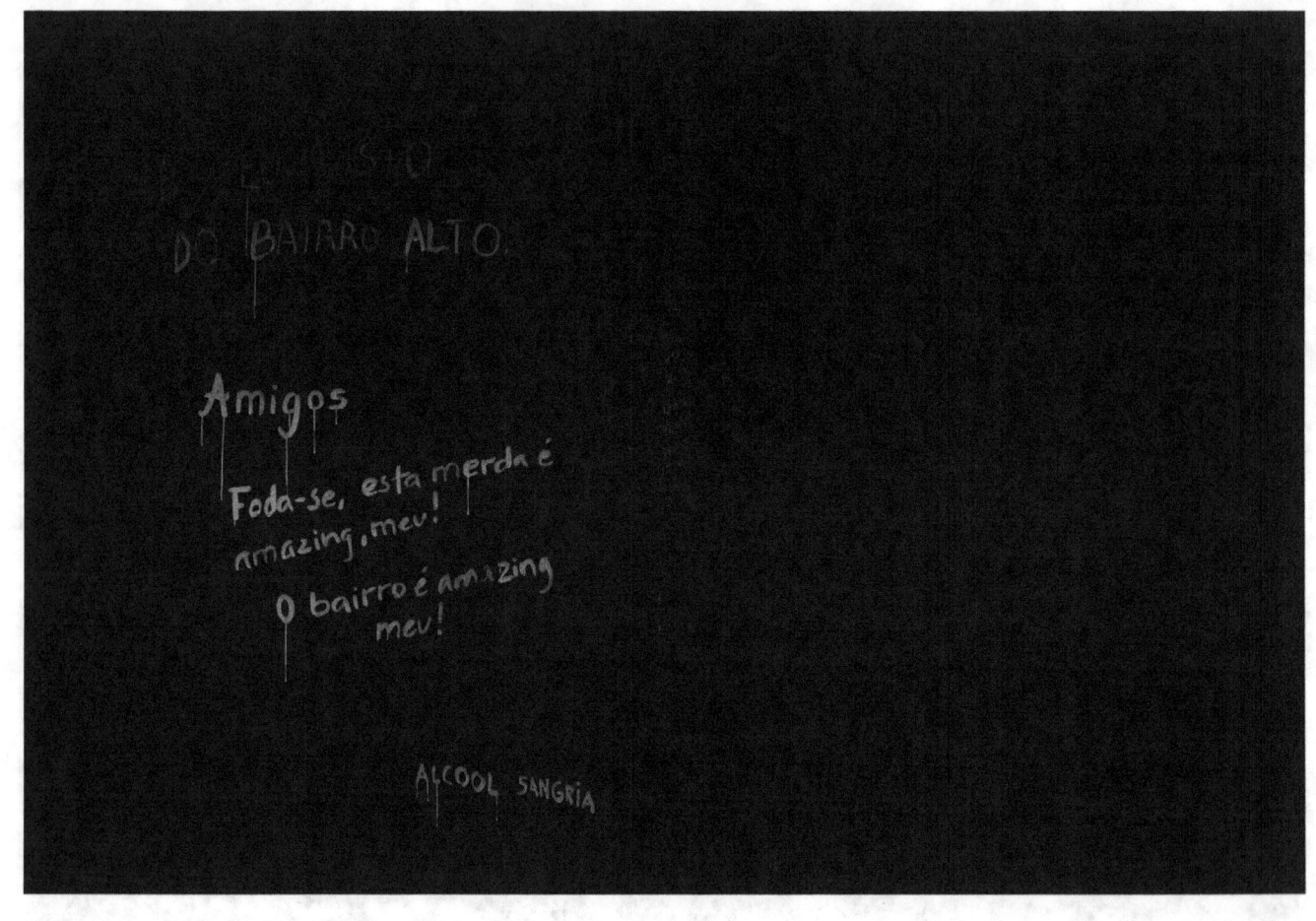

Figure 9 - What is, for you, the Bairro Alto? "dude, I like bairro alto"
"friends"
"fuck, this shit is amazing, man! the 'bairro[1]' is amazing, man!"
"alcohol, sangria"

---

1 "the "bairro", as it is often called by people, is frequently used indifferently as the short name for Bairro Alto, as well as for quarter/district/neighborhood…

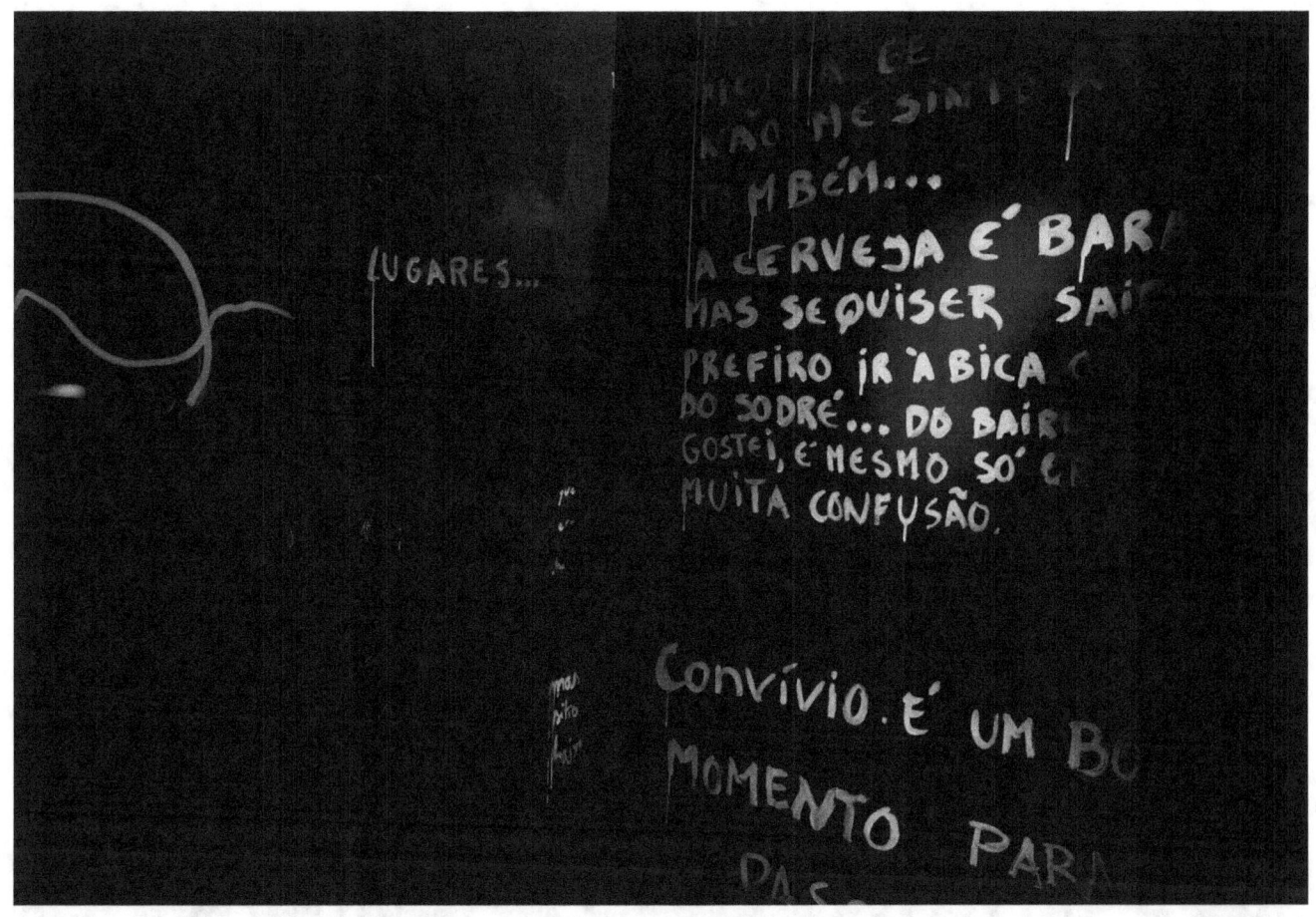

Figure 10 - What is, for you, the Bairro Alto?
"[under aged, drunk people, confusion, lots of people…] I'm not comfortable, as well.. the beer is cheap, but to go out I prefer to go to Bica or Cais do Sodré… I've never liked Bairro Alto, it is just Erasmus and lots of confusion"
"Conviviality. It is a good moment to spend"

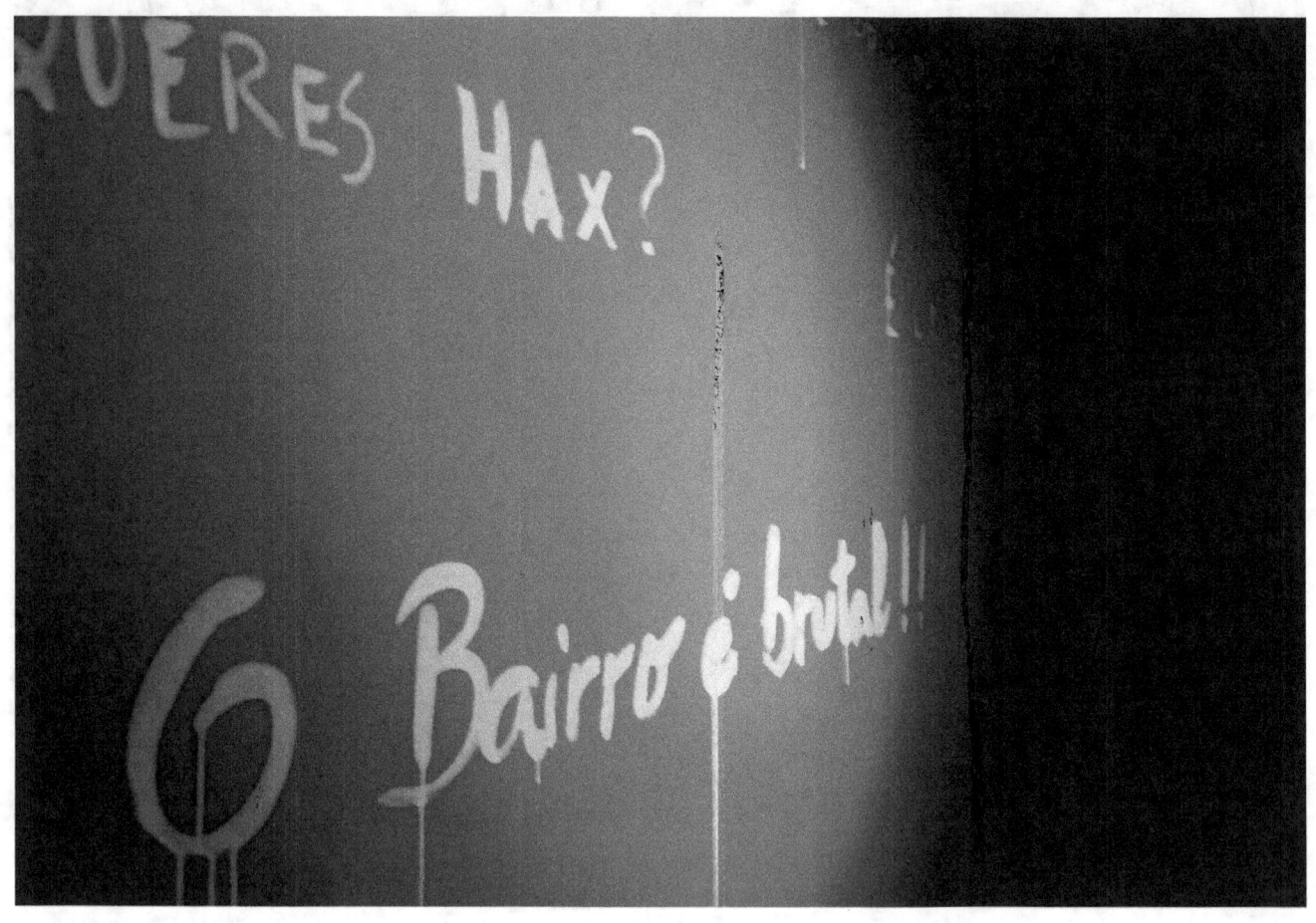

Figure 11 - What is, for you, the Bairro Alto?
"do you want hash?"
"The 'Bairro' is brutal!!" (Portuguese expression often used also to express the sense of overwhelming)

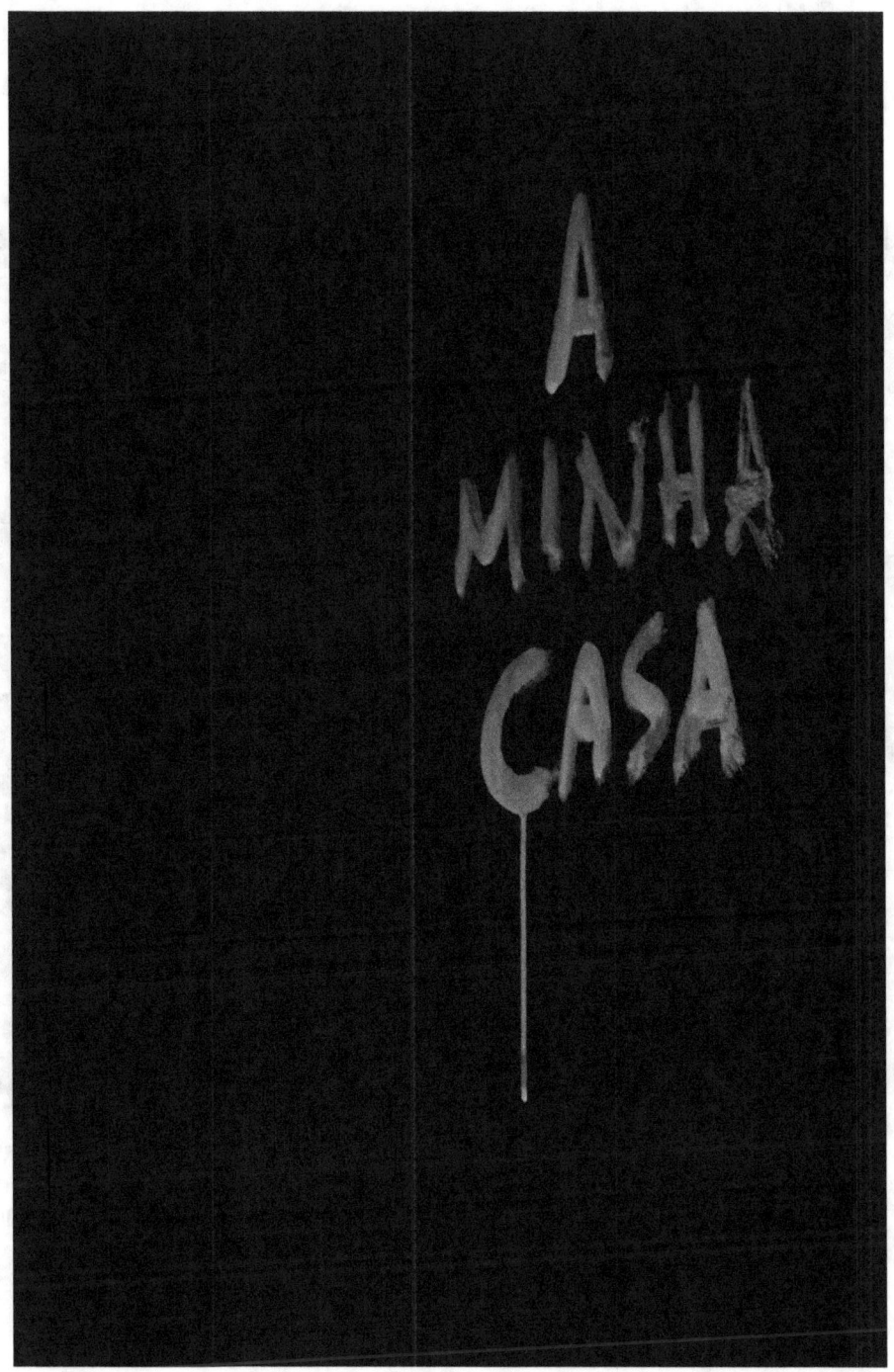

Figure 12 - Name an important place, for you, at Bairro Alto
"My home"

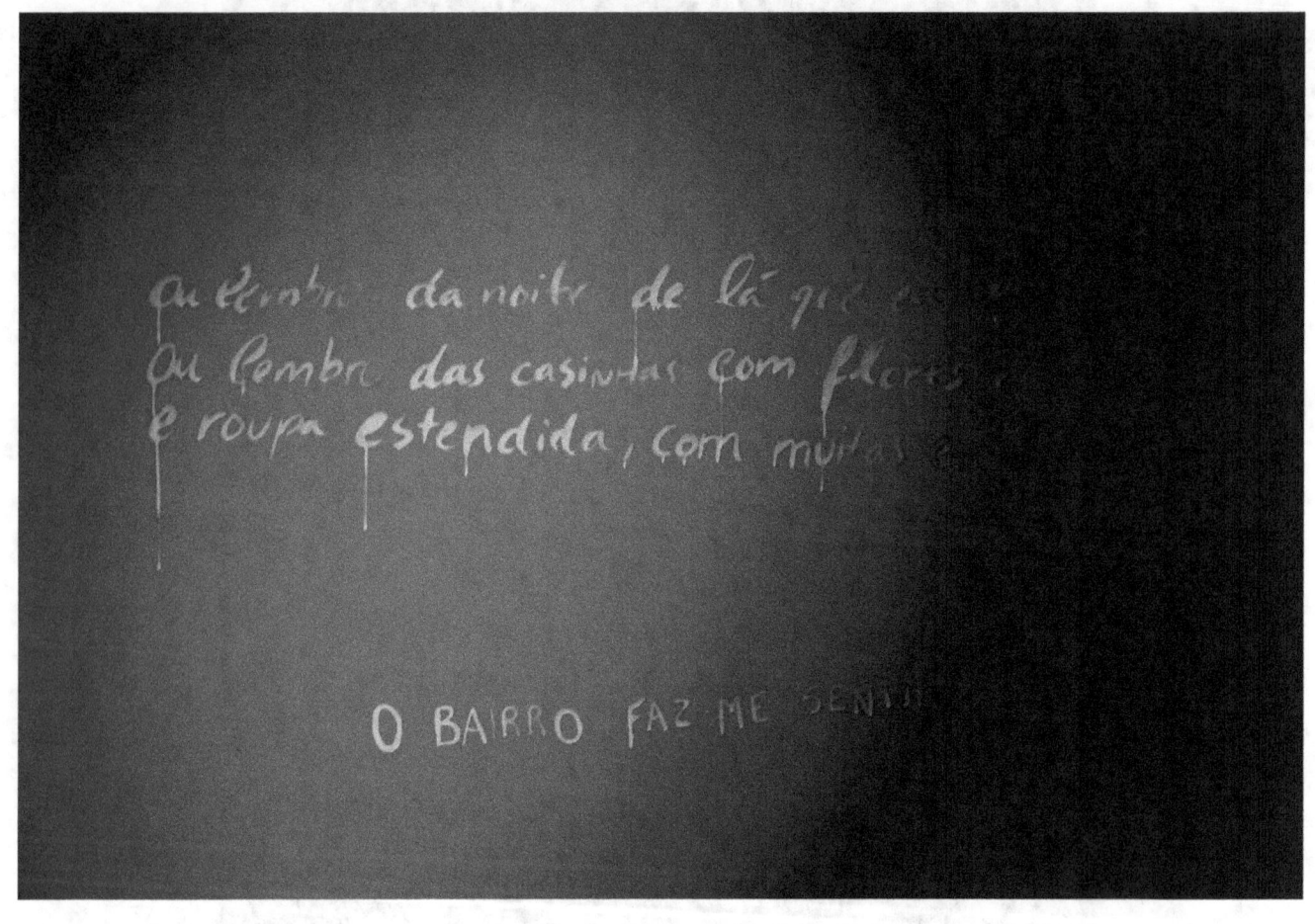

Figure - 13 - What is, for you, the Bairro Alto?
"I remember its nightlife, which I hate, or I remember the tiny houses with flowers at the windows and the clothes drying, with a lot of stairs."
"the 'Bairro' makes me feel old"

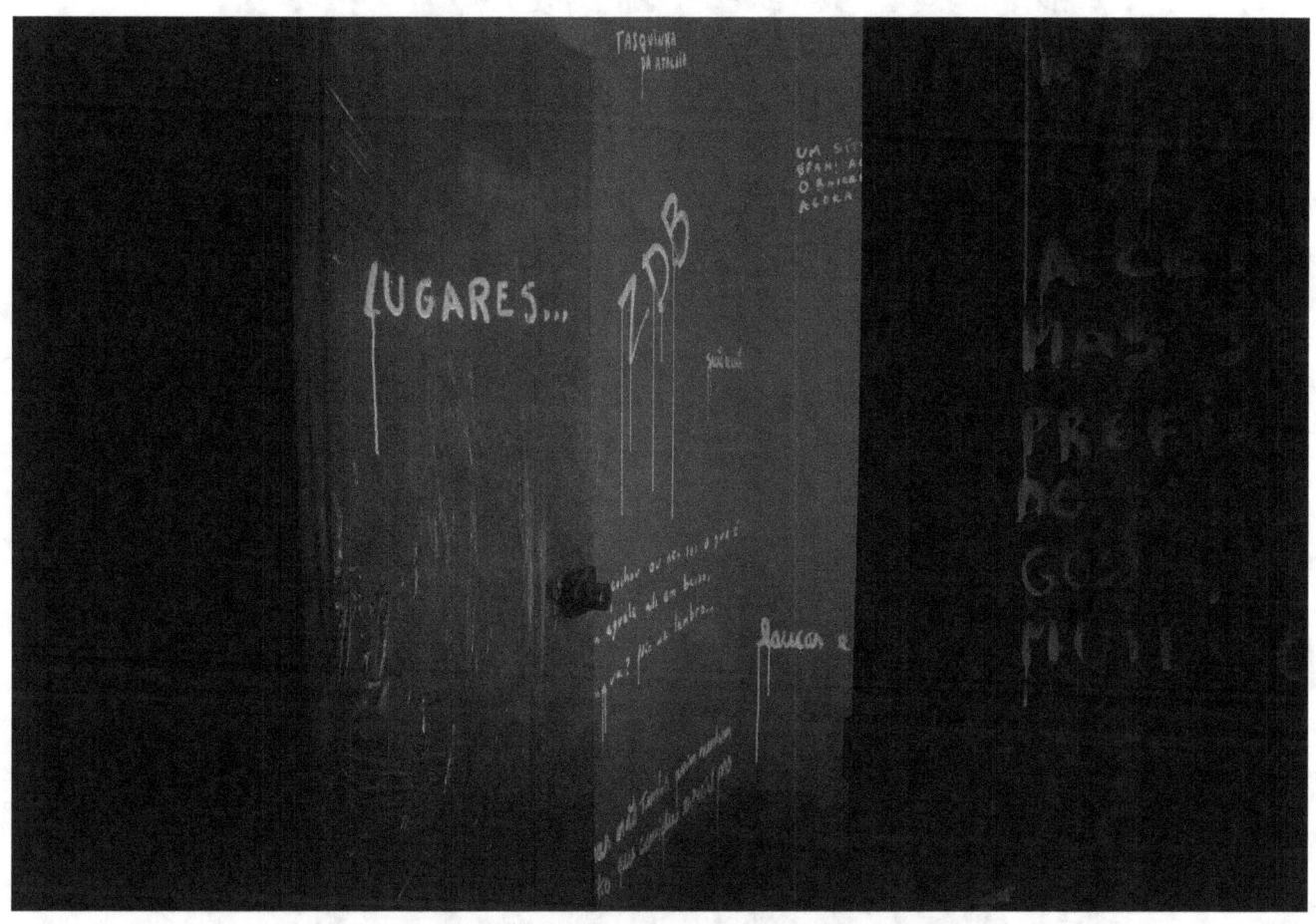

Figure 14 - Entrance to the room where the answers to the second question, asking people for a suggestion of "their" place in Bairro Alto, were displayed; "Places…"

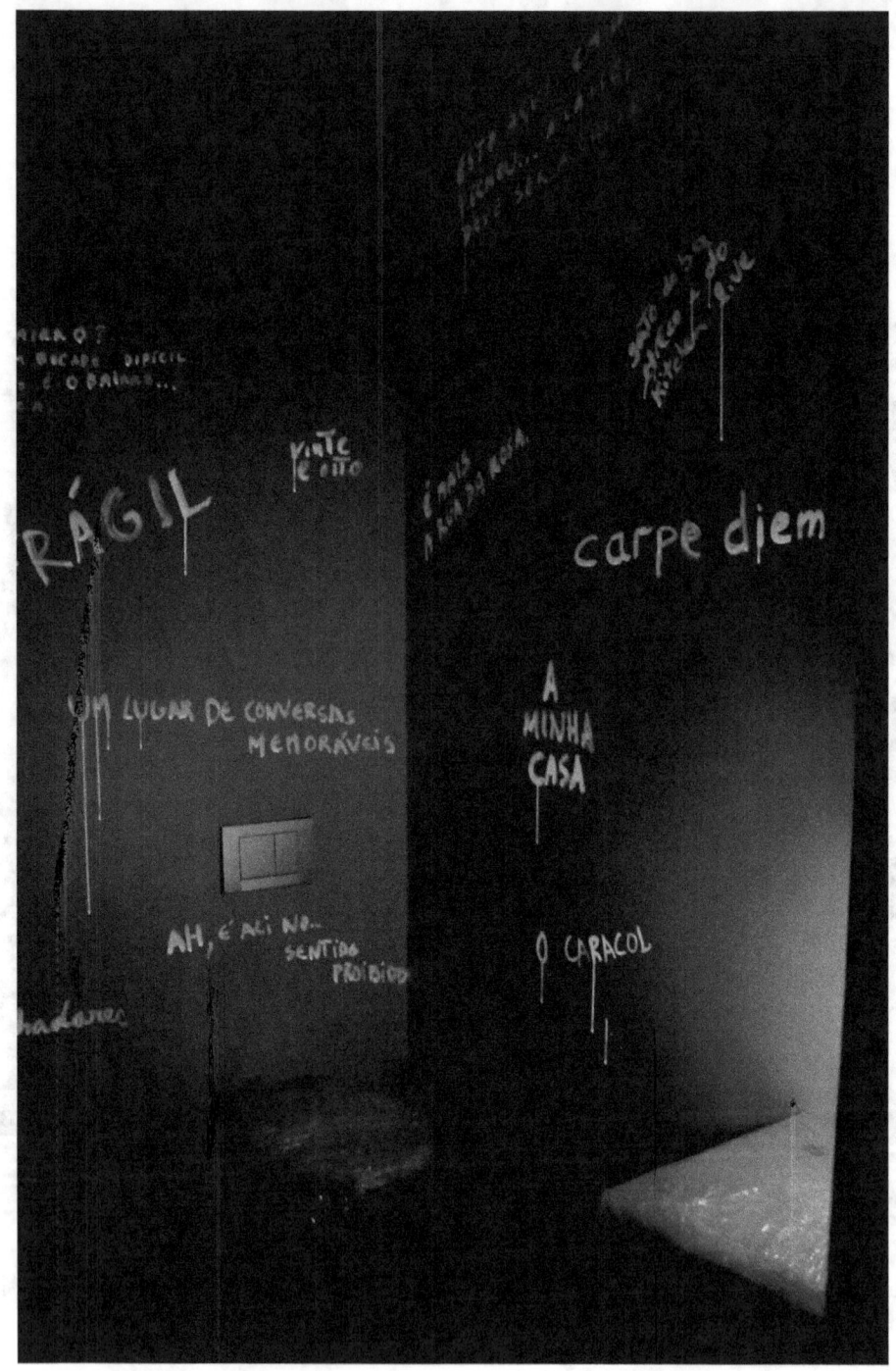

Figure 15 - Name an important place, for you, at Bairro Alto
"I like Etílico bar and Kitchen live" (bars) "My home" (which can be read very
pragmatically or more poetically) "The Caracol" (restaurant) "Oh, it's there, at Sentido
proibido" (bar) "Frágil" (bar) "Vinte e oito" (bar, club) "Carpe diem" (visual arts center)
"It is more Rosa street" "a place of memorable talks"

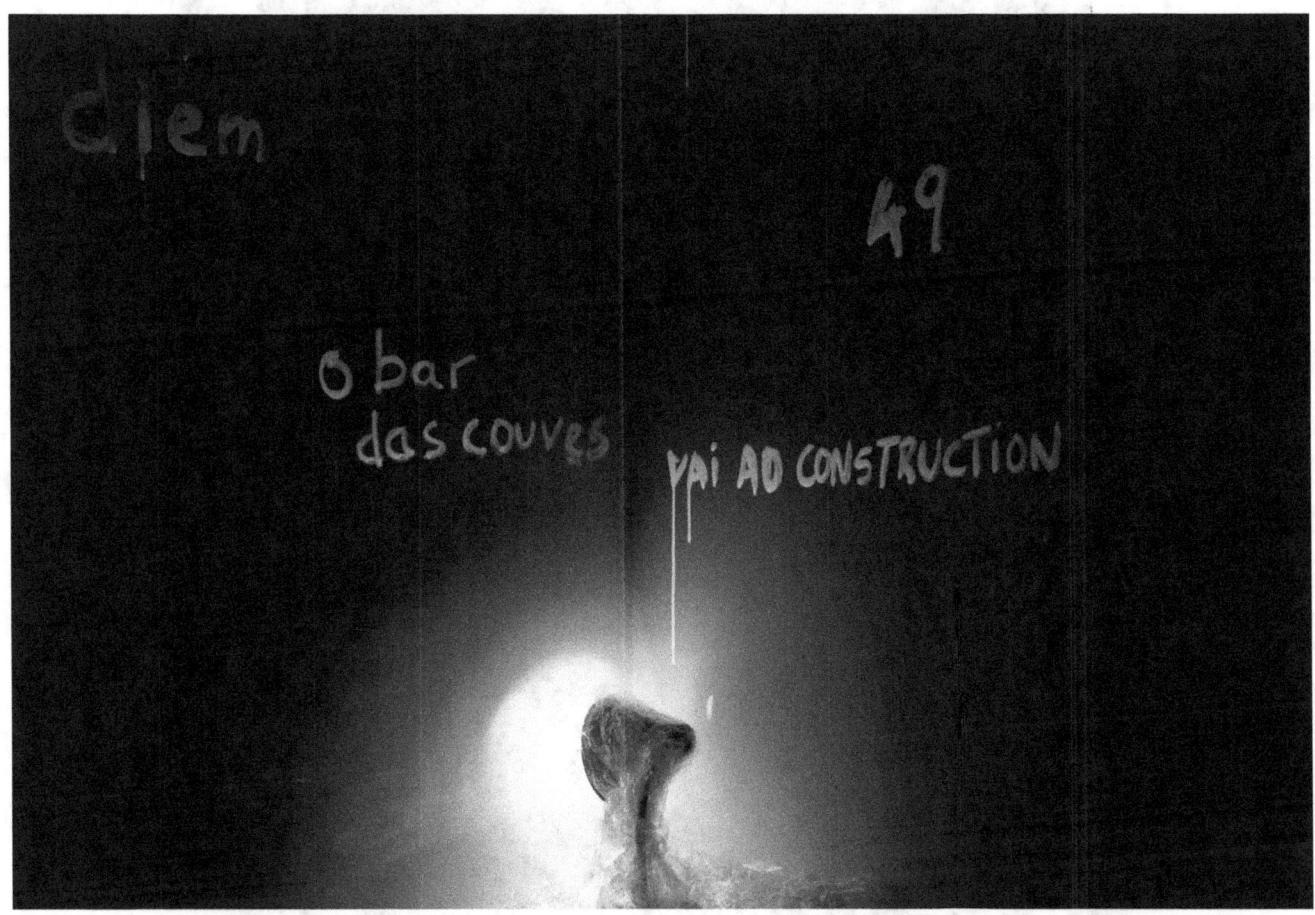

Figure 16 - Name an important place, for you, at Bairro Alto. "[carpe] diem" (visual arts center) "49" (bar) "the bar of cabbage" (reference to Mahjong, one of the most important bars of the 80's and 90's, which has now some lamps in the form of cabbage..) "go to construction" (reference to a LGBT bar)

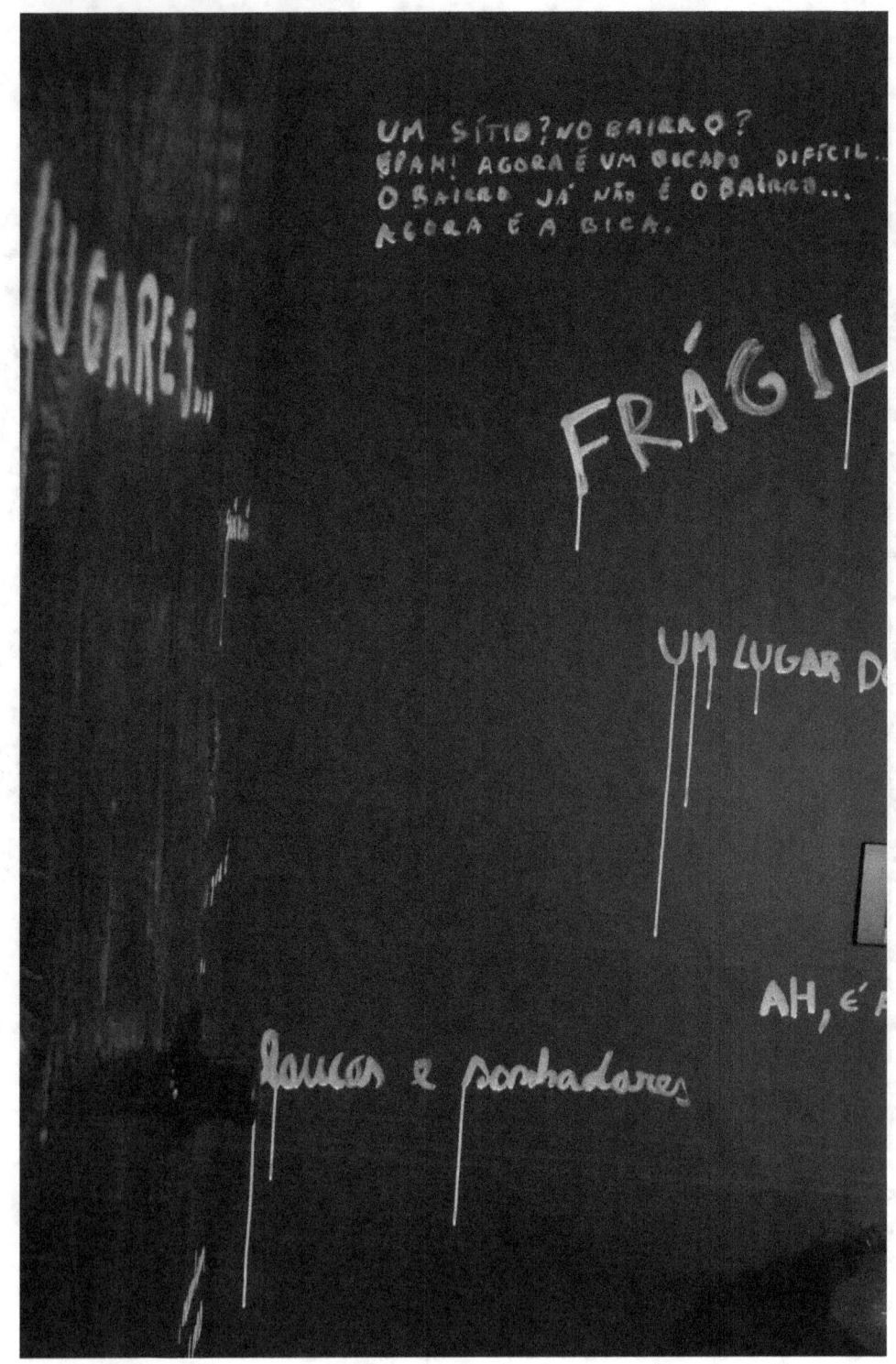

Figure 17 - Name an important place, for you, at Bairro Alto
"A place? In the quarter? So! Now it's a bit difficult… The Bairro is no more the Bairro… Now it is Bica"
(contiguous neighborood, to where many nightlife alternative activities spread in last decade)
"Frágil" (club, the most influential in the 80's)
"Loucos e sonhadores" (bar/association)

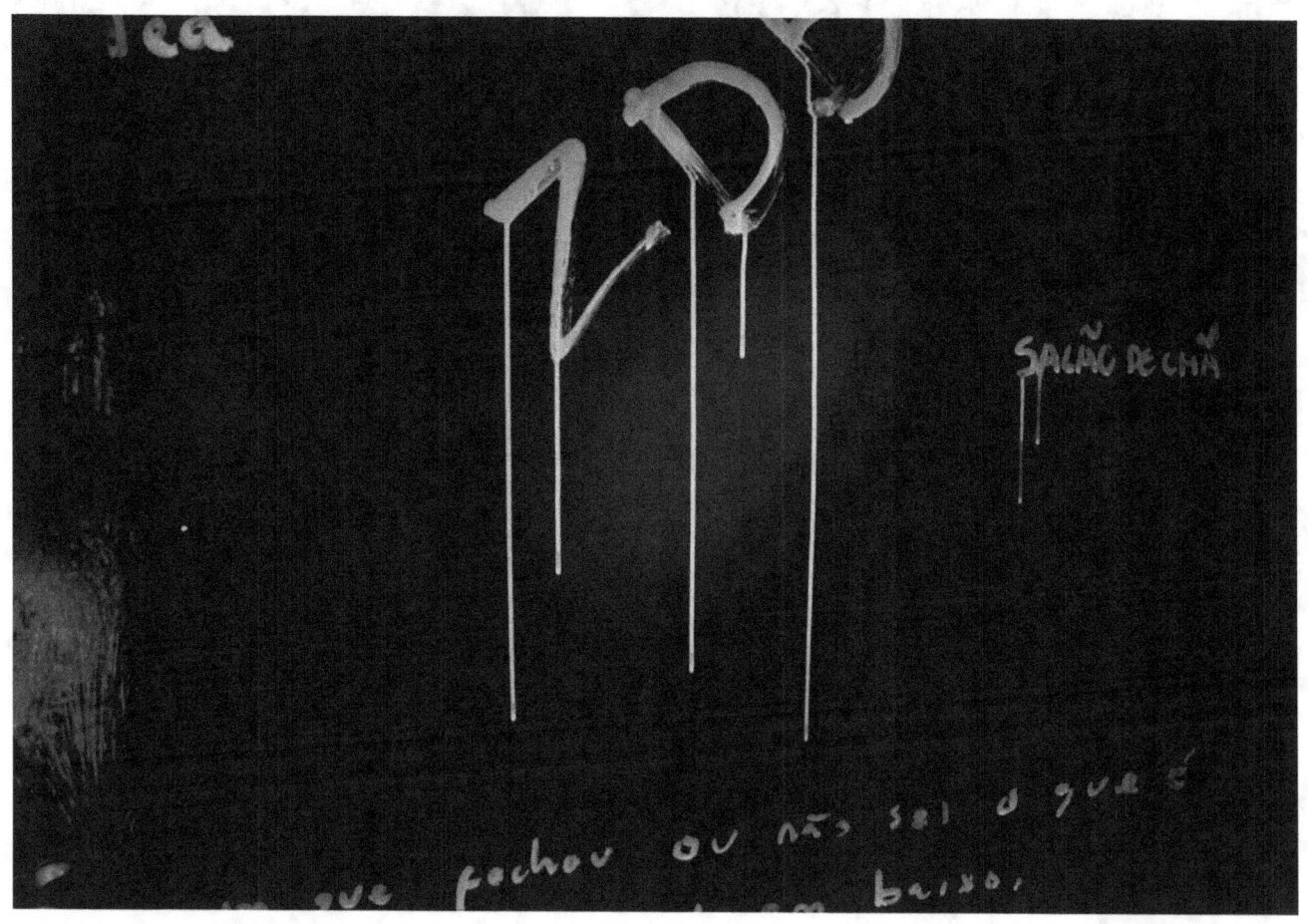

Figure 18 - Name an important place, for you, at Bairro Alto
"ZDB" (most important and influential underground gallery and performing/visual arts center in the neighborhood)
"tea house"
"one that is now closed… I don't know what it is…downthere"

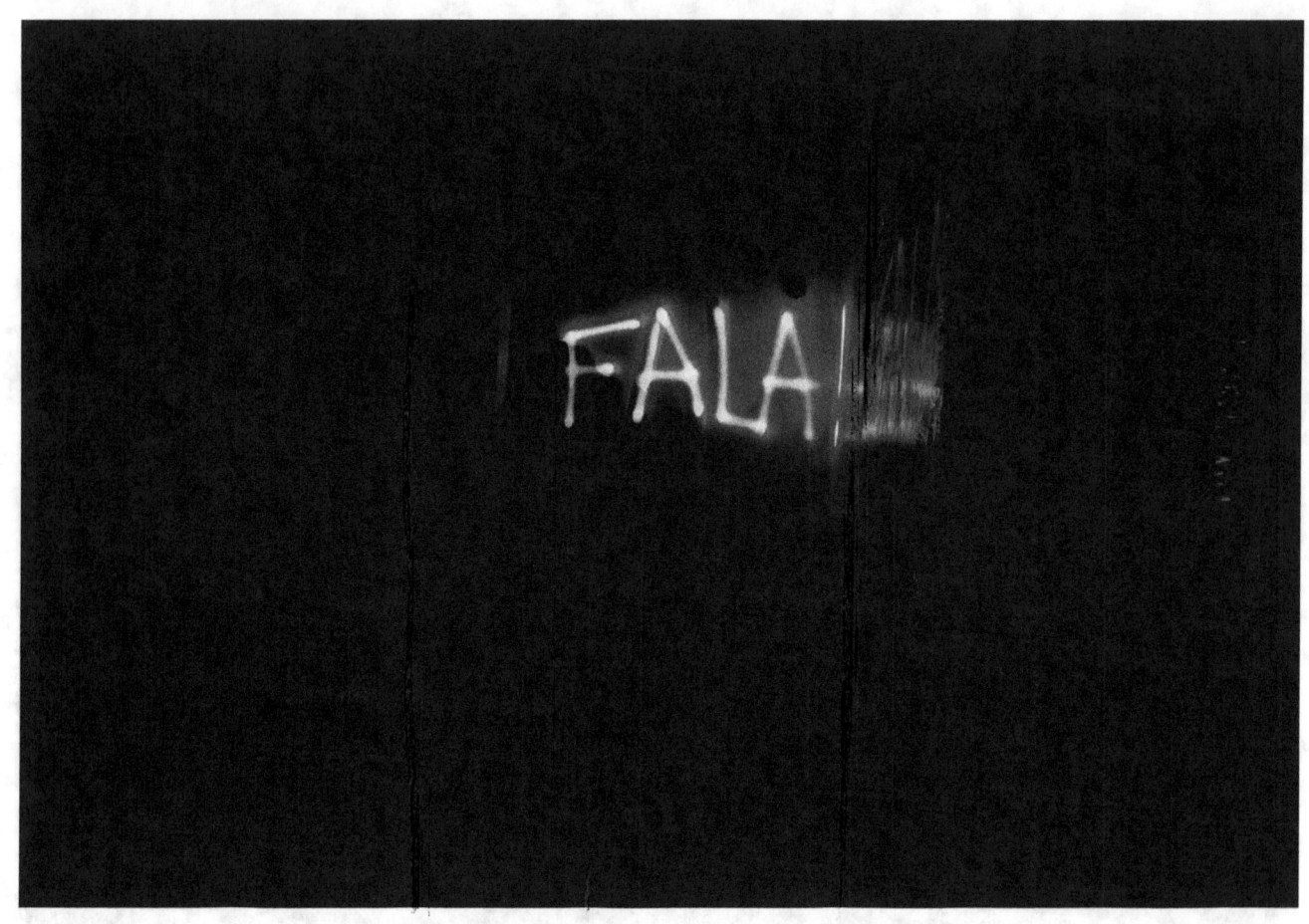

Figure 19 - Expression displayed by us at a specific room where it was set a recording device to people to express their opinion about Bairo Alto, during the happening – with results which not corresponded fully to authors' expectations: "TALK!"

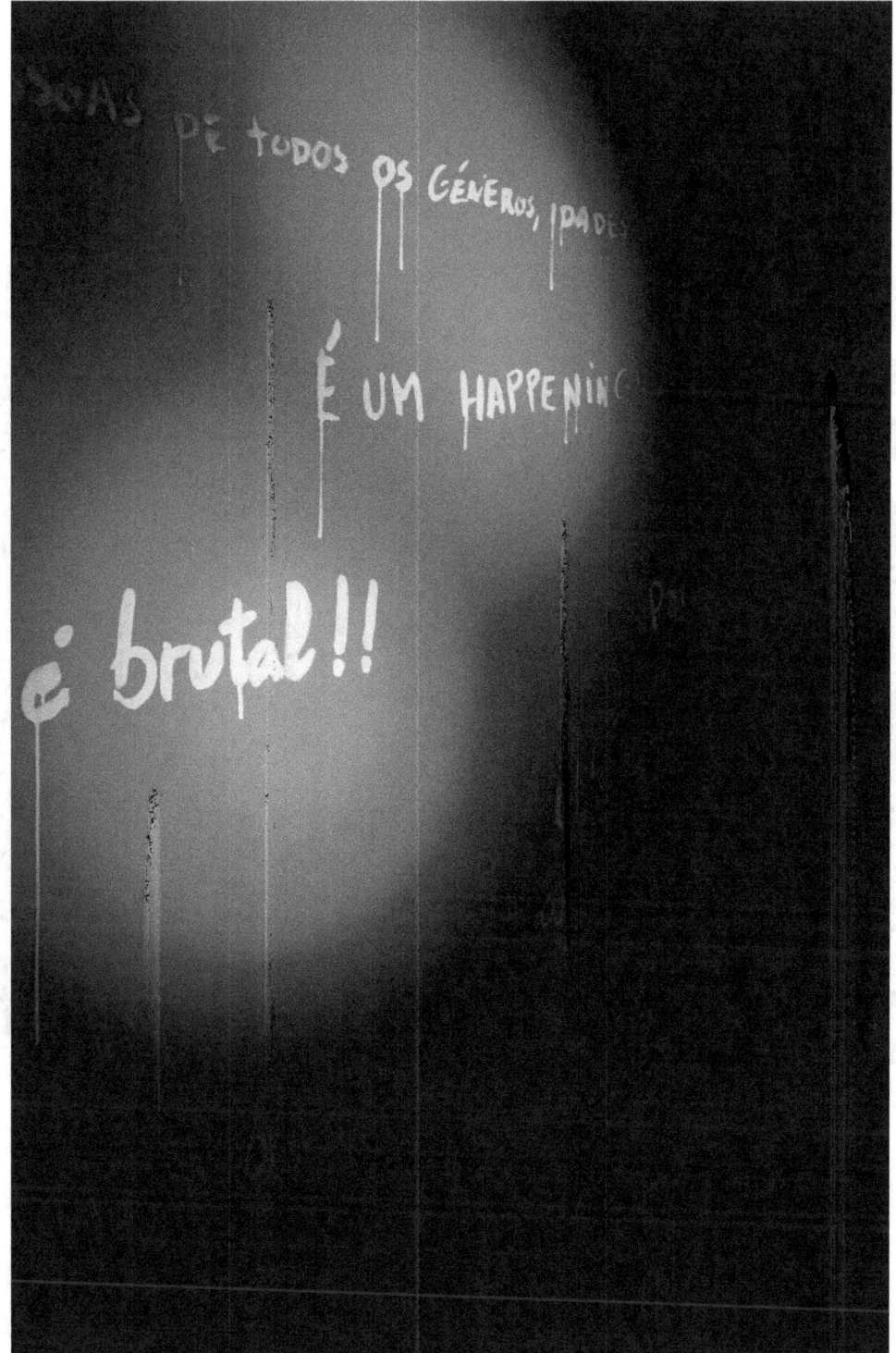

Figure 20 - What is, for you, the Bairro Alto?
"…people of all genres, ages."
" it is an happening!"
" it is brutal!!"
"for me it is work"
"it's sexy, and smoky"
"Insane. When people pass from Camões [main square at the entrance of Bairro Alto] to this side, everyone becomes mad"

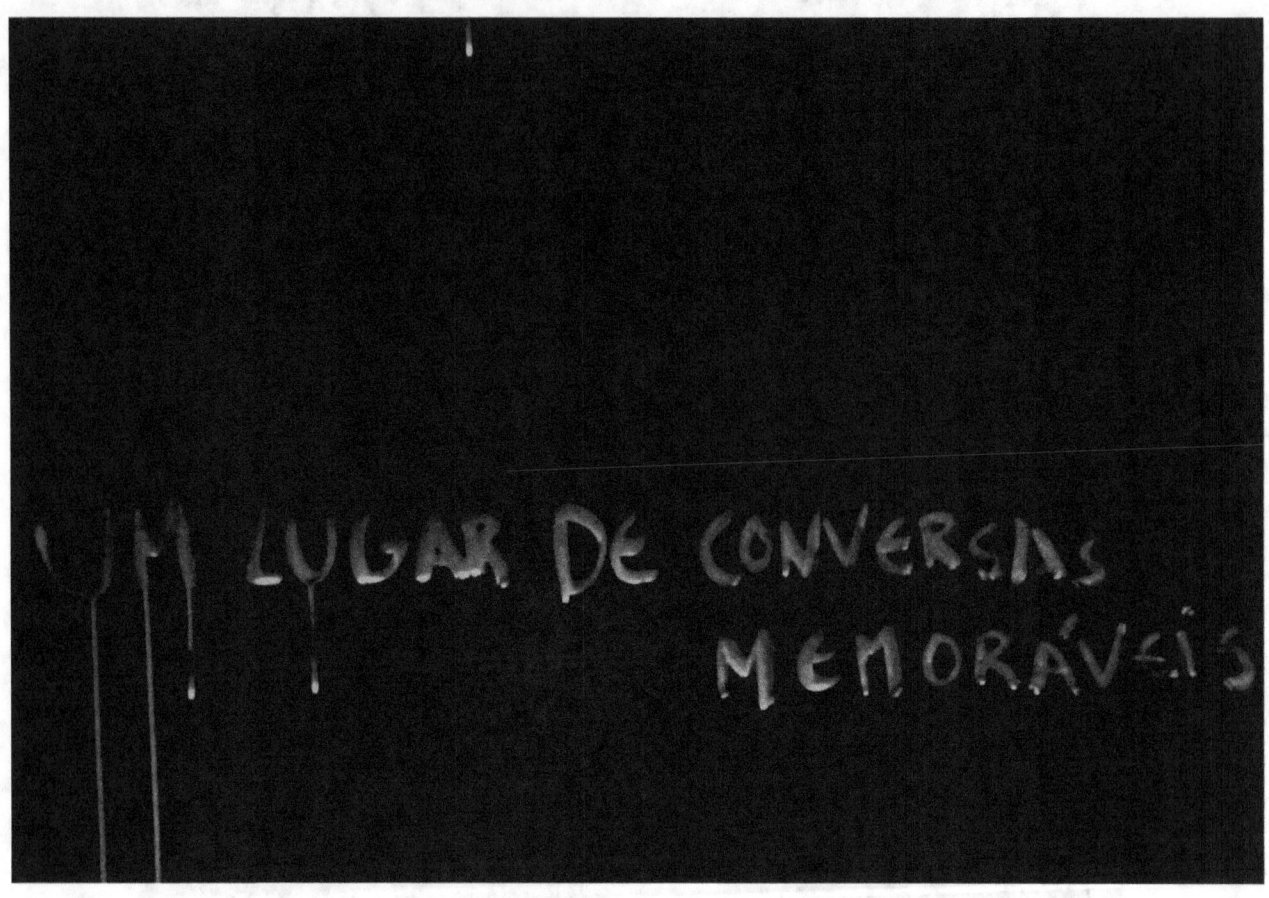

Figure 21 - What is, for you, the Bairro Alto?
"a place of memorable chatting"

5. Concluding note

Cities are changing every day (as always in history, but increasingly faster) and people are connected in networks that are driven by different rhythms, habits and identities; they tend to generate different layers of codifications and uses, not always pacific between all the users, as we can interpret through the sentences written on this intervention. However, it is this diversity and the critical masses associated to it (the "old" dimension, density and heterogeneity arguments) that make the cities being so appellative organisms to a constant change of experiences, ideas, opinions and knowledge, and then, to creative dynamics.

The aim of this photo-essay was to bring to discussion the different layers of codification of Bairro Alto. Drawing upon a research-action based methodology, some results and impacts of one of the experiences of urban intervention developed by the authors were briefly presented. These ephemeral artistic interventions introduced in the city new spaces of public use, performing different public and private spaces, and bringing them to the public sphere, creating also "new" zones that re-gain a certain utility in the city, contributing to the vitality and symbolic centrality of this area. Blurring the ambiguous and flexible boundaries between public and private spaces, and evidencing the usual conflicts verified on this kind of creative milieus, it was also possible to launch the discussion on how to keep these places as vernacular as possible and to try to avoid (or at least postpone) gentrification processes (recognizing however that authenticity is no more than a myth, a social construct). In this specific case, this was particularly notorious as the object of discussion was centered on the multiple layers of codification of the quarter and people were confronted with them, both at the side of "targets" of the experience (as "contributors" to whom were asked the phrases that were displayed at the exhibition), and at the side of audience and participants of the artistic event itself (at the time they were confronted with these expressions).

We do not want to make a systematization or an interpretation of this. The images speak for themselves, and that will be the relevance and substance of a photo essay such as this one. We just highlight that diversity, and the way it crosses the several divides we can identify in the area and a set of issues we've also identified in other works developed in this area, from the multiplicity of practices and identities of its users (e.g, splitted by their age, by their cultural practices, by their cultural capital, by their gender, by their spatialities), to their perceptions of the use conflicts (e.g., traditional vs newcomers; alternative vs mainstream; culture vs commerce;…), or from their identity traces (e.g, valorization of distinction, valorization of hedonism and diversion, valorization of tradition,…) to their political agendas (e.g. diverse economic interests, cultural or urban policy motivations, gender issues, etc.).

And of course we highlight the heuristic potential of an urban intervention such as this one to the empowerment of the community and to the achievement of a reflexive practice by its members, as well as its importance to the in-deepening of the academic knowledge, complementing other more traditional instruments and methodologies of scientific analysis. The potential for co-creation of knowledge between the researchers and the community observed is enormous, and could be very interesting and fruitful for both sides. On our side, we are certainly strongly committed to continue exploring the potential of these approaches to develop our knowledge on the cultural quarters and their effective creative dynamics.

References

Arantes A. (1997), "A guerra dos lugares: fronteiras simbólicas e liminaridade no espaço urbano de São Paulo". In Fortuna, Carlos (org.), Cidade, Cultura e Globalização – Ensaios de Sociologia, Oeiras, Celta, pp. 259-270

Bell D., Jayne M. (eds) (2004), City of Quarters: Urban Villages in the Contemporary City. Aldershot: Ashgate.

Camagni R., Maillat D., Matteacciolli A. (Eds.) (2004), Ressources naturelles et culturelles, milieux et développement local. Neuchatel: EDES.

Campos, R., A. Mubi Brighenti, L. Spinelli (2011), Uma cidade de imagens: Produções e consumos visuais em meios urbanos. Lisboa, Editora Mundos Sociais

Cartiere C., Willis S. (2008), The Practice of Public Art. New York: Routledge

Cooke P., Lazzeretti L. org. (2008), Creative cities, cultural clusters and local development. Cheltenham: Edward Elgar.

Costa, P. (2007), A cultura em Lisboa: competitividade e desenvolvimento territorial, Lisboa: Imprensa de Ciências Sociais

Costa, P. (2009), Bairro Alto – Chiado: Efeitos de meio e desenvolvimento sustentável de um bairro cultural, Lisboa: Câmara Municipal de Lisboa - DPPC

Costa, P. (2012), "Gatekeeping processes, reputation buiding and creative milieus: evidence from case studies in Lisboa, Barcelona and São Paulo", in Lazzeretti, L (Ed.), Creative industries and innovation in Europe: Concepts, measures and comparatives case studies", Routledge, pp. 286-306

Costa, P. (2013), Bairro Alto Revisited: Reputation and Symbolic Assets as Drivers for Sustainable Innovation in the City, DINAMIA-CET Working Paper n° 2013/14

Costa P, Magalhães M., Vasconcelos B., Sugahara G. (2008), "On 'Creative Cities' governance models: a comparative approach". The Service Industries Journal , Vol. 28, n°3-4, April-May 2008, pp. 393-413.

Costa P., Vasconcelos B., Sugahara G. (2011), "The urban milieu and the genesis of creativity in cultural activities: An introductory framework for the analysis of urban creative dynamics", Cidades, Comunidades e Territórios, N° 22, Dezembro 2011, pp. 3-21

Costa P., Lopes R. (2011), "Padrões locativos intrametropolitanos do cluster da cultura: a territorialidade das actividades culturais em Lisboa, Barcelona e São Paulo", REDIGE – Revista de Design, Inovação e Gestão Estratégica, Vol. 2, n. 02, 2011, pp. 196-244

Costa, P., Lopes, R., 2013. "Artistic intervention in public sphere, conflict and urban informality: an international comparative approach to informal dynamics in cultural districts", Cidades, Comunidades e Territórios, n° 2, Junho de 2013

Costa P., Lopes R. (2011), (2015) Urban Design, Public Space and the Dynamics of Creative Milieux: A Photographic Approach to Bairro Alto (Lisbon), Gràcia (Barcelona) and Vila Madalena (São Paulo), Journal of Urban Design, 20:1, 28-51

Costa, P., Lopes, R., (2016a, forthcoming), "Artistic Urban Interventions, Informality and Public Sphere: Research Insights from Ephemeral Urban Appropriations on a Cultural District", submitted for publishing on a double blind refereed journal, forthcoming.

Costa, P., Lopes, R., (2016b forthcoming), "Dos dois lados do espelho: diálogos com um bairro cultural através da intervenção urbana", submitted for publishing on a double blind refereed journal, forthcoming.

Gehl J. (1987), Life between buildings: using public space. New York: Van Nostrand, New York

Jacobs, J., (1989 (1961)), The Death and life of American Cities. New York: Vintage Books, a Division Random House

Lefebvre H. (1991), The production of space. Cambridge, Mass: Blackwell Publishers.

Lopes R. (2012), Intervenções artísticas efémeras e apropriação de espaço público em contextos urbanos informais: análise de cinco "bairros criativos": Bairro Alto e Cais do Sodré, Gràcia, Vila Madalena, Brick Lane e Kreuzberg SO36, ISCTE-IUL, Lisboa

Miles M. (1997), Art, space and the city – Public art and urban futures. London: Routledge.

Scott A.J. (2000), The Cultural Economy of Cities. New Delhi, London- Thousand Oaks: Sage

Traquino, M. (2010), A construção do lugar pela arte contemporânea. Ribeirão, Portugal: Húmus,

White, W. (1980), The social life of small urban spaces. Washington: The Conservation Foundation

www.ingramcontent.com/pod-product-compliance
Lightning Source LLC
Chambersburg PA
CBHW082107220526
45472CB00009B/2074